THE CORPORATION IN THE 21ST CENTURY

ALSO BY JOHN KAY

Other People's Money

The Long and Short of It

Foundations of Corporate Success

Greed is Dead (with Paul Collier)

Radical Uncertainty (with Mervyn King)

Obliquity

The Truth About Markets

THE CORPORATION IN THE 21ST CENTURY

Why (Almost) Everything We Are
Told About Business Is Wrong

JOHN KAY

Yale UNIVERSITY PRESS

NEW HAVEN & LONDON

Yale University Press books may be purchased in quantity for
educational, business, or promotional use. For information, please e-mail
sales.press@yale.edu (U.S. office) or sales@yaleup.co.uk (U.K. office).

Printed in the United States of America.

Library of Congress Control Number: 2024939696
ISBN 978-0-300-28019-7 (hardcover : alk. paper)

A catalogue record for this book is available from the British Library.

This paper meets the requirements of ANSI/NISO Z39.48-1992
(Permanence of Paper).

10 9 8 7 6 5 4 3 2 1

CONTENTS

INTRODUCTION: BUSINESS IN SOCIETY

And no one puts new wine into old wineskins; or else the
new wine bursts the wineskins, the wine is spilled, and the
wineskins are ruined. But new wine must be put into new
wineskins.

Mark 2:22, New King James Version[1]

In 1901 financier J. P. Morgan orchestrated the creation of US
Steel, then by almost any measure the largest company in the
world. Two years earlier, John D. Rockefeller had consolidated
his activities into Standard Oil of New Jersey, which controlled
around 90 per cent of refined oil products in the United States.
Steel and oil were essential elements in the rise of the automobile industry, which would transform both everyday life and the
ways in which people thought about business.

Business historian Alfred Chandler documented the rise of
the modern managerial corporation in his magisterial *Strategy
and Structure* (1962).[2] The book showcased General Motors,
along with chemical giant DuPont, retailer Sears Roebuck and
Standard Oil of New Jersey. These companies dominated their
industries in the United States and increasingly operated internationally. They exerted political influence, and their turnover
exceeded the national product of many states. Their combination of economic and political power seemed to secure their
dominance in perpetuity.

It didn't. In 2009 General Motors (GM) entered Chapter
11 bankruptcy. GM is still – just – the top-selling US automobile supplier, but its global production lags far behind that of

Toyota and Volkswagen. DuPont has broken itself up, and Sears Roebuck is more or less defunct. These failures are not because people have ceased to drive cars and shop or because business no longer requires chemical products. Incumbents lost out because other businesses met customer needs more effectively. Among Chandler's examples only Standard Oil of New Jersey – now ExxonMobil – continues to enjoy its former leadership status. Somewhat quixotically, in view of the widespread demand for a transition from fossil fuels.

In the 1970s you might presciently have anticipated that information technology would be key to the development of twenty-first-century business. And many savvy investors did; their enthusiasm made IBM the world's most valuable corporation. The leading computer company of the age would surely lead the race to the new frontier. That wasn't how it worked out.

On Wall Street they called the upstarts 'the FAANGs' – Facebook (Meta), Apple, Amazon, Netflix and Google (Alphabet). Then the fickle fashion of finance favoured the 'Magnificent Seven', with Netflix replaced by Nvidia, and Tesla and Microsoft added to the list – the latter restored to fortune after missing out on the Apple-led shift to mobile computing in the first decade of the new century. Microsoft is actually the longest established of these titans of the modern economy, famously founded in 1975 by Harvard dropouts Paul Allen and Bill Gates. Four of these businesses began trading only in the twenty-first century. None of the FAANGs is a manufacturer (I will explain Apple later.) The employees of these companies are not the labouring poor, victims of class oppression; many hold degrees from prestigious universities. (I will come back to Amazon later.) The workers *are* the means of production.

In 2023 investors believed that the 'Magnificent Seven' represented the future of business. They clamoured to buy their stock, as they had once clamoured to buy US Steel, General Motors and IBM. And these investors are likely to be right – for a time. But experience suggests the dominance of the seven is likely to be as transitory as that of the large businesses of earlier generations. As I write this, negotiations are proceeding for the rump of US Steel to be bought by Nippon Steel of Japan, and Andrew Carnegie and the Gilded Age have become a footnote to history. Thus the mighty fall – or just slowly fade away.

A central thesis of this book is that business has evolved but that the language that is widely used to describe business has not. The world economy is not controlled by a few multinational corporations; such corporations have mostly failed even to control their own industries for long. In the nineteenth and twentieth centuries capital was required to build, first, textile mills and iron works, then railways and steel mills and subsequently automobile assembly lines and petrochemical plants. These 'means of production' were industry-specific – there is not much you can do with a railway except run trains along it, and if you want to be an engine driver you need to seek employment with a business that operates (but, as I will explain, does not necessarily own) a track and a train.

The leading companies of the twenty-first century have little need of such equipment. The relatively modest amounts of capital they raise are used to cover the operating losses of a start-up business. The physical assets required by twenty-first-century corporations are mostly fungible: they are offices, shops, vehicles and data centres which can be used in many alternative activities. These 'means of production' need not be owned by the business that uses them and now mostly they are not.

Thus the owners of tangible capital, such as real estate companies and vehicle lessors, no longer derive control of business from that ownership. Labour is no longer subjected to the whims of capitalist owners of the means of production. Often workers do not know who the owners of the physical means of production are, or who the shareholders of the business they work for are, and they don't know because it doesn't matter. They work for an organisation that has a formal management structure but whose hierarchy is relatively flat and participative.

Necessarily so. In modern businesses the 'boss' can't issue peremptory instructions to subordinates, as Andrew Carnegie and Henry Ford did, because modern bosses don't know what these instructions should be: they need the information, the commitment and, above all, the capabilities which are widely distributed across the organisation. The modern business environment is characterised by radical uncertainty. It can be navigated only by assembling the collective knowledge of many individuals and by developing collective intelligence – a problem-solving capability which distinguishes the firm from its competitors, and even its own past. Relationships in these businesses cannot be purely transactional: they require groups of people working together towards shared objectives, and such cooperative activity necessarily has a social as well as a commercial dimension.

Collective knowledge is the accumulation of the facts and theories we can find in libraries and on Wikipedia, augmented by insights from our own experience and that of others. Other animals mostly know what they have learned for themselves. We understand science and appreciate art because of the endeavours of great scientists and famous artists and the efforts of our teachers to explain their achievements to us. Collective knowledge also includes what we have learned about ourselves and each other through our social and business interactions. When to praise and when to criticise, when to follow and when to lead. Collective knowledge is sometimes described as 'the wisdom of crowds', but the wisdom of crowds lies in the *aggregate of knowledge* rather than the *average of knowledge*. No one knows everything about anything or much about everything.

The twenty-first-century corporation is defined by these human capabilities, not its physical capital. The successful firm builds distinctive capabilities and distinctive *collections and combinations* of capabilities – capabilities such as supplier or customer relationships, technical and business process innovations, brands, reputations and user networks. These things can only be – at most – approximately replicated by competitors. Such differentiation among firms means that the structure of modern industry is very different from that of the past, which featured an economy in which essentially similar farms, mills and steelworks competed in the production of essentially similar products in capital-intensive and purpose-specific facilities.

As a result, what we call 'profit' is no longer primarily a return on capital but is 'economic rent'. The term 'economic rent' came into use in what was still a predominantly agricultural economy to describe the return that accrues to landowners because some lands are more fertile or better located than others. Today economic rent is used to describe the earnings that arise because some people, places and institutions have commercially valuable talents which others struggle to emulate. Economic rent accrues to silver-tongued attorneys, brilliant brain surgeons, dashing dealmakers and to sports and film stars. Economic rent is earned by Taylor Swift, and by businesses and house owners in Silicon Valley; economic rent is derived from the unique attractions of Venice and the enthusiasm of world-wide supporters of Manchester United.

But economic rent also describes and explains the revenue that is generated because some firms are better than others at providing the goods and services that their customers want. The economic rent earned by Apple and Amazon, like the economic rent accruing to Swift and Manchester United and arising in Silicon Valley and Venice, is the result of doing things better than other people, places and organisations. All these people, places and organisations have monopolies – of being their impressively differentiated selves. The traditional association of economic rent with monopoly is thus true, but trivial.

And we should welcome that differentiation and its associated 'monopolies'. The perfectly competitive market in which every product is homogeneous and every producer is equally efficient is not an ideal but a stationary equilibrium in which enterprise and innovation are absent. The purpose of economic organisation is to create combinations of factors of production that yield more value than the same factors would in alternative uses. And to do so successfully is to create a source of economic rent.

But when the term 'economic rent' *is* mentioned in modern texts on economics, business and politics, it is most often in the context of 'rent-seeking': the attempt by individuals and companies to appropriate some of the value created by other individuals and companies, by establishing monopolies or providing unneeded intermediary services. Such rent-seeking is indeed a major blight on modern economies, and a better appreciation of the nature and origins of economic rent will better equip us to tackle it. We need to rein in the excesses of financial intermediation. We need to limit the use of political influence to gain favoured positions; to win contracts, to establish monopolies, to secure incumbent-friendly regulations. It is not the purpose of this book to propose remedies for rent-seeking: the implications of my analysis for business and public policy, both of which should promote the rents that arise from innovative differentiation and eliminate the ones that are the result of the abuse of political institutions, will be the task of a successor volume. My objective here is to promote what I regard as an essential preliminary: a better understanding of how business works, and an explanation of how it does not work in the ways many people – both critics and apologists – think.

An understanding of the concept, origins and effects of economic rent is essential to understanding not only the financial accounts of firms but also the distribution of income and wealth in the modern economy. But the inherited terminology of capital and capitalism gets in the way of that understanding. Even sophisticated investors examine 'return on capital employed' (ROCE), although the return often has no more connection to the capital employed than it has to the amount of water used (ROW) or the number of meetings held (ROM).

Economic rent is not an anomaly but a central and valuable feature of a vibrant economy. Economic advance occurs when people and businesses create rents by doing things better, and it progresses further by inspiring others to try to compete them away. If this is capitalism, then I am a supporter of capitalism. But the process I describe has very little to do with 'capital' and nothing whatsoever to do with any struggle between capitalists and workers for control of the means of production. The economic system I favour and the one described in this book is better described as a market economy, or better still a pluralist economy, than as a capitalist economy. A pluralist economy is one in which people are free to do new things (and often fail at them) without requiring the approval of some central authority. A pluralist economy is a system in which consumers are able to make their wants known in a competitive environment that rewards success in meeting those wants.

But the pluralism of a market economy also requires a discipline in which failure is acknowledged and leads to change. Bureaucratic organisations find such self-awareness hard. IBM, General Motors and US Steel failed economically for more or less the same reasons that the Soviet Union failed economically: the difficulty centralised authorities encounter in adapting to changing technologies and changing needs. These institutions were slow to move and slow to acknowledge failure. However, the economic underperformance of IBM, GM and US Steel led only to the decline of these companies. Microsoft and Apple, Toyota and Tesla, Nucor and Arcelor Mittal were able to take their place. But the economic underperformance of the Soviet Union led to the decline, and ultimately demise, of an entire political system.

The term 'capitalism' came into being to describe an economy designed and controlled by a bourgeois elite. Both supporters and critics of modern business frequently conflate this historic caricature of 'capitalism' with today's reality of a market or pluralist economy, whose essential characteristic is that it is not controlled, or not controlled for long, by anyone at all. The mismatch of language and reality extends further. In the second half of the twentieth century, business evolved from an industrial structure characterised by large-scale production facilities staffed by low-skilled workers to one populated by knowledge workers sharing their collective intelligence in a cooperative environment. But the dominant narrative of how the business world did and should work evolved in the opposite direction. Economic relations were defined in purely transactional terms; intrinsic motivation and professional ethics were replaced by targets and bonuses. The purpose of business, MBA students were told, was not to meet the needs of customers and society but to create 'shareholder value' for anonymous stockholders.

The further, but closely related, paradox is that as capital became less central to the operation of business, the financial sector expanded greatly in size and remuneration. And the degraded values of parts of the financial sector spread to business. Both business founders and senior executives rewarded themselves handsomely for their profession of devotion to the cause of shareholder value. As a result of the erosion of business ethics and the evidence of indefensible inequalities, the twenty-first-century corporation faces a crisis of legitimacy. Today the public hates the producers even as it laps up the products. And, as I shall describe all too graphically, the managerial proponents of shareholder value often ended up destroying not only shareholder value but also the very businesses that their abler and better-motivated predecessors had created.

Both the intellectual origins and the practical application of these approaches, promoting individualism and emphasising shareholder value, come from the United States. But the influence of these ideas has been global. Business operates internationally, but all businesses are subject to the laws, regulations, customs and societal expectations both of the country in which they are registered or incorporated and of the countries in which they operate. It should hardly be necessary to say that these laws, regulations, customs and societal expectations differ from country to country. But it *is* necessary to say that they differ, because so much of what is written about business fails to recognise that both the legal duties and the expected behaviour of company directors and executives depend on where the company is based and where it is doing business. The relevant differences are not just those between the US and Russia, or Canada and Japan, but also between Delaware and California and – I shall give these countries specific attention – between Britain, Germany and the United States. And the differences and similarities between these jurisdictions and those of Asian societies are likely to be crucial to the development of the twenty-first-century corporation.

This is a book written by a British economist, and I offer no apology for the fact that much of my own business experience and knowledge is derived from the UK. Britain had a central role in the emergence of modern finance, modern law and modern institutions, and engaged in a colonial project that spread these developments around the world. The Industrial Revolution began in the UK, and the most influential business texts of the eighteenth and nineteenth centuries – Adam Smith's *Wealth of Nations* and Karl Marx's *Capital* – were written close to my boyhood home in Edinburgh and my current office in London respectively. Economics was the foundational discipline for an understanding of business for both Smith and Marx – although, as I will explain, modern economics has contributed less to an understanding of modern business than might reasonably have been hoped.

Still, if one were to seek twentieth-century works of similar significance, one would have to look to the United States. Perhaps to Chandler's *Strategy and Structure,* noted above, or to *The Modern Corporation and Private Property*, in which Adolf Berle and Gardiner Means first documented the transition in American business from the robber barons of the Gilded Age to the managerially controlled businesses of the twentieth century.[3]

If any individual exemplified that transition it was Alfred Sloan, the General Motors executive who was perhaps the greatest businessman of the twentieth century. As Sloan and his Chief Financial Officer, Donaldson Brown, approached retirement, they were anxious to ensure that the lessons that they had learned would be preserved for subsequent generations. Brown hired Peter Drucker, one of the numerous Viennese intellectuals who had fled the increasingly Nazified Europe for the United States, to tell the story.

The result was a business classic, *Concept of the Corporation*, which made Drucker the first management 'guru'.⁴ Sloan and his colleagues did not like the book, and publishers were sceptical that a book about business would sell. How wrong could they have been! Seventy-five years later *Concept of the Corporation* is still in print.

And every bookshop now has a section devoted to business books. Mostly, they fall into one of two categories. One type has titles such as '*Flexagility™ – the Secret of Delighting Customers and Raking in Enormous Profits*'. You will find them in airport bookstalls, not far from the self-help manuals. Their authors make a living, often a rewarding one, from consultancy or the delivery of 'motivational speeches'. The contents of these volumes are unlikely to engage your attention through even the shortest flight. Another genre comprises books with titles like '*Fleeced, Poisoned and Spied Upon – How Capitalism is Fuelling Inequality, Damaging our Well-Being and Destroying the Planet.*' These are written for people who welcome confirmation of what they think they already know.

This book fits neither of these categories. I hope that thoughtful executives – and there are many – will find something of interest in it, but I do not set out to offer tips for ambitious young managers. My target audience is people who would never normally pick up a business book – people who read popular science or history, but might welcome an intellectually serious, even sometimes challenging, approach to a subject with whose detail they are unfamiliar. I hope this book might stimulate students and young people who might be thinking of a business career or would just like to learn more about business. I would like to think they might read it and even enjoy it – and perhaps conclude that a career in business has more to offer than just financial reward.

PART 1

THE BACKGROUND

We have many and ambivalent relationships with business – in our multiple roles as consumers, employees, savers and citizens. Without the products of modern business our lives would be, by twenty-first-century standards, not only economically but also culturally impoverished. In fact, without the products of modern business most of us, including the author of this book, would be dead. And yet not only do most intelligent and thoughtful people have a negative view of business, especially large business; twenty-first-century business has described itself in terms that invite that negativity.

1

LOVE THE PRODUCT,
HATE THE PRODUCER

Senator Levin: 'When you heard that your employees in these emails and looking at these deals said "God, what a shitty deal" or "God, what a piece of crap", when you hear your own employees or read about these in emails, do you feel anything?'
David Viniar, CFO Goldman Sachs: 'I think that is very unfortunate to have on email.' [Laughter]

Senate Investigations Committee, 2010[1]

The whole organization is focused on the highest level of client service, taking a long-term view, really thinking about their needs, their interests.

David Solomon, CEO, Goldman Sachs,
interviewed by Jim Cramer, 2022[2]

As I began writing this book, Arkansas Teacher Retirement System was leading a proposed class litigation by a group of investors against Goldman Sachs, widely regarded as the world's premier investment bank. The plaintiffs claim to have been misled by the official ethics and values statement of Goldman Sachs, which began (and still begins) 'our clients' interests always come first'.[3]

You might have expected that the bank would respond by providing evidence to document the strength of its commitment to its clients with testimonials from customers, depositions from senior executives, illustrations of instances in which profit had

'Carbolic Smoke Ball', *Illustrated London News* (1893)

been sacrificed because 'our clients' interests always come first'. You would have been quite wrong.

The *defence* attorneys produced more than thirty press reports that alleged that Goldman had acted in ways that benefited the firm and its employees but disadvantaged its customers. They supplemented their submissions with expert analyses showing that these revelations of apparent malpractice had little impact on the stock price.[4] Market participants, the defence argued, did not take the company's ethical claims seriously and hence were equally indifferent to lapses from them. In legal terms, the press reports constituted a 'corrective disclosure' of the misrepresentations in the ethics and values code, like an erratum slip correcting a typo in the annual report. The statement of business principles was 'generic'; it represented 'puffery', akin to claims that 'Heineken refreshes the parts other beers cannot reach'.[5] No reasonable person would regard them as statements of fact on which they might rely. US courts had ruled in an earlier case that

J. P. Morgan's claims that the company had 'risk management processes [that] are highly disciplined and designed to preserve the integrity of the risk management process' and that the bank 'set the standard for integrity' were 'puffs' like 'Red Bull gives you wings', and hence unactionable.[6] To someone outside the arcane world of US class litigation, however, the difference of tone and substance between 'our clients' interests always come first' and 'refreshes the parts other beers cannot reach' seems clear and substantial.

The term 'puff' in legal circles dates from a case in which the future British prime minister Herbert Asquith unsuccessfully defended the Carbolic Smoke Ball Company. The company had advertised that users of its product would not contract influenza and further promised £100, a considerable sum at the time, to anyone who did use the smoke ball and contracted the disease.

The story that Red Bull was sued by someone who found himself unable to fly is an urban myth, although the manufacturer did settle a case brought by consumers who claimed that the company exaggerated its energy-giving properties.

The US Courts dismissed a claim by Ted Martin, purported holder of the world record for kicking hacky sacks – a kind of footbag – against the manufacturer of Five Hour Energy shots: 'long lasting energy with no sugar and zero net carbs. When you need an extra boost you don't want to wait!' The firm had released an advertising video in which the narrator claimed that in the five hours after consuming the beverage he had swum the English Channel, disproved the theory of relativity and broken the world record for kicking hacky sacks. Illinois Judge Tharp began judgment with a quotation from Oscar Wilde: 'It is a curious fact that people are never so trivial as when they take themselves seriously.'[7]

The Arkansas Teacher action was resolved in August 2023: the Supreme Court had referred the issue back to the lower court with a strong indication that it should uphold the arguments of the defence. As a result, the class action could not proceed. Kannon Shanmugam, acting for Goldman Sachs, noted that 'It was an enormously important case for the client; beyond the financial stakes, the client felt very strongly that it had not made any misstatements'.[8] Nevertheless, the Arkansas Teacher claim to have been duped is a little far-fetched. Matt Taibbi's 2009 denunciation of Goldman Sachs as 'a great vampire squid wrapped around the face of humanity, relentlessly jamming its blood funnel into anything that smells like money' went viral and must surely have spread as far across the internet as Little Rock.[9]

The revelation of blatant conflicts of interest in the broader financial sector during the 'new economy' bubble of 1999–2000 was followed by evidence of the promotion of mortgage-backed securities based on home loans that borrowers were unlikely to be able to repay. The global financial crisis that followed these abuses, and in part resulted from them, drove reputations in the financial sector to successive lows. Banking is not the respected business it once was, and perhaps its standards should not be regarded as representative of business as a whole.

> At the Davos meeting of the global business elite in 2020, CEO David Solomon announced that 'effective July 1, Goldman Sachs will only underwrite IPOs in the US and Europe of private companies that have at least one diverse [sic] board member'. This was, he explained, 'a component of our firm's holistic approach to driving sustainable, inclusive economic growth'.[10] And Goldman stood ready to offer a slate of suitably 'diverse' candidates. Solomon could hardly have illustrated better the degree to which the ESG (environmental, social and governance) and EDI (equity, diversity and inclusion) movements which have gripped modern business have allowed companies to substitute virtue signalling for genuine engagement with business ethics.

The Senate investigation in which Mr Viniar was embarrassed

had focused on the Timberwolf and Abacus transactions. These were among many similar trades featured in the film and book *The Big Short*, in which Goldman Sachs had marketed securities based on pools of subprime mortgages selected as particularly likely to fail. They not only *were* a shitty deal – they had been *designed* to be a shitty deal.

Not just the finance sector

And yet ... the US Chamber of Commerce has rushed to Goldman's defence, filing an *amicus curiae* brief with the court. The brief observes that 'Virtually every company says: "Our clients' interests always come first"; "We are dedicated to complying fully with the letter and spirit of the laws, rules and ethical principles that govern us"; and "Integrity and honesty are at the heart of our business."' The document goes on to warn that 'The import of the holding below [i.e. the finding of the court] is that companies now make those statements at their own peril.'[11] The Chamber's brief does not consider the possibility that those who make such statements could minimise this peril by taking reasonable steps to ensure that they were true.[12] Or that the members of the Chamber might tone down these 'generic statements' to more modest claims of ethical standards that they would actually seek to observe. But the Chamber was joined in a similar *amicus curiae* brief by the Securities Industry and Financial Markets Association, Bank Policy Institute, American Bankers Association and American Property Casualty Insurance Association.

Of course, these documents are drafted by cynical attorneys who perceive a duty to present the best legal defence available to their clients. But it is inconceivable that such representations are placed in the public domain without the approval of senior executives, who are evidently unaware of, or indifferent to, the effect on the reputation of the particular businesses involved and business in general.

Boeing

In October 2018 and again in March 2019 Boeing 737 MAX aircraft crashed soon after take-off, killing everyone on board. All
planes of this type were grounded by aviation regulators. In the
month after the second accident, Dennis Muilenburg, then chief
executive of Boeing, made the following public statement:

> As we work closely with customers and global regulators
> to return the 737 MAX to service, we continue to be driven
> by our enduring values, with a focus on safety, integrity
> and quality in all we do. … Safety is our responsibility, and
> we own it … When the MAX returns to the skies, we've
> promised our airline customers and their passengers and
> crews that it will be as safe as any airplane ever to fly. Our
> continued disciplined approach is the right decision for
> our employees, customers, supplier partners and other
> stakeholders.[13]

How should air passengers interpret these observations?
As honest declarations of the company's intentions? Or should
they shrug their shoulders cynically and observe, as does the
US Chamber of Commerce, that 'virtually all companies make
statements of this kind'?

Muilenburg was sacked with a substantial pay-off eight
months later, as the planes remained on the tarmac. And a
further eight months later a congressional inquiry revealed
that 'In several critical instances, Boeing withheld crucial information from the FAA, its customers, and 737 MAX pilots. This
included concealing the very existence of MCAS [the corrective
software implicated in the crashes] from 737 MAX pilots.' Most
significantly, 'Boeing concealed internal test data it had that
revealed it took a Boeing test pilot more than 10 seconds to diag-
nose and respond to uncommanded MCAS activation in a flight
simulator, a condition the pilot found to be "catastrophic".'[14]
That activation was the source of the problem that caused the
two 737 MAX crashes. Flights and deliveries of 737 MAX aircraft

resumed in 2021, after the company had paid around $2.5 billion in compensation and penalties.[15]

In September 2022 Muilenburg personally paid $1 million and Boeing a further $200 million to settle charges; these payments were not restitution for the hundreds of deaths but reflected penalties levied by the Securities and Exchange Commission (SEC) for misleading investors (not passengers) in statements of reassurance made after the crashes.[16] Responding to the announcement of the settlement, Boeing said that the company had now made 'fundamental changes that have strengthened our safety processes and oversight of safety issues, and have enhanced our culture of safety, quality, and transparency'. A real change of culture? Or just another statement of the kind that 'virtually all companies make'?

As I completed this manuscript in January 2024, two events made headlines in the business press. Fresh troubles at Boeing, after a panel flew out of an Alaska Airlines 737 MAX, leaving a gaping hole in the fuselage. (The plane returned safely to its departure airport.) And the 2024 meeting at Davos adopted as its theme 'Rebuilding Trust'. Well it might.

Stakeholders

Klaus Schwab, founder and impresario of those Davos events, has long talked enthusiastically of 'stakeholder capitalism', and in 2021 published a book on the subject to help launch a conference around the theme of 'The Great Reset'. Muilenberg spoke of making 'the right decision for our employees, customers, supplier partners and other *stakeholders*'. The term 'stakeholder' was popularised in 1984 in a book by R. Edward Freeman, who used it, as Muilenberg did, to refer to the range of people and organisations who have a legitimate interest in the performance of a business.

It is obvious that no organisation can succeed unless it has regard to the needs of all its stakeholders. And it is also obvious that these interests do not necessarily coincide. Is it the responsibility of management to strike a balance between these conflicting interests? Or is there an overriding shareholder interest, and are other considerations, such as the needs of consumers and the welfare of employees, relevant only instrumentally? Is regard for them required only insofar as it contributes to the capitalist imperative of maximising profits? This may seem an extreme view but, as I will describe, it is one that has been strongly asserted by influential scholars, lawyers and businesspeople.

The tension between these perspectives – stakeholder capitalism or shareholder priority – is a recurrent theme throughout this book. Some people would like to believe that no resolution is necessary – that all interests are essentially aligned and the problem can be dissolved in a warm bath of generalised goodwill. This is naïve, and Boeing illustrates the reality of conflict between competing interests, as I shall describe much more fully in Chapter 22. And yet the history of Boeing, like that of some of the other businesses described in that chapter, points the way to a more compelling resolution.

As almost everyone knows from personal experience, instrumentality – which posits that the interests of others matter only as means to ends – is destructive of social relationships. And the success of modern business depends on strong social relationships between and among stakeholders. In the long run, the corrosive influence of instrumental behaviour damages, perhaps irrevocably, the collective and cooperative behaviour that is necessary for commercial success. Few companies illustrate that issue more clearly than Boeing.

One is Bear Stearns, the investment bank which famously proclaimed, 'We make nothing but money' and ended up not even making any of that. (In the spring of 2008, six months before the collapse of Lehman and as the global financial crisis began to unfold, Bear Stearns ran out of cash. The Fed orchestrated a rescue by J. P. Morgan. The terms effectively wiped out shareholders – it was widely believed that the harsh terms were payback for Bear Stearns's failure to cooperate in similar operations in the past. The payout was improved after share-holders threatened a class action.)

The loss of confidence

Business reputation has suffered many blows in the last two decades. The collapse of Enron in 2001 was symbolic of a decade of excess in the 1990s; the revelation of the company's frauds demonstrated the scale of hubris that characterised the heady years of 'the new economy'. Other collapses occurred at that time: cable operator Adelphia Communications failed after being looted by its chief executive, John Rigas; at telecoms business WorldCom, former basketball coach Bernie Ebbers's defence that he had little grasp of what was going on may have had more truth than the court acknowledged in sentencing him to twenty-five years' imprisonment.

The financial crisis of 2008 had an impact on public confidence which continues; executives were exposed not only as greedy and corrupt but also as lacking the fundamental skills needed to run successful financial services businesses. In contrast to the earlier jailing of Rigas, Ebbers and Enron's CEO Jeff Skilling, only very junior individuals found themselves in prison after the global financial crisis. Some more recent scandals have led to criminal charges against executives responsible. Volkswagen had falsified data on emissions from its cars, and Wells Fargo created 2 million bogus customer accounts.[17] Silicon Valley celebrity Elizabeth Holmes attracted luminaries to her board. She achieved adulation in US business magazines and a $10 billion valuation for her company before it was revealed that the blood-testing product she was promoting did not exist. In 2022 she was convicted – not for misleading patients but for misleading investors – and sentenced to eleven years in prison.

But many perpetrators of egregious behaviour have remained within the law. The elaborate artificial tax avoidance schemes that have become commonplace among large multi-national companies attract increasing public attention. And the widening gap between the remuneration of chief executives and the earnings of ordinary workers has caused broad concern. Some of these billionaire executives are no superstars: individuals such as Philip Green, who extracted nine-figure sums from retailer BHS before selling the company to multiple bankrupt Dominic Chappell for £1, Mike Ashley, the domineering boss of the retailer Sports Direct, and Eddie Lampert, who inflicted similar destruction on Sears, for a century America's leading store chain. The lifestyle of these executives contrasts with the fate of their businesses. The 90-metre yachts of Green and Lampert make good newspaper pictures. Green's is moored in the harbour of the tax haven of Monaco, where he is resident, while Lampert's is named *Fountainhead*, after Ayn Rand's turgid paean to individualism.

In 2017 Jeffrey Blue, an investment banker advising Ashley, took him to court, claiming that 'after four or five pints in the Horse and Groom public house Ashley had promised him £15 million if the share price of Ashley's company rose to £8'. Witnesses gave evidence that Ashley frequently made business deals while under the influence of alcohol. However, in his judgment Mr Justice Leggatt, echoing Illinois Judge Tharp, opined: 'The fact that Mr Blue has since convinced himself that the offer was a serious one, and that a legally binding agreement was made, shows only that the human capacity for wishful thinking knows few bounds.'[18]

And then the poster children of the internet world became the companies everyone loved to hate. Google's slogan 'Don't be evil' was ridiculed and replaced by the motto 'Do the right thing', itself quietly dropped not long afterwards. Lina Khan's essay excoriating Amazon, published in 2017 while she was still a student at Yale Law School, received wide attention and in 2021 President Biden nominated her as Chair of the Federal Trade Commission. Mark Zuckerberg – still resembling the Harvard student who had launched Facebook from his dorm – became a reviled figure. For Adrienne LaFrance, no demagogue but the editor of the respected *Atlantic* magazine, Facebook was 'an entity engaged in a cold war with the United States and other democracies', 'a lie-disseminating instrument of civilizational collapse'.[19]

The successful businesses that define the modern economy are not well regarded, especially by the young people who are often the most committed users of their products. In 2022, 40 per cent of adult Americans under the age of thirty felt positively about capitalism; but slightly more – 44 per cent – felt positively about socialism.[20] (The poll allowed respondents to approve of both capitalism and socialism. Among those over sixty-five, capitalism was far ahead.) Of course, this finding leaves open what respondents to the poll understood by 'socialism' – the term has been construed very differently by Lenin, Xi Jinping and Bernie Sanders.

Or what respondents understood by 'capitalism'. In his 1946 essay, *Politics and the English Language*, George Orwell observed that 'The word *Fascism* has now no meaning except in so far as it signifies "something not desirable".' Orwell continued: 'It is almost universally felt that when we call a country democratic we are praising it: consequently the defenders of every kind of régime claim that it is a democracy.'[21] (This heuristic remains valid today: the regime over which Kim Jong-Un presides styles itself the Democratic People's Republic of Korea; cynics have observed that every word except 'of' is misleading.)

Something similar has happened to the word 'capitalism'; it has become a term of disapproval, or more rarely approbation, without more specific content. Mostly 'capitalism' is something that the speaker blames for an outcome that he or she dislikes. In the words of journalist Annie Lowrey, '"late capitalism" became a catchall for incidents that capture the tragicomic inanity and inequity of contemporary capitalism. Nordstrom selling jeans with fake mud on them for $425. Prisoners' phone calls costing $14 a minute. Starbucks forcing baristas to write "Come Together" on cups.'[22] More seriously, popular critical discourse emphasises the connection between 'capitalism' and 'inequality', usually without defining either of these complex and ambiguous terms or explaining the relationship between them.

Love the product, hate the producer

And yet ... Boeing created the modern civil aviation market, bringing affordable travel to millions of people worldwide.[23] Every day people step off a Boeing plane to begin their holidays, attend a business meeting or reunite with friends and relatives. Both Facebook and Google have over 2 billion active users – far more customers than any other companies in world history.

In the three centuries since the beginning of the Industrial Revolution business has created previously unimaginable comfort and prosperity for much of the world's population. People trust their employer more than they trust the government, although in the US only Congress is trusted less than big business.[24] Americans regard small business as highly trustworthy. Most readers of this book will recently have met employees who really did put the client's interests first: the helpful shop assistant, the reassuring flight attendant, the devoted nurse or doctor, perhaps even a financial adviser who took time to understand the particular needs of the client.

About 6 million businesses are registered in the UK and over 30 million in the United States. The vast majority of these businesses employ fewer than five people.[25] Typically, they are convenience stores, plumbers and electricians, community lawyers and physicians. Of course, some plumbers are more competent than others, but the trade they all practise is much the same, and they are mainly distinguished from each other by the location in which they operate.

This book is not about these microbusinesses, essential though they are to modern economies. This book is about Goldman Sachs and Boeing, Merck and Pfizer, Google and Apple. These are businesses with distinctive combinations of capabilities that have enabled them to scale their operations, operate globally and employ thousands or tens of thousands of people. Businesses that add value as organisations to the talents of the individuals who work in them. Businesses whose activities impinge on the everyday lives of millions and influence the politics and societies in which they operate.

2

A HISTORY OF PHARMACEUTICALS:
A CASE FOR TREATMENT

> If there was a company that was selling an Aston Martin at
> the price of a bicycle, and we buy that company and we ask
> to charge Toyota prices, I don't think that that should be a
> crime.
>
> Martin Shkreli, CEO of Turing Pharmaceuticals, defending
> a decision to raise the price of a 62-year-old drug to fight
> parasitic infection from $13.50 a tablet to $750, 2017[1]

The pharmaceutical industry has a chequered history. The Carbolic Smoke Ball was typical of the industry's products at the
end of the nineteenth century. Promoters made baseless claims
that their product would cure a wide range of diseases. Widely
advertised elixirs (patent medicines) often contained cocaine and
alcohol.[2] These potions may have made patients feel better but
did little for their health. The term 'snake oil' is still used today
to describe worthless propositions from persuasive salespeo-
ple; medicinal 'snake oils' were once promoted to the gullible
– some really did contain oil from snakes.[3]

The rise of scientific medicine

Some control of medicines had long been practised through
pharmacopoeias: lists of drugs recognised by the medical professionals of the time. But the harsh reality of pre-scientific
medicine was that doctors and apothecaries knew little more
than their patients. Medical practice relied on folk wisdom,

snake oils and an unwarrantedly confident bedside manner.

Drug regulation began in 1906. Congress passed the Pure Food and Drug Act in response to the abuses in the meatpacking industry exposed by Upton Sinclair and the exposé of fraudulent patent medicines described by Samuel Hopkins Adams.[4] Science and medicine were gradually introduced to each other. Aspirin, one of the first drugs with demonstrated efficacy and possibly still the most widely used, was trademarked by the German company Bayer in 1899. (Aspirin became a generic term in the US and UK when Bayer's assets outside Germany were confiscated by First World War belligerents.[5]) Sulfonamides derived from coal tar had been used as dyestuffs for decades. In the 1930s German scientists at Bayer, by then part of IG Farben, conjectured that these compounds might have anti-bacterial action and successfully demonstrated this effect for a drug labelled Prontosil. Thereafter therapeutic sulfonamides were widely marketed.[6]

Events immediately revealed the pharmaceutical industry's potential for both good and harm. A Tennessee company, Massengill, manufactured Elixir Sulfanilamide in 1937 to meet demand from doctors and patients for a liquid formulation. The solid product was dissolved in toxic diethylene glycol, which today is widely used as an anti-freeze. More than a hundred people died; the company's chief chemist, who had not understood the implications of his formulation, committed suicide. Proposals for tighter regulation of new pharmaceutical compounds had been controversial in Congress but were now quickly passed into law.[7]

In the 1950s the German company Chemie Grünenthal marketed Thalidomide, a sedative widely prescribed for morning sickness in pregnant women. The Distillers Company, the poorly managed dominant producer of Scotch whisky, obtained a British licence for the product. The drug was linked to birth defects and withdrawn from the market in 1961, but tragically not before many children in Britain and Germany had been born with seriously deformed limbs.[8] A campaign to obtain compensation for the victims dragged on for many years.[9] In the United States,

Frances Kelsey documented the Elixir Sulfonamide tragedy when she was a graduate student. Later, as a reviewer for the Food and Drugs Administration, she thought the information provided on the safety and efficacy of Thalidomide inadequate and refused to authorise its use. President Kennedy subsequently awarded her a medal for distinguished public service.[10]

Antibiotics

The anti-bacterial properties of penicillin were observed in 1928 by Alexander Fleming at St Mary's Hospital in London. Still, this discovery attracted little interest. Stop there for a moment: for a decade, neither government nor business pursued one of the most important innovations of the century – and one with huge commercial potential. Shortly before the outbreak of the Second World War, however, the Rockefeller Foundation funded research by Howard Florey and Ernst Chain at Oxford University who were trying to find a way to synthesise penicillin.[11] They would go on to share a Nobel Prize with Fleming.

The war concentrated minds and released funds – similar effects were observed in many other areas of innovation. Florey visited the US to evangelise for penicillin and found an enthusiastic supporter in George Merck, president of the company that bears his name. The Distillers Company's ill-fated diversification into pharmaceuticals originated in an invitation from the British government's wartime Ministry of Supply to manage a newly constructed penicillin plant in Liverpool. The Ministry had evidently perceived some similarities between whisky distillation and the synthesis of penicillin. Sulfonamides and penicillin were the first antibiotics, and over the following decades this category of drugs would cure millions of people who would otherwise have died of infectious diseases. The life-changing potential of pharmacology was now apparent – as was the opportunity to create profitable new business ventures.

Merck was one of the first companies to recognise that potential – and to benefit from it. George Merck senior had emigrated to the United States at the end of the nineteenth century to establish a branch of his family's German pharmacy business. The company describes the 'Merck Manual' of those times as 'a widely used medical reference' – it advocated bloodletting as a treatment for bronchitis and arsenic as a remedy for impotence.[12] Merck Manuals are still a widely used medical reference, though they now contain more reliable information. The American branch of the German company was nationalised in 1917, and when the war ended, George himself purchased its stock from the US government. German and American Merck were then, and remain, wholly separate businesses.[13]

George senior's son, George W. Merck, turned the company into a research-oriented business that has been listed on the New York Stock Exchange since 1927. After his meeting with Florey, and following the attack at Pearl Harbor, Merck made a commitment to mass production of penicillin; supplies were made available not only to the military but also to other companies and researchers. In 1944 Merck launched streptomycin, another antibiotic, discovered by Rutgers chemist Selman Waksman.[14] The first patient successfully treated with streptomycin was US Army Lieutenant Robert Dole, subsequently Senate majority leader and Republican presidential candidate, who lived for another seventy-five years.[15] This drug was not just the first effective treatment for tuberculosis; it was a cure. George Orwell, dying from the disease, persuaded David Astor, the rich Anglo-American editor of the *Observer* (for which Orwell was a columnist) to purchase a supply of streptomycin from the US. But the author of *1984* responded badly to the drug and died in 1950.[16] Penicillin and streptomycin were licenced freely, but in future, pharmaceutical companies would guard their intellectual property much more closely.

In 1950 Merck famously told students at the Medical College of Virginia: 'We try never to forget that medicine is for the people. It is not for the profits. The profits follow, and if we have remembered that, they have never failed to appear. The better we have remembered it, the larger they have been.'[17] Johnson &

Johnson's 308-word credo, published in 1944, is the work of R. W. Johnson, another member of a founding family. Its emphasis on profit as a result rather than an objective resembles the sentiment of George Merck.[18] In what became a classic business-school case on ethics and corporate reputation, the company's executives applied the credo in 1982 to implement a speedy product recall of Tylenol, the business's best-selling painkiller, after a criminal spiked containers with cyanide.[19] Middle managers did not have to be told to take the products off the shelves; they knew that was the right thing to do and were correctly confident that their bosses would support them.[20]

In the 1980s Merck chemists suspected that a veterinary product they had developed might treat river blindness, a disease caused by a parasite that grows inside the human body and leads to immense suffering for millions in sub-Saharan Africa. Merck created an appropriately modified version of the drug and confirmed its efficacy. Failing to persuade governments or charities to fund further development, the company decided to give the medication away to all who might benefit and continues to do so. (The cost of this philanthropic gesture is less than might be imagined because it is sufficient to take the tablet once a year.[21])

For many years Merck topped *Fortune* magazine's list of most admired companies.[22] The company was an exemplar of successful long-term corporate strategy in business guru Jim Collins's 1994 classic *Built to Last*. Collins's research method was to pair what he described as 'visionary' companies – Merck was one – with more pedestrian but similarly large companies in the same industry. Collins compared Merck to Pfizer and contrasted George Merck's 'medicine is for the people' with the emphasis of his counterpart at Pfizer, John McKeen: 'so far as humanly possible, we aim to get profit out of everything we do.'[23] Collins's argument stressed that, *judged by stock returns*, the 'visionary' companies, including Merck, had far outperformed their comparators.

The tide turns

The post-war pharmaceutical industry enjoyed an implicit contract with the public and the government. The arrangement was complex: drug pricing was, and remains, controversial. The most profitable drugs were not the lifesavers – such as antibiotics and vaccines – but those that alleviate but do not cure chronic diseases suffered by rich people – depression, hypertension, excess stomach acidity. Pharmaceutical products benefit from patent protection, and regulation both constrains their use and restricts competition. But overall, the industry was permitted extraordinary profitability in return for the businesses behaving as exemplary corporate citizens. Yet those days have long gone.

Drug companies came under pressure from Wall Street to demonstrate their commitment to securing value for shareholders. The pay-off from marketing is immediate whereas the pay-off from research is delayed, and industry strategy came to reflect that difference. Merck stumbled – the company would feature again in a 2009 book by Collins, *How the Mighty Fall*. Ten years earlier, Merck had marketed a new painkiller, Vioxx, not just for the minority of patients who derived a unique benefit but for many who might just as advantageously for them, if less profitably for the pharmaceutical industry, have taken an aspirin. US law permits direct advertising of prescription drugs to patients, and for a time Vioxx was the most heavily promoted product in that category.[24] As Ray Gilmartin, then Merck CEO, explained in the company's 2000 annual report: 'as a company, Merck is totally focussed on growth.'[25]

That is not a good strapline for a healthcare company; demand for its products is a regrettable necessity. Vioxx was linked to heart conditions in some patients. Merck withdrew the product in 2004 amid recrimination and lawsuits. Even the revered Johnson & Johnson would find its reputation tarnished by the regulator's discovery of bad practice – and inadequate management responses – at the company's McNeil consumer products group.[26] Merck and Johnson & Johnson deservedly remain respected businesses – 2020's *Fortune* list put J&J at 26 and Merck at 49 in its top fifty admired companies.[27] But they are now outliers in their industry.

When Michael Pearson took over as chief executive of Valeant Pharmaceuticals in 2008, he adopted a new strategy. Others in the industry had been edging towards this approach, but Pearson made it explicit. Valeant bought established drug companies, stopped research and development, emphasised marketing and raised substantially the prices of the proven products to which it had acquired the rights. For a time, the company's profits and share price responded favourably, and Pearson and other executives rewarded themselves accordingly. Some senior employees revelled in the atmosphere of unfettered greed sufficiently thoroughly to commit fraud. When illegality was revealed, Pearson was forced out and the company's shares plummeted; the business has since rebranded itself as Bausch Health, taking the name of the respected eyeglass supplier it had acquired.[28]

Valeant's approach found imitators, however. Martin Shkreli adopted an even more extreme strategy of price gouging at Turing Pharmaceuticals, increasing the cost of Daraprim, on the market since 1953, from $13.50 to $750.[29] In 2007 generic drugs producer Mylan acquired the rights of the long-established EpiPen® – used to provide urgent relief to people with severe allergies – and over the next ten years gradually raised the price sixfold.[30] The company paid almost a billion dollars to settle – 'without admission of liability' – claims that it had violated antitrust laws and defrauded Medicaid.[31] In 2019 Mylan merged with a divested subsidiary of Pfizer and renamed the business Viatris. 'Deriving its name from Latin, Viatris embodies the new company's goal of providing a path – "VIA" – to three – "TRIS" – core goals: expanding access to medicines, leading by innovating to meet patient needs, and being a trusted partner for the healthcare community worldwide.' Chairman Robert J. Coury declared 'We are creating a company unlike any other – a company focused on building a more hopeful and sustainable healthcare journey, empowering patients to live healthier [*sic*] at every stage of life.'[32] But, as the American Chamber of Commerce reminds us, all companies make statements of this kind.

But the most egregious abuse was the aggressive marketing of addictive drugs. Purdue Pharma, privately owned by the Sackler family, is now notorious for promoting opioids to small-town America. And even Johnson & Johnson agreed to contribute $5 billion to a settlement, led by the Sacklers, in acknowledgement of J&J's role in 'deaths of despair'.[33]

The Sackler family have been generous philanthropists, making donations to museums and galleries in London and New York and to Oxford's Bodleian Libraries. This philanthropy has become controversial, with a campaign demanding that Sackler gifts be refused and the family name removed from the buildings that they financed.[34] The protest is led by the queer American photographer Nan Goldin, who battled an addiction to OxyContin (produced by Purdue Pharma). The issues are not straightforward: would critics prefer that the family spent its undeserved money on itself rather than on purposes of public benefit?

Drug companies continued to push the limits of customary behaviour. Insys Therapeutics had developed an opioid for terminally ill cancer patients, for whom its highly addictive properties were of no consequence. But this market was doubly limited: only the terminally ill were customers, and they soon ceased to be customers (although they were replaced by newly diagnosed cancer patients). The head of sales for Insys, Alec Burlakoff, hired a stripper to persuade physicians to promote and prescribe the opioid to non-terminal patients, giving a new interpretation to the term 'hooker'.[35] In an interview with the *Financial Times*, Burlakoff acknowledged that he did not have 'morals, ethics and values'.[36] He described his thinking once he realised that prosecution was likely: 'Not only is the company going to get fined an astronomical amount of money, which I've seen a million times, but worse [*sic*] case scenario, which I've never seen before, they might actually take *my* money.'

Burlakoff and his fellow executives were prosecuted under federal racketeering legislation aimed at criminal gangs; they are now serving prison terms. A pharmaceutical industry that once seemed to exemplify a constructive relationship between private enterprise and public benefit had become widely and justifiably detested. In 2019 Gallup asked Americans whether their view of a list of twenty-five activities was favourable or unfavourable. Only four had net negative ratings – federal government, public relations, healthcare and pharmaceuticals – and pharma's score was much the worst.[37]

The quest for a Covid-19 vaccine

On the last day of 2019, China notified the World Health Organization of an outbreak of a novel coronavirus around the city of Wuhan. In 2020 the virus spread across the world, overwhelming hospital facilities. By the end of the year the illness was implicated in the deaths of millions of people. Lockdowns crippled many businesses and resulted in massive losses of economic output.[38]

Within a few weeks the genome of the virus had been identified, and work began to produce a vaccine. There were two strands of development: the traditional approach to vaccine production, which employs a weakened or modified strain of the virus to provoke the production of antibodies, and a still experimental procedure, modified ribonucleic acid (mRNA), that trains the body to generate its own immune response – an idea that would win a Nobel Prize in 2023 for its pioneers Katalin Karikó and Drew Weissman. In the US and Britain, governments offered funding for vaccine development by pharmaceutical companies and placed large advance orders for successful products. The European Union did something similar on behalf of member states but more slowly and less effectively.[39] Within a year four companies – AstraZeneca, Johnson and Johnson, Moderna and Pfizer – had taken their vaccines through clinical trials and obtained emergency use authorisation in several countries.

Fortune's 2021 most admired companies list showed that the rankings of Johnson & Johnson and Merck had risen by more than ten points. Merck's rating had improved even though the company's vaccine product had failed in trials. The speed and overall effectiveness of response had done something to restore the industry's damaged reputation. And yet the negative consequences of past abuses lingered. The conspiracy allegations that circulated on the wilder fringes of the internet can perhaps be discounted – there has always been an audience for such stories. But take-up was inhibited even among otherwise reasonable people by baseless claims of unacknowledged side effects. In Gallup's 2020 survey, pharma's net favourability rating had improved by seven points. But it was still the lowest of any industry sector.[40]

A Case for Treatment

The pharmaceutical industry illustrates modern business at its best and worst. Its products – antibiotics, anti-hypertensives, statins, vaccines and many others – have saved hundreds of millions of lives and improved the quality of life for almost everyone. Its revenues have funded new research and made large profits for investors. Since stock in companies such as Merck, Pfizer, AstraZeneca and Roche is widely held by individuals and institutions, these returns have contributed to the retirement funds of many people. The profits have also supported the philanthropy of Merck and, even though one should hesitate to applaud, the benefactions of the Sacklers. The Novo Nordisk Foundation, which owns a controlling stake in the Danish drugmaker, is the largest charitable foundation in the world, and the Wellcome Trust, by far the biggest educational endowment in Britain, has funded British science to remarkable effect.[41] Thus two of the four largest charities globally are the result of the philanthropy of the leaders of the pharmaceutical industry: the Danes August

Krogh and Harald Pedersen and the British Henry Wellcome.[42] (The list of leading charitable foundations is completed by those established by Bill Gates and by Sweden's Ingvar Kamprad, founder of furniture chain IKEA.)

But the same industry also illustrates all the features that have led to public mistrust of big business. Many of its executives have demonstrated standards of behaviour far below those that any modern society could accept or should tolerate from people occupying positions of responsibility whose actions bear crucially on the welfare of others.

The pursuit of 'shareholder value', the belief that profit is the defining purpose of a corporation, was one element in the decline of ethical standards. Yet the pharmaceutical industry is also a powerful counterexample to a simplistic view of the problem of 'short-termism'. Venture capitalists cluster around bright academics who have innovative ideas with possible commercial potential. Many established companies invest heavily in the development and trials of new products, the majority of which will fail, and few of which will yield revenues for many years.

This is an important and underappreciated point: there is no shortage of 'patient capital' – institutions such as pension funds and university endowments are naturally looking for investments that may only pay off in the long term – but there is a shortage of patient individuals working in the finance sector, an industry remunerated almost entirely by transactions. The result is a constant flurry of financial activity engaging senior executives, investment professionals and advisers which rarely adds to, and often detracts from, the effectiveness and success of the underlying business. The financial pressures that motivated strategy at Merck and Valeant not only damaged the standing of the businesses and their products but also diminished the returns to their shareholders in the long run. In later chapters I will show that these are far from exceptional cases.

The history of pharmaceuticals illustrates much that is right and wrong in the relationship between business and society. I have described four problem areas: the motivation and standards of behaviour of leaders of the industry; the interface between business and finance; the difficulty of constructing a regulatory regime that is relevant and effective; and the sometimes too tenuous relationships between prices, costs and values. None of these issues is unique to the pharmaceutical sector: similar questions arise in every kind of business, and the answers are necessarily specific to industry, time and place. But in this book – and another that will follow – I will illustrate principles and directions of travel.

3

ECONOMIC MOTIVATION

[They] are employed in contriving a new form of
government for an extensive empire, which, they flatter
themselves, will become, and which, indeed, seems very
likely to become, one of the greatest and most formidable
that ever was in the world.

Adam Smith in *The Wealth of Nations*, 1776[1]

In 1776 Britain's American colonies rebelled. Fifty-six delegates to
the Second Continental Congress, including Benjamin Franklin
and Thomas Jefferson, signed the Declaration of Independence.
In the same year Adam Smith, often described as the founder of
economics, published his masterwork. His Scottish homeland,
united with England seventy years earlier, was experiencing the
beginnings of the Industrial Revolution.

Smith's assessment of the future of the United States of
America was prescient. But he is remembered best not for his
political acumen but for his economic insight. 'It is the great
multiplication of the productions of all the different arts, in consequence of the division of labour, which occasions in a well
governed society that universal opulence which extends itself to
the lowest ranks of the people,' he wrote.[2] And that would be
the experience of both Scotland and the United States.

The economist's usual measure of output and income is
Gross Domestic Product (GDP), and inflation-adjusted GDP
per head in Britain has grown more than tenfold since 1776.[3]
But that statistic gives little insight into the scale of the change.
Smith wrote the manuscript of *The Wealth of Nations* with a quill

pen. His Edinburgh residence did not have running water and was lit by candlelight. It stood just off the Royal Mile, the city's principal artery, which ran from the castle to the palace of Holyrood House and stank of horse droppings. Panmure House, recently restored by Edinburgh Business School, is in Lochend Close, a narrow street that ran down to the eastern end of the Nor' Loch, which received the sewage of the Old Town. After being drained (work was beginning as Smith was completing his manuscript) the Loch became Princes Street Gardens and is today one of the city's most attractive features. But in Smith's time, the view across it was obscured for most of the year by the smoke of coal-burning fires which gave the city the nickname of 'Auld Reekie'. Most children then did not survive infancy, and when Smith died at the age of sixty-seven he would have been regarded as a very old man.[4]

The Wealth of Nations famously begins with a description of a pin factory:

> I have seen a small manufactory of this kind where ten men only were employed. ... Each person, therefore, making a tenth part of forty-eight thousand pins, might be considered as making four thousand eight hundred pins in a day. But if they had all wrought separately and independently, and without any of them having been educated to this peculiar business, they certainly could not each of them have made twenty, perhaps not one pin in a day.[5]

The story of Smith's book is the story of how 'the great multiplication of the productions of all the different arts, in consequence of the division of labour', the accumulation of collective knowledge and the combination of specialist capabilities took us in two and a half centuries from the business world of the pin factory to the business world of the iPhone, the Facebook and the Airbus.

Collective activity

Humans are social animals. Like other animals, humans compete – for material possessions, for sex, for primacy – but we are distinguished from other mammals by the extent of our capacity to communicate and cooperate. The scale of this combination of communication and cooperation gives humans capabilities unrivalled by any other species.

We need to belong, we need affirmation and we understand that we can accomplish things through collective action that would be far beyond the capacity of any individual. Competition is a spur to effort, innovation and creativity; cooperation is necessary to make that effort productive and to realise the fruits of innovation and creativity. National economic success depends on the effectiveness with which societies manage the tension between the human impulse to compete and the human pleasure in successful cooperation. And so does business success.

> A strand of research in social psychology, beginning with the 'Robbers' Cave' experiment of Muzafer Sherif, observed human tendencies both to create 'in' groups (cooperation) and to reinforce that identification by shared hostility to 'out' groups (competition). This phenomenon, now described as 'affective polarisation', is widely discussed in the context of contemporary political developments.

Organisations exist because humans can do things collectively that they cannot achieve individually. In 2009 designer Thomas Thwaites set out to build a toaster – on his own, from scratch.[6] It took nine months, costing him 250 times as much as a toaster from the local shop. And his product wasn't as good as the shop-bought toaster. It was at least possible for Thwaites to build an – inferior – toaster unaided. But no individual could build an iPhone or a nuclear power station and no individual even knows how to. Rousseau observed that a group could hunt stags while individuals could only catch hares.[7] You can read this book because of the joint efforts of many people whom neither I, the author, nor you, the reader, will ever know.

People establish sports clubs, and members join them to enjoy the benefits of collective endeavour. Parliament author-ised a National Gallery and many people have donated pictures to it or allowed works they own to be displayed there. Millions from around the world enjoy the collection. Professionals work together in schools, hospitals and universities because they know they can serve students and patients better and advance knowledge more effectively by sharing their knowledge and experience than by working independently. Humans can't fly, but a group of humans working together can build an airliner. And a pilot, with the assistance of thousands of other people in the air and on the ground, can fly it around the world with several hundred people on board.

The test of the success of any organisation – the stag hunt, Airbus and Boeing, the publishing company, the sports club, the National Gallery, the school, hospital or university – is that the product of the joint endeavour is more valuable than the product of the sum of individual actions. Attempts by individuals to fly are laughable, but groups of people can build and operate air-craft. The role of a publisher is to combine and coordinate the range of activities, from author to editor to printer to bookseller, needed to put this volume in your hands. Combination and coor-dination are key to business – and to progress of all kinds.

The medieval monk's manuscript was available to very few. But once allied with the printing press of inventor and busi-nessman Johannes Gutenberg, the cleric's erudition was open to many. Exercise with others is more enjoyable, and the club can access facilities that an individual alone cannot provide. The National Gallery gives more pleasure to more people than the same pictures hung in multiple private locations. The univer-sity can deliver a better education if its students can access the wisdom of many scholars. The effective professional service organisation – school or hospital, law firm or consultancy – bene-fits from the aggregation of knowledge of many individuals with different capabilities and experiences. That aggregation yields a collective knowledge available to all which can be the basis of a collective intelligence – the shared knowledge and capabilities of people working together – that can deliver fresh insights and offer solutions to business, social and scientific problems.

Opportunities to add value by collective action are all around us. Even the lonely long-distance runner derives pleasure from participation in an organised marathon. I shall use sporting illustrations frequently in this book. I have little more than a passing interest in sport. But sport reveals the benefits of the human capacity to compete and cooperate simultaneously – and most people can talk about sport without bringing to that discussion the preconceptions that colour their thoughts about business. Few events exemplify the combination of competition and cooperation more clearly than the gathering together of 50,000 people so that each can run 26 miles around the streets of London or New York.

Sources of motivation

Thus the rationale of collective action is rarely purely economic. Few participants in marathons do so for financial reasons – probably not even Tata Consultancy Services, part of the family-controlled Indian conglomerate and the lead sponsor of the race in both cities. Many run to raise money for charity. Nothing illustrates affective polarisation more clearly than the crowds at sporting events; 'No one likes us, we don't care' runs the chant. And even in the workplace, where the underlying rationale of collective action *is* primarily economic, the social dimension is conjoined.

The most influential description of the sources of human motivation, and the one best known outside the strictly academic literature on psychology, is Abraham Maslow's hierarchy of needs. People have basic physiological needs for food and shelter, and then for security; once these requirements are satisfied, they are able to seek belonging and affirmation; and then, as they achieve these, they can pursue the ultimate goal of self-actualisation. Subsequent research and its popularisation – such as Martin Seligman's 'positive psychology' – tend to recognise the notion of multiple needs but are less supportive of Maslow's hierarchical ordering.[8] Even poor people in poor countries, in common with most people in rich countries, express a need for belonging and affirmation.

Employees, of course, go to work expecting a pay cheque that will fund the groceries and the rent. But in a well-functioning organisation they also look forward to the camaraderie of the workplace. They welcome acknowledgement of their skills and contributions from their colleagues and bosses. Employees take satisfaction from being associated with the creation of fine products and satisfied consumers. The bonus is valued as a symbol of affirmation as well as for its cash value. Even in corrupt environments – whether Mafia clans or among the traders who conspired to fix interest rates at the time of the global financial crisis – there is a need for the approbation of co-workers.

The psychologist Mihaly Csikszentmihalyi finds that when people are asked to report on their state of happiness at a particular moment pleasure is found more often at work than at home. And he describes 'flow', the elation that comes from complete engagement in the successful performance of a difficult task.[9]

The experience of 'flow' is what drives people to risk their lives climbing mountains in weather that would lead others to flee for safety. However, the experience of flow is most often realised in the context of a collective activity. To recognise the power of flow, watch Lionel Messi's goal against Getafe, Steve Jobs launching the iPhone in San Francisco or Claudio Abbado conducting the Berlin Philharmonic Orchestra at the BBC Proms in the same year.[10] I vividly recall attending a play in a London theatre starring Sir Alec Guinness when there was a disturbance in the auditorium. Guinness exited the part, pointed at the culprits and said, 'Would you stop that?' before resuming as if nothing had happened. I had seen a consummate professional in flow.

But Guinness was not performing for reasons of altruism.

Few experiences flatter the ego as much as commanding an audience from a West End stage, or fill the wallet as amply as appearing, as Guinness did, in *Star Wars*. Messi is one of the best-paid sportspeople in the world. It is difficult to see any public benefit from Reinhold Messner's solo ascent of Everest, and public benefit was certainly not what he had in mind in undertaking it. In all these cases vanity and self-interest were not the only motives, but undeniably they *were* motives.

I might leave the last word to Steve Jobs: 'The only way to be truly satisfied is to do what you believe is great work. And the only way to do great work is to love what you do.'[11] As with Guinness, Messi and Messner, Jobs's career illustrates that high professional skill is often associated with extreme self-absorption. Claudio Abbado, who seems to have been distinguished from most conductors by a degree of personal modesty, explained why he had chosen not to conduct American orchestras: 'they finish the rehearsal not because the music is finished, but because the time is finished.'[12] A powerful expression of the difference between a group of people working together towards a common objective and individuals fulfilling their contractual obligations.

Another account

These observations are so immediately consonant with our everyday experience as to seem banal, even trivial. Yet much of what is written about business – by supporters, by critics and also by scholars – tells a very different story. One strand of thought finds its origins in Marxist thinking – business represents the front line of a class struggle that pits the bourgeoisie against the proletariat. Another is mechanical – the firm is defined by its production relations, akin to physical or chemical processes that deliver predictable output from specified inputs. Both of these approaches find their origins in the observation of nineteenth-century business.

And they remain influential despite dramatic changes in society, politics and technology. Class and status do play a role in business, although a rather different one from that which they played in 1850. Then almost half the English population was illiterate; now almost half attend university.[13] Then Parliament was dominated by a hereditary aristocracy; now universal franchise has been in operation for a century.[14] Then the board of a British corporation – a bank or railway – would be composed of grandees, while persons concerned with operational matters – the general manager or the chief locomotive engineer – would be left in no doubt of their subordinate status.[15] Today the members of the board are more likely to defer to the acknowledged and admired wisdom of the CEO. Or perhaps to recognise that their fees are contingent on the continued display of such deference.

The United States had broken free of the hereditary aristocracy and achieved widespread literacy more quickly; but it quickly came to acquire a class structure of its own, based in the first instance on acquired wealth rather than noble birth. But by the end of the Gilded Age New York society featured Mrs Astor's 'four hundred': 'If you go outside that number you strike people who are either not at ease in a ballroom or make other people not at ease', in the words of her consigliere, Ward McAllister.[16] Even within the 'four hundred' old wealth was more favoured than new, symbolised by the struggles of the Vanderbilts to gain acceptance. But Mrs Vanderbilt triumphed, and in the twentieth century the 'swells' eclipsed the 'nobs' in the US, in Britain and – less decisively – in continental Europe. Throughout the Global North today status is mostly the product of personal achievement or celebrity, of a varied but not always admirable kind.

The modern counterpart to Mrs Astor's balls is the annual gala of the Metropolitan Museum of Art. Tickets reportedly cost $50,000, and attendees need to be vetted by a panel chaired by *Vogue* editor Anna Wintour, who in 2023 was joined by Penélope Cruz and Roger Federer. In 2021 progressive Congresswoman Alexandria Ocasio-Cortez attended in a dress featuring the exhortation 'Tax the Rich', an injunction that might not have passed the scrutiny of Mrs Astor's footmen.

The United Nations Commission for Trade and Development (UNCTAD) adopts the following classification: 'The developing economies broadly comprise Africa, Latin America and the Caribbean, Asia without Israel, Japan, and the Republic of Korea, and Oceania without Australia and New Zealand. The developed economies broadly comprise Northern America and Europe, Israel, Japan, the Republic of [i.e. South] Korea, Australia, and New Zealand.' Reflecting the (approximate) geographical location of these countries, it is now common to refer to these groups as the 'Global South' and 'Global North' respectively. Despite the obvious anomalies, I follow this convention.

The tripartite linkage

For most of history, and into the Gilded Age, the word 'capital' was used to describe both personal wealth and the physical means of production. Before the Industrial Revolution land was the main constituent of both. (And it is a principal component still, although it is urban land not agricultural land which dominates. Today the word 'capital' is often used loosely to describe both capital as a factor of production and capital as financial assets which need not be connected, directly or indirectly, to any tangible object. The term 'capital' is also used as a measure of the net worth of an individual or a corporate entity. The many meanings of the word 'capital' and in particular the distinction between capital as wealth and capital as factor of production are discussed more fully in Chapter 29.)

The connection from personal wealth to the provision of productive capital to control of business was a defining characteristic of the Industrial Revolution. I describe that connection as 'the tripartite linkage' and throughout this book we will see its dissolution. Indeed the linkage was eroding even as the Industrial Revolution progressed; prior business success came to play a larger role than inherited land and property in providing tangible capital for new ventures.

There is a certain hubris, or perhaps just a lack of imagination, in believing that the language and models devised to describe a business landscape of textile mills and ironworks described by Adam Smith and Karl Marx and a financial system moulded by Aaron Burr and Alexander Hamilton can easily be adapted to describe the business world of Apple and Google. For J. P. Morgan 'the first thing in credit is character'; today the most successful financiers are pioneers of algorithmic trading, conducted anonymously by computers. And slogans calling for the overthrow of capitalism are carried on fashionable dresses at the Met Gala rather than on picket lines at Andrew Carnegie's Homestead Steel Works.

In the last half-century economists and legal scholars have emphasised personal rather than class identity. The language of individualism has been central to political and economic thought and today underpins much political philosophy. John Rawls and Robert Nozick each drew on the perspectives of modern economics to develop new social contractarian theories of the state. Rawls's emphasis on the welfare of the worst off appealed to the political left, Nozick's concern for the protection of property rights to supporters of the right.

Rawls and Nozick set out their views in major books published in the 1970s: *A Theory of Justice* and *Anarchy, State and Utopia* respectively. Rawls asked the question of how we would like society to be structured if we were behind a 'veil of ignorance' and did not know which position we would occupy in that society' He concluded that self-interest would lead us to want to protect the worst off. In contrast, Nozick's 'entitlement theory' protected property acquired through 'just acquisition' or 'just transfer' and viewed the state as a social contract individuals make to protect their own rights. His conclusion was that a just society was one where people were relatively unconstrained, even if this meant that some did much better than others – the state should not, for example, be engaged in redistribution of income.

Both these philosophical approaches polarise agency between the individual and the state, with the right emphasising personal autonomy and the left looking to the government to regulate and enforce collective action. In doing so, both schools minimise the role of communities: the communities of place and of work which are critical to our economic as well as our social lives. And they marginalise the competition and cooperation between these communities which is the basis of our prosperity – and our culture.

The nexus of contracts

A 1976 article by Michael Jensen and William Meckling is one of the most widely cited modern academic expositions of the dominant model of the business organisation, with more than 130,000 works referring to it. Jensen and Meckling assert that 'most organisations are simply legal fictions which serve as a nexus for a set of contracting arrangements among individuals.'[17] They describe the firm as a nexus of contracts, a group of people who – for the time being – find it advantageous to do business with each other.

Meckling died in 1998. Michael Jensen, who died as this book went to press, underwent an epiphany after his daughter introduced him to the self-help guru Werner Erhard.[18] Erhard (real name Jack Rosenberg) was a controversial figure whose career seemed to have been destroyed when allegations of tax evasion and sexual abuse were featured in a CBS documentary; these allegations were subsequently discredited, and it has been claimed they were orchestrated by the Scientology movement.[19] Jensen's most recent writings, in partnership with Erhard, involved complex arguments on the theme of integrity.

In the application of such individualistic thinking to business, the social instincts that are essential aspects of human behaviour – including economic behaviour – have been subordinated to an almost exclusive emphasis on response to incentives. Rationality has been reduced to little more than acquisitiveness. Investment bankers salivate at the approach of bonus season as Pavlov's dogs did to the chiming of his bell; they learn to press levers, as Skinner's rats did, to obtain their rewards.[20] These assumptions about agency and motivation tend to become self-fulfilling when organisations are designed around them. And the organisations that are designed around them are mechanical, not social.

In my book *Foundations of Corporate Success*, published in 1993, I was sympathetic to the 'nexus of contracts' approach, believing – as I still do – that the essence of the firm was an assembly of relationships among individuals. But I did not then realise, as I now do, that the advocates of this idea visualised these relationships as transactional rather than social. A central argument of the present book is that by excessive emphasis on the transactional nature of business relationships we have undermined not only the relationship between business and society but also the effectiveness of business, even in transactional terms.

PART 2

A BRIEF HISTORY OF BUSINESS

In medieval and Renaissance times, business was conducted by guilds and merchants. The Industrial Revolution of the eighteenth century led to the emergence of production lines facilitating repetitive manufacturing processes. In the Global North, the economic role of such manufacturing peaked in the mid-twentieth century. Thereafter, business increasingly provided services rather than goods, and manufactured products became knowledge-intensive rather than resource-intensive. Business organisation and business finance evolved in line with these changes in the nature of production. But the language and models used to describe them did not.

4

THE MECHANICAL FIRM

If God had meant there to be more than two factors of
production, He would have made it easier for us to draw
three-dimensional diagrams.

Robert Solow, *c.*1956[1]

Every beginning economics student is introduced to the model
of a production function pioneered by Philip Wicksteed (1894).
Output is the result of the combination of capital and labour.
Some nineteenth-century commentators, such as the economist
Alfred Marshall, still saw land as a third factor of production,
but, as agriculture declined as a share of national income and
industry grew, this third factor almost disappeared from economic analysis. Somewhat strangely. The fertility of land may
not matter much now, but its location does. If you think the
world is flat, look at a cityscape of Manhattan or Canary Wharf.
And ask why so much modern wealth is attributable to urban
land.[2]

But two-dimensional diagrams were easier, and the two
chosen dimensions were capital and labour. The economic
description of the firm as production function and the Marxist
view of the firm as the front line of the class struggle both
embraced this two-dimensional description, although in quite
different ways and with quite different implications. Late nineteenth-century economists such as John Bates Clark and Knut
Wicksell explained that businesses could choose to install more
machinery or less, depending on the relative scarcity and prices
of capital and labour. The Marxist view saw the distribution of

the value added by the business as the outcome of a bargaining process in which the odds were stacked against the property-less workers. Thus the division of the surplus of production between the two factors was the outcome of economic forces – the relative contribution of the two factors of production – and political forces – the relative power of the providers. Classical economists emphasised the economic forces, Marxists the social.

The more capital and labour are used, the more output there will be: doubling the application of the two factors of production will double output, or perhaps a little more than double output, if there are economies of scale. Labour and capital can be substituted for each other, but there will be diminishing returns if more capital is applied to a fixed quantity of labour or more labour is applied to a fixed quantity of capital. (The most commonly used example of this mathematical relationship is known as the Cobb–Douglas production function, named after mathematician Charles Cobb and economist Paul Douglas; the latter served as US senator for Illinois for twenty years.[3]) A firm seeking to minimise the cost of any desired level of output would choose a mix of capital and labour reflecting the relative prices of the two factors of production – the interest rate or cost of capital and the wage of labour.

With imitable technology and little ability to restrict potential competition, all firms have similar production functions, and many will therefore produce much the same output from the same quantities of capital and labour. If the price of the good concerned is such that the value of output is greater than the cost of production, given wages and interest rates, it will be profitable for established firms to expand and for new firms to enter the market. Conversely, if demand and prices fall and the output is worth less than the production cost, firms will contract production and weak firms may go out of business.

The assumption that production functions are common to all firms and potential firms and do not change over time is key to this model and its implications. That model was a reasonable approximation to the reality of production in the ironworks and textile mills of the Industrial Revolution. And perhaps remained descriptive of the new manufacturing processes that came into operation in the nineteenth and twentieth centuries.

Twentieth-century economists such as John Hicks, Roy Harrod and especially Robert Solow recognised that production functions might change over time. A simple modification to the basic model allows output from any given combination of capital and labour to increase over time as a result of technical progress, or simply from greater experience of repetitive tasks. Technical progress was something that just happened, described by some sceptics as 'manna from heaven'; technical progress might augment the productivity of capital, or labour, or both. In this latter case it was described as a rise in 'total factor productivity'. Such technical progress was an explanation – of sorts – of the very obvious phenomenon of the growth of economic output far in excess of the rate of growth of capital and labour.

In a further modification, Paul Romer developed the idea that such technical change was not 'manna from heaven' but was endogenous, the result of prior investment by the firms that benefited from it.[4] In 1994 the rumbustious Conservative politician Michael Heseltine reduced the audience at a party conference to helpless laughter by parsing the phrase 'neo-classical endogenous growth theory' in a speech. 'It's not Brown, it's Balls,' he roared, referring to the opposition finance spokesman (and future prime minister) Gordon Brown and his economist aide (and future cabinet minister and star of *Strictly Come Dancing*) Ed Balls.[5]

'Scientific' Management

Perhaps Heseltine had a point. This model has no concept of business as social organisation. The firm is a collection of assets owned by people called capitalists, who employ workers and order them to attend their premises and operate their plant and machinery. The most senior workers, titled executives, deliver

instructions to subordinate managers, and so on down an organisational hierarchy.

Frederick Taylor worked in and around the industrial plants
of Pennsylvania at the beginning of the twentieth century. He
summarised his thinking, based on the politics and economics
of the assembly line, in *The Principles of Scientific Management*
(1911). Taylor sought to break down the business process into
individual components which could be measured and monitored. 'Taylorism' asserted that ignorant workers needed to be
given precise job descriptions and not only required but benefited from this exercise of authority. Indeed Taylor described
and interacted with working people in ways that sound grossly
offensive to a modern ear: 'When he could not persuade workers
to try his new systems, he fired them, one by one, until they fell
into line.'[6]

But 'some of the best workers who are, however, either
stupid or stubborn, can never be made to see that [Taylor's] new
system is as good as the old; and these, too, must drop out.'[7]
Initiative from workers was completely counter to the spirit of
the transformation: 'no gang boss is fit to direct his men until
after he has learned to promptly obey instructions received
from any proper source, whether he likes his instructions and
the instructor or not, and even though he may be convinced
that he knows a much better way of doing the work.'[8] Despite
claiming an affinity with, and understanding of, workers, Taylor
did not hold back when they got in his way: 'Certain men are
both thick-skinned and coarse-grained ... the severity of both
words and manners should be gradually increased until either
the desired result has been attained or the possibilities of the
English language have been exhausted.'[9]

What would Taylor see and think if invited into a twenty-
first-century corporation? A row of people sitting in front of
screens and pressing keys. How, he might wonder, did they
know which keys to press, and who was telling them to do so?
When the CEO took him aside, she would explain the difficulty
she encountered in applying Taylor's principles. The scale and

complexity of modern business mean that capitalists and senior managers are often unable to directly monitor the adherence of workers to their instructions. Further, junior employees may hold critical information not available to their superiors.

Still, she would explain, scientific management was possible, but with the aid of remuneration consultants rather than mechanical engineers. If our CEO had taken an economics course, and that would surely have been part of her MBA, she would have been able to describe the issue of securing conformity by the workers to the purposes of the capitalists as the 'principal–agent problem'. And further, that the solution to the principal–agent problem is to devise incentive schemes that will induce conformity, and thus ensure that all workers, from the shop floor to the executive offices, use their knowledge for the benefit of the business rather than for themselves. Managers and junior employees alike are thus to be rewarded by reference to their success in implementing the goals of the capitalists, and the goals of all are generally assumed to be to make as much money as possible for themselves. Marx had outlined one solution in the nineteenth century: 'piece-wage is the form of wages most in harmony with the capitalist mode of production.'[10]

In this model, individuals are selfish, objectives are narrow and behaviour is instrumental. Workers are uncooperative factors of production, responsive only to material incentives and abuse. The piece-wage may even be extended to the C-suite, the modern term for the group of executives grand enough to have the word 'chief' in their job title. Salary and corporate perks may not be enough for the modern CEO, who, sometimes as 'thick skinned and coarse grained' as Taylor's workforce, needs a bonus to induce him to do the job well. It is not surprising that so many young people and intellectuals have a poor opinion of capitalism. What is more surprising is that many businesspeople have themselves embraced this unappealing description – though the lure of the bonus may give a clue to the explanation.

The most grand position is that of Chief Executive Officer, but often the operations of the business will be in the charge of the Chief Operating Officer, leaving the CEO to focus on 'strategy', which typically means dealmaking. There will always be a Chief Financial Officer. A firm attuned to the latest corporate trends may have a Chief Diversity Officer or Chief Sustainability Officer. The C is important for the public statement of corporate priorities as well as for the ego of the individual.

A central thesis of this book is that this transactional account of business is not just repellent but mistaken. It does not describe how successful business works – or could work – in modern society. Individuals do, of course, respond to incentives, but a better description is that individuals tend to behave in line with the behaviours expected in their environment; they are led to do what the community approves, both through praise and material reward. Social aspects of work, including both relationships within the workplace and those between business and society at large, are crucial to both personal productivity and personal fulfilment.

5

THE RISE OF MANUFACTURING

> The surest way to continued leadership is to adopt a
> policy of selling a few finished articles which require large
> tonnages.
>
> Andrew Carnegie, 2018[1]

The mechanical model of the firm was inspired by, and influenced the development of, manufacturing industry from the dawn of the Industrial Revolution to the mid-twentieth century. And even if, as I shall explain, the relevance of that model to the twenty-first-century corporation is much diminished, its legacy remains influential.

The economic historian Sir John Clapham chided Smith, as he might have chided many economists, for failing to undertake empirical or institutional research. 'It is a pity that Adam Smith did not go a few miles from Kirkcaldy to the Carron Works to see them turning and boring their cannonades [sic], instead of to his silly pin factory which was only a factory in the old sense of the word'.[2]

It is unlikely that Smith did visit a pin factory. Adam Ferguson, another major contributor to the Scottish Enlightenment of which Smith and philosopher David Hume were the best-known figures, had ten years earlier published his *Essay on the History of Civil Society*. In that book Ferguson introduced the concept of the division of labour, and had apparently referred in lectures to the productivity of the pin factory. Smith and Ferguson accused each other of plagiarism; Ferguson responded that both authors had drawn the example not from a factory

Diderot's pin factory, from Diderot's Encyclopédie

visit but from a drawing in Diderot's French encyclopaedia published a few years earlier.[3] (Normandy in northern France was a
centre of artisanal pin-making.) Smith may have seen the 'small
manufactory' in the encyclopaedia rather than real life. And the
dispute paused the friendship of the two Scottish sages until the
later years of their lives.

Not everyone was enthused by the Industrial Revolution.
Scotland's greatest poet, Robert Burns, did make the trip to the
Carron Works and was not impressed:

We cam na here to view your works,
In hopes to be mair wise,
But only, lest we gang to hell,
It may be nae surprise.[4]

Another visitor at the time of the publication of *The Wealth of
Nations* observed that the Carron Works employed 1,200 people

and suggested that it was the largest industrial site in Europe – and therefore almost certainly the world – at the time.[5] David Hume thought the number of employees was greater; in a letter to Smith during the recession in the Scottish economy at the beginning of the 1770s he wrote: 'The Carron Company is reeling, which is one of the greatest calamities of the whole, as they gave employment to near ten thousand people. Do these events any wise affect your theory, or will it occasion the revisal of any chapters?'[6] But despite his great erudition, Hume was probably not a strong empirical economist. The figure of 'ten thousand' is inconsistent with what we know about the turnover of Carron Works or the industry of the time.

As Smith had not recognised, but Clapham understood well 150 years later, the ironworks and the textile mill were the signature activities of the Industrial Revolution. The Carron Works used the innovative iron-smelting processes developed at Coalbrookdale in the English Midlands. Richard Arkwright's mill at Cromford in Derbyshire combined steam and water power with innovative textile machinery. As the nineteenth century began, Sir Robert Peel – father of the future prime minister of the same name – may have been one of England's largest employers, owning a string of Lancashire textile mills.

Arkwright's spinning frame had been invented by John Kay (no known relation to the John Kay who had a generation earlier invented the spinning jenny, or to the John Kay whose caricature of Adam Smith is the only known likeness of the sage, nor any known relation of the present author). Neither of these inventive Kays derived much financial benefit from their innovations despite attempts to enforce patent claims.

The processes of Arkwright's mill and Coalbrookdale were readily imitable, and patents provided little protection, as the two John Kays learned to their cost. Trade secrecy was another weapon against competition, which may be why Burns did not gain admission to the Carron Works:

But when we tirl'd at your door,
Your porter dought na hear us;
Sae may, shou'd we to hell's yetts come,
Your billy Sattan sair us![7]

But mostly these pioneers of the Industrial Revolution enjoyed little success in protecting their collective knowledge from either their domestic competitors or their incipient American and German ones. Francis Cabot Lowell, son of John Lowell and Susan Cabot, was the epitome of Boston brahminhood, as recorded in the old rhyme:

And this is good old Boston
The home of the bean and the cod
Where the Lowells talk only to Cabots
And the Cabots talk only to God.[8]

Lowell visited Britain in 1810–12 on what can only be described as a tour of industrial espionage designed to take the newly decolonised state of Massachusetts far beyond the bean and the cod. The export of textile machinery from Britain was prohibited, so Lowell memorised the designs. On returning to Massachusetts, he established a textile mill at Waltham on the Charles River. After his death, his Merrimack Manufacturing Company built a second, larger mill on Pawtucket Falls. The product was homogeneous, and the industrial process was linear and repetitive, ready for the application of Taylorism. These businesses required concentration of production in large facilities to facilitate the division of labour, allow specialisation and benefit from the economies of scale of water-driven and subsequently steam-powered engines.

The next phase of the Industrial Revolution was made possible by the construction of railways after 1830. These businesses demanded hierarchical, disciplined organisation. They even mimicked the uniformed display of rank of the military. The train could run on time only if every person and vehicle was in the right place at the right moment. And time itself was subordinated to business necessities; formerly each municipality's clock had proudly shown the local time, but now towns and cities across the UK adopted a common 'railway time'. The British Empire imposed Greenwich Mean Time as a world standard. These improvements in transport made possible the industrialisation and centralisation of the production of formerly artisanal products such as beer and meat. It would be to the magnates Edward Guinness and Philip Armour, not the local brewer and butcher who had served Mrs Smith, that future generations would speak.

One of Smith's most-quoted passages runs:

It is not from the benevolence of the butcher, the brewer, or the baker, that we expect our dinner, but from their regard to their own interest. We address ourselves, not to their humanity but to their self-love, and never talk to them of our own necessities but of their advantages. Nobody but a beggar chuses to depend chiefly upon the benevolence of his fellow-citizens.[9]

Adam Smith never married. He lived with his mother, who predeceased him by only two years. It is unlikely that the taciturn Smith addressed the butcher on his humanity, his self-love or anything at all: Katrine Marçal noted that 'Adam Smith only succeeded in answering half of the fundamental question of economics. He didn't get his dinner only because the tradesmen served their own self-interest through trade. Adam Smith got his dinner because his mother made sure it was on the table every evening.'[10]

The logic of linear repetitive manufacturing processes led to the assembly line. With this innovation Henry Ford, supported by the Danish-born engineer William (Bill) Knudsen, transformed the automobile industry – and in due course many

other industrial activities. In 1909, the first full year of production, Ford manufactured 10,000 Model T automobiles. Six years
later, this number had risen to a quarter of a million, and the
price of the car had fallen by more than 50 per cent. After the
end of the First World War the price was reduced still further,
and annual sales topped a million.[11]

If a manufacturing process is sufficiently repetitive, most
uncertainties are resolvable because they can be described
probabilistically. 'Student', whose 't' is familiar to all beginning
students of statistics, was the pseudonym of W. J. Gossett, who
joined the Guinness brewery in Dublin in 1899. The company's
management acquiesced in his anonymous contribution to
scholarship. He repaid them with his achievement in successfully establishing the company's first brewery in England at Park
Royal, in west London. Motorola and GE (General Electric)
would later put statistical jargon into popular usage with 'Six
Sigma' (six standard deviations) as a descriptor of low tolerance
of defects in repetitive manufacturing processes. These prob-
abilistic models were widely applied in financial services – the
CFO of Goldman Sachs notoriously declared the evolving 2008
financial crisis a 'twenty-five' sigma event. But financial services
is very different from repetitive manufacturing, as GE would
learn to its cost. And the activities of most modern firms are
different still.

Ford's River Rouge complex became the largest industrial
facility in the world when completed in 1928. 'The Rouge' was
built as a car factory, full of specialist equipment owned by the
corporation. It extended over 2,000 acres – you could drop both
London's Hyde Park and New York's Central Park on the site
and they would cover less than half of it. By the middle of the
twentieth century, Ford and General Motors were archetypes of
the large manufacturing companies that dominated business for
most of that century.

Capital

The Carron ironworks was built by four Roebucks, two Cadells and a Garbett: established businesspeople who provided the capital for the works and the equipment within it.[12] They also supplied funds to buy the raw materials of coal and iron ore; many of their customers – such as the Royal Navy – may not have been prompt payers, even if reliable ones. Therefore, like all businesses of the Industrial Revolution, the Carron Works needed fixed capital for plant and working capital for inventories. Talented engineers with few financial resources – such as James Watt – might find rich individuals – such as Matthew Boulton – with more money but less imagination and enter mutually productive partnerships.[13]

In Marx's account, the rise of capitalism was associated with the decline of European feudalism. Marx called the enclosure of the common land (and later the exploitation of colonies) 'primitive accumulation' – curiously following Adam Smith, who had emphasised 'accumulation … previous to the division of labour'.[14] But while Smith was inclined to attribute prior accumulation to thrift and frugality, Marx likened primitive accumulation to theft; the reality was somewhere between the two but probably closer to the Marxist version.

Thus the Carron Works was a traditional capitalist enterprise of the Industrial Revolution. The wealth of its founders originated in agricultural land; successful business enterprise subsequently enhanced their fortunes. These founders built and owned the Carron plant. And they controlled its day-to-day operations. These operations were based on the tripartite linkage: the deployment of personal wealth, the ownership of plant and machinery and the exercise of managerial authority.

That tripartite linkage was central to Marx's account of a system whose demise he confidently predicted. The capitalists exercising that managerial authority would control the distribution of the value added by the enterprise (value added properly attributable to the workers) and direct it to themselves. Marx envisaged, wrongly, that the proletariat would displace the wealthy and themselves take ownership of the plant and thus control the activities within it and the distribution of its produce.

Communism as actually practised in the Soviet Union – 'really existing socialism' or 'developed socialism' – maintained a similar tripartite linkage after the expropriation of the assets of the wealthy. (The phrase 'really existing socialism' is attributed to a 1977 speech by Soviet leader Leonid Brezhnev, in which he attempted to explain the difference between the practical experience of eastern European economies and the Marxist ideal to which they had aspired.) Under 'really existing socialism' the privileged rich were replaced by the privileged *nomenklatura* of party bosses. The state that the *nomenklatura* controlled determined the distribution of income and wealth, owned the means of production and directed the activities of the business.

The Marxist account of the distribution of income and wealth emphasised the importance of social roles and political power; thus organisation of the working class was key to securing for workers the fruits of *their* labour. The economists' description of the production function allowed for the substitution of labour for capital, and the elasticity of substitution was a critical determinant of the share of income going to labour and capital. In the Taylorist account, capitalists carefully monitored the rewards to workers to secure their maximum productivity, combining elements of the political and economic explanations. Relative productivity mattered to the distribution of revenues within the firm and so did relative power. A similar combination of politics and economics governs income distribution today, although the mechanisms through which these factors operate differ substantially.

Labour

As the common land was privatised, a new class of landless peasants became wage labourers. The men employed in the Carron Works had been drawn from the fields of lowland Scotland, driven by population pressures on the available land to seek the wages offered in the new factories. With nothing to offer but their labour, and lacking the common organisation of guilds, they worked for subsistence wages. Mr Pennant, reporting on his eighteenth-century *Tour of Scotland*, commented that 'This work [Carron] has been of a great service to the country, by teaching the people industry, and a method of setting about any sort of labour, which before the common people had scarce any notion of.'[15]

As industrialisation proceeded, they headed in increasing numbers to the rapidly expanding cities. The leaders of the Industrial Revolution built not just factories but communities, constructing housing and other facilities for their workers. Some went beyond this. After cholera hit the industrial town of Bradford in 1848, the Yorkshire textile magnate Sir Titus Salt devoted his wealth to the welfare of his employees; Saltaire is today both a living town and an industrial heritage site.[16] Soap magnate William Lever and chocolatier George Cadbury each built model villages in an Arts and Crafts style to house their workers – respectively Port Sunlight and Bournville, the latter regarded by many as the first 'garden city'.[17] On Pawtucket Falls, Francis Cabot Lowell built the town that still bears his name. He recruited New England farmers' daughters to operate his mill and provided them with board and education.

But these factory jobs in steelworks and textile mills were boring and required physical, not mental, labour. Workers were lightly trained and could be switched between routine tasks. And this was equally true of the twentieth-century auto plants of Detroit, largely manned by recent immigrants to the United States and by African Americans who had fled the plantations of the South. Labour was regarded as a commodity by both the ironmasters of Carron and the executives of General Motors.

At Ford's River Rouge plant much of the defining terminology of capitalism seemed as relevant as it had been for the Carron ironworks. From the eighteenth century to the twentieth, the principal industries were capital-intensive. Constructing an ironworks, a railway or an automobile plant was costly, and the capital involved was specific to the purpose of producing iron, operating trains or building cars. Those who controlled the capital controlled … pretty much everything. The capitalist might be benevolent, like the Cadburys or Titus Salt. But, absent the countervailing power of a trade union or the weak protections of legislation, you were at the mercy of the owner of the physical capital – premises and equipment – which was essential to your job.

Today there is no production at either Saltaire or Port Sunlight; only Cadbury, now a subsidiary of US-based conglomerate Mondelez, retains a manufacturing facility at Bournville. After the Second World War, the last mill facilities on the Charles River closed (although Harvard and MIT, further downstream, expanded). Lowell enjoyed a brief renaissance as the headquarters of Wang Laboratories, the now defunct pioneer of word-processing, and, like Saltaire and Port Sunlight, the town is now an industrial heritage site – a museum of the Industrial Revolution.

Labour fights back

Lowell was one of the first of the new factories to encounter a strike. US textile production was growing rapidly, which lowered prices. When wages were cut in 1836 in an attempt to preserve margins, some of the mill girls 'turned out'. This early industrial action was unsuccessful, as had been the famous attempt by some English farm hands to form a union of agricultural workers two years earlier: the 'Tolpuddle Martyrs' were transported to Australia for their effrontery in taking a secret oath of solidarity. It would be another half-century before organised labour became a force to be reckoned with.

But as the Gilded Age developed, the confrontational relationship between capital and labour which Marx had predicted became more of a reality, in part as a result of the intellectual and political movements stimulated by his prediction. In 1871 British legislation permitted the formation of trade unions, and American courts became less ready to support employers against the embryonic union movement. But the iconic US strikes of Pullman railroad workers and at Andrew Carnegie's Homestead Works both ended in failure; the Taff Vale judgment of 1901 made British unions liable for the economic damage imposed by strikes, effectively rendering industrial action futile.

In 1911 fire spread through the Triangle Shirtwaist Company, owned by Max Blanck and Isaac Harris, which occupied the three top floors of the (triangular) Asch building in New York. The doors to the stairwells and exits had been locked to discourage theft and unauthorised breaks. One hundred and forty-six people, mostly young women, died, many by jumping to the ground. Blanck and Harris were charged with manslaughter but were acquitted.[18] Fresh legislation introduced after the tragedy continued a process of statutory control of working conditions which had begun with the UK Factories Act of 1833 and the Massachusetts Factory Act of 1877.

The growth of trade unions gave labour more power to demand better wages and conditions, and the extension of the franchise gave political power to working-class voters. In the British general election of 1906, the Liberal Party won a landslide victory. The Conservative prime minister, Arthur Balfour, was defeated in his own Manchester constituency, and the Labour Representation Committee, which had previously held only two seats, won 29 and renamed itself the Labour Party. Legislation to override the Taff Vale judgment followed immediately. Less than twenty years later, the Labour Party would form the government. The workforce was increasingly educated, acquiring and developing skills on the job. At the end of the First World War, socialist parties became a material political force in Europe. In Russia, the Bolsheviks seized power and established the first government to identify itself as Marxist.

The modern assembly line

Assembly lines are still used to manufacture automobiles, although if Henry Ford toured a Toyota or Tesla plant he would wonder where all the people were. In 1962 General Motors sold more than half the automobiles in America, and Ford's US market share was 27 per cent. But that year represented the peak of these companies' dominance. Today their combined US market share is less than one-third.[19] The 1960s was the decade in which the then dominant model of business organisation, based on a closely monitored assembly line, peaked and began its decline.

The largest such lines today produce aircraft. The factory at Paine Field, near Seattle, that Boeing built to assemble the 747 is the biggest building in the modern world. Its volume is around 13 million cubic metres, equivalent to the contents of 5,000 Olympic swimming pools. But the site it stands on is only 100 acres, less than 5 per cent of the size of the River Rouge complex, illustrating both the extraordinary scale of Henry Ford's achievement and ambition and the simultaneously more concentrated and more dispersed nature of modern production.

The Airbus assembly facility in Toulouse is the largest building in Europe. (The list of the world's largest buildings is completed by Tesla's new Texas gigafactory, the Russian auto plant at Togliatti – acquired by Renault after privatisation but now on 'loan' to the Russian government following the invasion of Ukraine – and the Grand Mosque at Mecca.[20]) The modern civil aircraft may be the most complex product ever to be mass manufactured. It is a long way from the pin factory and the Carron Works to the production lines of Boeing and Airbus.

6

THE RISE OF THE CORPORATION

> Corporation: An ingenious device for obtaining profit
> without individual responsibility.
>> Ambrose Bierce, *The Devil's Dictionary*, 1911[1]

Corporations have a long history. The word 'corporation' is derived from the Latin *corporatio*; there were corporations in Roman times. The origins of the City of London Corporation, which today manages public services in London's financial district and acts as a lobby group for its business interests, are lost in the mists of time.[2] The Corporation received a royal charter from William the Conqueror in 1067 but this merely confirmed rights it had held since at least the time of Edward the Confessor.[3] Within the 'square mile' of its boundaries, guilds – of silversmiths and fishmongers, bakers and brewers – regulated their trade, supervised apprenticeships and monitored quality while restricting entry and fixing prices. These corporations existed by royal charter; the king's approval legitimised their existence and conferred their monopolies.

Guilds and livery companies survive into the twenty-first century as dining and drinking societies, and many support charitable causes. But you would rarely find a practising fishmonger in Fishmongers' Hall, and the only fish would be the sole meunière served at feasts – although in 2019 a narwhal tusk was pulled from the wall and used to subdue a terrorist who had murdered two people at a conference on offender rehabilitation.[4]

The colonial corporation

The essence of a corporation was to be an institution that could hold assets and make agreements without these assets being the property of, or the agreements binding on, any particular individuals. Thus the corporation had many of the rights and obligations of a natural person; this is the origin of the legal doctrine of 'corporate personality' which is central to modern corporate law. The rules of the corporation defined its purpose and its membership. The corporation's members would choose a smaller group, generally from among their number, to supervise the management of its affairs.

As Europeans sent ships to explore the world in the sixteenth century, they established corporations to handle the large investments and risks involved. Towards the end of her reign, Queen Elizabeth I granted a charter to the East India Company to conduct trade with the newly accessible territories of South-East Asia. Two years later the fledgling Dutch Republic persuaded a group of Amsterdam merchants to form the Vereenigde Oostindische Compagnie (VOC) to pool their interests in the spice islands further east.

Historically, a *company* was simply a group of people who worked together in some shared, loosely commercial endeavour; that group became a *corporation* when it acquired some special legal status, as did the East India Company. That status might include the important provision of limiting the liability of the members for the obligations of the venture. However, this privilege required some special process of approval, such as a royal charter or an act of parliament.

In 1606 King James, the Scottish king who had succeeded Elizabeth on the English throne, gave charters to the Virginia Company and its northern subsidiary the Plymouth Company to begin the colonisation of North America. These American companies were not successful commercially – Virginia did not have the deposits of gold which the promoters of the company had claimed were likely to be found – and the ventures were replaced by colonial administrations directly responsible to the

Crown. The Harvard Corporation – which is still today the senior body in the governance of that university – claims to be the oldest corporation in the Western hemisphere. It received its charter in 1650 from the legislative assembly of the Massachusetts colony.

In the seventeenth century many other corporations were authorised by the king, some as colonial ventures, some representing monopolies conferred as a reward for support of royalist causes. The fortunes of these corporations continued to be mixed. James had united the Scottish and English monarchies but not the parliaments; the failure of the Company of Scotland, which embarked on a misconceived (or at least centuries premature) expedition to settle the Panamanian isthmus as a Scottish colony, crippled many landed Scottish families financially in the 1690s and led to full parliamentary union between England and Scotland.

The loss of Dutch colonies to Britain in the late eighteenth century ended the life of the VOC, but the East India Company continued to expand and in the first half of the nineteenth century the Company was in effect the government of India. After the (failed) 1857 Indian Mutiny (which modern Indians reasonably prefer to call the War of Independence) the East India Company was effectively nationalised and ceased to be a trading entity. Soon after, Queen Victoria was declared Empress of India. Colonisation was henceforth a public rather than a private activity.[5]

Finance for business

The idea that one might deal in tradable securities that represent *claims* to tangible assets, independently of the assets themselves, has a long history. Along the Silk Road, merchants used notes to save themselves the burden of carrying coins. Shares in a corporate venture might be traded without disturbing the underlying capital assets – ships, cargoes, plant and machinery – which made the venture possible. The return on the shares would depend on the success, or otherwise, of the venture.

Similarly, banknotes were initially claims against the gold in the vaults of the banker. Banks soon discovered they could issue more notes than they had gold. That observation is the basis of the idea that banks 'create money', but the phrase is often misunderstood. A properly conducted bank has assets more than equal to its liabilities. It does not conjure wealth out of thin air. The modern equivalent of the gold in the vault – the asset that is the counterpart to your deposit – is a loan the bank has made. Historically these loans were used to buy tangible assets: houses, offices, manufacturing plants. If there is magic, it is the magic of *maturity transformation* – because not all depositors will demand their money back at the same time, the bank can borrow short and lend long.

English banks such as Lloyds and Barclays trace their foundation to the last decade of the seventeenth century and gradually broadened their activities and client base. The 1690s also saw the establishment of the Bank of England (now the central bank of the UK) and the Bank of Scotland (which collapsed in 2008 and is now owned by Lloyds). Merchant banks, so-called for their involvement in international trade, emerged slightly later. Barings (founded by two sons of a German immigrant, Johann Baring) was founded in 1764. In 1798 the Frankfurt banker Mayer Amschel Rothschild sent his son Nathan to London to establish a bank there, the first of the 'five arrows' which are still the symbol of the Rothschild dynasty. The London house prospered during the Napoleonic Wars, although the stories of its profits from early knowledge of the outcome of the Battle of Waterloo appear to be apocryphal. Banks such as Barings and Rothschild specialised in securities markets and were the precursors of modern investment banks.

The Amsterdam Bourse was established in 1602 by the VOC as a venue for trading its own shares, and twenty years later the VOC allowed a second company to offer securities in the building which housed it. The invention of the coffee shop provided a venue for philosophical speculation – the Grand Coffee House which still stands today on Oxford's High Street claims to have been the first such institution in England. But the coffee shop was also a venue for financial speculation – the restoration of the monarchy in 1660 diminished the Puritan resistance to gambling. Traders in the coffee shop that Jonathan Miles opened in the City of London in 1680 dealt not only in royal debt but also in the stock of corporations. Jonathan's is today celebrated as the origin of the London stock market (and Edward Lloyd's nearby coffee shop is recognised as the origin of the London insurance market).

Only three years after the Declaration of Independence some Manhattan merchants perceived the new American republic's urgent need for a venue for securities trading and gathered under the buttonwood (American sycamore) tree on Wall Street to establish a New York exchange. The railway boom of the first half of the nineteenth century was the trigger for the growth of widely dispersed stock ownership and anonymous market trading.

A modern, but less successful, reprise of the gathering under the buttonwood tree played out as American troops stormed into Baghdad in 2003. A twenty-four-year-old real estate salesman, Jay Hellen, followed close behind the invading army. Hellen had been recruited by the Department of Defense to head the immediate establishment of that vital institution of liberal democracy – a modern stock exchange. Hellen's Republican credentials were impeccable but his financial credentials less so.[6] Once the Coalition Provisional Authority was disbanded in 2004, Iraqi officials abandoned the attempt to implement electronic trading systems and establish a Securities and Exchange Commission on US lines and resumed the practice of setting the prices of the five quoted stocks on a whiteboard.

The institution of a secondary market in the shares of corporations provided opportunities for speculation and outright fraud. Around 1720 such trading became a frenzy. In England the South Sea bubble inflated and burst; the Scottish murderer and confidence trickster John Law, exiled to Paris, promoted his eccentric monetary theories and his fraudulent Mississippi Company from that city. Severe restrictions on the formation and promotion of corporations were imposed for the century that followed.[7]

But only for a century. The railway would change almost every aspect of economic life – including both the organisation of business and the organisation of production. The first railways and railroads were generally promoted by local businessmen who saw the advantages to their trade of fast and reliable transport links. They secured corporate charters from the crown or state. Building a railway was capital-intensive, and the promoters and other well-off individuals provided funds in return for promised dividends on their stock. The Great Western Railway, for example, was established by Bristol merchants who sought a rapid connection to London. They hired the brilliant young engineer Isambard Kingdom Brunel to supervise construction of the line.

The imminent arrival of the railway, and the social upheavals it portends, is a central theme of George Eliot's novel *Middlemarch,* set in the years 1829–32. The death of William Huskisson – Member of Parliament for Liverpool and a former cabinet minister who was killed by a locomotive while standing on the track at the opening of the Liverpool and Manchester railway – is recalled repeatedly as a symbol of the opportunities and dangers, while Eliot's fictional character Caleb Garth is caught up in the process of surveying land for the new line.[8] The progress of railroads in the United States was slower but ultimately even more momentous; in 1869 Leland Stanford hammered a golden spike to mark the completion of the first transcontinental railroad.

By the 1840s the economic potential, as well as the social impact, of the new development was becoming widely apparent. Britain succumbed to 'railway mania'. Share prices peaked in 1845–6; stock in the largest company, the London and North Western Railway, which connected London with Birmingham, Liverpool and Manchester, peaked at £250 against a launch price of £100 before falling to £110 by the end of the 1840s.[9] The new infrastructure was financed by drawing on the savings of the English middle class; US railroads were funded similarly. William Deloitte, founder of the eponymous accountancy business, made his reputation by instituting processes to reassure the shareholders of the Great Western Railway of the soundness of that business amid the rampant fraud seen during the railway boom.

Even the Brontë sisters (daughters of a country parson in remote Yorkshire) were caught up in the railway mania. In 1846 Charlotte wrote to an acquaintance:

I thought you would wonder how we were getting on, when you heard of the railway panic, and you may be sure that I am very glad to be able to answer your kind inquiries by an assurance that our small capital is as yet undiminished. The York and Midland is, as you say, a very good line; yet, I confess to you, I should wish, for my own part, to be wise in time. I cannot think that even the very best lines will continue for many years at their present premiums; and I have been most anxious for us to sell our shares ere it be too late, and to secure the proceeds in some safer, if, for the present, less profitable investment. I cannot, however, persuade my sisters to regard the affair precisely from my point of view; and I feel as if I would rather run the risk of loss than hurt Emily's feelings by acting in direct opposition to her opinion. C.B.[10]

Charlotte was only partly right; the York and (North) Midland was the centrepiece of the empire of the 'Railway King', George Hudson; at a shareholder meeting in 1849 Hudson was exposed as a fraudster, was forced out of the York and North Midland and ultimately fled the country to avoid imprisonment. This story may resonate with observers of the modern boom in crypto 'assets'.

Restrictions imposed after the bursting of the South Sea Bubble and the failure of the Mississippi Company a century earlier were gradually relaxed. In 1856 legislation allowed promoters in Britain to establish a limited liability company without the need for a royal charter or special act of parliament; simple registration was sufficient. France and several US states had already permitted such incorporation.

Many observers doubted that the public would want to deal with institutions that limited their liability and at the time did not even have to publish accounts. (In 1880 the Institute of Chartered Accountants was formed to educate and regulate auditors, but only in the twentieth century were companies – even the largest – required to employ them.) Such doubts were magnified when the banking house of Overend, Gurney & Company adopted limited liability in 1865 and failed the following year, provoking an economic downturn.

The magic of maturity transformation may be dispelled if too many depositors want their money back at the same time. And if you think this might happen, you will want to be at the front of the queue – this is the phenomenon of the bank run. A seminal article in *The Economist* magazine by its editor, Walter Bagehot, promoted the idea that central banks could relieve such problems by acting as 'lender of last resort', a concept that survived into the very different financial environment of the twenty-first century and would be amply deployed in 2008, albeit not in quite the manner Bagehot had recommended.

Yet the result of bank failures was to reinforce, not halt, the progress of incorporation. In 1878 the City of Glasgow Bank, which had expanded internationally and opened over a hundred branches, collapsed. The bank had emphasised the unlimited liability of its 1,800 shareholders – to their cost, as over 80 per cent of them were bankrupted.[11] The City of Glasgow failure was the death knell for unlimited liability in retail banking in the UK. Within months the directors were in jail. Some commentators noted that when the two major Scottish banks failed in 2008 the outcome was very different.

But despite these continuing waves of speculation and fraud, by the end of the nineteenth century the rise of the limited liability company was unstoppable. The corporate structures which had financed the railways were used in banking and to finance resource exploration and in due course extended to manufacturing companies. The initial public offering (IPO) of Guinness, the Irish brewer, in 1886 was the signature flotation of an industrial company on the London Stock Exchange. The issue was heavily oversubscribed; the shares rose at the opening from £10 to £16. Edward Guinness, soon to become Lord Iveagh, obtained £6 million by the sale of 65 per cent of the stock of the company.[12] The Baring partnership, the architect of the flotation, derived more than £500,000 for its efforts,[13] and the Baring family, whose bank organised the issue, had shrewdly retained one-third of the issue for themselves.[14]

Edward (Ned) Baring was ennobled in 1885 in recognition of his bank's role in the development of late nineteenth-century finance. It would take only five years for his triumphs – gaining a peerage as Baron Revelstoke, pulling off a financial coup and having a town (Revelstoke) named after him to commemorate his role in financing the Canadian Pacific Railway – to unravel. The bank was one of the first, but by no means the last, financial institutions to incur heavy losses in Argentina. Barings itself was rescued by the Bank of England, but the bank was an unlimited liability partnership. The country estate and Mayfair townhouse of the man recently elevated to the aristocracy were sold to satisfy creditors.

The reconstruction of Barings after the 1890 debacle involved incorporation as a limited company, although most other London and New York investment banks remained as partnerships for another century. So when Barings failed once more in 1995 (as a result of fraud by 'rogue trader' Nick Leeson), the shareholders lost their investment, but the elegant Georgian Baroque-style mansion in Oxfordshire owned by a later generation of Barings rests in the family still.[15]

Across the twentieth century, the notion of personal

accountability for failures of financial management became eroded. Dick Fuld, CEO of Lehman, whose failure provoked the 2008 global financial crisis, opened his fresh advisory business less than a year later, its reception adorned with the text 'That was then, this is now.'[16] But some may prefer the maxim attributed to legendary investor Sir John Templeton: 'the four most expensive words in investing are "This time it's different".'

The detail of legislation to govern corporate entities varies considerably from country to country and even across different American states. Today a whole range of acronyms around the world describe slightly different legal formulae: LLC (Limited Liability Corporation, US), Inc. (Incorporated, US), PLC (Public Limited Company, UK), SARL (Société à Responsabilité Limitée, France), AG (Aktiengesellschaft, Germany) etc. Critical factors in the choice of business structure are the limitation of personal liability, reporting obligations, the tax treatment applied, and whether the business has or plans to have more than a handful of shareholders and/or to offer shares to a wider public.

The European Commission has sought some degree of commonality across the EU and has usefully created the concept of a Public Interest Entity, spelling out the principle that the conduct of large businesses is properly a matter of public interest. But the application of that idea is in the hands of member states, with the consequence that nothing much has happened. A European corporation can now register as a Societas Europaea, and Airbus SE is the archetype of the modern European company, but the fact that it was necessary to resort to Latin for the title is indicative of the difficulty of securing continent-wide solutions, an observation equally true of the United States. The words 'corporation' and 'company' are today used more or less interchangeably, a practice I shall generally follow in this book. American English tends to favour 'corporation' and British English 'company'.

The twin inventions of marketable securities – which enabled people to buy and sell shares in a business without disturbing the conduct of the business – and of maturity transformation

– which allowed liquid saving to fund long-term investment – are of immense historical significance. Without them, it is hard to imagine how international trade could have developed, how the Industrial Revolution could have happened or how the railways and other infrastructure indispensable to a modern economy could have been built.

The end of British hegemony

Britain and its empire dominated the global industrial scene in the nineteenth century. But that leadership was increasingly challenged by the growing economic power of Germany and the United States. In the 1860s Otto von Bismarck unified Germany under Prussia and industrialisation continued apace. Deutsche Bank was founded in Berlin in 1870 with the industrialist Werner Siemens as one of its (two) directors. In Germany the banking system, rather than the stock market, was and remains the principal conduit by which the savings of the public were directed towards industry. When Siemens sold shares to the public in 1897, the purpose was not to enable the founders to monetise their holdings, in the manner of Edward Guinness, but to raise capital to expand the business; most of the new capital was subscribed by banks. Even today the mainstay of the German banking industry is not the international banks such as Deutsche, but rather the state-supported *Landesbanken* and the community savings institutions which still function in most German towns.

America entered the 'gilded age' in which the 'robber barons' – men like John D. Rockefeller (oil), Cornelius Vanderbilt (railroads), Andrew Carnegie (steel) and James Duke (tobacco) – 'consolidated' their industries, buying up competitors in an attempt to establish monopolies. They were assisted by financiers such as E. H. Harriman and Jay Gould. They sought power – the power to set prices, the power to determine the future of their industries and the power to dictate to their workforce and to governments. They believed their ever-expanding empires could benefit from ever-expanding economies of scale.

But the greatest of all bankers of the time was J. P. Morgan. Barings' financial success in the Guinness flotation was eclipsed when Morgan created US Steel in 1901 by amalgamating Carnegie Steel with several other businesses. The resulting combination was the largest company in the world. US Steel debuted on the New York Stock Exchange with a capitalisation of $1,450 million. The profits of Morgan and associates amounted to just over $100 million.[17] Even by modern standards, this figure takes the breath away – especially since the largest contributor (or victim) was Andrew Carnegie. Perhaps Carnegie, aged sixty-five and taking the opportunity to retire from business to devote the remainder of his life to philanthropy, had lost interest in driving a hard bargain and was content with the $450 million he took from the flotation.

The introduction of antitrust laws – the first such statute was the 1890 Sherman Act – was a distinctively American phenomenon. The names of many of the largest British companies in the period before the First World War attest to the intentions and scale of ambitions of the men who attempted to run them: Imperial Tobacco, United Alkali, the Calico Printers Association, Associated Portland Cement Manufacturers. Partly in reaction to the international success of US business, consolidation had more appeal than competition for European governments. Leslie Hannah, an eminent business historian, has shown how the 'rationalisation' of industry, which was favoured by the British Government (represented by the Bank of England), set the stage for the new 'corporate economy' which would characterise Britain for decades.[18] The 1920s saw the creation by merger of ICI (chemicals), the Distillers Company (Scotch whisky) and Unilever (soap and margarine). A similar wave of mergers in Germany established IG Farben and Vereinigte Stahlwerke as the dominant chemical and steel producers respectively. (Both these companies were dissolved by the victorious Allies in 1945.)

The consolidation of US Steel by Carnegie and Morgan

survived the trustbusters; Rockefeller's Standard Oil did not. The contrast in subsequent performance is striking. One hundred and twenty years after the formation of US Steel, Japan's Nippon Steel offered shareholders just $14.1 billion for it, while the Dow Jones index, of which US Steel was long a principal component, has risen three hundredfold. Many of the more than thirty companies that emerged from the break-up of Standard Oil prospered, and ExxonMobil (which finds its origins in the New Jersey and New York subsidiaries) is unique among the world's leading companies for its longevity.

New century, new businesses

Transportation by railways and railroads, the availability of mechanical power in factories, the institutions of incorporation and public capital markets: these factors, working together, had created a new business landscape. And this was just the beginning; the new century would see the rise of new industries based around the transformational innovations of the automobile and electricity.

Many entrepreneurs and engineers perceived the potential of the automobile to transform society: Henry Ford, of course, but also Antoine Cadillac, Walter Chrysler and Ransom Olds; outside the United States, Karl Benz, William Morris and Louis Renault. The nascent industry did not escape the attention of rationalisers and consolidators. Billy Durant took over the Buick company and used it as a base for acquisitions of many competitors and suppliers. In 1909 alone he added the names of Cadillac, Oldsmobile and Pontiac to his stable of brands.

Durant's talents as salesman and dealmaker exceeded his capacity to run a business, and the banks that had financed his acquisition spree took control of the cash-stretched company and sacked Durant. But he responded to the setback by buying Chevrolet and developing a vehicle comparable to Ford's Model T. This commercial success enabled Durant to regain control of General Motors. But by 1920 the company was again in financial difficulty. Pierre du Pont, a member of the du Pont chemical family and the company's largest shareholder, once more forced Durant out of the corporation. Alfred Sloan, who had come to General Motors when that company had acquired his roller bearing business, gained du Pont's support and in 1923 became president of the company with a plan to manage Durant's unwieldy empire. With the assistance of Bill Knudsen, who could no longer work for the irascible, autocratic Henry Ford, GM overtook its principal rival to become not only America's leading automobile company but the largest manufacturing corporation in the world.

Concentration continues

It is often forgotten that the British nationalisation programme of the 1940s was more about consolidation than public ownership and control, which already existed in many cases. The names of the British Railways Board, the Central Electricity Generating Board and the National Coal Board illustrate that centralised government direction was a primary goal.

As in the 1920s, the post-war growth of international trade stimulated a period of state-sponsored consolidation in Britain in the 1960s. The establishment of the Industrial Reorganisation Corporation (IRC) was followed by the creation of the somewhat oxymoronic National Enterprise Board. The three flagship achievements of the IRC were the merger of all major surviving car companies into British Leyland, the absorption of all British computer interests into ICL and the consolidation of the major electrical companies into the General Electric Company (GEC). The answer to international competition was domestic scale.

But it wasn't. The automobile flagship, British Leyland, collapsed in 1974, was nationalised and eventually broken up. The computing flagship ICL failed in 1981 and was absorbed into the Japanese manufacturer Fujitsu (as I write, Britain's most reviled company for its role in the persecution of victims of its flawed Post Office accounting system). The electrical flagship GEC survived until its 2001 disintegration, described in Chapter 22.

The National Enterprise Board was hardly more effective. Alongside an unsuccessful investment and expansion plan for British Leyland, it promoted national champions in machine tools (Alfred Herbert, failed 1983), semiconductors (Inmos, sold in 1989 to STMicroelectronics, which was jointly owned by the French and Italian governments) and consumer electronics (Sinclair Radionics, failed 1980). Only Rolls-Royce, which had been taken into public ownership in 1971 following the company's crippling cost overruns in its RB 211 aero engine, survived as a successful company. While the iconic automobile brand was sold to BMW the (subsequently privatised) aero engine division is today one of the three dominant global producers.

As mass manufacturing grew in significance, many goods could be traded across borders, and globalisation led to international competition in tradable commodities such as steel, oil and consumer goods. In the first half of the century protectionist lobbies attempted to resist this opening of markets, but the world economic system established after the Second World War promoted free trade in manufactured goods. While the common pattern of international trade in the colonial era was one in which raw materials were bartered for manufactured goods, by the end of the twentieth century most international trade represented industrial economies exchanging manufactures – and increasingly services – with each other.

Both businesspeople and critics of business, then and now, exaggerate the benefits of size. The advantages of scale are technological and appear visible; the disadvantages are mostly human and less immediately apparent. If pricing power is not eroded by competition, as it usually is, regulation will generally follow. Large organisations develop entrenched interests which inhibit the development of collective intelligence and the adoption of new business methods and innovative products. We have Intel and Microsoft, not IBM, to thank for our laptop computers; Apple, not AT&T and Verizon, to thank for our smartphones; and Tesla, not General Motors, for pioneering electric and autonomous automobiles.

In the 1920s General Motors competed for market leadership with Ford and Chrysler in the United States, and in Europe through its Opel and Vauxhall subsidiaries. But it would eventually lose pole position to firms that had not yet been created in countries that had not then experienced an Industrial Revolution. British consumers can today buy Fords made in Germany, Volkswagens made in Spain, Hyundais made in Korea and Nissans made in Sunderland. And they can choose between smartphones designed in California and assembled in China or designed in South Korea and assembled in Vietnam. And all these goods are available more or less everywhere.

7

CHANGING FORTUNES

All fortune is good fortune; for it either rewards, disciplines, amends or punishes, and so is either useful or just.

Boethius, *The Consolation of Philosophy*,
written in 524, while in jail awaiting execution[1]

The business magazine *Fortune* published a list of the largest 500 US corporations in 1955 and has continued to do so annually ever since. The subsequent fate of the initial top ten provides a powerful rejoinder to the claim that large businesses acquire a scale that leaves them masters of their environment.

That 1955 list contains two automobile companies: General Motors, which easily topped the rankings, and Chrysler. General Motors entered Chapter 11 bankruptcy proceedings in 2009 and after restructuring is today the fourth-largest car manufacturer in the world, after Toyota, Volkswagen and Hyundai. Hyundai had not manufactured a single automobile in 1955 and no Toyota had ever left Japan. At the time of writing Tesla, founded in 2003, is America's most valuable car company.

Chrysler ran into financial difficulties in 1970, was rescued by the US government, disposed of its European operations and revived for a time under the leadership of the publicity-conscious Lee Iacocca.[2] An unsuccessful merger in the 1990s with Daimler, German owner of the Mercedes marque, ended when the Chrysler business was bought out by a private equity consortium in 2007. Chrysler also filed for bankruptcy in 2009 and was then purchased by the Italian company Fiat, which participated in the refinancing with the United Auto Workers pension fund and the US government. In 2021 Fiat–Chrysler merged with the French producer PSA and is now known as Stellantis.[3]

There were two food processing companies on the 1955 list: Swift and Armour. After numerous vicissitudes and ownership changes, the rumps of these businesses are now controlled by Brazilian and Chinese companies respectively.

Three oil companies made the cut. Standard Oil of New Jersey acquired its rival Mobil (also in the 1955 list) and is now ExxonMobil, the only business to appear in both 1955 and 2020. After an attack by corporate raider T. Boone Pickens in 1984, Gulf Oil found a 'white knight' in Chevron (Standard Oil of California), which retained some of its assets and disposed of many. (The term 'white knight' describes a friendly bidder who is called in to support incumbent management by offering stockholders an alternative to a hostile takeover.)

The 1955 list is completed by three manufacturing companies. US Steel subsequently continued its century-long decline. The chemical giant DuPont was a poster child for the modern professionally managed business during the interwar years and was one of the four corporations singled out in Alfred Chandler's *Strategy and Structure*. With Britain's ICI and Germany's IG Farben, DuPont straddled the world market for chemical products. But subsequent events would demonstrate that Chandler was describing the past, not anticipating the future. After decades of indifferent performance and an unsuccessful acquisition of Conoco, another of the successor companies to Standard Oil, in 2015 DuPont merged with Dow, the other leading US chemical producer. The business was then divided into three separate units, one of which retains the DuPont name.

General Electric was for much of the century regarded as the best-run company in the United States – not only developing its own talent but exporting it to other businesses. Its chief executives were always among America's most revered businessmen. Jack Welch, who held the position from 1981 to 2001, to great contemporary acclaim, brought focus to the business, famously declaring that he was interested only in markets where

GE could be number one or number two.[4] Welch presided over the expansion of a financial services operation which for a time became a driver of profits and revenues for the whole corporation. Following Welch's retirement and the global financial crisis of 2008, it became clear that the growth of financial services had served to conceal weaknesses in the underlying core businesses.

The Fortune 500 list did not include retailers. If companies had been ranked by sales, the list would have then been led by America's three great shopping giants: Sears Roebuck, Montgomery Ward and JCPenney. Their fate was one of steady decline. In 2000, Montgomery Ward filed for bankruptcy. In 2019 Sears did the same and in 2020 JCPenney followed suit.

The disappointing fortunes of these businesses are not the result of being in declining industries. Global demand for automobiles, food, oil, steel, chemical products and particularly electrical goods has continued to grow. Consumers still shop. But none of these 1955 companies is today the dominant firm in its industry. Cars are Toyota and Volkswagen; food is Nestlé; steel is ArcelorMittal, which took over much of the excess capacity located in the former Soviet Empire. Germany's BASF is the world's leading chemical company. And electricals – well, it depends on what you mean by electricals but, whoever you regard as market leader, it isn't GE. Within America, cars are still General Motors – unless you look at market capitalisation and hence to Tesla. But food is PepsiCo and Tyson, steel is Nucor and Pfizer leads in chemicals. Retail is Walmart – and Amazon. Only ExxonMobil and some of the DuPont and GE subsidiaries remain among the global leaders in their fields.

A journalist impressed by the strength of the FAANG corporations today once asked me if there were historic examples of once dominant companies which had lost that dominance. I told her the more interesting question was to find a historically dominant company that had retained that dominance. It was not always so. Of the top ten companies on the Fortune 1955 list, all except Chrysler (1904) had been founded in the nineteenth century or were recognisably successor companies to one that had been. (Buick, the precursor of General Motors, was established only in 1899, but then the first automobile only hit the road in 1886, in Germany.)

The Fortune 500 now

In 2020 the Fortune 500 looks very different. *Fortune* now includes service businesses, so the two top companies by sales are retailers – as would also have been true in 1955. But the current leaders are retailers that did not exist in 1955: Walmart and Amazon. No fewer than four companies are names that probably mean little to non-US readers – they are intermediaries in the fabulously costly US healthcare system. United Health is an insurer, McKesson and Cencora (previously known as AmerisourceBergen) are distributors of pharmaceutical products and CVS Health is both insurer and retailer.

The one manufacturing company on today's list is also in the healthcare sector: Johnson & Johnson. Berkshire Hathaway, the investment vehicle of the legendary 'sage of Omaha', Warren Buffett, has some manufacturing subsidiaries. The AT&T on the modern list is a different company from the American Telephone and Telegraph company whose 'Bell system' monopolised US telecommunications until it was broken up by antitrust action in 1982. Southwestern Bell was the smallest of the businesses (Baby Bells) created by that break-up, but it was the one with the most ambitious executive, Richard Pope. When restrictions were gradually relaxed, Pope led an acquisition spree. Southwestern Bell then bought several other Baby Bells and also the long-distance network which had remained with the original AT&T. The company then assumed the impressive name of its acquisition. The corporation also acquired and subsequently disposed of satellite broadcaster DirectTV and media conglomerate Time Warner. The modern top ten is completed by the perennial ExxonMobil, the only survivor from 1955.

In 1955, most of the world's largest companies were American, and all were either American or European. This is no longer true, reflecting the economic rise of Asia, exemplified by Hyundai, Toyota, Samsung and Sony. In 1955 or 1975 the idea that a Chinese company would be a global leader in any industry would have seemed risible. No one is laughing now. Alibaba, Baidu and Tencent are among the world's most valuable companies.

In 1955 the list of leading businesses was much the same whether the ranking was based on sales, employment, assets, profits or stock market ranking. This also is no longer true. Businesses with many employees are generally facilities companies such as Compass, G4S and ISS, which provide services such as cleaning or catering to other companies, or logistics businesses, delivering goods to customers or firms, either at retail – Walmart, Home Depot, Target – or directly to their homes – UPS, FedEx and, of course, Amazon.

Fortune excludes banks from its rankings of companies by assets because otherwise these companies would overwhelm the list. Of course, it is in the nature of banking that these very large volumes of assets are matched by liabilities of similar magnitude. Or sometimes, as in 2008, more than matched. Other asset-rich companies include those which provide specialist infrastructures, such as AT&T, Verizon and Comcast. A few manufacturing companies, such as Ford and General Electric, remain among the largest by revenues or assets. Probably not for long.

But the best guide to the leading corporations of the twenty-first century is perhaps found by asking which companies have the largest profits and stock market value. As I write, there are six trillion-dollar companies – Alphabet (Google), Amazon, Apple, Nvidia, Meta (Facebook) and Microsoft. Some way behind are Berkshire Hathaway, ExxonMobil, Tesla and Taiwanese chip manufacturer TSMC.[5]

Adam Smith described the pin factory, in which ten different employees undertook eighteen different operations. Even if he had been writing in the mid-twentieth century, he could not have envisaged the degree of corporate specialisation that characterises the twenty-first-century economy. Some companies – such as Compass Group – provide little but labour; others – banks and investment companies – little but capital. I will describe in Chapter 22 how large but little-known businesses provide capital services – renting to operating businesses the assets that the companies operating them once owned.

Some modern corporations – such as United Health – provide, inter alia, a specialist administration service, like the accounts department of a traditional company, and indeed there are businesses – like Sage – that offer such bookkeeping services to smaller companies. Other companies, such as Google or Meta, provide a platform whose content is generated by others. Despite their omnipresence, Google and Meta do not make top positions by sales revenues, as they neither buy their principal inputs nor sell their principal outputs. Most of their revenues come from advertising and feed directly into profit. The twenty-first-century corporation is very different from those which competed to feature in Fortune's 1955 list.

8

THE DECLINE OF MANUFACTURING

The physical weight of our GDP is growing only very
gradually. The exploitation of new concepts accounts for
virtually all of the inflation-adjusted growth in output.
Remarks by Chairman Alan Greenspan, 1988[1]

Where in the hell is it written that America can't lead the
world in manufacturing again? Where is that written? I don't
know where it's written and it's not going to be written on
my watch.
Speech by President Biden at Springfield, Virginia, 2023[2]

In traditional societies more than half of the population will
be found in the fields. In the first British census, held in 1801,
one-third of workers were employed in agriculture. By 1861
this proportion had fallen to 27 per cent and by the end of the
century it was below 10 per cent.[3] It was obvious where the
field hands had gone; in that 1861 census 40 per cent of British
workers were engaged in manufacturing.

Manufacturing's share of employment has declined ever
since. At first only slowly: in 1960 manufacturing still provided
30 per cent of UK jobs. The US proportion was virtually the
same, at 29 per cent. By 2019 these figures had both fallen to 8.5
per cent.[4] Many people (including both President Biden and his
predecessor) find this trend disturbing.

What I describe as manufacturing fetishism – the idea that
manufacturing is the central economic activity and everything
else is somehow subordinate – is deeply ingrained in human

thinking. The origins of this belief lie deeper still. A perception that only tangible objects represent real output and only physical labour constitutes real work may have been formed when economic activity was a never-ending search for food, fuel and shelter. In prehistory, man hunted, fished and made primitive implements. His wife and children prospered if he was good at these things; if not, they languished or even died. Women also worked hard – perhaps harder – but it was the activity of men that was seen as economically productive. For Aristotle, *theoria* ('contemplation') was the highest form of human activity.[5] Still, he conceded that:

> the art of getting wealth out of fruits and animals is always natural. There are two sorts of wealth-getting, as I have said; one is a part of household management, the other is retail trade: the former necessary and honourable, while that which consists in exchange is justly censured; for it is unnatural, and a mode by which men gain from one another.[6]

From primitive times we have inherited the notion of a hierarchy of needs in which food and shelter rank ahead of chartered accountancy and cosmetic surgery. And from the hierarchy of needs comes a perception of a hierarchy of productive activities: agriculture, extraction of primary resources and basic manufacturing rank ahead of hairdressing, wholesaling and television programming.

But such thinking ceased to have economic relevance once collective intelligence and economic institutions had advanced enough for it to be unnecessary to hunt and till all day to get enough to eat – a state of affairs reached centuries ago. Once our ancestors achieved this level of economic progress, they started to add discretionary activities to the fulfilment of their basic needs. The services they craved then remain representative of the services we buy today. The priest would ward off evil; the political leader would organise looting of the resources of alien tribes; the repairman would sharpen stones and knives; and eventually the insurance agent would organise a scheme of mutual support for unlucky villagers whose cow died or whose house burned down. With the rise of this market economy came Adam Smith's division of labour. Specialist tasks were assigned to those best qualified to fulfil them. Some would hunt and others meet demands for services.

'Surely you don't think that an economy can survive on hairdressing and hamburgers?' manufacturing fetishists roar. No, I don't, any more than I think an economy can survive on steel and automobile production. Modern economies are necessarily diverse. But diversity of consumption is entirely compatible with specialisation of production. As Smith noted, the division of labour was limited by the extent of the market, and the growth in the geographical scope of markets has steadily increased the geographical division of labour. Switzerland and Denmark are among the richest countries in the world, but neither produces automobiles.

> Contrary to many people's images of a society focused on tourism and banking secrecy, Switzerland is an outlier in the Global North, with 20 per cent of the working population engaged in manufacturing, particularly speciality chemicals and precision engineering.[7] But little of this manufacturing is of the kind that requires its exhausted workers to wash off the dust and sweat of the day as they return home.

As economies passed beyond the basic and all-consuming requests for food, fuel and shelter, the scale of rewards from production became divorced from the order of their output in the hierarchy of needs. You only got paid for producing goods that people wanted, but it soon became apparent that repairs and priestly services and (later) insurance and cosmetic surgery were among the things people wanted. The earnings from different activities came to reflect the availability or scarcity of the talents needed to undertake them and the position of the actor in the power structure of the tribe. Specialist skill explains why the insurance agents, surgeons and repairmen did well, and hierarchy accounted for the relative prosperity of the political leader and the priest.

Those who are lucky enough to possess rare talents or occupy positions of authority sometimes feel embarrassed by earning more than those who work to satisfy more basic elements in the hierarchy of needs. Often they also engage in occupations that are less arduous and more fun. Such embarrassment at one's good fortune is rarely very great, and in recent decades many people – especially in the finance sector and corporate boardrooms – appear to have overcome it entirely. They have persuaded themselves that they deserve their generous remuneration – or simply do not care what others think.

The Industrial Revolution was built on the substitution of mechanical work for human – or animal – labour. The flying shuttle and the spinning jenny replaced skilled craftsmen with machine power. Then the internal combustion engine displaced the horse, and the fibre optic cable made the running of marathons necessary only as a recreational activity. Today a robot can undertake almost any repetitive task that once required manual labour. Assembly line functions are now mostly delegated either to workers in low-wage countries or to machines. But however far globalisation and automation advance, many services can only be performed by people close to the beneficiary of the service. And low-skilled jobs in an advanced economy will mostly be found in these service activities. Workers in China can assemble your iPhone, but they cannot cut your hair, collect your refuse or give your grandmother a bath.

The manufacturing fetishist often denies that these service activities are 'real jobs'. Making money through manual labour in primary activity is 'necessary and honourable', but – at least in a commonly held view – the subsequent addition of value by people who sit in offices and design iPhones, study the aerodynamics of wing designs or plan the logistics of distribution networks is not. Two millennia after Aristotle, a 'red wall' voter explained to *The Economist* in 2021 during the pandemic lockdown that 'It's not a real job if you can do it in your pyjamas.'[8]

This is largely a gender issue: when you ask for examples of 'real jobs', they will usually be functions that have traditionally been undertaken by men. Mining and metalworking are 'real jobs'; cooking and caring, however skilled or arduous, are not. Manufacturing was once the principal source of low-skilled male employment. But this is no longer true in advanced economies. Thus the decline of manufacturing is associated with the emasculation of the workforce and has led to the destruction of related male social bonds and units of political organisation. The principal manufacturing industry that has always employed a majority of women – textiles – is the industrial analogue of the traditional female activity of making clothes for the family, and is barely acknowledged by manufacturing fetishists as a source of 'real jobs'.

And much manufacturing was undertaken in large plants that dominated their communities, many of which have now closed, as experienced in Britain's 'red wall' and America's 'Rust Belt'.[9] The automobile plants of Detroit and the steelworks of Pittsburgh once defined their towns, but few service activities are undertaken at similarly large facilities. There are some exceptions, such as hospitals and universities. These institutions have shown more permanence than the firms that built assembly lines; Oxford University is seven centuries old, but the Oxford plant of Morris Motors, which opened in 1922, closed seven decades later and was demolished in 2002. The founding of Oxford's Radcliffe Infirmary in 1770 is almost contemporaneous with the beginning of production at the Carron Works. But the Carron Works is shuttered while the modern John Radcliffe Hospital employs 11,000 people. Rochester, once synonymous with Kodak and Xerox, is now known for its university and the Eastman School of Music (a leading conservatory).

Universities and conservatories employ highly trained professionals, with low-skilled workers only in less prestigious supporting roles. The assembly line worker at River Rouge had no doubt that it was *his* product, not the work of the bean counters and stopwatch monitors, that attracted customers and revenues, and may have wondered what useful work the managers were doing. The janitor may similarly wonder what useful work the professors are doing but cannot doubt that it is the activity and reputation of the faculty that bring revenues to the university. If the Industrial Revolution began with the substitution of mechanical labour for human and animal labour, it continued with the substitution of collective intelligence for physical labour.

The manufacturing obsession has no economic basis but considerable social and political significance. Many of the roots of the white working-class resentment which in the US supports Donald Trump and in the UK voted for Brexit are to be found in the disappearance of traditionally masculine jobs in the Global North as a result of economic globalisation. It would be an absurd response to look nostalgically at pictures of men whose bare torsos were covered in sweat as they worked in the light and heat of rivers of molten iron, or who heaved coal as they spent their day working underground; these may have been 'real jobs', but they were awful jobs, and our society is better off for no longer needing them. But their very awfulness generated solidarity and stability that have been lost. Martin Wolf has written powerfully on the social and political consequences of that loss, which are reflected in the fragility of today's political order, while recognising the vast gains that globalisation has brought.[10]

The unbearable lightness of modernity

In the modern economy, value comes not from building something bigger or heavier but from creating something smarter. You can buy a business suit from Amazon for £25. It will be practical – ready to wear, polyester-blended, ideal for a gangland funeral and machine-washable so that your moll can pop the bloodied trousers in the washing machine and they will come up good as new. You can pay ten times as much at Marks & Spencer for Italian tailoring and good-quality wool fabric. And you can pay ten times as much again for a bespoke suit from Savile Row. You need to decide whether you want a stylish suit or just a suit: a customised suit or just a good-looking suit. You need not pay much for a suit but you will pay a lot for style, and a lot more for personalisation.

The carronade was a type of short cannon developed at the Carron Works in 1776 to provide greater firepower for less weight than the long cannons then commonly in use, thus allowing ships to carry a battery of hostile weapons. Napoleon supposedly blamed his defeat at Trafalgar on the impact of the Royal Navy's carronades. And guns have continued to improve their power and cost-to-weight ratio; the real (inflation adjusted) price per kilogram of the SA80A2, the British Army's standard-issue combat rifle, is two orders of magnitude greater than that of the carronade. The most powerful weapon ever used – 'Fat Man', the atomic bomb dropped on Nagasaki – weighed the same as five carronades. The armour of Nelson's flagship, the HMS *Victory*, would have weighed at least sixty times as much as 'Fat Man'.

'In this war' – Napoleon wrote to his minister of marine in 1805 – 'the English have been the first to use carronades, and everywhere they have done us great harm. We must hasten to perfect their system.'[11]

Henry Ford's Model T car, first produced in 1908, was priced at $850 when American average annual earnings were around $500: by 1926 the price had fallen to $260 and the average wage had risen to $1,500.[12] The Airbus A380 is affordable for almost no one, which is why production has been discontinued: airlines baulked at the price and Airbus wasn't recovering its production costs. But a commercial failure can still be a technological marvel, and the design means, per kilo, you paid an order of magnitude more for the A380 than the Model T.

If you want the latest iPhone, be prepared to pay more (per kg) still – Apple has consciously tried to reduce the weight of its flagship product, although it is still a little heavier than the original iPhone. And Pfizer's Covid-19 vaccine, although seemingly inexpensive at £15 per dose, is the most costly of all these products per unit of physical resource because a dose weighs only 30 micrograms.

New Product	Date developed	Price per kg at 2020 prices[13]
Carronade[14]	1776	£2
SA80A2 Rifle[15]	2000	£200
Model T Ford[16]	1908	£27
Airbus A380[17]	2007	£1,250
Empire State Building[18]	1931	£1.40
Burj Khalifa[19]	2010	£2.70
DynaTAC mobile phone[20]	1984	£10,000
iPhone 15 Pro Max	2023	£5,000
Pin[21]	Price from 1821	£11
Pfizer Covid-19 Vaccine[22]	2020	£500,000

Construction has always been more resource-intensive than manufacturing; the Empire State Building, completed in a year and the tallest skyscraper of its day, was far less costly per kilo than the Model T. But for modern buildings, as for men's suits, value has increasingly migrated from materials to design, from simple functionality to perceived utility. The tallest building in the world today – Dubai's Burj Khalifa, twice the height of the Empire State Building – is twice as expensive per kilo of weight as the New York icon.

Better, not more

As former Federal Reserve chairman Alan Greenspan observed in the remark that began this chapter, modern economic growth in developed economies is largely about better and more complex rather than bigger and more. Once, the badge of poverty was not having enough to eat; now we describe not having a home computer as 'digital poverty'. Today obesity is a problem of the poor, while the rich buy fresh food and gym subscriptions and obsess about 'wellness'. In the Global North we spend more than 10 per cent of our income on healthcare, not because we are more ill but because there is so much more that can be done to treat us, and we have prophylactic access to contraceptives, vaccines and antibiotics.

My own grandparents never travelled more than a few miles from the small Scottish village where they were born. (My paternal grandfather died there at a young age in 1916, though some of his friends were buried in France.) Some of their relatives had emigrated to the United States; their newfound prosperity and generosity enabled my father to make the much shorter journey to attend university. Today that village exports Highland Spring water globally, and its residents can and do visit distant places and explore other cultures.

Economic growth is Facebook, Google and Siri, email, instant access to a million songs. Economic growth is low-cost air travel and the immediate arrival of an Uber, the availability of counselling and gene editing. Economic growth is varifocal spectacles and bluetooth-connected earphones, satnavs and mobile banking. Economic growth is promoted by ideas that seem banal and obvious once invented but which make our lives easier: shipping containers, ring-pull cans, wheels on bins and suitcases. Some of these things are mixed blessings and many – such as internet connections – fulfil needs we never knew we had but now seem indispensable products. In the face of a modern concern for limits to growth or even advocacy of 'degrowth', it cannot be stressed too strongly that economic growth in developed economies is not primarily about 'more stuff'. Modern economic growth is about building collective intelligence into familiar resources to create new products and still more advanced capabilities.

The significance of this point – evident though it is from our personal experience – is not fully appreciated, even among economists. The benefits we derive from the product and process innovations listed in the last paragraph are poorly recorded, if recorded at all, in measures of national output such as GDP. Statistical offices try to make some allowance for new goods and quality improvements, but there are nearly intractable issues of principle in estimating how much better off we are from consuming goods – such as iPhones – that we did not imagine we wanted until they became available.

In a brilliant and widely noted but insufficiently seminal paper William Nordhaus calculated the price of light over millennia as measured by the human effort required per lumen – from the times when gathering and setting fire to wood was the only means of illumination, giving way to tallow candles whose light shone on the manuscript of *The Wealth of Nations*, and in due course to the electric light on Nordhaus's desk.[23] He noted that traditional measures of the cost of light (which could not fully account for these new methods of lighting) suggested it had risen since 1800: perhaps by an order of magnitude, perhaps by just a factor of three. His index, on the other hand, showed that the cost had *fallen* by over two orders of magnitude. What price indices measure is the rising cost of things we use to make light – but what we want is light, rather than candles or light bulbs. Remarkably, since Nordhaus wrote there has been a further and largely unmeasured fall in the price of light as LEDs have replaced incandescent bulbs. You can run a modern, bright LED bulb for twenty-four hours at a cost of about 2 pence – including the (pro-rated) price of the bulb itself.[24] This is about ten times cheaper than achieving the same illumination from a modern incandescent bulb.[25]

This is not intended to be another contribution to the endless criticisms of GDP measurement for its failure to incorporate things the critics – mostly rightly – believe to be important. Matters such as 'well-being', the natural environment, the quality of social and personal relationships, levels of inequality and the safeguarding of human rights. My critique of GDP measurement in practice relates to its inability to report sufficiently accurately what it is *intended* to measure: the value of economic output. And pronouncements based on such data about long-run trends in income or the rate of increase of productivity should be taken with a grain of salt – or several. When pundits fret over whether the latest figure for GDP growth is an annual rate of 1.8 per cent or 1.9 per cent, they are fussing over differences that are insignificant in relation to the fundamental and inescapable uncertainties in the data they are citing.

> This does not mean that calculated GDP figures convey no actionable information. In conversation with someone engaged in GDP forecasting in an investment bank, I was shocked to realise that she had – like most economics students today – taken no course in National Income Accounting and did not really understand what GDP was. But, on reflection, I recognised that this did not really matter for the purposes of her job. She was employed to forecast what the statistics office would say GDP was, because that would influence markets. And because the statistics office had access to many data sources, its reports did give a useful indicator of some trends in the economy, and would certainly influence market reactions and business behaviour. But it was a salutary reminder of the dangers of using economic data without asking questions about where the data comes from and what it means.

Much of the world has not yet enjoyed the benefits of the Global North's transition to an economy that is mostly about better rather than more, although large parts of Asia are moving rapidly towards it. Access to the collective intelligence already developed in the West allows Asian countries to achieve rates of economic growth without precedent in history. And increasingly Asia itself now adds to that collective intelligence, potentially enabling the world as a whole to move forward faster. But,

particularly in Africa, economic growth of the traditional kind –
more stuff – is required to meet the basic needs for food, shelter
and primary healthcare. Physical resources and energy will
subsequently be required for transport and consumer durables,
which were the essential preliminaries to Western prosperity. It
would be a double tragedy if by misunderstanding the nature
of our own success we were – in the name of sustainability – to
deprive others of the opportunity to achieve theirs.

Failure to recognise that economic growth is mostly *better*
rather than *more* is why the sages who have repeatedly predicted
that growth must end because we will run out of – first it was
wood, then it was coal, then nitrates and then oil – have always
been wrong. We haven't run out of arable land and our progress will not be halted by a shortage of lithium. All physical
resources have finite limits, but human ingenuity does not.

PART 3

THE SECRET OF OUR SUCCESS

Humans have become better at almost everything as a result of the steady accretion of collective knowledge and its transformation into collective intelligence – a problem-solving capability characteristically found in teams of people. Successful businesses find new or distinctive combinations of capabilities to offer new or distinctive products, creating an output more valuable than the same resources could produce in alternative uses. Adding value in this way, business – and other – organisations create economic rents.

9

BETTER AT EVERYTHING

I've got to admit it's getting better (better)
A little better all the time

John Lennon and Paul McCartney, 1967[1]

The accumulation of collective knowledge and the development of collective intelligence have made humans better at – almost everything. Men have been trying to run fast for thousands of years. To warn of approaching armies, to report victories and to deliver the urgent messages of the sovereign. And they competed in sporting events. We do not know how fast the ancients ran, and only very recently could sprinters be timed with precision. But we can observe the productivity of modern runners – and see how it has increased. When Harold Abrahams won his gold medal in the 1924 Olympics, the race immortalised in the Oscar-winning film *Chariots of Fire*, he completed the 100 metre sprint in 10.6 seconds.[2] Usain Bolt currently holds the world record for the sprint at 9.58 seconds.[3] Note the improvement not just in speed but in chronometry.

The original marathon – a dramatic dash from Marathon to Athens – is probably an invention of the nineteenth-century poet Robert Browning. But Browning's creative imagination encouraged Olympic founder Pierre de Coubertin, at the suggestion of the philologist Michel Bréal, to schedule a marathon at the inaugural Olympics in 1896. The race was won in a time of just under three hours. In 2019 Eliud Kipchoge became the first person to complete the distance in less than two hours, and more than a thousand runners in the modern New York marathon achieved

times that would have won a gold medal in 1896. While Pheidip-
pides probably never made the fabled journey from Marathon to
Athens, there is some historical support for the claim that he ran
140 miles from Athens to warn Sparta of the Persian approach.
It took him two days. The leading participants in the modern
Spartathlon which commemorates his feat complete the run in
just over twenty hours, with the benefit of modern roads. But
now a fibre optic cable would transmit news of the conflict, or
the result of the race, in about one millisecond.

Abrahams employed a personal coach, Sam Mussabini,
before his 1924 Olympic victory. This was regarded as almost tan-
tamount to cheating, but today even club runners benefit from
extensive coaching, better diet and nutritional guidance, and
from the advice of friendly competitors.[4] Bolt runs 10 per cent
faster and Kipchoge 50 per cent faster than the earlier winners
in their events. These improvements in productivity have been
observed in an activity whose essential character has remained
unchanged for thousands of years. Mussabini could train Abrahams to win Olympic gold but could never have run the race
himself; Abrahams could run faster than any man alive but had
no understanding of sports mechanics. The combination was
more powerful than either alone. The power of combinations
of capabilities is the secret of our modern athletic prowess. And
of our opulence.

Supporting capabilities

The Scottish National Portrait Gallery organised a display
celebrating great Scots of the twentieth century. I visited to
admire their portrait of Sir James Mirrlees, my graduate super-
visor (more of him in Chapter 14). In the Gallery, Mirrlees was
facing Sir Kenneth Dalglish, aka Kenny Dalglish, Scotland's
most capped footballer.[5] Mirrlees was brought up in a small
village in Galloway and went from there to Edinburgh University, Oxford and Cambridge, and in due course to Stockholm to
receive a Nobel Prize.[6] Dalglish came from a run-down district

of Glasgow, Dalmarnock. Dalglish's skill had enabled him to escape Dalmarnock, travel the world and be honoured by the late queen. And earn a great deal of money.

A few days later, although only 40 miles away from Edinburgh's gothic portrait gallery and portraits of Scotland's honoured citizens, I was in what seemed another world. In a dingy office in Glasgow, I gained insight into the city's problems from someone working to provide help in estates like Dalmarnock, which suffer the most severe drug addiction problems in Western Europe.[7] One redeeming feature of the drug trade, I was told, was that it enabled entrepreneurial young people to acquire enough wealth to leave the area and bring up an honest family with a middle-class lifestyle.

Through practice and the acquisition of knowledge, the innate talent of a Dalglish or a Mirrlees becomes a capability: the ability to solve problems, problems as different as bypassing the English defenders and the nature of optimal contract design. But practice, the acquisition of knowledge and the development of capabilities are the product of the organisational context set by the institutions of the market economy. Celtic Football Club, whose Parkhead stadium abuts Dalmarnock, enabled Dalglish to build his talent into a productive capability admired by millions. But the Dalmarnock drugs trade enabled Keith Gartshore, now in jail for nine years for operating a drug supply business from a warehouse there, to develop his talents in a manner that any decent society will want to suppress.

The achievements of individuals such as Guinness and Lionel Messi are the result of both cooperation and competition. Without the aid of talented fellow players and coaches, and the systems of talent-spotting and training that took him to Barcelona and Paris, Messi would still be kicking a ball around the streets of his home town of Rosario and the pampas of Argentina. But football is a team game, and any of the members of the Barcelona and Celtic teams who helped Messi and Dalglish would have been outstanding players at another club. Guinness collaborated with great directors such as David Lean and George

Lucas.[8] But his performances also required the services of other talented actors and the support of stagehands, camera operators and the cashiers who took the money at the box office. Without them Guinness would have lodged in seedy boarding houses as he played minor roles on the provincial stage.

> Srinivasa Ramanujan was a clerk in the Madras Ports Office who engaged in mathematics in his spare time. He sent notes of his discoveries to several famous mathematicians. Few replied, but one who did was G. H. Hardy, who realised the man's genius. Hardy organised Ramanujan's trip to Cambridge, where, over some opposition, he was elected to a fellowship at Trinity College; Ramanujan produced some remarkable mathematical results and was soon elected to the Royal Society.
>
> But Ramanujan did not fit in well to the unfamiliar context; the journey to Europe itself violated the precepts of his devout Hinduism; the weather and food of England did not suit; and he was frequently ill. His wife, whom he had married when she was ten years old, had remained in India. Eventually, Ramanujan returned to his native country, where he died aged thirty-two. Talent matters, but is most productive when deployed in context.
>
> Alec Guinness was born in London to a single mother, Agnes Cuff, who was certainly a drunk and probably a sex worker. However a wealthy banker, Andrew Geddes, paid for his education and enabled him to go to drama school. Was Geddes his father – or the agent of a still more famous parent?

The outstanding talents of Mirrlees and Ramanujan became productive only when developed in organisations and combined with complementary capabilities. But the different experiences of Gartshore and Ramanujan illustrate the importance of complementarity between talent and environment. Some of these complementary supporting capabilities originate in individual talents, but combining individual skills with more mundane complementary resources builds the distinctive capabilities of teams, and these assemble into combinations which represent the distinctive capabilities of organisations.

Globalisation and inclusivity

Runners' times have also fallen because the pool of talent from which elite athletes are drawn has widened. The athletes against whom Abrahams competed in 1924 were white men who had received a university education in Britain or the United States. Strikingly, today most short-distance and extreme-distance champions are, respectively, of West African and East African descent.[9] Inclusivity – which allowed people from diverse nationalities and social classes to compete for gold – together with sports engineering, the scientific analysis of the determinants of performance, nutritional advance and systematised training protocols, gave us sub-ten-second sprints and sub-two-hour marathons.

In 2021 the Italian Marcell Jacobs was the surprise victor in the Olympic 100 metre sprint. Although Jacobs has spent almost all his life in Italy, his father is an African American serviceman. Every other gold medal in that event since 1984 has been won by a black athlete from the US or West Indies. (The US did not participate in the 1980 games and Allan Wells, a white Scot, was the surprise victor.) Following Abebe Bikila's stunning barefoot victory in the Olympic marathon of 1960, Ethiopia has won four marathon golds, Kenya two and Uganda one. Different regions of the world, including Britain and Scandinavia, have had similar periods of outperformance despite having very different geographies, societies and genetic pools. All these factors may play a role; currently there does not appear to be a consensus explanation for any of these phenomena.

More tempting

The product of the first recorded commerce – the apple in the Garden of Eden which was the precursor to so much trouble – has improved immeasurably in quality as it has fallen in price. The Garden of Eden could not have been located in Western Europe or the United States, whose native crab apples are almost inedible. But the fruit of the tree which Eve had picked 'was good for food, and … pleasant to the eyes, and a tree to be desired to make one wise'.[10] If Eden was located in modern Iraq, as many believe, the fruit might have been the small wild apple that originated and still grows widely in Kazakhstan. Almost all the apples we eat today are thought to result from cross-breeding the crab apple with this Asian variety. The apple probably travelled along the Silk Road from Kazakhstan. It reached ancient Greece and Rome, and the Roman Empire spread it throughout Europe, including Britain. Apples were imported from there to the United States, and America has led the world in selective cross-breeding that has steadily improved their taste and texture. Today Eve could tempt Adam with the modern Braeburn and Honeycomb, and in 2022 the new hybrid Cosmic Crisp, developed at Washington State University and applauded for its flavour and long shelf life, became widely available.

We run faster because of the accumulation of collective knowledge about sports engineering and nutrition. With the aid of coaches this knowledge becomes collective intelligence – know *that* becomes know *how*. We eat better apples because plant species were carried across the world and because of the accumulation of collective knowledge of techniques of cross-breeding. The collaboration of Sam Mussabini and Harold Abrahams won an Olympic gold medal, and the collaboration of botanists at Washington State University, local growers and breeders and marketing and branding agencies produced the Cosmic Crisp.

By accumulating collective knowledge, applying collective intelligence and practising the division of labour on a global and inclusive basis, humans have become better at … almost everything.

There is one important recent exception to the proposition that humans have been getting better at almost everything. Individual performance on intelligence tests improved steadily – until the 1970s, when it stalled in Western Europe. (This historical trend of improving test results is often described as 'the Flynn effect'.) The author is too modest to take pride in being part of the most intelligent generation that has ever lived. And before American readers engage in any self-congratulation, they should note that the US continues to perform poorly relative to other countries of the Global North in the PISA tests of comparative scholastic achievement. (The top-scoring countries are all in East Asia).

The measurement of human intelligence by applying tests based on abstract problems is an idea pioneered by statistician Sir Francis Galton (of whom more below) and developed in practice at the beginning of the twentieth century. Although some practitioners claim otherwise, it seems inevitable that the content of the test is to a degree culturally specific, and this must influence the interpretation of differences over time and between groups. There will be further occasions in this book for scepticism about the significance of time series constructed over long periods in which many things have changed.

Competition and cooperation

I have used the examples of running and apple breeding in order to emphasise that the growth of collective knowledge and collective intelligence is not simply about what we think of as 'technology' – the arrival of gadgets such as automobiles and transistors. Of course, technology has contributed to social and economic progress, but automobiles and transistors are the result, not the cause, of the growth of human capabilities. The psychologist Cecilia Heyes has written of 'cognitive gadgets' to

emphasise the key role of culturally developed cognitive capabilities: the ability to assemble disparate and developing components
of human knowledge into problem-solving capabilities. While
collective intelligence is the product of cooperation, it is competition between individuals, teams and firms that provides the
spur to its development. In the late nineteenth century competition between Western Union and the Bell companies, between
Thomas Edison and Nikola Tesla, between Westinghouse and
General Electric, led to the first commercial applications of electricity. And a century later competition between IBM and Digital
Equipment, between SRI's Don Nielson and CERN's Tim
Berners-Lee, between Netscape and Microsoft, gave us the internet and its first commercial applications. By 1900 the Wright
brothers were among many pioneers trying to make flight a
reality. Two decades later, many businesses would be striving to
establish commercial aviation. And then the jet engine, envisaged by many but made a reality by groups of engineers in
Britain and Germany, transformed international travel.

It is common, and natural, to tell the history of innovation
through the exploits of men of genius, such as Edison and Tesla,
and pioneers such as Berners-Lee and the Wright brothers. But
if the Wright brothers had not flown in 1903, someone else
would have done something very similar in some other location. Collective intelligence develops when the accumulation of
collective knowledge reaches a point at which talented people
identify problems that this shared knowledge can be employed
to solve. And it is also common, and natural, to describe the
history of innovation through the introduction of new gadgets,
from aeroplanes to iPhones. I have taken running and apples
as examples to emphasise that the growth of collective intelligence has a range and applicability that extends well beyond
technology.

For evolutionary anthropologist Joseph Henrich, the progressive growth of our collective intelligence is the 'secret of our
success' as a human species.[11] We are distinguished from other
animals by our capacity for social learning – gaining knowledge

not just from our own experience but from the experience of others – and the acquisition of such learning is immeasurably enhanced by our ability to communicate. Together we know far more than any individual can know. No individual has either the knowledge or the skills necessary to build an Airbus, but 10,000 people working as a cooperative group do.

The significance of this observation cannot be exaggerated. The psychologist Michael Tomasello has noted that 'You never saw two chimpanzees carrying a log together.'[12] Some primates have developed sufficient collective intelligence to enable them to – on occasion – hunt together and to plan to attack the territory of another tribe. But humans have developed sufficient collective intelligence to build aeroplanes and iPhones and even enough collective intelligence to realise that attacking other tribes is mostly a stupid thing to do. The unprecedented prosperity of the modern world is the result of the growth of our collective intelligence.

The assembly of varied knowledge to solve problems is why we have faster times and better apples, why Edinburgh's Lochend Close no longer leads to a cesspit, why you can see to the end of it even on a winter evening, and why Adam Smith at sixty-seven could today have expected to live for many more years. And that is why opulence, although still not universal, is widely experienced throughout the Global North.

10

BETTER AT BUSINESS

It was getting darker, and soon the candles were lighted. Macak [Tesla's cat] took a few steps through the room. He shook his paws as though he were treading on wet ground. I looked at him attentively. Did I see something or was it an illusion? I strained my eyes and perceived distinctly that his body was surrounded by a halo like the aureola of a saint!

I cannot exaggerate the effect of this marvellous night on my childish imagination. Day after day I have asked myself 'what is electricity?' and found no answer. Eighty years have gone by since that time and I still ask the same question, unable to answer it.

Nikola Tesla, aged eighty-three, in letter to Pola Fotić, 1939[1]

For many centuries, a range of natural phenomena admitted only supernatural explanations, or none. Some eels could stun their prey by emitting sparks. Forks of lightning might briefly light up the sky. Two metals immersed in liquid could cause the muscles of a dead frog to twitch. After the Renaissance and the Enlightenment, scientific explanations challenged the supernatural. In the early nineteenth century scientists began to realise that these disparate observations were all manifestations of the force we know now as electricity. Understanding of electricity advanced steadily through the eighteenth century. But such knowledge was a curiosity rather than a discovery with practical application.

So who 'discovered' electricity? Was it the American Benjamin Franklin, flying his kite in a thunderstorm (in 1752)? Or the Italian Alessandro Volta, who (in 1799) created an electrical charge chemically? Or the Dane Hans Oersted, who (in 1820) demonstrated the connection between electric current and magnetism? Or the Englishman Michael Faraday, who (in 1831) described magnetic force fields at London's Royal Institution? Or the Scot James Clerk Maxwell, whose equations (in 1873) assembled previous discoveries into a unified theory? All of these people 'discovered' electricity. The nature of collective knowledge is that it is the creation of many and the property of all.

This steady advance of collective knowledge about electricity led to the development of collective intelligence: the application of this knowledge to practical problems. Franklin's experiment led to the installation of lightning conductors on tall buildings – notably the State House of Maryland. It was a modest beginning to the useful application of emergent understanding of electricity. The German mathematician Carl Gauss had pioneered the idea that electrical impulses could be used for communication – he could not have conceived how much communication would follow from that idea! With the considerable technical assistance of Joseph Henry of Princeton (who had done something similar to Gauss at that institution), Samuel Morse, who had enjoyed a career as a portrait painter, persuaded Congress to fund the construction of a telegraph. Morse became wealthy from the proceeds – wealthy enough to take an ultimately unsuccessful claim to a patent on most forms of electrical communication to the Supreme Court.

Alexander Graham Bell took advantage of this freedom. He studied speech vibrations to help him communicate with the profoundly deaf Mabel Hubbard, whom he subsequently married. Bell realised that these vibrations could be transmitted and reproduced electrically; the telephone was the result. With help from Mabel's father, the Bell companies were established and dominated American telephony until broken into the 'Baby Bells' by court order in 1982.

Others had related ideas. Western Union, threatened by Bell's telephone, hired Thomas Edison to improve it; Edison went on to patent the phonograph and became a prolific proponent of commercial applications of electricity, most famously electric lighting. Edison had many rivals, including Nikola Tesla, a Croatian émigré to the United States, working for Westinghouse. Tesla successfully promoted alternating current (AC) over Edison's direct current (DC). And if you search for 'inventor of the electric motor' you will be offered a choice of at least a dozen names.

> Elon Musk named his automobile company after Nikola Tesla, whose victory in the 'current wars' helped define the modern world. Will the same be said of Musk 150 years from now? No other contemporary figure has displayed that ambition more openly.

Three centuries after Franklin launched his kite into the thunderstorm, we cannot imagine a world without the universal application of electricity. A world in which the only means of communication had been the messenger. A world in which the only source of power in the home had been individual effort. A world in which even after the establishment of a factory, the processes in it relied on a single engine.

The history of flight

The possibility of manned flight has stirred the imagination since ancient times. Icarus fell to earth after he flew too close to the sun, which melted the wax attaching his wings to his arms. Since birds flew with flapping wings, it seemed obvious that flapping wings were the key to flight. But it was not until the scientific enlightenment of the seventeenth century that humans began to understand the mechanisms behind flight. And even today, while scientists and engineers know how to build planes that remain airborne, we do not have a complete understanding of *why* they do so.[2]

Robert Hooke was the English polymath widely credited with the recognition that objects need not fall to earth if they were possessed of sufficient forward thrust – it had long been observed that javelins and discs could travel some distance before they returned to the ground. But there was no mechanism for achieving that thrust for a chariot or a carriage: until the invention of the steam engine, animals, including human animals, were the primary source of power, supplemented by wind, water and – in a critical flowering of collective intelligence – wheels.

James Watt's condenser (1769) greatly improved the efficiency of Thomas Newcomen's (1712) steam engine. The iconic product of the early years of the Industrial Revolution resulted from the addition of Watt's technical breakthrough to existing technology. Still, the development of Watt's engine required not just the capital but also the business acumen of Matthew Boulton. And the continued pre-eminence of the firm of Boulton and Watt owed much to the inventive genius of William Murdoch – who had walked 300 miles to offer his services to the partnership and made many critically important, incremental improvements to Watt's designs. The deployment of efficient steam engines may have been the single most important catalyst of the Industrial Revolution. It was the outcome of the collective knowledge that accumulated in the scientific revolution which began in the seventeenth century. Combined with the technical expertise of Murdoch, the business skills and financial resources of Boulton and the inventive genius of Watt, it became the capability to build steam engines – and to continue to improve them. The development of the iPhone 250 years later would be the result of a similar combination of collective knowledge and complementary skills.

Many people experimented with using the engines of Newcomen and Watt to propel a boat, with little commercial success, but in 1804 Richard Trevithick had a different idea: an engine mounted on wheels. George Stephenson persuaded the promoters of the Stockton and Darlington Railway, built to take coal to the port, to use a wheeled steam engine as well as horses to pull freight cars. At the opening in 1825 a carriage labelled *Experiment* carried local dignitaries. The next step was obvious – and revolutionary. Few *people* wanted to travel from mine to dock, but many wanted to travel between Liverpool and Manchester. The line linking the two cities opened for passenger traffic in 1830. Less than half a century later, railroads connected the Atlantic and Pacific coasts of the United States. The nineteenth century saw

steady advances in technology and business organisation until by
its end steamships were crossing the Atlantic. But the power-to-
weight ratio of early engines was far short of that needed to make
aviation a realistic possibility. The development of steam turbines
revolutionised seaborne traffic. Still, the concept of a coal-fired
aircraft, which makes us smile today, was – if barely – within the
imagination of visionaries in the nineteenth century. The Scottish chemist James Young recognised the potential of mineral
oil and partnered with Edward Binney and Edward Meldrum
to extract it from shale. (As a small boy in Edinburgh I regularly
passed the shale 'bings' of West Lothian but did not appreciate their historic significance – these piles of residue are now a
scheduled monument.) The new fuel opened up a different path
of evolution and was followed by the development of the internal combustion engine, which would be the preferred means of
propelling the horseless carriages we now know as automobiles.
As every schoolchild knows, Wilbur and Orville Wright built the
first fixed-wing aircraft to take off under its own power.

Manned flight happened at the beginning of the twentieth
century as a result of an accumulation of collective knowledge
(by scientists) and its translation into collective intelligence (by
engineers). In the century that followed, businesspeople would
combine these technical capabilities with the organisational
capabilities required to develop commercial products. In 1967 the
first Boeing 737 entered service. In the following fifty years over
ten thousand of these aircraft would be built.[3] The 747 jumbo jet
took to the air in 1969. The European Airbus consortium would
rival these planes with the short-haul A320 and the wide-bodied
A380, the latter the biggest commercial plane in the skies.

The Airbus A320 is one of the most complex manufactured
products of the present era. There is not and could not be any
manual that describes the whole process of plane assembly, flight
planning and aircraft management. The Airbus consortium is
itself a complex international network: the A320's forward fuselage is built in Saint-Nazaire, France, the horizontal stabilisers
in Getafe, Spain, and the wings in Broughton, Wales; and many

other parts are built at other sites across western Europe. A complex dedicated transport network shifts the parts for assembly in Toulouse. Airbus even has its own specially designed aircraft for transporting those parts; the completed plane is flown from France to Germany for fitting out in Hamburg.

The term 'learning curve', now used casually and widely, came into being to describe the phenomenon that Adam Smith identified and claimed to have observed in the pin factory.[4] Individuals become better at routine tasks, though usually at a decreasing rate, as they repeat them. The 'experience curve' describes the same phenomenon in a collective endeavour.[5] This effect was first quantified in aircraft manufacturing: the cost of each plane decreased with each successive unit of production, so that each doubling of cumulative output led to a reduction in unit costs, estimated for airplanes at 15 per cent.[6] (The experience curve is dynamic, related to cumulative output, in contrast to static scale economies, which describe the cost reductions associated with greater volume of output at a point in time.) The experience curve is the result of the growth of collective intelligence – mostly knowing how, but also knowing what – in developing the capabilities of groups.

The design of aircraft has evolved step by step since the Wright brothers first flew, and involves extensive trust, cooperation and the willing sharing of knowledge. Thousands of incremental advances took us from the plane that carried Orville Wright one hundred yards to an aircraft that transports 400 passengers 17,000 miles. The 'fly-by-wire' system based on myriad developments in informatics means that, in principle, an aircraft can fly from London to Sydney without a pilot. And flying to Sydney (or anywhere) requires another complex network involving booking systems, ground handling, airline consortia and international air traffic control. Adam Smith's masterwork was published twelve years before the First Fleet landed on the shores of Australia and more than two hundred years before the first Airbus did. But Smith might still recognise – and no doubt be awed by – the effectiveness of the modern division of labour. But the division of labour requires exchange. And exchange requires a concept of value.

> The concept of 'the wisdom of crowds' is often said to originate with Aristotle, a figure who appears frequently in this book. The modern popularisation of the phrase is attributable to the American journalist James Surowiecki.[7] His intriguing essay on the subject of the wisdom of crowds begins with a famous observation by Francis Galton: in a competition at a country fair, attendees were invited to guess the weight of an ox. Galton noted that the median (or perhaps average) of all the widely dispersed guesses was close to the correct weight.[8]
>
> Galton's observation is closely related to the (not then formulated) efficient market hypothesis, a pillar of modern financial economics, and to the legendary investor Benjamin Graham's distinction between markets as voting machine and investing as weighing machine. 'The Parable of the Ox', which introduces my book *Other People's Money*, offers a light-hearted take on these issues.[9]
>
> But Aristotle did not have in mind weight-guessing competitions or the efficient market hypothesis when he described the wisdom of crowds; he intended to refer to the aggregate, not the average. 'Impure food mixed with what is pure', he continued, 'makes the whole more nourishing than the small amount of pure food alone.' He acknowledged the genuine importance of expertise: 'it might be held that the best man to judge which physician has given the right treatment is the man … who is himself a physician.'[10] Flying a plane benefits from the assembled expertise of pilots, schedulers, air traffic controllers etc., but not from the average opinion of the passengers.

11

VALUE

Catch a parrot and teach him to say 'supply and demand,'
and you have an excellent economist.
> Popularly attributed to Thomas Carlyle but first traceable to
> Irving Fisher, 1907[1]

What is a cynic? A man who knows the price of everything
and the value of nothing.
> Oscar Wilde, 1892[2]

We might as reasonably dispute whether it is the upper or
the under blade of a pair of scissors that cuts a piece of
paper, as whether value is governed by utility or cost of
production.
> Alfred Marshall, *Principles of Economics*, 1890[3]

The rationale of economic organisation is that it adds value. But
what is meant by 'value'? A theory of value is the foundation
of economics. Early economists – Adam Smith (1776), David
Ricardo (1823) and Karl Marx (1867) – subscribed to versions of a
labour theory of value. The division of labour breaks a complex
task into components and reassembles these components into
the whole. That process necessitates reciprocity and exchange,
implying both a social dimension and a commercial dimension.
The man who receives the wire and the man who straightens
the wire rely on each other, and they stand only a few yards
apart. And there needs to be a commercial arrangement that
recognises the contribution of each to the output of all. It is easy

to understand why an economy characterised by processes such as pin-making developed a labour theory of value. You could look round the factory and see who was really doing the work.

These early theorists thus perceived value as a tangible property of the object – the result of the direct and indirect human effort put into its creation. But such an 'objective' definition of value encountered problems. Despite the resources Thomas Thwaites devoted to his toaster, his creation was less useful than the product available at the corner store. The extensive and continuing labours of Sisyphus had no value not only because the boulder never reached the top of the hill but also because the activity was inherently pointless.

A subjective definition of value focused instead on the utility of the output. From this perspective, value was found in the mind of the consumer rather than originating in the effort of the producer. This led Adam Smith to the diamond–water paradox: why are diamonds, which only look pretty, much more expensive than water, which sustains life?

In the second half of the nineteenth century Stanley Jevons (1863), Carl Menger (1871) and Léon Walras (1874) provided a resolution that took elements from both sides of the debate. Value was subjective because it could not exceed the pleasure or use that the consumer derived from the product. If no one wanted a boulder rolled up a hill, then boulder rolling had no value, no matter how much work Sisyphus put into it. But the objective cost of production was also relevant. Diamonds are valuable not just because they are beautiful but also because they are hard to find, and their extraction and cutting entail much labour. But we flush gallons of water down the toilet daily because water is plentiful and easy to find and distribute.

The further resolution of the diamond–water paradox is that, although the value to you of *some* water is immense – you would die without it – the value of the last gallon used when you indulge for an unnecessary extra minute in the shower is small. The marginal litre is much less valuable than the first litre or the average value of all the litres you use. If diamonds were plentiful, little value would be attached to them, and we might have diamond-bladed pocketknives and letter openers as well as diamond earrings. The significance of this difference between the *average* and the *margin* was one of the great insights of late nineteenth-century economics. An appreciation of its impor- tance still marks people who have studied an elementary course in economics from those who have not.

Price

The argument above makes no mention of prices or markets. Diamonds, the *Mona Lisa*, the Grand Canyon and apartments overlooking Central Park are valuable because they are both desirable and scarce. Since water is plentiful, people of the Global North attach little value to it and use it in wasteful ways; populations in arid areas where water is hard to find treat it as a precious resource. These things would be true in any society, whatever its economic or political organisation. And in every society prized objects tend to be appropriated by those who have power: power that may have been acquired by economic or polit- ical means or simply by brute force. This relationship between societal position and societally valued wealth is evident for dia- monds and apartments on the Upper East Side but also observed in cultures with quite different preferences and resources, from the Australian outback to the Amazonian jungle.

Democratic societies have been able and willing to provide public access to the *Mona Lisa* and Grand Canyon (and the Palace of Versailles and the tiger forest of the former Maharajah[4]) because these goods, although scarce, can be enjoyed by many with only limited damage to the enjoyment of any. But only one household can occupy a particular apartment, and only one person can wear a particular diamond ring at any particular time.

In 2017 *Salvator Mundi*, another painting by Leonardo da Vinci, was sold for $450 million, the highest price ever paid for a work of art. Mystery and controversy surround the sale. The attribution to Leonardo is disputed. There are around thirty similar paintings from Leonardo's workshop. A head for business appears to have been among the skills of this remarkable Renaissance polymath. The seller in the recent transaction, Dmitry Rybolovlev, a Russian oligarch, claims to have been the victim of a large-scale fraud perpetrated by Swiss art dealer Yves Bouvier. The purchaser was ostensibly Prince Badr of Saudi Arabia on behalf of the state of Abu Dhabi but is widely believed to have been Mohammed bin Salman (MBS), the Saudi crown prince. The current whereabouts of the painting are unknown.[5] The rich are different.

The most valuable houses on the Upper East Side are occupied by the current (Eric Adams) and former (Michael Bloomberg) mayors of New York and a Mexican billionaire (Carlos Slim). The blocks between 63rd and 65th Street on New York's Fifth Avenue housed Alfred Sloan, Laurance Rockefeller, Rupert Murdoch, Charles Schwab, and Ken Griffin.[6]

The most valuable diamonds in the world are probably the Cullinan diamonds, cut from a stone discovered in South Africa in 1905 and one of which is now in the possession of the British royal family. Another is owned by the king of Thailand. The more recent Centenary diamond has been valued at $100 million; De Beers will not disclose the identity of the purchaser.

Carlton House Terrace and Gardens, a stone's throw from Buckingham Palace and probably London's most prestigious address, was once home to Gladstone and Palmerston but now accommodates Ken Griffin (an American hedge fund billionaire), the Hinduja brothers (Indian businessmen) and Saudi royals – as well as the Royal Society, the Turf Club and the head office of BAE Systems (defence contractors). Such is the varied nature of power in the modern world.

Among these many uncertainties, some facts are beyond dispute. Leonardo will not be producing any more paintings.

And his most famous work – the *Mona Lisa* – is in the custody of the French state and will not be coming on the market soon – or ever. This fundamental, irremediable scarcity is key to the value of the *Mona Lisa*, and perhaps the value of *Salvator Mundi*.

But it is the combination of uniqueness with the vanity of wealthy men that explains the eye-watering price of *Salvator Mundi*. After all, you can buy a decent print of the *Mona Lisa* for $20. For less than $500 an artist will paint a reproduction that could only be distinguished from the original *Mona Lisa* by forensic examination. The price of these reproductions reflects their cost of production because there are few limits to their supply. Yet your friends would probably not be much impressed by the *Mona Lisa* above your mantelpiece because they know it is not the – scarce – real thing. The economist Fred Hirsch described items such as old master paintings as *positional goods*, whose value is enhanced – even dependent on – the fact that other people cannot have them.[7] This analysis of value as the product of the interaction of supply and demand, the relationship between the opportunity cost of production and the utility of consumption, underpins modern economics. No other approach now receives or deserves serious attention.

Some modern philosophers, sceptical about what they regard as the excesses of capitalism, write critically about value in economics, notably Elizabeth Anderson and Michael Sandel. In particular, Sandel insightfully explores the widely held intuition that many social relationships are damaged if viewed in purely transactional terms – an observation that will be a theme of this book. We disapprove of prostitution and are sceptical about paid organ donation or surrogacy. But this observation does not refute, or in any real sense challenge, the observation that value is the joint product of utility and cost.

Markets

Willingness to pay is the combined product of need or want and ability to pay. A poor person may value bread very highly but

not have money to pay for it. Conversely, however passionate he
may be about art – there is nothing to suggest any such passion
– MBS could pay $450 million for *Salvator Mundi* only because he
is one of the world's richest men. And MBS is one of the world's
richest men because he is a descendant of Ibn Saud, who in 1932
established the kingdom of Saudi Arabia; because a group of
American companies led by Standard Oil of California (now
Chevron) discovered and developed the world's richest reserves
of oil; because political tensions in the Middle East enabled
oil-producing countries, coordinated by Sheikh Yamani, to
wrest more of the value of their output from multinational oil
companies and their customers; and because MBS managed the
complex politics of the Saudi royal family with sufficient skill
to establish a dominant role for himself. Business is embedded
in a social, political and cultural environment, and we cannot
understand its outcomes without understanding these interre-
lationships. Nor seriously maintain that the outcome of market
allocation is a distribution of resources based on desert – the
moral rather than the sandy kind.

In a market economy, price is a source of information about
values and costs. As young children, we want anything and
everything. As we grow up, we are introduced to the concept
(implicit or explicit) of budgets – you can't have everything – and
the idea (implicit or explicit) of prices – if you want this, you can't
have that. The singular virtue of a competitive price mechanism
is that it aims to achieve a property that economists describe as
incentive compatibility: the best course of action is to tell the
truth, to disclose honestly what you want and are capable of
paying, by attaching a price. These incentive-compatible properties of the price mechanism are most effective where there are
many buyers and sellers. Consumers ask themselves, 'Does the
value to me of this good or service exceed the price?' If it does,
buy it. Producers ask themselves, 'Is the cost to me of providing
this good or service less than the market price?' If it is, make it.

Incentive compatibility is more problematic if there are
few potential buyers and sellers. Then there is room for the

haggling familiar to anyone who has bought a house, or a used car, or visited a bazaar. Still, mostly – though not always – trade will occur if there is an opportunity for a mutually beneficial exchange. And the price agreed will yield useful information for buyer and seller – and perhaps others – for use in future deals.

A need for further treatment

In the pharmaceutical industry prices are a poor indicator of value. Neither the doctor who prescribes a pill nor, in most cases, the patient who takes it pays the cost; usually the bill will be picked up by an insurer or a healthcare system. This fact alone differentiates pharmaceuticals from typical consumer products.

But there are further complications. Witness the delight – most fully reflected in the share price of manufacturer Novo Nordisk – in the development of Wegovy as a treatment for obesity, another chronic disease of many rich people. The condition returns as soon as you stop taking the drug. Paradoxically, antibiotics are less attractive commercially because they work so well – a course lasting a week will often achieve a permanent cure, and there is less research than one might hope on new drugs which will compensate for the declining effectiveness of traditional antibiotics.

'Orphan drugs' treat rare diseases; there is no vaccine against Hepatitis C, a viral infection uncommon in the Global North but which persists and causes severe liver damage if untreated. The most effective current treatment is SOVALDI, produced by Gilead Scientific; at the standard price of $1,000 per pill, a twelve-week course costs $84,000. The public outrage at the cost is easy to understand. But it saves lives. And that is why NICE (the National Institution for Health and Care Excellence), which assesses value for money by reference to the additional QALYs (Quality-Adjusted Life Years) gained from treatment, approved SOVALDI for use in the British National Health Service at tax-payer expense. And while SOVALDI is an extreme case, the structure in which most of the cost of production is an initial set-up cost and the cost of manufacturing an additional unit is low is common, and increasingly so. It is true of this book, for example, especially if you are reading an electronic version. It is true of the software and apps that you use. And Google and Facebook charge the costs of establishing their platforms to advertisers and offer their product to you for free.

What is an appropriate price for a product such as SOVALDI, which will only ever be used by a small number of people but will transform their lives; which represents the outcome of years of research and which must undergo the same rigorous testing as a drug prescribed for millions? This question has no easy or obvious answer. And it is separate from the question of who – the individual, an insurer or the state – should pay that price.

The price mechanism is an indispensable method of eliciting information about values and costs. But as QALYs show, not everything that is valuable has a price. In fact, most of what is valuable falls outside the scope of the market economy. And not everything that has a price is valuable. There are many things people buy because they know no better, such as Goldman Sachs's Timberwolf and Abacus securities and Purdue Pharmaceuticals' opioids. And not everything that destroys value imposes a cost on the destroyer. Businesses and individuals may damage the environment without paying for the harm they cause – Colin Mayer, a management professor, has argued forcefully that companies who are supposed to solve social problems are often indifferent to creating them.[8]

Prices and markets are indispensable sources of information about value, but must not be fetishised. We can, should and do make political decisions about the cultural environment we experience and the values we hold as a society. Production is not just about stuff, and there is more to life than consumption. But consumption is a large part of our lives and production occupies half our waking hours. And the societies whose leaders determined centrally what should be produced and who should benefit from it scored poorly on almost any measure of well-being or human development. Reflect on the costs imposed by

Mao Zedong's 'Great Leap Forward' and 'Cultural Revolution', by Stalin's forced collectivisation and the consequent Ukrainian Holodomor.

12

STANLEY MATTHEWS CHANGES TRAINS

> Money is not a motivating factor. Money doesn't thrill me or make me play better because there are benefits to being wealthy. I'm just happy with a ball at my feet. My motivation comes from playing the game I love. If I wasn't paid to be a professional footballer I would willingly play for nothing.
>
> Lionel Messi[1]

Cost and utility were the two blades of Alfred Marshall's scissors. The rationale of economic activity is to add value: to create utility in excess of cost. Economic rent is the difference between the utility of output, as measured by what people are willing to pay, and its cost, as measured by what they would be willing to pay for the same factor, or combination of factors, in alternative uses.

Messi and Matthews

In 2017 Lionel Messi signed a new contract with Barcelona Football Club which promised him over 650,000 euros per week over four years.[2] When his contract with the Spanish club ended in 2021, Barcelona could not afford to retain him, and he signed for the Qatari-backed Paris-St Germain for a similar or larger sum.[3] When that contract expired, Messi rejected an offer reportedly worth $500 million from Saudi Arabia in favour of a move to Inter Miami, a team in the Major Soccer League (MSL) which is attempting to promote the world's most popular game in the United States.

Messi is widely regarded as the finest soccer player in the world, but he has few other evident talents. If he were not employed as a footballer, his earnings would probably be modest, as were those of Sir Stanley Matthews, regarded by many as England's greatest-ever footballer. Matthews's autobiography describes a somewhat different lifestyle from that of Messi. One of his most memorable matches was a post-war celebration of the resumption of international football in 1948. England met Scotland at Hampden Park before a crowd of 135,000 people (England won). A letter from the Football Association encloses Matthews's match fee of £14 (about £500 at current prices) and refunds his (third-class) return rail fare from Blackpool to Glasgow. But his claim for 6d (about £1 today) spent on a cup of tea in the station buffet at Carlisle while waiting for the train to Scotland was rejected: it was not a reimbursable expense.[4]

The difference between what Messi is paid and what Matthews earned reflects economic rent. Economic rent is the difference between the returns to an activity and the opportunity cost of the resources needed for that activity – the returns to these resources in their best alternative activity. The term 'economic rent' puzzles many – the ordinary meaning of rent is what you have to pay if you don't own a house. The usage dates from a time when agriculture was the principal form of economic activity. The concept is generally attributed to the English economist David Ricardo, but the idea was set out fifty years earlier by Adam Smith's contemporary, a Scottish gentleman farmer and scholar called James Anderson.[5] Scotland won this match of precedence in economic theory.

For Adam Smith, the cause of prices in excess of the cost of production had been monopoly: 'the monopolists, by keeping the market constantly under-stocked, by never fully supplying the effectual demand, sell their commodities much above the natural price.'[6] But Anderson explained that without need for monopoly prices would exceed cost simply by virtue of differences in capabilities: in his example, differences in the fertility of different areas of land. Some land would barely repay the cost of farming it, and some would not even do that – this unproductive territory is described as 'the margin of cultivation'. Smith never absorbed Anderson's theory of rent, although he did recognise that more fertile or better-located land would command higher rents. It seems the two men were acquainted but not well acquainted; Smith received a copy of Anderson's treatise and expressed an intention to respond, but there is no evidence that he ever did.

> In every country there are various soils, which are endued with different degrees of fertility; and hence it must happen that the farmer who cultivates the most fertile of these can afford to bring his corn to market at a much lower price than others who cultivate poorer fields. But if the corn that grows on these fertile spots is not sufficient fully to supply the market alone, the price will naturally be raised in that market to such a height as to indemnify others for the expense of cultivating poorer soils. The farmer, however, who cultivates the rich spots will be able to sell his corn at the same rate in the market with those who occupy poorer fields; he will, therefore, receive much more than the intrinsic value for the corn he rears. Many persons will, therefore, be desirous of obtaining possession of these fertile fields, and will be content to give a certain premium for an exclusive privilege to cultivate them; which will be greater or smaller according to the more or less fertility of the soil. It is this premium which constitutes what we now call rent, a medium by means of which the expense of cultivating soils of very different degrees of fertility may be reduced to a perfect equality.
>
> James Anderson (1777)[7]

Differences in capabilities that give rise to economic rents exist in all activities. Boys are kicking a ball around in every urban centre in the world, and many of them aspire to be professional footballers. Few are sufficiently talented to attract the attention of a club – the majority are, in the language of Anderson and Ricardo, 'outside the margin of cultivation', not worth the attention of trainers. Those aspirants who just make it into the professional game – the (relatively) mediocre players in (relatively) mediocre teams – can expect to earn little more than they could as unskilled workers. Perhaps even less: the possibility of the fame and earnings of players like Messi attracts many who will never make it into the league of well-remunerated professionals, just as celebrity and wealth accrue to a few successful stars of stage and screen who coexist with many unemployed actors struggling to make ends meet. But clubs and their fans will pay much more to obtain the exceptional talent of Messi, and audiences and studios will do the same to benefit from the star appeal of Leonardo di Caprio and Taylor Swift.

The extraordinary talent of Messi and Matthews meant that their employment as professional footballers was immensely more valuable than their employment in another occupation. Messi saw that difference in his pay packet; Matthews did not. Only in competitive markets are distinctive capabilities turned into economic rents. Competition to recruit top soccer talent – once suppressed, now vigorous – explains why Matthews was paid so little but Messi earns so much. Competition for the services of superstar actors explains why they accrue rewards many times those of only marginally less talented, or perhaps only less recognised, thespians.

In competitive markets – and only in competitive markets – organisations similarly derive rents from their distinctive capabilities, from doing things other organisations cannot or do not do equally well. In 1955 America's largest companies were just – large. Large in terms of revenues, number of employees, assets, profits or stock market capitalisation. Today each of these measures yields significantly different rankings. This change is an indicator of the extent to which corporate success today depends less on size than on the ability of corporations to generate economic rents – and to create an expectation that they will be able to sustain and continue to appropriate these rents. Valuable organisational rents are the product of distinctive capabilities that are both appropriable by the organisation that enjoys them and sustainable over time.

Rent, class and power

Why does Messi earn so much while Matthews made so little? Matthews's third-class ticket is a significant detail – we can assume that Football Association officials did not travel third-class to Glasgow. The difference demonstrates the social milieu within which Matthews worked. At the end of his football career, in the early 1960s, he received the then maximum wage of £20 a week, roughly the average earnings of a manual worker.[8]

In Britain, the threat of a players' strike in 1961 led to abolition of the wage cap.[9] But the footballers' revolt was only the proximate cause; the social changes of the 1960s eroded many traditional class barriers. When I was first taken to a Test match as a child, the scorecard I avidly maintained listed amateur cricketers ('gentlemen') as 'Mr P. B. H. May' and 'Mr E. R. Dexter'. The professionals ('players') appeared with surname first and without honorific: as 'Titmus, F. J.' and 'Trueman, F. S.' When Titmus made his debut for Middlesex against Surrey in 1950, a famous announcement corrected the card: 'For "Mr F. J. Titmus" read "Titmus, F. J."'[10] Titmus had signed as a (paid) professional.[10] The distinction between gentlemen and players in cricket was abolished in 1962. The award of a knighthood to Stanley Matthews in 1965 was a symbolic event; he was the first footballer to be honoured.

So was pre-1960 football an example of capitalist exploitation brought to an end by the power of organised labour? Not quite. If Matthews was exploited, and it is hard to argue otherwise, it was mainly for the benefit of football fans. In 1948 the standard admission price at an English football ground was 1s 3d, the price of two and a half cups of tea in the waiting room at Carlisle station.[11] The cheapest tickets to Premier League matches now cost £30. In January 2021 I investigated the price of a ticket for the England–Scotland international in June; the lowest price I was quoted was £200.[12]

I have a photograph of a queue for entry to that 1948 Hampden Park match. A row of men – there are no women – almost all dressed in cloth caps and cheap dark suits, anxious to join the 135,000 crowd that stood on the terraces to cheer Scotland. The locomotive works and shipyards that employed many of them have since closed. Today the capacity of the all-seat Hampden Stadium is only 50,000. As the ticket prices have changed, so has the social composition of the crowds. And the organisation of football clubs. And the earnings of footballers.

Control of football clubs was always a vanity project, but control was exercised benignly. In Matthews's day, the shares of football clubs were typically held by local businessmen, who ran the clubs more for the benefit of the local community than for their personal profit. But television arrived, and English football went global. The British traveller abroad is now often asked by the cab driver in India or the barman in Singapore, 'Which team do you support?'

Bidding for television rights meant that revenue from football grew rapidly. And as the game became global, so did vanity. A Russian oligarch, a Thai tycoon and Sheikh Mansour of Abu Dhabi bought controlling stakes in Chelsea, Leicester City and Manchester City respectively. PSG could afford to recruit Messi because the club is funded by the Emir of Qatar, himself the beneficiary of the economic rent derived from the state's gas fields. These individuals are so wealthy that money is inconsequential, and they enjoy the public profile and prestige of association with a famous English football club. And many are willing to invest in their passion – when Vichai Srivaddhanaprabha, chairman of Leicester City, died when his helicopter crashed in 2018 as he left the club's stadium after a match, supporters and players were moved to tears at a tribute ceremony.[13] His financial and practical support led the club to league victory in 2016, when bookmakers were offering odds of a thousand to one against.

But not all club directors are so benign. The fraudster Robert Maxwell, as greedy as he was vain, may have been the first to realise the potential for extraction created by global interest in English football. Maxwell had derived much of his wealth by purchasing rights to publish academic journals, then, as now, written and reviewed for free by naïve academics. He then raised the price charged for prestigious journals, indispensable to major university libraries, by astonishing amounts. Maxwell was thus alive to the potential of strong franchises to generate economic rents, and in this spirit he bid unsuccessfully for Manchester United in 1984.

Mike Ashley, whom we encountered lounging on his Mediterranean yacht and making foolish commitments in the Horse and Groom bar, was the unpopular owner of the football club Newcastle United. In 2021 Ashley sold his shares to a Saudi-led consortium for £300 million. Ashley celebrated his financial coup, and Newcastle United supporters celebrated the change of ownership, each with copious quantities of beer.[14]

Following the failure of Maxwell's approach to Manchester United, rival media magnate Rupert Murdoch, who had a similar nose for economic rents, bid for the club. But the acquisition was rejected by the Monopolies and Mergers Commission. Malcolm Glazer, an American entrepreneur who brought complex financial engineering to sport, obtained control of Manchester United in 2005. He and his family (Malcolm died in 2014) have extracted value they had little role in creating. Most supporters of the club would shed only tears of joy at their departure.[15] (In 2023 Ineos, the oil products company controlled by Jim Ratcliffe, now Britain's second richest man, bought a 25 per cent stake in, and took managerial control of, the club.)

Economic rent in organisations

All productive activity is directed to adding value through organising resources in such a way that they are more valuable than they would be in an alternative configuration. That is what we mean by productive activity. And thus successful organisations create economic rents. Barcelona Football Club created value that could never have been achieved if Messi had still been kicking a ball around the streets of Rosario, the club's matches had never been broadcast and its merchandise did not carry the Barça logo. The successful business similarly creates an output more valuable than could have been achieved if its employees had been working in other firms or industries, its customers had made do with different products and its investors had placed their money elsewhere. If different firms have different capabilities, as different plots of land have different fertilities and prospective footballers have different talents, then the firms with superior capabilities will earn economic rents just as do the beneficiaries of better land and greater soccer skills.

If the marginal land had a voice – it doesn't, of course, but those who work on it, enclose it and today own it do – it would like to imitate the fertile land. The boys who kick a ball around Argentinian towns would like to be Lionel Messi. There are many football clubs – and their fans – that aspire to be Barcelona or Manchester United. Silicon Valley is populated by groups of enthusiasts who hope to be the next Microsoft or Google. These plots, these clubs and these start-ups mostly don't succeed because they cannot replicate the particular combination of capabilities that constitutes a productive field, a footballer of outstanding talent and a team with the sustained record of success of Barcelona and Manchester United. Or which replicates the mixture of inspiration, perfect timing and simple good luck that contributed to the success of Microsoft and Google. And although much has been written about both these companies, there is no blueprint that a new generation of start-ups can replicate.

At the margin of cultivation, yields barely compensate the costs of agriculture. Some aspiring footballers, the sporting analogue of the margin of cultivation, are good enough to be selected for 'the farmhouse', Barcelona's youth training academy, but never make it into the team. These are the analogue of semi-successful businesses, which make enough to keep going but not enough to pay their proprietors and employees more than they could earn elsewhere, or to make more than a slight difference to the lives of their customers and suppliers. And of course there are the millions of microbusinesses, those local tradespeople whose economically and socially necessary capabilities differ from those of others in the same trade only in respect of the location at which they are delivered and who earn enough only to pay the rent of the shop or office from which they work.

And many firms would aspire to be Apple or Amazon, Walmart or Goldman Sachs. They don't succeed because they cannot reproduce the particular combination of characteristics that is Apple, Amazon, Walmart or Goldman Sachs. Organisations create economic rents because they enjoy distinctive capabilities or distinctive combinations of capabilities. A successful organisation is one whose capabilities are appropriable and sustainable – they can be deployed for the benefit of the organisation and its stakeholders on a continuing basis. These differentiated firms, which earn substantial economic rents, are the focus of this book.

The division of rents and the extent of the market

Before the land of Scotland was enclosed, there were significant differences between the earnings of the fortunate peasants who tilled the fertile soil of the common land of East Lothian and those less lucky tillers of soil who worked the barren land by the Clyde. Enclosure enabled landowners to appropriate for their own benefit the superior returns from superior land, the phenomenon Anderson and Ricardo observed at the end of the eighteenth century.

The development of canals and then railways, which tended to equalise grain prices in the two regions, benefited workers in the west, who enjoyed cheaper grain, and landowners in the east, who encountered increased demand for their produce. These gains were secured at the (lesser) expense of workers in the east, who experienced a rise in food costs but did not earn commensurately higher wages, and landowners in the west, whose crops were no longer in such scarce supply. Lesser expense because the relative expansion of production on the fertile lands of the east made Scottish agriculture as a whole more efficient.

This process is an early example of globalisation at work, and a precursor of the changes, and redistribution of incomes, that later globalisation would bring. The greater the extent of the market, the greater the rents accruing to those who still have distinctive capabilities in the larger market. The rents accruing to Mercedes rise when Mercedes is able to sell to China; those accruing to Chinese rickshaw manufacturers fall, as Chinese entrepreneurs prefer chauffeur-driven limousines to rickshaws. But by less, since China is better off with cars than rickshaws. China taken as a whole benefits, but some Chinese workers and businesses lose out.

As Anderson was the first to argue, to comment on the amount and distribution of economic rent we must begin by understanding the mechanisms that gave rise to it. He might have been anticipating the furore over bankers' bonuses when he asked what might happen if 'the gentlemen of Clydesdale, from an extraordinary exertion of patriotism, and an inordinate desire to encourage manufactures, should resolve to lower their rents. … Would the prices of grain fall as a consequence of this? By no means … Readers of penetration will be able of themselves to finish the sketch', he concluded.[16] They must do so again today.[17]

Good and bad rents

Economic rent gets a bad press. The definitive Oxford English Dictionary referred me, to my surprise, to *Fabian Essays in Socialism*, edited by the great polemicist George Bernard Shaw. In one of these essays Sidney Webb wrote: 'The landlord in France was an obvious tyrant: here he certainly caused (by the abstraction of the economic rent) an artificial barrenness of the workers' labour; but the barrenness was so old and had been so constant that it was not seen to be artificial, and was not resented as such.'[18]

When I asked Google – of course – for a more modern definition of economic rent, the first response from the folks at Mountain View took me to Investopedia.[19] There I was offered 'takeaways':

- Economic rent is an amount of money earned that exceeds that which is economically or socially necessary.
- Market inefficiencies or information asymmetries are usually responsible for creating economic rent.
- Generally, economic rent is considered unearned.

Messi undoubtedly earns more than is economically or socially necessary. The absence of other players as good has created, perhaps, a market inefficiency; but humanity has benefited greatly from the monopolies of talent enjoyed by Aristotle, Shakespeare and Newton. And anyone who considers Messi's remuneration 'unearned' should watch again his 'goal of the 21st century'. And wonder why they used Google as their search engine and YouTube to watch him score.

Parasitic rent extraction by agents such as financiers and corporate executives is today a major economic issue. But much of the economic rent generated in modern economies is the result of unique capabilities – such as those of Messi – or unique combinations of capabilities – such as those of Google. The content of Economics 101 typically describes a world of perfect competition in which all footballers are equally talented, all firms have the same conditions of production, and if there are innovations they are instantly replicated. Fortunately, that is not the world in which we live. Nor is it a world dominated by those corporations that featured in Fortune's 1955 list.

PART 4

THE AGE OF INDIVIDUALISM

The 1960s were the zenith of the large manufacturing corporation, which many believed would permanently dominate, even control, the global economy. But despite, or perhaps partly because of, this tribute to the power of collective action, the era also saw the rise of individualist political philosophy and social and economic liberalism. Both the philosophy and the reaction to it had profound consequences.

While the first half of the century had witnessed the replacement of the robber barons of the Gilded Age by the professional management style epitomised by General Motors, in the second half of the century a dominant narrative arose in which business was viewed in essentially financial terms. The purpose of the corporation was the creation of 'shareholder value'.

13

MONEY CAN'T BUY YOU LOVE

Sexual intercourse began
In nineteen sixty-three
(which was rather late for me) –
Between the end of the 'Chatterley' ban
And the Beatles' first LP.

Philip Larkin, 1967[1]

The 1960s was an era of social and political turbulence. The Beatles revolutionised popular music. Skirts shortened, and the contraceptive pill became widely available. John F. Kennedy was elected the youngest president of the United States. After he was assassinated, his vice-president, Lyndon Johnson, a career politician, delivered civil rights legislation and a Great Society programme through Congress.

The corporation was by this point sufficiently entrenched in society to be the butt of humour, as in W. H. Whyte's *The Organization Man* or Sloan Wilson's fictional account in *The Man in the Grey Flannel Suit*. There were critics of the growing social, political and economic power of the corporation: Eisenhower's valedictory address on relinquishing the presidency to Kennedy in 1961 warned of the dangers of what he christened 'the military–industrial complex'; J. K. Galbraith's *The New Industrial State* in 1967 claimed that the corporation controlled its environment to such an extent that it transcended the traditional sources of 'countervailing power'.[2]

The foundational literature on corporate governance (Berle and Means, 1932), the theory of the firm (Coase, 1937), organisational theory (Drucker, 1962), business history and corporate strategy (Chandler, 1962) and business strategy (Ansoff, 1965) was written in the context of a commercial landscape dominated by large manufacturing corporations. As a result, these texts all describe – implicitly or often explicitly – General Motors. And General Motors was the epitome of Galbraith's 'technostructure' and the target of Ralph Nader's critique of corporate irresponsibility. In the 1960s a student could spend several days in a business library without realising that in the twentieth century American business extended beyond a single firm based in Detroit, close to the freshwater of the Great Lakes.

But that student's attention might have been distracted by the noise outside. In April 1965 the first US troops landed in Vietnam, and the resulting war polarised American society and mobilised young people: some into the military, others to demonstrate against the draft and the war. In 1968 students in many countries took to the streets in imitative protest. The outcome unseated the presidents of both the United States and France.

Rudi Dutschke led German student demonstrations in what became known as the 'extra-parliamentary opposition'. The fracturing of the political left in that country was accelerated by the 'grand coalition' formed in 1966 which brought the conservative Christian Democrats (CDU) and the leftist Social Democrats (SDP) together in government.[3] The 'Baader–Meinhof Gang' (later the 'Red Army Faction') engaged in political terrorism. Across the world the largest demonstrations, violent but not murderous, were in Paris in 1968; trade unionists joined with students led by Daniel Cohn-Bendit (a German whose expulsion from France did nothing to quell the protests) and brought large sections of the French economy to a halt.

As stones were thrown at police in the boulevards of Paris, the critique of big business was no longer framed in the nuanced language of Eisenhower and Galbraith; the 'soixante-huitards' were calling for the overthrow of 'capitalism'. The would-be revolutionaries drew inspiration from various intellectual sources such as Antonio Gramsci and Herbert Marcuse in Europe and Noam Chomsky in the US.[4]

The revolt had many consequences. Dutschke coined the phrase 'the long march through the institutions' (a phrase intended to be redolent of Mao's 'long march', the 5,000-mile trek he led which was a precursor to the communist takeover of China) to describe a much longer-term strategy of 'infiltrating' professions with left-inclined young graduates. Half a century later, some conservative commentators, such as Robert Kimbell and Charles Murray, would suggest that, like Mao's, this long march had enjoyed a measure of success. (The first members of the 'baby boomer' generation (born 1946–1964) became fifty in 1996; the last will be sixty-five in 2029.)

Sticks and stones were supplemented by words. Yale professor Charles Reich claimed in his widely noted *The Greening of America* that the counterculture of the 1960s was an 'unstoppable force that would destroy traditional bureaucratic organisation'.[5] Rachel Carson's *Silent Spring* denounced the despoiling of the land by chemical companies and might be regarded as the foundational text of the modern environmental movement. Paul Ehrlich warned in *The Population Bomb* that 'in the 1970s hundreds of millions of people will starve to death'.[6] With this Ehrlich began a routine of apocalyptic projections, revised in each decade as each predicted apocalypse failed to materialise. The damage Nader's criticisms had inflicted on GM was compounded when it was revealed that the automobile company had engaged in harassment and intimidation, hiring prostitutes to attempt to lure him into compromising situations.

An unexpected outcome

This increasing hostility to business in intellectual circles provoked a reaction that in many respects proved more powerful and enduring than the original critique. Milton Friedman's notorious article in *The New York Times Magazine*, which may be the most-cited piece to have appeared in that newspaper, was an early example. His argument is summarised in the title: 'The Social Responsibility of Business Is to Increase its Profits'. The tone is strident. 'Businessmen who acknowledge responsibilities for providing employment, eliminating discrimination, avoiding pollution … are preaching pure and unadulterated socialism … they are unwitting puppets of the intellectual forces that have been undermining the basis of a free society in these past decades.'[7]

In 1971 Lewis Powell, a corporate lawyer, prepared a brief for the US Chamber of Commerce – the body which fifty years later would warn of the dangers of holding companies to the truth of statements such as 'honesty and integrity are at the heart of everything we do'. Powell's lengthy memo offered a more measured and thoughtful response than Friedman's to the criticisms levelled against business in the previous decade. Powell stressed the importance of education. He proposed that the Chamber should encourage the establishment in universities of a body of scholarship which addressed business issues sympathetically.[8] Soon afterwards Powell was nominated by President Richard Nixon to the Supreme Court, where he served with some distinction.[9] In 1972 Fred Borch of General Electric and John Harper of Alcoa took the lead in founding the Business Roundtable, a group composed of the chief executives of most of America's largest corporations. Today, with a staff of around fifty in Washington, the Roundtable has become a powerful lobbying group.

Powell's memo was influential, and his approach proved effective. 'The long march through the institutions' was a strategy available to the right as well as the left. Scholarship congenial to business interests was funded both directly by corporations and via charitable foundations established by rich businesspeople. Conservative think tanks such as the Heritage Foundation (founded 1973) and the Cato Institute (founded 1977) became effective providers of political ideas in Washington.

Rudi Dutschke had urged radical students to take their ideas with them into the workplace. Powell encouraged business, traditionally unintellectual and at times anti-intellectual, to engage with the world of ideas. It is not fanciful to see the origins of the culture wars of the 2020s in these events of half a century ago.

> Although firmly conservative, Powell's legal reasoning resisted the political polarisation now too characteristic of the US judiciary. He delivered the majority opinion in *Dirks v. SEC*, asserting the common-sense position that the public interest in exposing criminality outweighed that of maintaining an orderly market in the shares of a fraudulent company. He provided an influential supporting opinion in *Bakke*, establishing the legality of affirmative action. However, Powell also delivered the majority opinion in *First National Bank of Boston v. Bellotti*, a judgment that paved the way for the 2010 ruling in *Citizens United v. FEC*, which gave companies broad scope to make political donations, and helped promote the retreat of antitrust enforcement by his rulings in *Sylvania and Matsushita v. Zenith*.

The neo-liberal turn

While West London celebrated the swinging sixties on King's Road and Carnaby Street, equally momentous changes were in progress on Threadneedle Street in the east of the metropolis. The Bank of England encouraged the development of the Eurodollar market, in which both American and European banks traded dollars outside the purview of the Federal Reserve System. This was the beginning of a process of rapid expansion, internationalisation, deregulation and reregulation of financial markets which continued until the crisis of 2008.

The Bretton Woods Conference of 1944 had established the International Monetary Fund and World Bank and set out a world financial system based on fixed exchange rates. But the Vietnam War had economic as well as political consequences. Through the 1960s and into the decade that followed, inflation accelerated in the Global North. In 1971 President Nixon abandoned the gold standard, and currencies were left free to fluctuate in

value. The Yom Kippur War between Israel and the Arab states
was the trigger for an oil price shock which entrenched inflation
further and reordered global finances in favour of Saudi Arabia
and other Gulf states.

Much has been written about the political influence of the
Mont Pelerin Society, founded in 1947 by Friedrich Hayek.
A brilliant, difficult and combative economist, Hayek is
detested on the left but equally strongly admired on the right
– a widely repeated anecdote has then prime minister, Margaret Thatcher, slam a copy of Hayek's *Constitution of Liberty*
on the table with the assertion 'This is what we believe.' But
the practical political role of the Society – essentially a dining
and debating club for right-wing intellectuals (and some
others with intellectual pretensions) – has been far less than
that of the institutions and movements I describe above,
which are linked directly to the changes in the political and
business climate that began in the 1970s.

I have attended one meeting of the Mont Pelerin Society;
the purpose was to discuss the important question of the
role of evolution in business and economics. The meeting
brought together people from many disciplines and across
the political spectrum and was appropriately but also imprac-
tically held in the Galapagos islands. The event was blighted
by a string of accidents to the mostly elderly attendees, with
a tragic conclusion when the thoughtful conservative political theorist Kenneth Minogue died on the plane returning
participants from the islands to the Ecuadorian mainland.

The political developments which followed these events had
major financial and economic consequences. In Britain in 1974
Edward Heath's flailing Conservative government gave way to
its Labour opposition. But the new regime's leftist programme
collapsed in 1976 in the aftermath of the recessionary and infla-
tionary influence of the 'oil shock'; Britain was forced to seek
assistance from the International Monetary Fund. In 1978–9

('the winter of discontent') industrial troubles were a source of constant disruption and in May 1979 Margaret Thatcher led a right-wing Conservative party to an election victory. In 1980 incumbent US President Jimmy Carter was defeated by Ronald Reagan. Thus in the 1980s the political leaders of both Britain and the United States professed adherence to market-oriented, business-friendly policies which became widely known as neo-liberalism (never used as a term of approbation).

Britain and the United States had moved sharply right, but France went in a different direction. In 1981 perennial French presidential candidate François Mitterand finally secured election. He began his term by dissolving the National Assembly, and voters delivered for him a Socialist majority in the new Assembly. The result was a programme of nationalisations (which included several banks) and a wide extension of welfare programmes. Mitterand's leftist dalliance ended after less than two years, as inflation accelerated and the value of the French Franc declined. He announced the 'tournant de la rigueur' ('return to austerity').

Mitterand's U-turn might also be regarded as the last gasp of socialism in the Global North (although in 2018 the plans of elderly leaders Jean-Luc Mélenchon in France and Jeremy Corbyn in Britain bore a marked resemblance to the programmes of the parties they had supported forty years earlier as optimistic 30-year-olds). Sweden's Social Democrats were defeated in 1976 after forty years of unbroken power. In Germany the Grand Coalition was replaced in 1987 by a rightist government drawn from the Christian Democrats and the market-friendly Free Democrats (FDP). Between 1989 and 1991 the Soviet Empire collapsed, and with it 'really existing socialism'. The world had changed a lot since 1960, when General Motors was hegemonic and presidential candidate Kennedy had campaigned on the 'missile gap', the supposed superiority of Russian military capability resulting from the supposed superior performance of its planned economy. But what was to follow? And what were the new ideas that the neo-liberal turn would bring to an understanding of business?

14

OR PERHAPS IT CAN: THE MODERN
THEORY OF THE FIRM

> If economists wished to study the horse, they wouldn't go
> and look at horses. They'd sit in their studies and say to
> themselves, 'What would I do if I were a horse?'[1]
>
> attributed to Ely Devons by Ronald Coase

Clapham's criticism of Smith in the 1920s for his failure to visit
the Carron Works (or, as we now suspect, any other industrial
premises) was written in the context of a broader controversy
among the academics of Cambridge, UK. Clapham wrote of
'empty economic boxes', suggesting his colleagues spent time
theorising about productive activities without engaging with the
practicalities of business.[2] The critique presented by Clapham
and Devons still resonates today. David Sainsbury, a businessman and former government minister, argued that economics
as a discipline still conceptualises firms like this.[3]

Igor Ansoff was a polymathic Russian émigré whose career
had taken him from the Rand Corporation to Lockheed to the
Graduate School of Industrial Administration (now the Tepper
School of Business) at Carnegie Mellon University in Pittsburgh.
Carnegie Mellon sought to develop a more scientific approach
to the business school curriculum than the case-study-based
approach associated with Harvard Business School. Ansoff and
Harvard's Kenneth Andrews are often described as the founders of the subject of strategic management, which became a
key element in the MBA programmes of the rapidly expanding
number of business schools.

Ansoff justified his approach to corporate strategy with the claim that microeconomics had contributed little to the subject he tried to elucidate.[4] He observed that 'study of the firm has been the long time concern of the economics profession. Unfortunately for our present purposes, the so called microeconomic theory of the firm which occupies much of the economists' thought and attention, sheds relatively little light on decision-making process in a real world firm.'[5]

Ansoff's critique had considerable justification. In 1982, soon after the retirement of Joe Bain from UC Berkeley, the American Economic Association elected him 'distinguished fellow' and described him as 'the undisputed father of modern Industrial Organization Economics'.[6] In his classic 1959 text *Industrial Organization: A Treatise,* Bain defined the scope of his analysis:

> I am concerned with the environmental setting within which enterprises operate and in how they behave in these settings as producers, sellers and buyers. By contrast, I do not take an internal approach, more appropriate to the field of management science, such as could inquire how enterprises do and should behave in ordering their internal operations and would attempt to instruct them accordingly … my primary unit for analysis is the industry or competing groups of firms, rather than the individual firm or the economy-wide aggregate of enterprises.[7]

Harvard's economics department, where F. M. Scherer developed the framework initiated by Bain, became the leading centre for academic analysis of industrial organisation. Scherer's *Industrial Market Structure and Economic Performance* (1970) succeeded Bain's on the bookshelf of a generation of graduate students – including this one. In the Structure-Conduct-Performance framework, industry structure determines behaviour, which in turn determines performance. The difference of emphasis between Ansoff and Scherer is illustrated by the latter's measures of performance: 'production and allocative efficiency, progress, full employment, and equity'.[8] Each of these measures refers to a public benefit from the activities of the industry, none to the private benefit to the stakeholders of the firms that comprise it.

In the 1970s Michael Porter literally and metaphorically crossed the Charles River, which divides the main campus of Harvard University from its Business School, in an attempt to bridge the gap between economics and strategy. Porter's widely discussed 'five forces' framework is effectively a translation of the S-C-P approach into business language.[9] The strategy of the firm is assumed to be determined by the 'five forces' of suppliers, customers, entrants and substitute products, mediated by competitive rivalry. Yet the limitations of that S-C-P/five forces model are immediately apparent. There is no explanation of why different firms, facing the same five forces, perform differently. Thus the main issue of corporate strategy – how to outperform competitors – is sidelined. And with no emphasis on differentiation, the only source of economic rent is monopoly (or lesser forms of market power).

As a result, Scherer and his colleagues had influence on business through the application of their framework to issues of antitrust and regulation, rather than through its use by businesspeople. A friend and colleague of mine undertook consultancy in the 1980s on market definition in the computer industry. He demonstrated that the old distinctions between the markets for mainframe computers and the market for other types of machine were rapidly disappearing. His client was delighted because this argument was of considerable assistance to them in the antitrust proceedings the company faced in both Europe and the United States. The client was, of course, IBM, and the notion that this analysis had any relevance to their business was not something that had occurred to the people in corporate affairs and the office of the general counsel who were tasked with fending off interfering regulators. And to the present day, economics continues to provide the primary framework for public policy towards business, while having very little influence on business policy itself. In my experience, most businesspeople think economics is about forecasting rates of growth, inflation and interest. They crave such forecasts but wisely attach little credence to them.

Economics and business

Sir Denys Henderson, a lawyer by training, was chairman of ICI, then Britain's leading industrial company, from 1987 to 1995. He accepted the honorific role of President of the Society of Business Economists and arranged a meeting to express his frustration at the inability of economists to make sufficient contribution to business. He began with a critique of the failure of economists to predict successfully the turbulent economic events of the 1970s and 1980s: a critique which had considerable justification.

The Society had lined up two of its members to respond. Sir Alan Budd, who served in numerous roles in the public and private sectors, including Chief Economic Adviser to the Treasury, explained that economic systems are complex and non-linear and that, while patterns may be identified, reliable prediction was impossible. I followed and suggested that microeconomic analysis of firms and markets might be more useful to businesspeople than macroeconomic forecasting. By the end of the evening, Henderson was almost tearing out (what was left of) his hair in frustration. 'I need to know,' he fumed, reiterating his demand for reliable prediction.

It was an event I would remember as I observed subsequent developments at ICI, described in Chapter 22. But the recollection came more often when someone approached me with a question like 'What will the dollar–sterling exchange rate be ten years from now?' My response – and I strongly believe the only appropriate response – was along the lines of 'If you tell me why you are asking that, I will try to help you formulate a more sensible question which it may be possible to answer.' But that reply was not often well received. Frequently the problem was that the individual concerned had been asked the question by their boss, who – like Sir Denys – had to be placated. Or they were building a spreadsheet and this number was required to fill a vacant cell. Or my interlocutor might observe that, if I could not give them an answer, there was someone else – probably at an investment bank – who would. And ring off.

The need to know

The 'need to know' is almost universal. Humans continue to crave certainties that are not available. The search for The Man Who Knows did not begin with the Oracle of Delphi and will not end with the identification of Superforecasters.[10] I was fortunate to combine a career in academic roles with the opportunity to meet practical businesspeople such as Henderson and to learn from them the issues and the problems they faced. It helped me understand both the uses and the limitations of economic models.

In models such as those of Michael Jensen and William Meckling, 'rational' maximising individuals pursue their own interests. These models describe 'small worlds'. All opportunities and constraints can be listed and prospectively quantified. Mathematical tools developed for science and engineering can then be applied to make predictions and derive solutions. A major strand of economic thought is based on the concept of 'rational' expectations. Agents in such models are themselves familiar with the underlying model, or behave as if they were, and make their 'rational' decisions accordingly.

These models are useful in helping us organise alternative ways of thinking about the problems of organising and managing firms. But they are not 'true' descriptions of the world in the sense that some models in the physical sciences may be regarded as 'true' descriptions of the world. Friedrich Hayek described the issues well in his 1974 Nobel Prize lecture, which he delivered under the title 'The Pretence of Knowledge.'[11]

Hayek observed:

I regard it in fact as the great advantage of the mathematical technique that it allows us to describe, by means of algebraic equations, the general character of a pattern even where we are ignorant of the numerical values which will determine its particular manifestation. ... It has led to the illusion, however, that we can use this technique for the determination and prediction of the numerical values of those magnitudes; and this has led to a vain search for quantitative or numerical constants.

He continued:

compared with the precise predictions we have learnt to expect in the physical sciences, this sort of mere pattern predictions is a second best with which one does not like to have to be content. Yet the danger of which I want to warn is precisely the belief that in order to have a claim to be accepted as scientific it is necessary to achieve more. This way lies charlatanism and worse. To act on the belief that we possess the knowledge and the power which enable us to shape the processes of society entirely to our liking, knowledge which in fact we do *not* possess, is likely to make us do much harm.[12]

Real businesspeople operate in 'large worlds', in which problems are ill defined and there are no objectively correct answers. Moreover, the 'right' answer will often not be apparent, even in retrospect. Effective decision-makers in large worlds are not maximising; they do not have and never can have the information needed to make the relevant calculations. They confront radical uncertainty. Often they not only do not know what will happen but do not even know the kinds of things that might happen.[13]

Although we must abandon 'the pretence of knowledge', individuals, institutions and businesspeople need to act in the face of uncertainties. The proper response is not to insist on receiving answers to unanswerable questions – 'I need to know' – but to reformulate the problem in ways that allow the preparation of information that relates directly to the issues faced by decision-makers.

Salt- versus freshwater economics

As Ansoff had observed, the corporation was an institution about which economists for long had little to say, despite the obvious empirical importance of the phenomenon. One reaction to Ansoff's critique came, appropriately, from nearer Detroit. The economist Robert Hall drew a distinction between 'freshwater' and 'saltwater' economics, observing that economists in institutions close to the Great Lakes – such as Chicago, Rochester and Minnesota – tended to adopt a more conservative stance than those of California (Hall taught at Stanford) and New England.[14] Milton Friedman, of course, came from the most distinguished of freshwater institutions.

Ronald Coase's 1937 article 'The Nature of the Firm' (based, he later explained, on ideas put forward five years earlier, when he was only twenty-one, and formulated after a travelling scholarship had allowed him to visit Detroit) remains seminal.[15] Coase's article initially attracted little attention. It was only after he moved to Chicago that his thesis became influential. Following a famous dinner party in 1960 at the home of Aaron Director, brother-in-law of Milton Friedman and himself a considerable economist, Coase moved to the windy city, where he remained for the rest of his life.

> It is the morbid practice of national newspapers to commission obituaries of distinguished people still living but mature in years; my obituary of Coase remained under lock and key at the *Financial Times* for almost twenty years before his demise in 2013 at the age of 102.[16]

In Coase's analysis, the boundaries of the firm were defined by the relative costs and efficiency of two methods of coordination: markets and hierarchies. Sometimes markets and the price mechanism were more effective; sometimes central direction and hierarchical management structures were more appropriate. The *market* contract was one in which the controllers of the firm (leave aside for the moment the important question of who these controllers were) specified their requirements and reached out to find the best price, as when the purchasing department sought tenders for the supply of red tape. With a *hierarchical* contract, the controllers hired people and told them what to do, as a traditional boss might employ a secretary to perform whatever duties he might require today and tomorrow. It was always costly to trade in markets. On the other hand, subordinates might not always carry out the wishes of controllers as diligently or effectively as superiors would wish.

The hold-up problem

The choice between markets and hierarchies was also influenced by the need for investment specific to the requirements of a commercial relationship, an issue particularly associated with the work of Oliver Williamson.[17] In 1900 a group of San Francisco fishermen agreed to sail to Alaska to catch salmon for a fee of $50 each. Once they arrived in Alaska – and it was too late for the canners to recruit alternative boats for the short fishing season – the Californians demanded an increase to $100. The canners reluctantly agreed. Their catch landed, the fisherman returned to San Francisco, where the canners refused to pay more than $50.[18] The several resulting cases of *Domenico v. Alaska Packers* are cited by lawyers even today. (Essentially, the fishermen lost.)

In all but the most trivial of business (or social) relationships, agents will make investments in the relationship – in the broadest sense of the term 'investment', which includes not only expenditure but also time and forgoing alternative opportunities. The fishermen sailed their boats to Alaska; the canners relinquished

the possibility of recruiting more cooperative crews. The difference in bargaining positions before and after agreements are made
is known as the 'hold-up' problem. The court rejected the blatant
exploitation of the 'hold-up' problem by the Domenico fishermen. But the merits and outcomes of other cases are less clear.

Yet it was not the salty Alaska fisheries that gripped the attention of the freshwater economists but the automobile plants by
the Great Lakes. In 1926 General Motors bought Fisher Body,
the company that produced the metal bodies for its cars. No
other business transaction has received so much attention from
economists. Fisher Body needed to build equipment to create
idiosyncratic patterns for stamping metal into the right shape.
But once they had been built, the only use for the machinery
was in making parts for General Motors, and General Motors
was dependent on Fisher Body for critical components. As in
Alaska, the bargaining positions were very different once the
necessary investments had been made.

Two of Coase's Chicago colleagues, Armen Alchian and
Harold Demsetz (1972), observed that the hold-up problem
could be avoided by writing a sufficiently detailed contract. In
their view, the only difference between market and hierarchy
would then be whether failure to achieve the wishes of the controllers was a matter for a judge, who might impose damages for
breach of contract, or the human relations department, which
might threaten the sack.[19] And since everyone would know the
inevitable outcome, neither court proceedings nor dismissal
would ever be necessary.

As is often the case with economic models, the value of this
argument is found not in its absurd conclusion but in understanding why the absurd conclusion is false. The world is radically
uncertain. Information is imperfect. No contract can anticipate
all possible contingencies. Not only do we not know what will
happen – we often have only limited insight into the range of
things that *might* happen. Unforeseen events will require adaptation. But by the time such adaptation is required, both parties
to the contract will have committed to the relationship.

A potential imbalance of power can be relieved by vertical integration: when a customer acquires its supplier or vice versa. Then there is no incentive to extract value from the other side because you *are* that other side. If manufacturing a part required specialist tooling and knowledge, then the related functions would, by this account, need to take place within an integrated firm. And so in 1926 General Motors bought Fisher Body. Or so the story went – and went on and on.

The nexus of contracts

Coase interacted with the conservatively inclined faculty of the Chicago law school. Another Chicago scholar, Richard Posner, led what became known as the 'law and economics' movement. Posner's career displayed prodigious knowledge and energy as he engaged in teaching and writing while also serving as a judge in the Seventh Circuit Federal Court of Appeals. The notion that underpinned his academic work, his books and his judgments was that the law can be viewed from the perspective of its contribution to economic efficiency – a more subtle perspective than that frequently attributed to him.[20]

Less distinguished academics and lawyers promoted these doctrines, and many US universities undertook research and teaching in 'law and economics'. The Olin Foundation was established by the chemical engineer and conservative businessman John M. Olin. In line with Powell's advocacy of working through academic institutions, the Foundation gave substantial financial support to the development of 'law and economics'. George Mason University in Virginia made a particular specialism of this approach. Despite its proximity to the tidal Potomac River, the University was associated with many strands of conservative 'freshwater' thought.

That 1976 article by Jensen and Meckling on the theory of the firm was seminal for the law and economics movement.[21] Within their framework, the corporation was simply an artificial convenience to facilitate the execution of agreements between individuals: shareholders, other investors, employees, customers and suppliers. The purpose of the corporate entity is to economise on the number of formal agreements and the cost of negotiating them. Agents are self-interested individuals, and all relations among them are transactional. Denying the significance of intermediate units of organisation, the 'little platoons' which the conservative thinker Edmund Burke described as 'the first principle of public affections', Jensen and Meckling and the body of scholars who followed them describe a world in which there is little scope for collective action or the development of collective knowledge.

The 'nexus of contracts' approach stands in sharp contrast to the long-standing and still influential legal doctrine of corporate personality. In this older tradition, the firm is no 'legal fiction' but has a life – 'personality' – distinct from that of its stakeholders. An entity in its own right, the firm – not the shareholders – owns assets and its directors and employees owe duties to it. This corporation has rights and obligations which may include rights of free speech and even religious freedom; it may be capable of criminal activity and is entitled to legal and political representation.

There is an obvious tension between the concept of corporate personality, which holds that the firm has an identity distinct from its stakeholders, and the Jensen and Meckling view of the firm as a 'nexus of contracts' among individuals. Frank H. Easterbrook and Daniel R. Fischel, writing in the 'law and economics' tradition pioneered by Jensen and Meckling, assert that 'The corporation is not real. It is no more than a name for a complex set of contracts among managers, workers, and contributors of capital. It has no existence independent of these relations.'[22] This approach was developed further by Easterbrook and Fischel in their seminal US text on the economics of corporate law.

Yet the 'nexus of contracts' is an approach that came to dominate academic thinking in law and economics, and to some extent accounting, in the latter part of the twentieth century.

The timing of this shift in philosophy seems odd. The economy had become dominated by large corporations controlled by professional managers, and the significance of sole traders and proprietors had diminished. Among these large corporations, manufacturing processes based on assembly lines which were managed hierarchically were giving way to businesses characterised by flexible teams of knowledge workers cooperatively extending collective intelligence. Observable reality and scholarly discourse were steadily evolving in opposite directions.

Thus we encounter the paradox that the thesis put forward by Jensen and Meckling from the Midwest of America in the 1970s is broadly consistent with the Marxist view of the capitalist firm proposed in Western Europe by Karl Marx and Friedrich Engels in their *Communist Manifesto* of 1848. It is also consistent with the account of Ayn Rand, whose libertarian rants inspired yacht-owning Eddie Lampert, whom we shall meet again at the destruction of Sears, Roebuck and Co. Left and right often agree when both are wrong.

The firm as a problem of contract design

But it is not only the future that is subject to radical uncertainty. Information about the present is also imperfect – and unevenly distributed. Knowledge and problem-solving capabilities that are necessary to achieve the objectives of the firm will be found among its employees, customers and suppliers. How can contracts be framed so as to ensure that the individuals or other businesses that are parties to them make the greatest possible contribution to the objectives of the organisation? Contract design might induce these multiple stakeholders to apply their relevant knowledge and capabilities towards these objectives: this is the principal–agent problem. Relationships within firms and between firms may thus be seen as problems of contract design.

This contractarian view led to convergence between economic and legal approaches to the theory of the firm, a convergence facilitated by the law and economics movement. The hold-up problem and the principal–agent problem would occupy the attention of economists for half a century. The Nobel Prize in economics was awarded to Coase (1991) and Oliver Williamson (2009) for their contributions to the market versus hierarchy debate and to James Mirrlees (1996) and Eric Maskin (2007), who had considered contract structures. The continuing centrality of these issues was recognised when a further Nobel Prize was shared in 2016 between Oliver Hart, for his work on the choice between markets and hierarchies, and Bengt Holmström, for his work on contract design. Hart used the issue to develop a theory of ownership, which is discussed in the next chapter.

The classic modern industrial organisation text by Margaret Meyer, Paul Milgrom and John Roberts displaced Scherer from the bookshelves of modern graduate students – although perhaps that text was itself superseded by that of Jean Tirole, who also received the Nobel award in 2014. For these more recent writers the principal–agent problem frames the structure of the organisation. Thus Meyer, Milgrom and Roberts write 'although delegating authority to those with the information needed to make good decisions is an important part of good organisation design, it is of little use unless the decision makers share the organisation's objectives. We have already mentioned incentives as a way to align individual and organisational objectives … incentives and delegated authority are complements: each makes the other more valuable'.[23] Their solution to the principal–agent problem is to create incentives such that the individual (with local knowledge unavailable to persons more senior in the hierarchy) will act as if the objectives of the organisation were his or her own. The principal–agent problem seeks solutions that will induce subordinates to pursue the objectives of the organisation. But what are the objectives of the organisation, and who identifies them?

15

THE MYTH OF OWNERSHIP

You are undone if you once forget that the fruits of the
earth belong to us all, and the earth itself to nobody.
Jean-Jacques Rousseau, *Discourse on the Origin of Inequality*, 1761[1]

Friedman's answer was clear – the objective of the organisation
is to maximise its profits. Although Friedman won his reputation – and Nobel Prize – as an economist rather than as a
lawyer or philosopher, the case he makes in his *New York Times
Magazine* article 'The Social Responsibility of Business Is to
Increase Its Profits' has little connection to economic efficiency.
Its essence is to be found in the following assertion: 'a corporate
executive is an employee of the owners of the business. He has
direct responsibility to his employers. That responsibility is to
conduct the business in accordance with their desires.'[2] Friedman summarises thus: 'the key point is that in his capacity as a
corporate executive, the manager is the agent of the individual
stockholders in the corporation and his primary responsibility
is to them.'[3]

The argument is social or legal rather than economic. And
it raises a number of issues. Are shareholders the owners of the
company? And – whatever answer is given to that question –
are managers permitted or indeed required to consider interests
other than those of shareholders in their conduct of the business? From the days of the Great Western Railway, the scale of
the activity and the dispersed nature of shareholding had made
day-to-day control by salaried executives inevitable. This need
for delegation poses a fundamental problem for the 'nexus of

contracts'. How can the principals (the shareholders) induce the agents (the executives) 'to conduct the business in accordance with their desires'?

Different cultures and different legal systems are likely to view these issues differently – and they do.

> The potential tension between the doctrine of corporate personality and the theory of the nexus of contracts – the relationship between the rights and obligations of the corporation and the rights and obligations of its members – is a feature of common law jurisdictions. These are the legal systems which are derived from medieval English law – broadly, former British colonies, including, of course, the United States – and attach weight to an evolving body of legal precedent. The courts of common law countries operate through the adversarial system familiar from television dramas.
>
> Most other countries, including the major EU states and, to a large degree, China and Japan, are civil law jurisdictions which rely on prescriptive codes, and the role of the judge is one of investigation and the application of relatively detailed and specific rules to particular cases.

Shareholders as owners of the corporation

In 1943, as the British government mobilised resources for the war effort, the aircraft manufacturer Short Brothers was taken under state control. The business was founded by two aeronautical enthusiasts but had become a public company with shares listed on the London Stock Exchange. At nationalisation, the stockholders received compensation based on the recent market value of the shares.

After the end of the war Oswald Short, who had remained a substantial shareholder until the takeover, sued the Treasury. The principal argument put forward by his legal team was that the government had acquired not just Short's shares but the whole company. They asserted that the right course – which Short believed would have offered significantly more compensation – was to value the assets of the company and divide this amount pro rata among the shareholders.

The case went to the House of Lords, then the highest civil court of the United Kingdom, and the shareholder claim was rejected. The Law Lords affirmed the finding of a lower court: 'shareholders are not, in the eye of the law, part owners of the undertaking.'[4] They had received a fair price for their *shares* and that was the end of the matter. The House of Lords considered the issue again in 2003. That case sought to establish the legal status of cash balances accumulated within a company, Laird Group. The Law Lords reiterated their earlier formulation, adding that 'the company owns its property beneficially and not in trust for its members'.[5]

Parents may hold property in trust for a child: the parents are the legal owners, but the property is held for the benefit of the child and the parents can use it only for purposes that benefit the child, who is the equitable or beneficial owner. In contrast, in English law company property is not held for the benefit of the shareholders but is owned by the separate legal entity that is the company. Any benefit to shareholders must come from dividends and from any increase in the value of their shares, not from the property itself. There is a further layer of complication. Most shareholdings today are held by a nominee – typically a bank or stockbroker – for the benefit of an individual or institution, and the institution – perhaps a pension fund or university endowment – may itself be acting on behalf of an individual or charity. The string of principal–agent problems may be lengthy.

In *Laird*, Lord Millett cited with approval an earlier judgment characterising a share as 'the interest of a person in the company, that interest being composed of rights and obligations which are defined by the Companies Act and by the memorandum and articles of association of the company'.⁶ An earlier judgment had identified these rights as normally comprising 'rights to receive dividends, if declared, rights to vote, rights in a liquidation to receive a share of surplus assets'.⁷

But then Lord Millett went on to muddy the waters. He referred approvingly to the then current edition of *Gower*, the standard text on English corporate law: 'the company is at one and the same time a juridical person with rights and duties of its own, and a *res* owned by its shareholders.'⁸ It is hard to avoid a suspicion that the Latin term *res* is employed in order to maintain an appropriate appearance of erudition while avoiding being more precise about exactly what is being said. We might agree with Lord Millett that 'the juridical nature of a share is not easy to describe'.⁹

Other jurisdictions

If we look to Germany, Friedman's argument falls at the first hurdle. Article 14 of the Basic Law – the constitution of the modern Federal Republic of Germany – states: 'Property and the right of inheritance shall be guaranteed. Their content and limits shall be defined by the laws. Property entails obligations. Its use shall also serve the public good.'¹⁰

The Basic Law is relevant to the obligations of the shareholder in respect of his or her shares, the obligations of the company in respect of its assets and any obligations of the shareholder in relation to the company. In each case, Germany requires that any exercise of property rights has regard to the public good. The Basic Law represents a reaction to the complicity of some corporations and wealthy individuals in the Nazi era. *Of course* property ownership in modern society carries duties as well as rights. Only the most rabid libertarians or followers of Nozick could think otherwise.

So what of the US? In the main, US courts and commentators have accepted without demur the proposition that shareholders are the owners of a corporation, although there is vigorous dispute in both the courts and academic journals about the implications of this proposition.

Since 1843 English law has followed what is known as the rule in *Foss* v. *Harbottle*. Harbottle was a director of a company established to develop the Victoria Park area of Manchester, and with some fellow directors had misappropriated the company's assets. Foss, a minority shareholder, sued. His claim failed; the fraud had been against the company, and it was for the company, not the shareholder, to bring an action. While this is an old case, the legal principle remains solid, and developed in the doctrine of 'reflective loss', reaffirmed in the Supreme Court in 2020.[11] Only in exceptional circumstances can a shareholder sue for damage done to the company, even though this will obviously reduce the value of his or her shares.

Mr Foss might have had a better chance at Delaware, in which 'There is no rule better settled in the law of corporations than that directors in their conduct of the corporation stand in the situation of fiduciaries. While they are not trustees in the strict sense of the term yet for convenience they have often been.'[12] In the controversial case of *Smith* v. *van Gorkom* in 1985, a Delaware Court found directors personally liable for damages of $23.5 million after agreeing a leveraged buyout of the company at what some shareholders considered a low price. Anxious to maintain the attractiveness of Delaware as a place where managers could safely register their corporations, the Delaware legislature quickly passed provisions freeing them from personal liability for breach of their duty of care.

Individual American states have their own corporate statutes and courts, and the law relevant to any corporation is primarily that of the state of incorporation. States have competed to be the favoured venue for corporate registration – a competition that has been convincingly won by Delaware, which is home to two-thirds of Fortune 500 companies but only 0.3 per cent of the US population. If you thought Google was based in Mountain View and Apple in Cupertino, both in California, and Walmart at Bentonville, Arkansas, then think again; the registered office of all these companies, and 300,000 others, is at 1209 North Orange St, Wilmington, Delaware. The consequence is that corporate litigation relating to these companies is brought under the law of Delaware, and this pre-eminence of the First State means that its jurisprudence, administered by specialist judges without juries, is largely determinative of the rights and responsibilities of American corporations.[13]

In practice, the decision on the place of corporate registration is made by corporate management. Lynn Stout, an American legal scholar who sadly died prematurely in 2018, observed that British law was more favourable to shareholders than US law, but this is not quite the key point.[14] The attraction of Delaware law is that it is particularly favourable to corporate executives. (Although perhaps not friendly enough for Elon Musk; in 2024 a Delaware court ruled that his $56 billion remuneration package was excessive.) But judges have given especially wide scope to the 'business judgment' rule – the courts will not challenge management decisions except in cases of obvious bad faith. That is why, as Stout noted, a variety of practices are commonly adopted in Delaware that law, regulation and societal expectations do not permit in the UK.

The practices described by Stout include many that favour executives at the expense of shareholders. A 'Poison Pill' is a device that enables Delaware corporations to issue shares on terms designed to dissuade hostile takeovers and 'activist' investors. 'Staggered boards' provide for board elections to take place at different times, thus inhibiting an acquirer from taking effective control of the business. There are no legal requirements for 'proxy access', a phrase describing the opportunity for shareholders to put forward their own resolutions, including resolutions to appoint directors, at meetings of the company – a right that is taken for granted in the UK. The SEC (Securities and Exchange Commission, a federal agency) has achieved some facilitation of proxy access but faces entrenched and influential opposition.

> The everyday modern usage of the word 'activist' describes a campaigner for some social or political cause. In the corporate world, the term is most often used when a financial investor takes a stake in a company with a view to effecting a change in corporate policy, most usually advocating an acquisition or disposal. Carl Icahn, who achieved notoriety by taking over and effectively winding up the airline TWA, has been a famed activist in the corporate sense for over four decades. But social activism related to business is increasing. In 2021 the newly formed investment fund Engine No. 1 secured the election of environmentalist Andy Karsner to the Exxon Mobil board. Sometimes corporate activists are active in both senses, as with Icahn's attempts to engage with McDonald's over animal welfare.

Federal legislation and regulation have chipped away at management tactics designed to keep shareholders at arm's length. In the aftermath of Enron and other corporate scandals at the turn of the century, Congress passed the Sarbanes–Oxley Act (SOX), named after the Democrat Senator Paul Sarbanes and Republican Congressman Michael Oxley who sponsored it. The Dodd–Frank legislation followed the 2008 financial crisis (both Senator Chris Dodd and Congressman Barney Frank were Democrats, but three Republicans supported the bill, just sufficient to secure its passage). The SEC imposes regulations on listed companies and is often a supporter of shareholder rights. But absent far-reaching Federal legislation to assert control of corporations, such as that proposed by radical Senator Elizabeth Warren, the primacy of management in US corporations remains. It matters little whether or not stockholders are owners of the corporation if there are many obstacles to the exercise of the rights of ownership. But what are the rights of ownership anyway?

What does ownership mean?

A widely cited approach to this question was developed by economists Sanford Grossman and Oliver Hart, who recognised the necessary incompleteness of contracts in the face of radical uncertainty. Their purpose was to explain how the 'nexus of contracts' approach could handle the resulting problems.

Grossman and Hart describe the owner of an asset as the person or entity that holds all rights over the asset not assigned explicitly to someone else. In this view, the owner is the person who decides what should happen when a situation arises which is not described, or not described fully, in any contract. The 'owner' had the residual authority to determine the unresolved contractual terms. The boss could tell subordinates what to do, but for 'non-human' assets it was the owner of the physical asset who enjoyed ultimate control. This right of residual control was, for Hart, the essence of ownership. The extent of the influence of property rights theory (PRT) on subsequent economic analysis of the firm was marked by the award of the Nobel Prize to Hart in 2016.[15]

Hart uses the example of the rental of a car. Suppose, he hypothesises, you rent a car for a period of six months and wish to install a CD player (this was 1995), but the rental contract has no provision for such modifications.[16] You will have to ask the person you rented the car from to agree to it: residual control over what happens to the car still rests with them.

This example deserves more scrutiny than Hart gives it. Although it is possible to rent a car for six months, such agreements are not very common. You may rent a car for a week when you are on holiday. That contract illustrates clearly that ownership is not the same as possession. During the week, you can park the rental car in your garage, you can drive it where you like (probably within some wide limits specified in the contract) and you can carry your kitchen sink or your life savings in the trunk. If you use the car to run over a pedestrian, it is you, not Hertz, who incurs civil and criminal liability. But few would dispute that the car is owned by Hertz, not by you.

It is also common to rent cars for *longer* than six months. When you take delivery of a new car, you are very likely to do so under some kind of financing agreement. There are many varieties of these agreements. Car loans, lease agreements and hire purchase are all widely used. What is normally common to all these arrangements is that legal title to the car is held by the institution that provides the finance. That title may be transferred to you after you have made a certain number of payments, or the agreement may provide an option for you to retain the car at the end of the lease period on payment of a pre-agreed sum. In Britain, the Driver and Vehicle Licensing Agency (DVLA) maintains a register of the 'keepers' of cars. The keeper is the person who accepts responsibility for traffic and parking violations and will be the first person the police approach if the vehicle has been used in criminal activity. A vehicle can legally be driven only if it has a registered keeper. In the United States, many jurisdictions make a distinction between the *registered owner* of an automobile and the *legal owner* of an automobile. The keeper or registered owner will usually refer to the car as 'my car'.

Similar issues arise in the ownership and occupation of real estate. And real estate is today much the largest category of asset used in business. As I shall describe in Chapter 28, most of the operating assets of modern corporations take the form of real estate, and most of that real estate is not owned by the company that occupies it. People 'buy' apartments within blocks which contain many such apartments. Even within common law jurisdictions that use the English language and are based on English law there are different legal structures designed to make this 'purchase' of a flat possible. Different rights and obligations are attached to the English leasehold, the American condominium and the Australian strata title. There are even substantial divergences between the relevant legal mechanisms of Scotland and England. Ownership has many dimensions, and even for physical assets subject to elaborate contractual arrangements the meaning of 'ownership' seems blurred.

An extensive body of statute and case law and collective

knowledge governs the occupation and leasing of real property. And the treatment of assets held under long leases is one of the most complex and evolving issues in the formation of accounting standards. Lawyers and accountants have devoted much time and skill, less to resolving these issues than to finding pragmatic and practical solutions to the business problems that emerged, and they were doing so many years before economists discovered them. The meaning of ownership is evidently complicated.

The badges of ownership

A useful elucidation of the concept of ownership was provided sixty years ago by the legal theorist A. M. Honoré. Honoré explained that ownership is neither a single nor a simple concept and that meanings of ownership vary across countries and over time. But, he argued,

> there is indeed a substantial similarity in the position of one who 'owns' an umbrella in England, France, Russia, China. In all these countries, the owner of an umbrella may use it, stop others using it, lend it, sell it, or leave it by will. Nowhere may he use it to poke his neighbour in the ribs or knock over his vase.[17]

But the relationship between me and my umbrella is simple. The relationship between Amazon and the warehouses from which it operates is more complex. And similarly the relationship between Amazon and its stockholders. Honoré suggested a useful method of appraising this complexity. Ownership, like friendship, has many characteristics. But, at least until Facebook came on the scene, there was no formal definition of what it means to be a 'friend'. If a relationship has a sufficient number of characteristics of friendship, the individual is a friend. Similarly, a relationship is one of ownership if it has a sufficient number of attributes of ownership.

Honoré went on to list eleven 'badges of ownership'.

Ownership typically confers the right to possess, the right to use and the right to manage. Ownership entitles you to any income that is earned, and to claim the capital value of the asset. Ownership imposes an obligation to refrain from harmful use. What you own can be seized to satisfy your unpaid debts. Owners may claim security against expropriation. And owners can pass on any or all of their rights to someone else. The absence of any time limit on these rights is another badge of ownership. And owners have an ultimate right of residual control. They continue to hold all rights they have not explicitly conceded to someone else. This last criterion is the one that received the attention of Grossman and Hart in their attempt to find resolutions to the hold-up problem. But, as the examples of the rented car, the property held on a long lease, the condominium and the many assets owned by nominees and trusts illustrate, the modern economy is far more complex than their formulation can accommodate.

Following Honoré's approach, when I say 'I own my umbrella', I declare that I can put it up, take it down, sell it, rent it, leave it in my will, throw it away. I can appeal to the police or the European Court of Human Rights if a thief or the government appropriates my umbrella. And I must accept responsibility for my misuse of it and admit the right of my creditors to take a lien on it.

When we run through these tests, we see immediately that stockholders own their shares in Amazon. All the criteria of ownership are met. But it is not at all apparent that the stockholders own Amazon itself. Their shareholding gives them no right of possession, no right of use. If they go to an Amazon warehouse, or its headquarters in Seattle or its registered office in Wilmington, Delaware, they will be turned away. Stockholders have exactly the same rights to use Amazon services as any other customers. They are not responsible for any harmful actions of Amazon, and the cash pile on the Amazon balance sheet cannot be appropriated to satisfy the unpaid debts of its stockholders. Shareholders have no right to the proceeds of the sale of Amazon assets, which may not concern them much since, as we will see, there really aren't any saleable assets.

Amazon shareholders do have rights to receive a share of surplus assets when the corporation is dissolved, but Amazon's trillion-dollar valuation would vanish in the event of liquidation; that valuation only makes sense on the assumption that the business continues to thrive for many years. Amazon stockholders do not have the right to manage, although they do have a right to appoint the people who do. Thanks to the restrictive provisions of Delaware law, this right is largely theoretical. They have a right to such part of the income as the directors declare as dividends. None as yet in the thirty years of Amazon's life. Of the eleven tests put forward by Honoré, the relationship between Amazon and its shareholders satisfies only two, and these are rather minor; three are satisfied in part; and six are not met at all.

If the position was not confused enough, it is complicated by the growing practice of class action in which shareholders, or former shareholders, sue the company. On 2 April 1993 (Marlboro Friday) Philip Morris announced that the company, concerned to pre-empt the introduction of discounted competitive brands, would reduce the price of a pack of its iconic brand of cigarettes by 40 cents. The stock price fell sharply. Groups of stockholders (or contingency fee-based lawyers supposedly acting on their behalf) launched cases seeking to recover the damage resulting from the share price losses. These losses were the result of the actions of the company those stockholders themselves supposedly 'owned'. (The lawsuits were dismissed by the judge.)[18]

The case brought by Arkansas Teacher described in Chapter 1 was a case against Goldman Sachs, the company the teachers and other stockholders 'owned', though several executives were also named in the suit. In March 2019 the ride-sharing company Lyft made an IPO (Initial Public Offering) on NASDAQ (the US stock exchange specialising in technology companies). The first class-action lawsuit by stockholders against the company was filed the following month.

Such litigation is not easy to reconcile with the theory that shareholders own the company. Can I sue my umbrella if it fails to protect me sufficiently from the rain? And so recover compensation from the owner of the umbrella – myself? That seemed to be the logic of the Philip Morris suit. Any settlement of lawsuits brought by stockholders against their own corporation basically comes out of the assets that the stockholders, *ex hypothesi*, already own. Since the outcome is accompanied by an extremely high transaction price in the form of lawyers' fees, the lawsuit will necessarily yield a net negative return.[19]

If a Martian were to arrive having read Honoré's article en route, if he paid a visit to Amazon facilities and was allowed in or turned away, if he were allowed to observe the company's decision-making procedures ... he would probably conclude that, if anyone owned Amazon, it was its senior executives. Of course, Jeff Bezos is the largest (although minority) shareholder in Amazon, but I suspect the Martian would be likely, applying Honoré's or similar tests, to identify Tim Cook rather than Laurene Jobs as the 'owner' of Apple.

So who does own Amazon or Apple? The answer is that no one does, any more than anyone 'owns' the Mississippi River, the Theory of Relativity, the Royal Economic Society or the air we breathe. A thing or – in Lord Millett's erudite terminology – a *res* can exist without being owned by anyone. There are many different kinds of claims, contracts and obligations in modern economies, and only occasionally are these well described by the term 'ownership'. The differences between the modern corporation and my umbrella are so wide-ranging that it is hardly likely that my relationship with them could usefully be described in the same way. Clear thought is constrained here by inappropriate analogy. As Charles Handy has expressed it, 'when we look at the modern corporation, the myth of ownership gets in the way.'[20]

16

MUST COMPANIES MAXIMISE PROFITS?

> We are concerned not with economics but with law. The
> distinction between the two is fundamental.
>
> Lord Goff, 1987[1]

It is neither necessary nor sufficient to determine whether
shareholders are owners of the corporation to decide whether
the company does, as Friedman asserts, have a responsibility to
maximise its profits. The legal duties of directors and executives
follow the law of the country where they operate. Here also
the relevant corporate law differs across countries and, indeed,
across different American states. And, within every legal framework, the actions of all but the most tone-deaf executives and
directors must be sensitive to the culture and expectations of the
society in which they operate. These cultures and expectations
also vary across the world.

Britain

In the UK, section 172 of the 2006 Companies Act defines the
relevant law:

> A director of a company must act in the way he considers,
> in good faith, would be most likely to promote the success
> of the company for the benefit of its members as a whole,
> and in doing so have regard (amongst other matters) to –

(a) the likely consequences of any decision in the long term,
(b) the interests of the company's employees,
(c) the need to foster the company's business relationships with suppliers, customers and others,
(d) the impact of the company's operations on the community and the environment,
(e) the desirability of the company maintaining a reputation for high standards of business conduct, and
(f) the need to act fairly as between members of the company.

This formulation is a masterpiece of ambiguity and compromise. The obligation is to promote the success of the company. The benefit to the members (generally, the shareholders) will follow from the success of the company. If the intention had simply been to require directors to act for the benefit of the members, the phrase 'the success of the company' could have been omitted, and the provision would read very differently in tone and substance. But that phrase was not omitted, and its inclusion resulted from long deliberation, not carelessness – the 2006 Act is the product of a company law review that extended over several years.

Section 172 requires that the objective of the success of the company be achieved 'with regard to' the various stakeholders listed there: employees, customers, suppliers. It is hard to imagine any reasonable definition of corporate success which could be achieved *without* regard to these groups. Or any proper definition of corporate success that would not, in the long run, be to the benefit of employees, customers, suppliers etc., taken as a whole (although possibly to the detriment of *some* employees, customers and suppliers). Suppose the company fired all its employees, sold its assets to a competitor and distributed the proceeds to stockholders. Or imagine that a monopoly provider of, say, electricity or water raised prices very substantially and somehow induced politicians and regulators to ignore the resulting outcry. These actions might benefit the members, but it is hard to see how they represent the promotion of 'the success of the company' – unless the success of the company is *defined* by the benefit to the members, which is not consistent with the words of the statute.

Section 172 singles out shareholders from other stakeholder groups without expressly giving them priority – it does not say and clearly does not intend that shareholders always come first. It allows executives to act in ways that benefit shareholders but disadvantage employees. It also seems to allow them to act in ways that advantage employees and do not advantage shareholders. It is unclear whether it would allow directors to advantage employees at the expense of shareholders – it would certainly be unwise for the board to *say* that this is what they were doing. The wording is a compromise between the stakeholder model of the corporation, which imposes on managers an explicit obligation to balance the interests of all stakeholding groups, and the 'shareholder first' model, which gives overriding priority to the shareholder interest. The formulation offers succour to both camps but victory to neither. The shareholder camp can observe that there is frequently little inconsistency between the maximisation of shareholder value and acknowledgement of the interests of stakeholder groups, the stakeholder camp that managers are obliged to have regard for the interests of all. Nevertheless, in my experience, most senior managers in the UK believe that company law, which they have not read, mandates shareholder priority.

German law allows no such ambiguity. The German commercial code provides that:

4.1.1 The Management Board assumes full responsibility for managing the company in the best interests of the company, meaning that it considers the needs of the shareholders, the employees and other stakeholders, with the objective of sustainable value creation.
4.1.2 The Management Board develops the strategy for the

company, agrees it with the Supervisory Board and ensures its implementation.[2]

This is an unambiguous stakeholder position. (Since Germany is a civil law jurisdiction, the commercial code is legally binding. The 'combined code' imposed by the Financial Conduct Authority (FCA) on UK-listed companies is promulgated by the Financial Reporting Council (FRC). The legal force of this latter code is limited to a regulatory requirement to 'comply or explain', a formulation applied in some other jurisdictions.)

The United States

The classic American case is that of *Dodge v. Ford*, a ruling that has recently celebrated its centenary.[3] Henry Ford, struggling to gain a foothold in the emergent automobile industry and with a poor credit record, reached an agreement in 1903 with the Dodge brothers, who would supply the components for his Model A. The arrangement gave the Dodges 10 per cent of the Ford Motor Company stock. Ford himself retained a majority stake. Early Ford cars enjoyed modest success, and in 1908 Henry launched the Model T. The following year he declared his vision:

> I will build a motor car for the great multitude. It will be large enough for the family, but small enough for the individual to run and care for. It will be constructed of the best materials, by the best men to be hired, after the simplest designs that modern engineering can devise. But it will be so low in price that no man making a good salary will be unable to own one – and enjoy with his family the blessing of hours of pleasure in God's great open spaces.[4]

Sales of the Model T increased year after year, but the assembly line production that Ford implemented enabled the company to keep reducing the price, and by 1915 the Model T was by far the best-selling car in America. Following this success, profits and cash balances mounted, and the Ford company paid regular special dividends. The Dodge brothers used the proceeds to expand their own car production. But the irascible Ford and the Dodges inevitably fell out, and Ford, who had ambitious plans to build what would become the massive River Rouge complex, ceased to pay special dividends.

The Dodges sued. Henry's testimony made it difficult for any court to find in his favour. The court observed that Ford had 'the attitude towards shareholders of one who has dispensed and distributed to them large gains and that they should be content to take what he chooses to give'. The judgment went on: 'His testimony creates the impression, also, that he thinks the Ford Motor Company has made too much money, has had too large profits, and that although large profits might be still earned, a sharing of them with the public, by reducing the price of the output of the company, ought to be undertaken.'[5]

A modern commentator has observed that 'It would be wonderful to know what advice Mr Ford's lawyers gave him before he testified so helpfully for the plaintiffs who were suing him.'[6] It is, of course, unlikely that he paid much attention to whatever his attorneys did say. The lower court findings were almost ludicrously hostile, the court even issuing an injunction against the Ford company investing at River Rouge. The Michigan Supreme Court reversed much of the judgment. But the court nevertheless ordered that Ford pay a special dividend, asserting that

> A business corporation is organized and carried on primarily for the profit of the stockholders. The powers of the directors are to be employed for that end. The discretion of directors is to be exercised in the choice of means to attain that end, and does not extend to a change in the end itself, to the reduction of profits, or to the non-distribution of profits among stockholders in order to devote them to other purposes.

The Michigan Supreme Court finding (although not binding in other states) has been influential in US jurisprudence throughout the century that followed.

Ford bought out the Dodge stake in 1919 for $25 million.[7] The Dodge brothers both died in the Spanish flu pandemic that followed the First World War, and did not have an opportunity to regret their legal success. But if they had lived, they would certainly have done so. Ford's strategy of investment in building new plant and acquiring market share paid off handsomely for continuing stockholders – principally Henry and his family and foundations. When Ford again became a public company, in 1956, the business was valued at $3.2 billion, making a 10 per cent stake worth $320 million. (The Dow Jones industrial index of American stocks increased threefold over that period, and the US consumer price index by 60 per cent.[8])

The scene shifts forward in time to 2010, and eastward in location to Delaware, to the somewhat similar case of *Newmark v. eBay*.[9] Craig Newmark was the founder of Craigslist, an internet site for classified advertising. Together with technology officer Jim Buckmaster, he owned a majority of the company's shares. Newmark and Buckmaster had little interest in money – most listings on their site were and continue to be free and the modest expenses of the business are covered by paid job ads from companies wishing to recruit the millennials who use the site to buy sofas and arrange hook-ups.

eBay was impressed by the success of the start-up and wanted to buy it. The internet auction site saw an opening; an early supporter of Craigslist had been given some equity in Newmark's rather casual style. eBay offered the minority shareholder $15 million for his stock. At that point, Newmark and Buckmaster decided they were not so uninterested in money after all and demanded and received $8 million each from eBay in return for agreeing to the stock transfer. From this unpromising start, the relationship between Craigslist and eBay ran steadily downhill and ended in a series of actions and counteractions in the chancery court of Delaware.

In an extended article in 2015 the then chancellor of the
Delaware court, the highly respected Leo Strine, asserted that
Delaware law dictates shareholder primacy. He rejected the view
of some academic legal scholars, such as Lynn Stout, that the
scope of the business judgment rule allows a stakeholder perspective. Strine relied primarily on the chancery court findings in *eBay*
(and an earlier case, *Revlon*, in which the court ruled that having
decided to put the company up for sale the board was required to
accept the highest offer).[10] Strine gave this view while expressing
a personal opinion that he wished the law were otherwise.

Yet it seems likely – as was probably also true for Henry Ford
– that if the Craigslist founders had been willing to make some
conciliatory noises about building value in the business over the
long run, the result would have been different. The Delaware
court ruled that

> the Craigslist directors are bound by the fiduciary duties
> and standards that accompany that [for profit] form. These
> standards include acting to promote the value of the corpo-
> ration for the benefit of its stockholders ... I cannot accept
> as valid ... a corporate policy that specifically, clearly, and
> admittedly seeks *not* to maximize the value of a for-profit
> Delaware corporation for the benefit of its stockholders.[11]

It is plain that any commercial activity that hopes to survive
must aim to make a profit. Like staff, directors, customers and
the local community, shareholders are stakeholders in the firm
and are entitled to their rewards. eBay had paid to acquire its
equity in Craigslist, and just as it would have been inappropriate – bad business – for Craigslist to sell ad space to companies
and then not promote their ads, so it was inappropriate to fail to
provide a way for eBay to profit from its investment. But it does
not logically follow that an obligation to make a profit entails
an obligation to maximise that profit; the Delaware Court may
seem to imply that but does not say so. As is often noted, we
breathe to live but that does not mean we live to breathe.

American corporate law is primarily state law, but the case of Hobby Lobby, an unlisted corporation registered in the state of Oklahoma, went to the US Supreme Court in 2014.[12] The federal courts became involved because the case concerned the constitutionality of a federal statute. Hobby Lobby operates a chain of arts and craft stores across the United States. The corporation was founded by David Green, a militantly evangelical Christian, and the Green family owns all its shares. Hobby Lobby claimed that the obligation on employers under the Affordable Care Act (Obamacare) to provide health insurance coverage which included abortion and contraception violated the constitutional right to religious freedom.

But could a *corporation* have a right to religious freedom? Five years earlier the same court had concluded in *Citizens United* that the First Amendment right to free speech extended to corporations. But the extension of this finding to religious freedom was a further large step. It was a step the majority of the court, led by conservative Justice Samuel Alito, was willing to take. (Justice Ruth Bader Ginsburg lodged a vigorous dissent.)

Corporate personality

The notion of corporate personality has many applications. Until 1965 a corporation in Britain was subject to income tax on the same basis as an individual. When the European Convention on Human Rights was formulated in 1949, it was decided after some debate that the convention extended to 'legal persons': i.e. corporations. In subsequent cases, the European Court of Human Rights (ECHR) confirmed the right of a company to freedom of expression and determined that the right to respect for one's home extended to the business premises of firms.[13]

This conflict between these collective and individualistic perspectives on the firm, between corporate personality and nexus of contracts, recurs frequently in the course of this book. And I come down firmly on the side of those who believe that corporate personality should be regarded as not just a legal doctrine but an empirical reality. I find it hard to imagine that anyone with knowledge of successful – or unsuccessful – business could think otherwise. Organisations have distinctive cultures and collective intelligences, and it is through these differentiating characteristics that they contribute to our economy and society.

> A further group of complications is introduced by the common law concept of 'directing mind'. To assert criminality it is frequently necessary to establish intent, but can a corporation have an intent? Only if it has a 'directing mind'. In an absurd series of English cases in 2018–20, Barclays executives were acquitted because the actions under investigation had been undertaken by the bank, and the bank was acquitted because the organisation was too large and diffuse to have a 'directing mind'.

This recognition of the reality of corporate personality does not necessarily mean that the rights and obligations of corporations are or should be the same as those of individuals, notwithstanding the decisions of the Supreme Court and the European Court of Human Rights cited above. Freedom of speech for individuals is an essential component of a vibrant democracy. But paid corporate lobbying is a threat to that democracy, and the 'religious freedom' of a business corporation seems a ludicrous concept.

German law is clear and adopts a stakeholder perspective. American law on corporate obligations is not at all clear; scholarly debate is extensive and continuing, but veers towards shareholder primacy. Britain is, as on so many issues, somewhere in between. But clarification of the legal issue is much less important than it may appear to be at first sight.[14] All three jurisdictions have sensibly framed their law, and the practice of their courts, to make it hard to challenge honestly made business decisions. As a result, managers are left with considerable discretion in practice in balancing the claims of different stakeholders. The manner in which they resolve these questions owes far more to the business climate and the expectations of society than to the precise definition of legal duties. Businesses are social organisations and operate within a particular society.

17

LEAKY PIPES AND OVERFLOWING SEWAGE

> We do not inherit the earth from our ancestors; we borrow
> it from our children.
>
> Widely attributed

In 1989 the water industry in England was privatised. Ten state-owned regional boards became companies listed on the London Stock Exchange. I recall a conversation soon afterwards with the former chief engineer of one of these companies, now designated a corporate CEO. He explained that almost everyone in his company was employed either to stop things going wrong or to fix them when they had. If most of the workforce were fired, he explained, water would continue to flow almost as normal, probably for quite some time. All you needed was a billing department; revenues, like the water, would continue to flow and profits would increase spectacularly.

Although there was no scientific way of computing the 'right' level of staffing, his view was that the nationalised industry had employed too many people. Under public ownership, the managerial imperative was not to be blamed for anything, and it had always been easy to avoid hard choices, especially in labour relations. In the business of water supply, there are many things that might happen for which one could be blamed, while customer demand was guaranteed.

But now regulation had capped prices so that any cost reduction would be of immediate benefit to shareholders and executive bonuses. The CEO anticipated that under the new regulatory regime and profit target his company, and others like it, would continue to drive down costs and reduce manpower. And then, he speculated, something would go badly wrong; and there would be an overreaction. That prediction was fulfilled not in the water industry but on the railways, where an accident attributed to neglected track maintenance killed four people in 2000 in Hatfield.[1] In the months that followed there was massive disruption of services as a result of speed restrictions and the renationalisation of the rail tracks followed two years later. (That CEO is long retired, but his company is now routinely criticised for its leakages and sewage discharges.)

> The Hungarian economist János Kornai developed the concept of the 'soft budget constraint', noting that enterprises in communist countries did have limited budgets but could rely on being rescued by the state if they breached them – so there was no need to make hard choices.[2] Soft budget constraints are not merely a feature of socialist economies, as citizens discovered when banks were bailed out after the 2008 financial crisis.

I realised that the water industry was an extreme case but also that what had been described was true to a greater or lesser extent in almost every business. What is the 'right' amount to spend on customer service, on attracting new customers, asset maintenance, fault prevention and fault fixing in order to sustain the business in the long run? There are no objectively correct answers to these questions, which can only be matters of judgement and experience. So it is always open to new management to decide to spend a little less and add the difference to earnings. In my mind, I have labelled it *leaky pipe and overflowing sewage* syndrome.

Soon after that conversation with the water company executive I stayed in a once elegant hotel and noticed that the carpets were a little frayed, the paintwork a little scuffed, the breakfast and the minibar significantly overpriced. An internet search confirmed my suspicion that the hotel group had been acquired by a private equity house with a reputation for buying businesses, quickly boosting earnings and flipping the company back into the public markets. Seven of the ten water companies that were floated in 1989 – including the one whose CEO provided that illuminating insight – are no longer listed on stock markets but are owned by private equity consortia. And leaky pipe and overflowing sewage syndrome is widespread.

Earnings management

In 2010 the play *Enron*, written by Lucy Prebble, was an improbable hit. The show begins with a champagne party hosted by Jeff Skilling, the mastermind of Enron's rise and fall. The event that set the corks popping was the receipt in January 1992 of a letter from the Securities and Exchange Commission. The letter gave Enron permission to use mark-to-market accounting to report earnings from long-term gas supply contracts.[3]

> Prebble's play was a critical and commercial success in England and ran for a year in London's West End. But a Broadway production received a hostile review from *The New York Times* – 'British and American tastes don't always coincide in such matters, especially when the subject is American' – and closed after only fifteen performances.[4]

All businesses report their earnings over an accounting year, and businesses that are listed on a stock exchange must report more frequently.[5] Annual reporting began when agriculture was the main economic activity. Crops were planted in the spring, which was also the lambing season. The harvest was gathered in the autumn, and the cycle would repeat itself the following year. There would be good years and there would be bad years. But the annual cycle was determined by the orbit around the sun.

Banking was different. Banks have always borrowed cheaply and lent more expensively. The old joke was 'borrow at 3, lend at 6, golf course at 3'. Banks can borrow cheaply because their lenders are reasonably confident that they will be repaid; they lend more expensively because lenders recognise a possibility that non-bank borrowers will default and seek to compensate for this by charging an interest rate premium. The bank collects the interest premium until the loan is repaid – or not. So banking is profitable – until it isn't. That makes banking a cyclical business. And it explains why many, including 'manager of the century' Jack Welch, have been attracted by the lure of easy profits in financial services for a business with a strong credit rating. Borrow at 3, lend at 6. Readers of Welch's autobiography may be surprised at how large a role golf played in his corporate and personal life.

But the length of the business cycle is longer, and more variable, than the seasons. And banking is not the only activity for which annual accounting may be misleading. Many businesses have many contracts or agreements with customers or suppliers which extend over much longer periods. It is then necessary to decide how the costs and revenues are to be distributed over several accounting periods.

Historically, accounting conventions were conservative: you booked revenues and costs as they fell due, and the profit from a contract would therefore be spread over the life of the contract. With mark-to-market accounting, however, you might take credit for all the profit you expected to earn from the transaction at the moment the contract was signed. As reported by Bethany McLean and Peter Elkind, Skilling was evangelical about the need to account in this way: 'A business should be able to declare profits at the moment of the creative act that would earn these profits. Otherwise, businessmen were mere coupon clippers, reaping the benefit of innovation that had been devised in the past by other, greater, men.'[6] This is not the only occasion reported in this book on which people were adroit in developing intellectual arguments that worked to their financial advantage. Or in overestimating their abilities and foresight.

Andrew Fastow, an accountant, was hired by Skilling and rose to become Enron's chief financial officer. Fastow was the man behind the creation of a series of 'special purpose entities' (played in Prebble's production by actors with reptile heads). These are associated companies whose accounts do not have to be consolidated with those of the principal business; hence they can be used in essentially fictitious transactions that yield profits or losses for the principal business and allow management (i.e. manipulation) of the reported earnings of the principal business. The 'badges of ownership' are fudged – or buried in many pages of accounting standards.

The impressive growth of Enron's reported earnings and stock price ended in the largest corporate bankruptcy in US history, the conviction and imprisonment of Skilling and Fastow, and the failure of Arthur Andersen, the company's auditors. However, the accounting techniques of mark-to-market accounting and transactions with special purpose entities were also employed by more reputable companies to enable them to report the steady pattern of earnings growth which financial markets came to regard as the hallmark of a well-managed, stable business. After the collapse of Enron, the new century would reveal the extent to which businesses such as General Electric and the government-sponsored mortgage insurer Fannie Mae had used these techniques. And mark-to-market accounting would be a principal source of the illusory profits reported by banks in the years before the 2008 global financial crisis.

18

THE DUMBEST IDEA IN THE WORLD

Shareholder value is a result, not a strategy ... Your main
constituencies are your employees, your customers and your
products.

> Jack Welch, CEO, General Electric, 1981–2001[1]

I'd be a bum on the street with a tin cup if the markets were
always efficient.

> Warren Buffett, 2013[2]

A possible answer to leaky pipes, overflowing sewage and
earnings management is to demand that managers, instead of
maximising profits, maximise shareholder value – the returns to
shareholders from dividends and stock price appreciation over a
long period, potentially the entire life of the company.

The era of shareholder value

In 1999 the ambitious Sandy Weill merged his Travelers Insurance Company with the venerable Citibank. For a brief period
John Reed, the CEO of the bank, and Weill were joint CEOs of
the newformed Citigroup. An American journalist recorded the
following exchange between the two.

> 'The model I have is of a global consumer company that
> really helps the middle-class with something they haven't
> been served well by historically, that's my vision, that's
> my dream,' said Reed. 'My goal is increasing shareholder

value', Sandy interjected, glancing frequently at a nearby computer monitor displaying Citigroup's changing stock price.[3]

Reed, representative of an older generation of bankers, was quickly forced out of the executive suite. What might Weill have learned from the monitor? Not enough, evidently; by 2008 most 'shareholder value' had been destroyed and the 200-year-old Citibank was rescued by the US government.

Jack Welch is widely credited with inaugurating the era of shareholder value in a speech at The Pierre hotel in New York in 1981 soon after he took over as CEO of General Electric. Welch did not in fact use the phrase 'shareholder value'. Alfred Rappaport, whose 1986 text is still the movement's bible, may have coined it.[4] Consultants took up the notion with evangelical fervour; Marakon Associates and Stern Stewart popularised the concept, and Rappaport founded his own firm, Alcar. The term 'shareholder value' became heard more and more widely in the two decades that followed. Only in 2009, some years into retirement, would Welch describe it as 'the dumbest idea in the world'.[5] A statement he partially retracted a few days later.[6]

"Maximising shareholder value doesn't count."

It is hard to imagine that any Walmart employee – from the checkout cashier to CEO Doug McMillon – is enthused by the task of maximising shareholder value. Or that business founders like Bill Gates and Jeff Bezos hope that 'he maximised shareholder value' will be the epitaph on their tombstones. Or even that their eulogists would be able to determine that they had indeed maximised shareholder value. But freshwater economists came to their aid.

Efficient markets to the rescue

The efficient market hypothesis (EMH) is a cornerstone of modern finance theory. In a 1978 paper surveying new critiques of the hypothesis Michael Jensen (of Jensen and Meckling) observed that 'There is no other proposition in economics that has more solid empirical evidence supporting it than the Efficient Market Hypothesis' (although he went on to say that cracks seemed to be appearing).[7] 'Efficient' here has a specific technical meaning: a securities market is efficient when all available knowledge relevant to the value of securities is incorporated in prices so that there are few, if any, profitable trading opportunities. Market efficiency is often conflated with a broader concept of economic efficiency: but there is nothing about the efficiency of a securities market that guarantees the efficiency of the enterprises whose securities are traded.

The Friedman doctrine required the firm to maximise its profits. The 'shareholder value' movement put a gloss on this obligation. The duty was now to sustain returns for shareholders – not to maximise profits this year but to maximise the present value of profits over the long run. Making such a calculation required extraordinary prescience, but here the efficient market hypothesis came to the aid of the manager. Since everything that could be known about the company was reflected in the stock price, maximising shareholder value could be equated to maximising the current value of the company's shares. Thus Sandy Weill could manage his company with the aid of the constant flow of share price information displayed on his computer monitor and benefit from the wisdom of crowds. As events proved, however, the stock ticker was a poor substitute for the wisdom of experienced bankers.

> If all available knowledge is already incorporated into prices, there is no incentive to engage in the research which generates that knowledge. So there is a tension, even a contradiction, in the efficient market hypothesis as a description of actual securities markets.[8]
>
> The tension is recorded in the notorious joke about the Chicago economist who fails to pick up a $5 bill on the street on the grounds that if it had been there someone would already have picked it up: a joke that deserves careful analysis. There are few $5 bills lying on the street, for precisely the reason the hypothetical economist describes; but there are some, and it is those occasional opportunities which are the source of profits in financial markets – and success in business more generally. In 2013 the Nobel Prize in economics was shared between Eugene Fama, for formulating the EMH, and Robert Shiller, for accumulating evidence that it was not true. This is not quite as paradoxical as it seems – the EMH is an illuminating concept without being true.
>
> Warren Buffett put it well: 'Observing correctly that the market was frequently efficient, they [academics] went on to conclude incorrectly that it was always efficient. The difference between these propositions is night and day.'[9]

Such magical thinking epitomises the inappropriate use of illuminating economic models. The efficient market hypothesis contains an important element of truth: public information influences stock prices. And thoughtful investors look at the long-run prospects for a company as well as its current profits. The price of shares in early-stage pharmaceutical or technology companies reflects hopes of profits far into the future. However, the management of these companies can only speculate on what these profits might be, and prospective investors can only speculate on the cogency of these managerial assessments. Any idea that the market knows more about the corporation's future than its management knows – or could or should know – represents the triumph of an abstract theory over common sense.[10]

Executive remuneration schemes

The move to shareholder value gave a new twist to the principal–agent problem posed by the separation of control and ownership. How were executives to be incentivised to maximise shareholder value? Jensen and Meckling's 1976 article focused on this issue and emphasised the need to align shareholder and managerial interests by designing appropriate executive incentive schemes. Their analysis proved highly influential, not least because its conclusions were so congenial to the executive managers themselves.

If managers were to be incentivised to maximise shareholder value, their pay could be linked to the price of the company's stock. Perhaps remuneration should be in stock rather than cash. Or related to the increase in the stock price during their term of office. Then, the rationalisation continued, the magic of the efficient market hypothesis would ensure that their reward accurately reflected the impact of their actions not only now but in the future. Prospective Jeff Skillings would not need to persuade the SEC to recognise the value of their achievements: Mr Market would do it for them. (In the original analogy of 'Intelligent Investor' Benjamin Graham, Mr Market was not an omniscient observer but a fickle manic depressive. Graham may have been wiser, and richer, but Fama collected the Nobel.)

There was a possible snag for the executive: stocks go down as well as up. The answer was the share option, which conferred the right – but not the obligation – to buy stock at some future date at a price fixed today. The manager would therefore benefit from a rise in the stock price but would not suffer from a fall. And – partly but by no means entirely coincidentally – the two decades from 1980 to 2000 saw a rapid increase in stock prices, with the Dow Jones Industrial Average rising tenfold.

Over the following decades, explosive growth in the use of stock options was associated with explosive growth in the remuneration of senior executives. Paradoxically, the measures designed to align shareholder and managerial interests would become the principal focus of friction between these interests. Managers, advised by the newly established profession of remuneration consultants, used incentive plans to help themselves and each other to larger rewards.

What advice can one give the newly appointed CEO, installed at a desk with a computer monitor showing the company's fluctuating stock price and enjoined to maximise shareholder value? Typically he, or now occasionally she, has five years or so to make an impact on the share price and be lauded as a corporate hero before luxurious retirement. The head of investor relations will tell the CEO that the stock market is fixated on reported earnings. Establish a consistent record of 'making the numbers' and look forward to golden years flitting by private jet between Manhattan penthouse, Florida beachfront and Montana ranch.

The winner's curse

The auction procedure at Christie's at which *Salvator Mundi* changed hands is another attempt to solve the incentive compatibility problem without using prices in an open market. The successful bidder need not reveal the value that he places on the painting but must reveal that it is higher than the value placed on it by the second-highest bidder. Thus if a trade takes place, the price arrived at will be less than or equal to the valuation of the purchaser but more than or at least equal to the minimum required by the seller: the often undisclosed reserve price.

And yet ... there cannot be anyone in the world who has not regretted a purchase as soon as they got the item home. Perhaps not even MBS. Since the winner of an auction is the highest bidder, the winner will often be someone who overestimates the value of the item being auctioned and rarely someone who underestimates it. All the bidders who offered far more than the pre-sale estimate of $100 million for *Salvator Mundi* had presumably convinced themselves that it was a genuine Leonardo; others who were more sceptical chose not to enter the bidding.

The 'winner's curse' describes the phenomenon that purchasers of idiosyncratic items will often include people who have simply made a mistake. Not just those who raised their hands in the saleroom at the wrong moment but buyers of the clothes that looked stylish in the shop but not in the mirror at home, and owners of the kitchen gadgets that seemed useful at the moment of purchase but now clutter the drawer or worktop. The term 'winner's curse' was first used to describe an issue that arose when exploration rights to offshore blocks were sold.[11] Oil companies discovered that many of their winning bids were in places where their geologists had misread the data and overestimated the potential.

Successful bidders for objects whose true value is unknown routinely turn out to have paid too much: they won because they were the most optimistic. When there are few publicly held shares in small companies whose success or failure is hard to predict, these shares are more likely to be held by people who overestimate their value than by people who underestimate it. Most such investments fail, but the losses might, though need not, be offset by occasional spectacular gains. The market value of a security is often a poor guide to the value likely to be created in the business over the long run.

Clarity of objective?

One argument presented in favour of the shareholder value position is that, whatever its limitations, a profit objective is clear and easy to implement, and it is clear whether it has been implemented. On reflection, this argument is simply false. The injunction 'Go and make money' actually provides very little guidance to the newly appointed manager of a business. It fails to distinguish between the roles you assume as chief executive of Apple, of Siemens or of Disney Corporation. All these jobs are completely different. What makes them different are the different characteristics, histories and prospects of the different organisations.

Intrinsic rather than instrumental motivation is required at all levels of the successful business and is a hallmark of such businesses. Disney employees are not told to go and make money for Disney. They are told to make sure the guests have fun. They feel they are part of a great business. The result makes a great deal of money for the Disney Corporation. It is all that way around.

And if maximisation of shareholder value provides no clear guidance in anticipation, it provides no clear measure in retrospect. Did Alfred Sloan or Steve Jobs maximise long-term shareholder value? I don't have the slightest idea, and nor did they. I do know, as did they, that they created great businesses and a great deal of shareholder value.

You can create shareholder value, as John D. Rockefeller did, by finding an industry that will grow dramatically for the next 150 years and setting out to build the dominant business in that industry. In 1865, at the age of thirty-one, Thomas Sutherland founded the Hong Kong and Shanghai Banking Corporation in the belief that trade between Europe and China would grow. It did, even if the exchange of opium for tea would metamorphose into the exchange of Mercedes saloons for 5G telecom equipment. The founders of BP (William D'Arcy) and Shell (Marcus Samuel) would benefit from the same insight as Rockefeller. These three companies emerged as the largest creators of shareholder value in Britain – in both present and past eras.

To create shareholder value is to build a great business – as did Charles Coffin, CEO of General Electric from 1893 to 1922, who melded the inventive capabilities of Thomas Edison, Elihu Thomson and Edwin Houston into a business that became not only one of America's leading corporations but one of its finest management schools. The father and son, Thomas Watson senior and junior, who established IBM aimed to create a great business – and succeeded. It would be hard to say the same of the bankers and executives who ran these long-established icons in the twenty-first century.

PART 5

HOW IT ALL WORKED OUT

*It is not a coincidence that the emphasis on financial metrics in busi-
ness occurred at the same time as explosive growth in the size and
remuneration of the financial sector. There were useful innovations,
such as the emergence of venture capital as a means of financing
start-up businesses. But the financial sector is primarily rewarded by
fees from facilitating transactions, not for the consequences of these
transactions.*

*Corporate executives engaged in a frenzy of dealmaking, buying
and selling existing businesses; incentive plans encouraged actions that
generated immediate revenues or cost savings, mostly with unmeasured consequences for the business in the long run. The result was the
destruction of many of the great businesses which an earlier generation of less well-rewarded managers had created.*

19

THE EVOLUTION OF FINANCE

No sooner did you pass the fake fireplace than you heard an
ungodly roar, like the roar of a mob ... It was the sound of
well-educated young white men baying for money on the
bond market.

Tom Wolfe, The Bonfire of the Vanities, 1987[1]

For most of history wealth consisted of physical assets. Tribal
chiefs occupied the best residences. Kings and princes lived in
palaces, sported finery and maintained armouries. Wealthy
aristocrats were marked out by their ownership of land, stately
homes and townhouses. In the early days of the Industrial Revolution the marks of wealth were still mostly tangible – Richard
Arkwright owned the textile mill, Abraham Darby the ironworks. The first financial assets were claims on physical assets:
the gold in the vaults of the bank, or shares, literally, of the ships
on the sea and the cargoes they carried.

But as finance evolved, the link between the financial and the
physical became more tenuous. Stocks were claims on the revenues of a commercial venture rather than shares of its assets.
Loans were traded. Currencies had once been physical objects
– gold and silver coins – but were now the debt obligations of
banks or governments. Businesses might borrow from financial institutions but could tap the savings of a wider public by
issuing bonds, which might themselves be tradable on securities markets. Rating agencies which had traditionally reported
on the creditworthiness of companies, useful for suppliers and
customers, extended their activities to assessment of the quality

of issued bonds, helpful to investors. Three companies – Fitch, Moody's and Standard & Poor's – dominate this market. The governments of Australia and Canada, Germany and Switzerland, along with Johnson & Johnson, achieve the highest AAA or 'triple A' rating. The bonds of less creditworthy borrowers such as the governments of the United Kingdom and the United States are still categorised as 'investment grade'. Securities that do not meet the standards of investment grade are described as 'junk'.

By the end of the nineteenth century, retail banking in England was already concentrated into a handful of institutions such as Barclays and Lloyds. (Scotland remained separate.) There was a clear distinction between the genteel world of investment (then called merchant) banking, which funded global trade, large businesses and governments, and the more proletarian activity of retail banking, which required branches in every significant population centre. In the first half of the twentieth century merchant banking in the City of London remained a gentlemanly affair. Scions of the Baring and Rothschild families, no longer outsiders, had been raised to the peerage. Merchant bankers had mostly been educated at public schools, had often served in the army rather than attended university, arrived at their offices late in the morning and enjoyed lengthy lunches lubricated with fine wines. Stockbrokers fitted this caricature even more clearly. Cleverness, particularly numerate cleverness, was frowned on. Hours were short, workloads undemanding. Much of their activity would now be regarded as improper and illegal insider trading.

In the United States, restrictions on interstate banking prevented the consolidation of retail banking that had occurred in England. But the leading banks of New York, such as J. P. Morgan and the National City Bank, became powerful internationally as well as in the US. The Glass–Steagall Act, passed in 1933 in response to the Wall Street Crash, mandated the separation of commercial and investment banking. This led to the divestiture of the investment banking operations of J. P. Morgan into Morgan Stanley. The universal banks of continental Europe funded industry in France, Germany and other countries where securities markets were (and still are) much less developed than in the Anglophone world. Small community banks coexisted there with national institutions such as Crédit Lyonnais and Deutsche Bank.

Venture capital

In the nineteenth century, and for most of the twentieth, a new business needed funds to fit out premises and acquire plant and machinery. The local bank manager would know the prospective founder, assess his (very rarely her) character and suitability, and probably require security on the business assets and the family home. That model remains relevant for many small businesses, especially those I have described as trades.

But in the later twentieth century this practice would change. Secured lending was inappropriate for a start-up that needed little in the way of fixed assets but was likely to lose money for several years. Founders sought equity investment; banks did not offer this and retreated from their traditional role of supporting small businesses and local entrepreneurs. Some of the necessary finance would come from 'angels' – well-off private individuals such as Mike Markkula, who provided $100,000 to Steve Jobs and Steve Wozniak as they assembled Apple computers in their garage. But specialist firms emerged to supplement the blessings of angels.

The fame and success of Silicon Valley was much facilitated by the activities of venture capital houses such as Sequoia Capital and Kleiner Perkins. Sequoia was the first external funder of Apple and Google; Kleiner filled this role for Amazon and Netscape. These seedcorn investments were both economically important and, in cases such as these, very rewarding for the investors. The business model of venture capital firms anticipates that many of the new companies they support will fail but hopes that a few successes such as these will more than compensate.

> Netscape's internet browser first made the web acces-
> sible to a mass audience. The company's wildly popular
> 1994 IPO launched the dotcom bubble. But Microsoft's
> Internet Explorer was introduced a year later, and by 2003
> Gates's company had achieved a 95 per cent market share
> in browsing. The then struggling Netscape was acquired
> by AOL, which then engaged in a disastrous merger with
> Time Warner. The Netscape browser has not been updated
> since 2008. Although the business ultimately failed, Kleiner
> Perkins had been able to cash out its $5 million investment
> for $400 million.

Venture capital funds such as these – and the private equity
and hedge funds described below – are typically structured
as 'limited partnerships'. The venture capital manager is the
'general partner' and usually does not pay for a stake in the fund,
but is entitled to a share of the proceeds, a practice known as
'carried interest'. The 'limited partners' – limited in both influence and liability – are typically well-off individuals, pension
funds and charities such as university endowments. The carried
interest enjoys tax advantages and obviously can be extremely
profitable; at Airbnb's IPO in 2020 Sequoia's carried interest was
worth around $15 billion.[2] Although the language might suggest
otherwise, the risks associated with unsuccessful investment are
assumed by the limited partners. The worst that can happen to a
carried interest is that it yields no profit. Thus the transaction has
the character of heads the promoters win, tails the investors lose.

Securitisation

The boundaries between loans and bonds have always been
blurred – banks had for many years syndicated large loans,
placing portions of them with other institutions, and bonds that
were notionally tradable were often not so in practice. Bond
issuance was more common in Britain and the US than in continental Europe, where bank financing is still predominant.[3]

Institutions such as the European Commission and European Central Bank have been anxious to promote the use of bonds in Europe, but the pressure seems to come from the aspirations of financiers rather than the needs of businesspeople.

Those boundaries were blurred further with the rise of securitisation, which began in the US in the 1970s. Packages of loans would be marketed as bonds and traded. A further refinement would involve the creation of multiple tranches of security within the package – the senior tranches would have the first claim to repayment and more junior tranches would receive what was left. The major rating agencies would pass judgment on the security offered by these different tranches.

The bankers who devised these products became skilled at seeing weaknesses in the models which the rating agencies used to assess the credit risk of bonds. Sophisticated financial engineers could secure favourable ratings for dubious securities. They also became skilled at selling the products to gullible buyers – as in the Timberwolf and Abacus deals. Purchasers were sought who were knowledgeable enough to be identified by regulators as 'eligible counterparties' – there are many restrictions on what can be sold to the general public – but nevertheless not knowledgeable enough to steer clear. Alongside these asset-backed securities (ABSs) and collateralised debt obligations (CDOs) were credit default swaps (CDSs), which paid out if the associated security defaulted. These swaps acted as insurance if you held the security and as a gamble if you didn't – a 'naked short' is a bet against an asset you do not own. This was the combustible mix of acronyms that caught fire in 2008.

Michael Milken, of Drexel Burnham Lambert, is credited with the invention of the 'junk bond'. Bonds often *became* 'junk', with high yields and a poor credit rating, when the company or government that issued them stumbled. But junk bonds were *intended* to be junk, with a high risk of default and correspondingly high yield, from the moment they were issued. Milken's idea was that individuals or institutions could put up small amounts of capital to buy large businesses with the aid of large amounts of junk bond financing. The debt would be secured on the assets and revenues of the acquired business. The junk bond further blurred the traditional distinction between debt and equity.

> Robin Potts QC delivered an opinion in 1997 to the International Securities and Derivatives Association in which he helpfully concluded that CDSs were neither gambling nor insurance products and hence outside the regulatory framework of either industry. With London thus poised to be the central market for such securities, the US adopted the Commodity Futures Modernisation Act (2000), which exempted these products from US regulation. In poor health, Mr Potts retired early to study history at Oxford but lived just long enough to see the havoc which he had helped cause.

Financial conglomerates

The 1960s were harbingers of many changes. The internationalisation of finance which had begun with the establishment of the eurodollar market also had wide repercussions, many of them unintended. The process is often described as 'deregulation', but the reality is that there is far more, and more detailed, regulation of financial services today than existed fifty years ago.

As finance became more global, and policies in Britain and the US more oriented towards liberalising markets, retail banks were allowed more operational freedom. Regulatory reform in Britain – popularly known as 'Big Bang' – occurred in 1986. In the US there was no 'Big Bang', but 'May Day' in 1975 similarly ended fixed stock exchange commissions, while Glass–Steagall's separation of retail and investment banking was steadily relaxed and finally repealed in 1999 to accommodate the boundless ambitions of Sandy Weill. Banks everywhere sought to operate internationally; American and continental European banks set up major operations in London, and Goldman Sachs and

Nomura were among the first to open London offices. Retail banks, which were better capitalised and, more importantly, enjoyed the resources of a large deposit base and the implicit state guarantee that supported these deposits, acquired investment banks. Deutsche Bank bought the venerable Morgan Grenfell.[4] Swiss Bank Corporation (now merged into Union Bank of Switzerland, UBS) purchased the upstart S. G. Warburg. The greedier and smarter dealmakers and traders from the investment banks soon wrested overall control of the new conglomerate businesses from the retail bankers. The age of the deal had dawned.

20

THE ART OF THE DEAL

It Is Theoretically Possible for the Entire United States to
Become One Vast Conglomerate Presided Over by Mr.
James L. Ling.
> *Saturday Evening Post* headline, 1968[1]

I do it to do it. Deals are my art form.
> Donald Trump, *The Art of the Deal*, 1987
> (ghostwritten by Tony Schwartz)[2]

'But what good came of it at last?'
Quoth little Peterkin.
'Why, that I cannot tell,' said he,
'But 'twas a famous victory.'
> Robert Southey, *The Battle of Blenheim*, 1796[3]

Until the 1960s mergers were typically *horizontal*, between companies in closely related lines of business, as at US Steel, ICI and
IG Farben. There were some *vertical* mergers; businesses bought
their suppliers, as General Motors had done at Fisher Body,
or, less frequently, bought their distributors, as when brewers
acquired collections of pubs. But in the later part of the twentieth century, many different arguments would be used to justify
proposed consolidations. The term M&A (mergers and acquisitions) would become central to the corporate lexicon. With the
emphasis on acquisitions.

The whole is worth more than the sum of the parts?

Tex Thornton was the commanding officer of a group of ten young, numerically oriented Harvard Business School faculty who transformed US military logistics in the Pacific during the Second World War by introducing methods of statistical control. At the end of the war Thornton wrote to Henry Ford II, who had just become CEO of the company on the death of his grandfather. He pitched the services of the group as consultants; Ford accepted, and some of the 'whiz kids' rejuvenated the business. The best-known 'whiz kid' was Robert McNamara, who became president of Ford (and was Defense Secretary to Kennedy and Johnson during the Vietnam War and subsequently president of the World Bank).

Thornton himself did not stay long at Ford. After a spell with Howard Hughes he borrowed money to buy a small electrical company, Litton, and began an acquisition spree. Litton was one of several conglomerate companies of the 1960s that expanded on the principle that superstar managers enjoyed skills that could be advantageously deployed in almost any business. Rival conglomerates included LTV, the empire of Jimmy Ling, and Henry Singleton's Teledyne.

Academic cheerleaders were also available here. In 1965 the

Chicago lawyer Henry Manne suggested a theory that might help link securities market efficiency with business efficiency: 'the market for corporate control'.[4] An active securities market in which takeover bids were common was, in effect, a market in which buyers and sellers traded the opportunity to manage businesses. Just as a market for apples and pears tended to put fruit in the hands of the people who most wanted it, a market for corporate control would put the management of companies in the hands of those who could exercise it most effectively. 'The market for corporate control' was a nicely chosen phrase, seeming to soften the bruising reality of clashing executive egos.

The standout 1960s conglomerate was International Telephone and Telegraph (ITT), a company with origins in the international development of telecommunications. In 1959 Harold Geneen was appointed CEO. Geneen began a bewildering series of unrelated acquisitions, including Sheraton Hotels, Avis Rent a Car and The Hartford insurance. Operating in many countries, ITT became engaged politically as well as commercially and was notoriously associated with the coup that toppled Salvador Allende's Marxist government in Chile in 1973. Geneen was forced out of the company in 1979, and his successor began a series of disposals that unwound the unwieldy accumulation of disparate activities. The conglomerate fashion was at an end. In 1970, only two years after that *Saturday Evening Post* headline, a restive board had forced Jimmy Ling out of the company he had founded. LTV finally went bankrupt in 1986. Litton also moved into disposal mode, and the rump of its business was acquired by Northrop Grumman in 2001.

The parts are worth more than the whole?

Mergers and acquisitions had once been a friendly business. It would be naïve to think that the smaller companies which sold to John D. Rockefeller were necessarily willing sellers. But they acquiesced in offers they could not readily refuse. The purchases of ITT and its rivals were mostly agreed upon, often expensively. The idea that a bidder might appeal to shareholders over the heads of incumbent management could arise only after the separation of ownership and control and did not become a common practice till the later part of the twentieth century.

The British financier Charles Clore is often credited with the invention of the concept and word 'takeover'.[5] In 1953 he mounted a bid for Sears, a chain of British shoe shops (unconnected with the US Sears Roebuck). Clore had recognised that the high street premises Sears owned were more valuable than the poorly run business. Clore's insight was that as a result of financial innovation and the dematerialisation of production, capital in the form of tangible assets was increasingly distinct from capital in the form of financial assets (which represented claims on future revenues). In subsequent chapters I will emphasise the importance of this insight in understanding the evolution of the modern corporation. For Charles Clore it was the route to a considerable fortune, much of which he devoted to charitable purposes.

Clore had been an outsider and had won control of Sears despite the opposition of the company's board and some anti-Semitic prejudice. Sir Ivan Stedeford, chairman and managing director of Tube Investments, was a consummate insider, a member of the Court of the Bank of England and a Governor of the BBC. But no less ambitious for that – he had built the company into an engineering conglomerate. And then he launched Europe's first major hostile takeover.

Stedeford decided to appeal directly to the shareholders of sleepy British Aluminium over the heads of its incumbent management. He obtained outside help from the American company Reynolds Metals and hired Warburgs, the upstart investment bank established in London in 1934 by a Jewish refugee from Nazi Germany. Stedeford probably had few alternative advisers; the City establishment gathered together to support British Aluminium. What Tube Investments and Warburg proposed was just not done. But the bid was successful, and what had been just not done was done more and more frequently.

Even by Imperial Chemical Industries (ICI), Britain's largest and most respected industrial company. Shortly after the British Aluminium takeover closed, ICI attempted to acquire its long-time rival Courtaulds, which had pioneered the development of artificial fibres but had fallen on lethargic times. ICI's bid failed mainly because an internal revolt within Courtaulds led by an assertive young chemist, Frank Kearton, began to revitalise the company. The market for corporate control was becoming a reality.

In 1974 International Nickel, advised by Morgan Stanley, made a hostile bid for ESB, an American manufacturer of batteries. Warburg had been an outsider in the clubby atmosphere of the City of London. What was pathbreaking about this bid was the involvement of Morgan Stanley, the Wall Street 'white shoe' investment bank, on the side of the aggressor. Goldman Sachs was called to assist ESB. The Goldman partners, in search of a 'white knight', turned to Harry Gray, a former colleague of Tex Thornton at the now-struggling conglomerate Litton Industries. Gray had just become CEO of United Aircraft. However, International Nickel (Inco) raised its bid above United Aircraft's competing offer and duly acquired ESB. (The combination was not a success, and seven years later Inco disposed of its loss-making subsidiary.) But Gray now had the bit between his teeth. Renaming the company United Technologies, he launched a successful hostile bid for Otis Elevator. This would be one of a series of assertive moves that built the company (which became Raytheon Technologies after yet another merger in 2020 and is now known as RTX) into one of the world's largest defence contractors.

The business world had for ever changed. No chief executive or chairman, however large their company, would ever feel quite secure: an early morning phone call might give notice – perhaps only a few minutes' notice – of the announcement of a hostile takeover bid. Advisers from investment banks, who would plan campaigns of attack or defence, became the regular confidants of top company managers.

A new era of dealmaking

Britain had its own conglomerate boom. In 1964 a young accountant, Jim Slater, joined with future Conservative cabinet minister Peter Walker to establish Slater Walker Securities, which became an aggressive bidder for companies with underexploited assets. Slater Walker put the term 'asset stripper' into common – and rarely favourable – discourse, but the firm collapsed in 1974 in the aftermath of the oil shock. Some aggressive British conglomerates had greater longevity, such as James Hanson's eponymous Hanson Trust and Owen Green's BTR. It is not an accident that all the conglomerates listed here, both American and British, are associated with the name of a dominant CEO.

The fall of Geneen and Slater might have signalled the end of the cult of the superstar manager. But the unwinding of the failed conglomerates of the 1960s only served to unleash a new frenzy of dealmaking. All companies, and all divisions of companies, were potentially for sale. This activity was fuelled by financial innovation and led to further financial innovation.

The success of the first venture capital houses led to the rapid growth of the sector. Financiers turned their attention from small new businesses to larger, established businesses. The next related innovation was private equity. Private equity managers bought established companies, usually spun out of bigger companies. Or they 'took private' a listed business, borrowing most of the money needed to pay off existing shareholders. These transactions had tax advantages because interest on borrowings, unlike dividends, could be deducted in computing the company's taxable profits. Blackstone, founded by Stephen Schwarzman, is today the largest private equity business, buying and selling an assortment of assets which have ranged from The Weather Channel to Madame Tussauds, from Butlin's holiday camps to Spanx 'shaping' underwear for women.

The 'management buyout' enabled some incumbent executives to take a larger stake, securing for themselves some of the gains otherwise available only to business founders or financiers. Some see this as an answer to the principal–agent problem.

Others take a less charitable view. 'Junk bond' finance made these transactions possible. Buyouts need not involve a private equity partner, but many did.

The signature deal of the 1980s was the takeover of the food and tobacco conglomerate RJR Nabisco, a public company with a market capitalisation of $12 billion on the New York Stock Exchange. RJR Nabisco was itself only three years old. As many other tobacco companies had done, the long-established R. J. Reynolds decided to pursue a future in which tobacco would play a smaller role and merged with Nabisco Brands – itself the product of the merger of a biscuit manufacturer and a packaged foods company.

Ross Johnson, CEO of RJR Nabisco, was the fortunate beneficiary of a generous executive incentive scheme and a wide range of perks. Most famously, these included access to what became known as the 'RJR airforce', a fleet of ten corporate jets and thirty-six pilots. The airforce's most famous passenger was Johnson's dog Rocco. But these benefits were not adequate reward for what Mr Johnson saw as his singular talents, and he proposed a management buyout, which would have installed him as principal shareholder with the aid of borrowed money secured against the business. The plan was foiled, however, when private equity house KKR intervened with a competing bid. Like similar private equity houses, KKR raised funds from institutional investors which it leveraged with junk bonds. KKR outbid Johnson, who was released to pursue opportunities elsewhere. However, the deal was not a success, in either business or financial terms.

In the most bizarre transaction of a decade of bizarre transactions, a Canadian real estate developer named Robert Campeau acquired a string of famous US department stores led by Bloomingdale's. Even Drexel had turned that deal away. The Campeau Corporation tumbled into bankruptcy.

At its worst, private equity has often been a means of extracting money from businesses by massaging short-term earnings. While cost cutting may begin with the winding down of the air force, it can end with leaky pipes and overflowing sewage. At its best, private equity can be a means of providing growth capital and supportive business expertise to small and growing businesses. In practice, however, the worst has been seen more often than the best.

> This description of private equity presents a puzzle. If the tactic of loading companies up with debt which often results in them failing is so destructive, shouldn't investors recognise this and charge a higher price for making those loans? The limited evidence available suggests they don't: junk bonds sponsored by private equity firms have tended to underperform relative to similar bonds.[6]

The band played on

The pace of dealmaking slowed in the 1990s as the junk bond market shrank and the failure of many earlier transactions became evident. But the 'irrational exuberance', in Alan Greenspan's famous phrase, of the later 1990s spilled over into the market for corporate control; the 'new economy' boom and bust excited markets. The century ended with some of the largest – and worst – deals in corporate history.

But, even after the 2008 Global Financial Crisis, the band played on. In 2016 the man for whom deals 'were an art form' was elected president of the United States. During the campaign Trump said he would nominate Carl Icahn as Treasury Secretary, having previously floated the name of Jack Welch. 'We made wonderful deals together,' Trump said on hearing of Welch's death.[7] (In the event, Trump made the safer appointment of Goldman Sachs alumnus Steve Mnuchin to the Treasury post.) Trump was not specific about the 'wonderful deals' he had made with Welch, the poster child of the era of shareholder value. And 'irrational exuberance' and 'wonderful deals' ended in the destruction of some of the greatest businesses of the twentieth century.

21

NOT A PRETTY PICTURE

We must dare to be great; and we must realize that
greatness is the fruit of toil and sacrifice and high courage.[1]
Theodore Roosevelt's address at the opening of the
gubernatorial campaign, New York City, 5 October 1898

Trump Tower is not the high spot of New York's architecture,
but it does represent a tangible legacy from the man for whom
'deals were an art form'. It is difficult to be as positive about
many of the deals described in the previous chapter. 'I do it to
do it' might be a better, and sufficient, description of an activity
which, taken as a whole, created little, if any, value.

Dare to be great

The commercial success of Trump's ghostwritten autobiography – the book topped *The New York Times* best-seller list for
three months – suggests that dealmaking skills, real or claimed,
are more widely admired than the political and administrative
abilities required to manage large organisations. Takeovers, especially hostile ones, have a natural dramatic structure. There are
moves, countermoves and a decisive climax. These have obvious
news value and propel the leaders who engage in them on to the
front pages. *Barbarians at the Gate*, the account of the battle for
RJR Nabisco by Bryan Burrough and John Helyar, reads like a
fast-paced thriller. No one has ever said that of Sloan's *My Years
at General Motors*.

The newsworthiness of the deal further personalised the

CEO role. 'The art of the deal' allowed many executives to lay claim to the heroic status attached to the founders of businesses. And since these executives could dispense much patronage, armies of advisers were anxious to collude in this flattery. The M&A business is now substantially driven by managerial egos and the fees it generates for bankers, lawyers and consultants. Mergers and acquisitions have always been part of corporate activity – but today finance professionals actually use the phrase 'corporate activity' to *describe* mergers and acquisitions, as though such deals were the primary purpose of corporations.

A central skill of investment bankers is the ability to cultivate and maintain a contact list that ensures that they will be called on when the transaction is envisaged. The effective 'rainmaker' who does not merely facilitate deals but also initiates them is valued and sought after not just by investment banks but by the lawyers and accountants who specialise in financial transactions. And is correspondingly rewarded.

The finance sector, and its associated legal and accounting advisers, is rewarded for making a transaction happen, not for the commercial success of that transaction. The 'advice' expensively provided is not primarily about the merits of the deal, but principally about how to get the deal done. Bruce Wasserstein, architect of KKR's takeover of RJR Nabisco, was the doyen of Wall Street M&A advisers for more than two decades before his death in 2009. Wasserstein became known as 'bid-em-up Bruce' for his role in encouraging his clients to pay whatever was necessary to get the deal done. The 'dare to be great' speech with which he massaged the egos of corporate executives became famous. While the businesses concerned paid his fees, his real client was the ambitious executive teams.

They appreciated his support in expanding their empire, even if their successors were often less enthusiastic. The two largest mergers in history (by value) both occurred in 2000; one between the American internet company AOL and Time Warner, the other involving the British phone company Vodafone and the German Mannesmann, the latter a long-established engineering business that had won a licence to operate a mobile telecoms network. Both mergers proved to be disasters of titanic proportions.

The photographs of Steve Case (AOL) and Gerald Levin (Time Warner) high-fiving each other and of Chris Gent (Vodafone) and Klaus Esser (Mannesmann) grinning like Cheshire cats as they announce their respective deals should be compulsory viewing for every acquisitive chief executive. Jeff Bewkes, who became Time Warner CEO in 2008, described Levin's deal as 'the biggest mistake in corporate history'.[2] Time Warner paid $183 billion for a business that proved to be virtually worthless. In 2008 Time Warner divested what was left of AOL (not much). The relic was later acquired for some reason or other by Verizon. Time Warner itself was bought by AT&T, in another attempt to obtain the imagined synergies of combining content with delivery. That fresh deal was finally consummated in 2018, setting a new record for adviser fees.[3]

In March 2000, immediately following the closing of the Mannesmann transaction, Vodafone shares peaked at over £5, making the company much the most valuable on the London Stock Exchange. Three years earlier, these shares had been worth around 70p. And as I write this in 2024, they are again worth around 69p. 'Advisers' walked away from both those epochal transactions with hundreds of millions in fees.[4]

But these salutary stories have done little to diminish the lure of the deal. More recently, consultants McKinsey explained why the pandemic year of 2021 saw a record volume of large corporate transactions: they described 'corporate leaders who found new reserves of time and attention by dialling in to meetings, rather than racing for planes'.[5] These titans kept dialling in, and resumed racing for planes; dealmaking has now become seen as a central skill of the chief executive.

Lunch with Jack Nicklaus

I am embarrassed to record that for several years I would use the

2000 acquisition of National Westminster Bank by Royal Bank of Scotland (RBS) as a prime example of a value-adding merger. And for a time it *was* value-adding; NatWest had been badly managed and was lumbered with bureaucratic overhead ripe for elimination. But the outcome was hubris at RBS. Bad lending, poor risk control and finally a disastrous further acquisition of the Dutch bank ABN AMRO followed. In a textbook illustration of the winner's curse, RBS and Barclays competed to complete the purchase of ABN AMRO; with hindsight (or with minimal foresight), the prize for the successful bidder was bankruptcy. RBS won the deal and the prize.

I remember sitting in disbelief in July 2007 as Sir Fred Goodwin (as he had become in 2004 and ceased to be after 2012) waxed lyrical over lunch on the merits of the about-to-be-completed ABN AMRO deal. By then it was obvious to me – and certainly should have been obvious to anyone with any knowledge of the industry – that the banking sector was headed for crisis. Bear Stearns would be rescued in March of the following year and the decisive collapse of Lehman would follow in September. A year after that lunch RBS warned the government that within hours its ATMs would be forced to stop issuing cash. The Bank of England responded with unlimited credit lines. This emergency support was followed by a taxpayer-funded injection which gave the British government a majority stake in the bank – which ironically has now rebranded itself as NatWest.

But Andrea Orcel of Merrill Lynch was reportedly paid a personal £12 million bonus, specifically for his 'advisory' role in the takeover of ABN AMRO by Royal Bank of Scotland. Orcel's bonus was part of an estimated £150 million RBS paid in fees associated with the fatal deal. Mr Orcel would later tell a parliamentary select committee that 'If we'd known [then] what we know today, we would have advised them not to proceed.'[6]

I had timidly remained quiet since I knew that Goodwin, nicknamed 'Fred the Shred', was known for his hostile reaction to opinions he did not wish to hear. But then I was only taking advantage of a free lunch rather than earning a £12 million bonus. And the conversation that day may have been inhibited by the presence of some of the sporting celebrities with which Goodwin surrounded himself. I suspect Jack Nicklaus was more interested in par values than credit default swaps. But Johnny Cameron, head of RBS investment banking, should not have been. ABN AMRO had exposure to almost \$1 billion of the Abacus and Timberwolf securities described in Chapter 1 – securities that subsequently became virtually worthless. 'It's around this time that I became clearer on what CDOs [Collaterised Debt Obligations] were,' Cameron subsequently explained.[7] According to reports, Goodwin had favoured Orcel and Merrill over John Cryan of UBS, a previous adviser. 'There is stuff in here we can't even value,' Cryan had said. 'Stop being such a bean counter' was Goodwin's response.[8]

Fred Goodwin was not the only successful regional banker whose aspiration to become a titan of international finance was frustrated by the global financial crisis. Goodwin's ambition for RBS was replicated by executives of several German *Landesbanken*, the partially publicly owned state banks which play a major role in financing German industry. *The Big Short* features traders making fun of the naïvety of German bankers; after the 2008 crisis most *Landesbanken* required state bailouts and the largest and most ambitious, Dusseldorf-based WestLB, collapsed following its own losses on US securities.

The economic impact of M&A

Before Warburgs broke the sleepy City club open, there had been too little competitive pressure on management; before Clore began identifying underpriced assets, too many resources had been used inefficiently. Although the opening of the market for corporate control represented a rude awakening, it helped shareholders nudge executives to run their businesses more effectively. But the managers have had the last laugh: the M&A process now overwhelmingly benefits executives, not shareholders. The Mannesmann transaction was consummated by the payment of large 'appreciation bonuses' to the retiring executives of the acquired company. Members of the Mannesmann board were prosecuted for the payment of what appeared to some to be bribes; litigation was settled when the beneficiaries agreed to donate much of their reward to charity.[9] It is unlikely that a similar case against directors would have made progress in Britain or the United States.

Stories of failure such as AOL Time Warner are extreme only in their scale: the general conclusion of the mini-industry analysing mergers and acquisitions is that overall the activity destroys value. This is not necessarily because of the winner's curse which fell on RBS: while bidders often pay too much, the overpayment is just a transfer of wealth from the shareholders of the acquiring company to the shareholders of the acquired company, minus the transaction costs. The important economic question is whether the composite company adds more value than its constituent parts did or could.

Systematic evaluation of merger performance is not easy. 'Event studies' estimate the impact news has on the price of a stock. (These were the kind of analyses Goldman Sachs commissioned to show that investors were indifferent to revelations of malpractice.) A slight variant of this technique is often used to measure the effect of the announcement and consummation of a deal. But to believe that the immediate response of the stock market to a merger is a good measure of the value it adds demands an extraordinary and unjustified faith in the efficient market hypothesis and the ability of 'the market' to assess correctly within days benefits that will be created only over years – or decades.

A better approach looks at the effects of the transaction on the output and costs of the combined business over a longer period. The problem here is the construction of a counterfactual – what would have happened in the absence of the merger? This seems easy in the extreme cases. Almost nothing could have been worse for Time Warner than the AOL transaction. (One would need to imagine Gerald Levin standing under the shower tearing up two hundred billion dollar bills, which would have been around a third of all US currency in circulation at the time.[10]) But the valuations of both Vodafone and Mannesmann, inflated in 2000 by the new economy bubble, would have collapsed even in the absence of the foolish transaction.

And even for successful deals, the counterfactual is not obvious. Disney's acquisition of Pixar, a pioneer of computerised animation developed by Steve Jobs, and Google's purchase of Android, which was developing an alternative to iOS for mobile devices, worked well for all the companies involved. But if Disney and Google had not engaged in these transactions, Disney would probably have still found it necessary to go digital and Google probably would have developed a mobile operating system. There are many different kinds of effective commercial arrangements between market and hierarchy. Would in-house solutions have been better or worse? We cannot know. But it is hard to avoid the general conclusion that managers would do better to focus on building, rather than acquiring, a great business.

What did it have to do with doing business?

Tourists in London know Harrods and Selfridges as the city's iconic department stores. Gordon Selfridge was an American who had begun his career as a stock boy in Marshall Field, the famous Chicago department store. After rising in the business and marrying an heiress, he retired to Britain and saw an opportunity at the then unfashionable Marble Arch end of Oxford Street, London's premier shopping location. The palatial building he erected there cost him £400,000 – perhaps £50 million at current prices.

Selfridge himself gambled extravagantly and died penniless. Lewis's, another department store group (not to be confused with the John Lewis Partnership chain) acquired Selfridges and was in turn acquired by Clore's Sears. The Lewis's group was put into administration in 1991 and Selfridges was in due course bought by Philip Green, owner of that Monaco yacht, and subsequently by Galen Weston, a British Canadian businessman. On Weston's death in 2021, ownership passed to a joint venture between a Thai store group and an Austrian developer of department stores; in 2023 the Austrian shareholder ran into financial difficulty, and at the moment of writing the Thai Chirathivat family are in exclusive control of the Oxford Street icon.

In the early 1980s, two men vied for control of the even more spectacular Knightsbridge building occupied by Harrods. 'Tiny' Rowland operated mostly in Africa and his activities had earlier been denounced in the House of Commons as 'the unacceptable face of capitalism' by then prime minister Edward Heath. Rowland lost the bidding war to the Egyptian Mohamed Al Fayed, best known as the father of Dodi, whose romantic attachment to Diana Princess of Wales ended tragically when both died in that Paris car crash. Fayed eventually sold the store to the Sovereign Wealth Fund of the State of Qatar, which owns it today.

Trophy assets – Selfridges, Manchester City, *Salvator Mundi* – have a growing and international appeal. Should we indulge this vanity, or see it as part of the 'unacceptable face of capitalism'? The frequent changes in ownership went more or less unnoticed by Selfridges' customers and the store's equally committed personnel. Harrods shoppers would certainly have seen the 'shrine to Diana and Dodi' (now removed) and the Egyptian kitsch that Fayed imposed in the store, but there was little change in the luxurious merchandise.

Oreo cookies are an American icon. The product was introduced in 1912 by the National Biscuit company (Nabisco). Today annual sales worldwide exceed $40 billion.[11] Oreos continued to be a Nabisco product until the merger which created RJR Nabisco in 1985. Three years later came the KKR takeover of RJR Nabisco. In 2000 the cookie division was sold to another tobacco company, Philip Morris, and incorporated into that company's Kraft subsidiary. In 2007 Philip Morris (now renamed Altria) divested Kraft, and in 2012 Kraft in turn divested the division which bakes Oreos into a new company, Mondelez.

The biscuit filling has undergone minor changes and the top pattern has been redesigned, but otherwise America's favourite cookie has evolved little over the century. Only the ownership of the brand has changed. Repeatedly. 'What did it have to do with doing business?', Bryan Burrough and John Helyar asked in the final sentence of their study of the KKR transaction, referring to the changes in corporate structure. It is an appropriate note on which to end this chapter.

22

THE FALL OF THE ICONS

When people say I changed the culture of Boeing, that
was the intent, so it's run like a business rather than a great
engineering firm. It is a great engineering firm, but people
invest in a company because they want to make money.
                    Harry Stonecipher, CEO of Boeing, 2004[1]

ICI was formed in 1926 by the merger of Brunner Mond, Nobel
Industries, United Alkali and British Dyestuffs. The architect of
the merger was Alfred Mond, a businessman who had also been
a member of parliament for twenty years and briefly a cabinet
minister. The company's imposing head office overlooking the
Thames (now converted into luxury flats) was adorned with
statues of the great chemists of the ages. I recall entering that
building in the 1980s with the same sense of awe that accompanied a visit to the Houses of Parliament only a few hundred
yards away.

ICI's long-standing business purpose was described in the
company's 1987 annual report:

ICI aims to be the world's leading chemical company,
serving customers internationally through the innovative and responsible application of chemistry and related
science. Through achievement of our aim, we will enhance
the wealth and well-being of our shareholders, our employees, our customers and the communities which we serve
and in which we operate.[2]

Those applications changed as technology and consumer needs evolved. In the early years of ICI, explosives and dyestuffs declined and fertilisers and petrochemicals took their place. In the post-war era, pharmacology opened a new frontier.

ICI's pharmaceutical business succeeded through the calibre of its people and the farsightedness of its strategy. ICI was then one of a relatively small number of important British companies with a reputation for valuing intellect, which enabled them to attract outstanding graduates. The most important recruit proved to be a young chemistry lecturer named James Black, who discovered beta-blockers, the first effective anti-hypertensive drug. The board of ICI accepted sustained losses in pharmaceuticals in the conviction that drugs would eventually provide future sales and profit growth. Only after two decades was this belief vindicated by the commercialisation of Black's discovery.

Successful institutions may grow fat and lazy, which ICI did. Perceiving a need for change, in 1982 the board made the unexpected appointment of John Harvey-Jones, a former naval officer, as chief executive. Harvey-Jones gave a jolt to a complacent culture. But his years were to be the beginning of ICI's path from national institution in the 1980s to ordinary company in the 1990s to oblivion in the following decade.

In 1991 Lord Hanson's eponymous conglomerate bought a 3 per cent stake in ICI. Lobbying of politicians and investment institutions saw off the threat of takeover, which was probably never real. But the company was, for the first time, answerable to the City and beholden to its investment bankers. A team from S. G. Warburg, led by John Mayo, came up with a scheme for hiving off the pharmaceutical business (now the Zeneca in AstraZeneca) at an elevated price/earnings ratio. ICI's strategy of using the cash flow from mature chemical businesses to finance the development of innovative new ones came to an end. In 1994 the mission had become 'to maximise value for our shareholders by focusing on businesses where we have market leadership, a technological edge and a world competitive cost base'.[3] Of course, a company with that objective would not have established a pharmaceutical division, far less nurtured it through years of losses.

Black left ICI not long after the successful launch of beta-blockers and joined another British pharmaceutical company, SmithKline, where he discovered Tagamet, an anti-ulcer medication. This breakthrough led Glaxo, a smaller company, to refocus its research and the outcome was Zantac, a similar therapy which became for a time the world's best-selling drug. Directly and indirectly, Black probably created more shareholder value than any other person in Britain.

I interviewed Black to discuss his departure from ICI. He told me:

> I used to tell my colleagues [at ICI] that if they wanted to make money, there were many easier ways to do it than drug research. How wrong could I have been! In business as in science, it seems that you are often most successful in achieving something when you are trying to do something else. I think of it as the principle of 'obliquity'.

In that exchange, Black gave me inspiration – and a title – for my 2010 book *Obliquity*.

In 1996 Tony Blair, the dynamic young leader of the Labour opposition, talked of a 'stakeholder society', and I was asked to talk at a conference of the Confederation of British Industry on what Blair's thinking might imply for business. I used the transition in ICI's statements to illustrate how the shareholder value movement had brought change – and not, I argued, for the better. The company's subsequent fortunes somewhat mirrored those of Tony Blair. Certainly its share price did. The stock market initially received ICI's restatement of purpose well, and in the spring of

1997, as voters swept Blair to power, investors swept the ICI stock price to an all-time high. And then a steady decline followed. After the disposal of Zeneca, ICI was left with its historic cyclical and slow-growing heavy chemical businesses. A new management team and its advisers devised an all too common 1990s business strategy: to sell off boring bits to fund exciting acquisitions. But, like other companies, ICI found it easier to overpay for new businesses than to make rewarding disposals of old ones. Burdened with debt and finding growth elusive, the stock price was only a fraction of what it had been a decade earlier. What remained of Britain's leading industrial company of the twentieth century was acquired in 2007 by the Dutch company AkzoNobel. Blair resigned the premiership in the same year.

Lights out

Chapter 6 described the state-promoted 'rationalisation' movements of the 1920s (which led to the formation of ICI) and the 1960s. This latter phase of consolidation was led by a newly established agency, the Industrial Reorganisation Corporation (IRC). Under the IRC the electrical flagship was to be GEC, which under the assertive but cerebral Arnold Weinstock was the smallest but best managed of the three major British firms in the industry. GEC duly acquired AEI and English Electric. Over the next two decades GEC and ICI were the two largest industrial companies in Britain.

Weinstock was famous for his emphasis on tight financial control. While GEC was able to secure substantial improvements in efficiency, the company was criticised for eschewing the new frontiers of information technology in favour of a focus on relatively 'soft' and mainly public sector customers in fields such as defence and telecommunications. Weinstock retired in 1996 after more than thirty years as chief executive. His successor was the industrialist George Simpson, who recruited a new finance director: John Mayo, the investment banker who had advised ICI and then joined Zeneca.

Under Mayo's influence, this company also began a strategy of disposing of its traditional businesses and buying new ones. The defence business was sold to British Aerospace. The proceeds of that sale, along with GEC's existing cash pile and large additional borrowings, were used to acquire ludicrously overpriced companies in the midst of the 1999 New Economy bubble. In 2001, the company having collapsed under its unmanageable debt burden, Mayo and Simpson were forced out and the shares became almost worthless.[4] Much of what was left was sold to the Swedish firm Ericsson and a residue survived as Telent. Telent was a strange company – a small trading business with the legacy of the huge GEC pension fund attached.

Britain's GEC should be clearly distinguished from America's General Electric (GE). The American company was for long the poster child of the shareholder value movement. While the term 'shareholder value' would not appear in GE's annual reports until the 1990s, the emphasis on the stock price was clear, as was the strategy of focusing on activities in which the company held, or could rapidly establish, market leadership. Welch soon acquired the nickname 'neutron Jack' after the neutron bomb, which is designed to kill people but not damage property.

GE was aggressive in earnings management, pleasing Wall Street with a record of smoothly increasing quarterly results. This achievement was facilitated by the growth of its financial services business, which soon became a major part of its revenues and earnings. GE was one of several large manufacturing corporations which had become accustomed to providing credit – the automobile giants had always provided such facilities to their retailers and became involved in financing their customers as well. The stellar credit ratings accorded to these sound manufacturing businesses were essential to the profitability of the financial transactions. In the 1980s GE expanded these subsidiary financial activities and offered other financial products, many unrelated to the traditional businesses of the company.

Between 1980 and 2000 the rise in GE's stock price – from $2 to $50 – was remarkable. Then Welch retired in 2001 and the story began to fall apart. The rise of financial services had masked issues in the core activities of aerospace, healthcare and plastics. When the global financial crisis hit in 2008, the business was ill prepared. Like other financial institutions, it needed to rely on support from the Federal Reserve System as credit markets dried up. A string of acquisitions and disposals did nothing to improve the situation. Even after the financial activities had been sold or closed, a legacy of underprovision on long-term insurance business continued to haunt the company. With the share price down 80% from its level at Welch's retirement, America's former leading conglomerate broke itself up into separate businesses for each of the three (historic) core activities.

Retail giants

Sears Roebuck was for long an American legend. The company's catalogue business, established at the end of the nineteenth century, brought the variety and convenience of the department store to millions across rural states. People who could previously access only the limited range and high prices of the general merchant were able to enjoy the range of goods formerly available only to inhabitants of big cities. In 1973 the company celebrated its success by building a new head office in Chicago, at the time the tallest building in the world.

Pride went before a fall. In 1962 Sam Walton opened the first Walmart store in Arkansas. In 1972 his company listed on the New York Stock Exchange and expanded across America. Faced with this competition, Sears decided that the appropriate response was not to try to match Walmart's global sourcing and its innovative use of developing information technology to manage inventory but to diversify into financial services. In 1981 the company bought a stockbroker (Dean Witter) and a real estate brokerage (Coldwell Banker) and announced plans for a major expansion of its Allstate Insurance subsidiary. In 1985 Sears launched a credit card, Discover. In the meantime, Walmart overtook Sears to become the largest retailer in the world.

A fresh strategic restructuring of Sears in 1993 led to the disposal of many of these financial activities: by the end of the century all had been divested. The Sears Tower was sold.[5] Sears discontinued its catalogue and closed its warehousing and fulfilment operations. In 1995 Amazon.com was founded. Someone else would build 'the everything store' for the twenty-first century.

The Sears department store chain continued its gentle decline, but the final phase borders on farce. In 2005 hedge fund manager Eddie Lampert, whose yacht featured in Chapter 1, took over the bankrupt Kmart and merged it with Sears. Lampert not only believes in the theory of the firm as a nexus of contracts but applies it with enthusiasm to business, wheeling physical and financial assets in a bewildering series of deals, and requiring units within stores to compete and trade with each other. Fresh investment was minimal. Sales fell steadily, and in 2018 Sears finally entered bankruptcy. Lampert then bid successfully to regain control of the failed firm from the federal judge. The chain, which once operated 3,500 stores, now has thirteen.

If Sears was America's iconic retailer of the twentieth century, in Britain that title belonged to Marks & Spencer. Michael Marks had operated a market stall in Leeds in 1884 under the strapline 'don't ask the price, it's a penny.' The business expanded under his son Simon into a chain of stores that was represented in every high street and dominated the supply of everyday clothing. Simon had befriended Israel Sieff at Manchester Grammar School, and each married the other's sister. The Marks and Sieff families controlled the executive management of the company for most of the twentieth century and regarded themselves as custodians of the corporate culture.

'Marks and Sparks' achieved a deferential affection among British middle-class consumers rivalled only by Queen Elizabeth, the NHS and the BBC. Employees were also devoted; if you fitted the disciplined corporate culture – and many recruits did not – you might stay for life, and senior management roles were almost entirely filled from within the company. M&S had a long-standing relationship with Prudential, Britain's leading insurance company, which was a major shareholder and financed much of the development of the company's property portfolio.

In 1988 Richard Greenbury, who had joined the company at the age of sixteen, became chief executive, and he subsequently became chairman. His accession marked the end of effective family influence on the company. Marks & Spencer's dominance of its established market was a constraint on growth, although an expansion into food had proved successful. Greenbury set an ambitious target of £1 billion in annual profit by the end of the decade. Prices were edged up, costs were trimmed and suppliers squeezed. In 1997 the profit target was achieved, and the share price reached £6.

And then sales fell off a cliff. The mantra of 'quality, service, value' had been quietly dropped from the beginning of the company's annual report, and customers had begun to notice the effect in the stores. A new management team induced some recovery – after a decade profit reached £1 billion again and the shares regained that £6 figure – but only briefly. Competition in the high street was intense and there Marks & Spencer was now only one store among many – too many – as online retailing grew steadily. By 2020 the share price had fallen to £1.

Boeing

In 1967 the first Boeing 737 entered service with Lufthansa. It is the most successful civil airliner in history, with more than 10,000 planes sold. The 747 jumbo jet appeared the following year. And in the same year Bill Allen, who had been CEO of the company since 1945, retired.

Jet planes had been deployed by both British and German air forces in 1944. But civilian jets were still almost a decade away when Allen took over at Boeing. The first civil jet aircraft were British de Havilland Comets, but after two crashes (caused by metal fatigue which had not then been properly understood) market leadership migrated to the United States. Although Allen was a lawyer, he declared an intention that he and his colleagues should 'eat, breathe and sleep the world of aeronautics'.[6] The 737 and 747 were the products of that culture. When a non-executive director asked for a financial evaluation of the 747 project, he was reportedly told that such an evaluation had been prepared but no one could remember the result.[7]

The commercial success of these aircraft established Boeing as the world's premier civil aircraft manufacturer, eclipsing its US rivals Lockheed and McDonnell Douglas. By the 1990s only the European Airbus consortium offered effective competition, and in 1997 Boeing acquired McDonnell Douglas. While legally the merger was a takeover by Boeing, culturally it was a takeover by McDonnell Douglas, whose cost-cutting executive Harry Stonecipher became president of the merged company. In May 2001 a plane carried the Boeing senior executive team to the company's new corporate headquarters, a location not disclosed until the plane had taken off. Would it be Denver, or Dallas, or Chicago? It was Chicago. As the then CEO Phil Condit – a Boeing lifer – explained, 'When the headquarters is located in proximity to a principal business – as ours was in Seattle – the corporate center is inevitably drawn into day-to-day business operations.'[8] Evidently a danger to be avoided.

Boeing boosted its stock price by aggressive share repurchases. In 1982 US regulations were relaxed to allow a company to buy its own shares, a practice previously viewed with well-founded suspicion. (The UK had introduced similar provisions permitting buybacks a year earlier.) It is not a coincidence that this change coincided with the rapid growth in the use of stock options to enhance executive remuneration/incentivise management to maximise shareholder value. Share repurchases tend to increase stock prices, and if the number of shares is reduced, earnings per share are arithmetically higher. If management pay is largely based on stock price or earnings per share, then buybacks help fill management's, as well as selling shareholders', pockets. In the ten years after 2010, Boeing spent $43 billion buying back its own shares.[9]

In 2011 Boeing recognised a competitive threat from a new generation of Airbus planes equipped with much more fuel-efficient engines. Rather than design a new plane to compete with Airbus, Boeing reconfigured the fifty-year-old 737 to accommodate the new engines. The decision saved money and time – there was no need to interrupt the share buybacks – and was popular with airlines, since minimal retraining was thought to be required for pilots accustomed to flying 737 aircraft. For a time the strategy worked. Boeing's stock price rose steadily, reaching over $400 in March 2019.

But the redesigned plane was the 737 MAX. And when these aircraft began to fall out of the sky, so did Boeing's stock price. A congressional report in September 2020 found that 'The MAX crashes were not the result of a singular failure, technical mistake, or mismanaged event. They were the horrific culmination of a series of faulty technical assumptions by Boeing's engineers, a lack of transparency on the part of Boeing's management, and grossly insufficient oversight by the FAA.'[10]

Twenty years ago I wrote in the *Financial Times* that I had once told students that Boeing was an exception to the rule that industry dominance was necessarily transient and liable to change. But I confessed then that I had changed my mind. Boeing's change in philosophy – from 'complete commitment to a market and market leadership' to a focus on shareholder value – left the field open to Airbus to pull ahead.[11] And so it proved: since 2019 Airbus has consistently outsold Boeing, and the A320 is about to overtake Boeing's 737 as the best-selling aircraft in history.[12]

Smaller Blue

In the 1970s and 1980s IBM was the most valuable company in the world. The Watsons, the father and son who had helped build the world's leading computer business, had stressed the corporation's 'basic beliefs': 'respect for the individual, superlative customer service, and technological excellence'.[13] And few companies had a corporate ethos as distinctive or bureaucratic or successful as that of IBM. 'IBMers' were a recognisable type, and the company had never laid off an employee.

In the 1990s, overtaken by the personal computer revolution it had played a part in launching, 'Big Blue' went into sharp decline; soon Microsoft, the fledgling company from which IBM had bought an operating system, overtook it in profits and market capitalisation. Yet the IBM whose very survival had once seemed in doubt recovered, reinventing itself as a provider of information technology services to the large customers who had once depended on its mainframes.[14]

Despite an embarrassing 'values jam' in 2003, in which all employees were invited to help update the corporation's basic beliefs, the new core mission became clear: to enhance the stock price, and with it senior executive remuneration. This was to be achieved by relentless cost-cutting, principally by offshoring customer support to less expensive locations such as Brazil and India. The target was earnings of $20 per share by 2015. But revenues were falling as customers deserted; earnings peaked at $15 per share in 2015 and declined thereafter. And so did the stock price, which had peaked at over $200 in 2013 but then fell steadily, despite the expenditure of almost $100 billion on share repurchases. The disappointing tenure of Ginni Rometty, one of the first women to head a major US corporation, ended in 2020.

Neither Boeing nor IBM are the companies they once were – their era of unrivalled dominance of their industries is long gone. Nor are they the companies they might have been – the markets for civil aircraft and information technology were, and still are, growing and full of attractive opportunities, and Boeing and IBM took advantage of few of them. But perhaps, given the scale of buybacks they were able to afford even as their businesses experienced relative decline, Boeing and IBM maximised shareholder value. We will never know. And nor did, or do, Phil Condit or Ginni Rometty.

Deutsche Bank

This book could be filled with depressing accounts of the evolution of businesses in the financial sector, and I have intentionally refrained from telling most of them, but in a chapter entitled 'The Fall of the Icons' one case cries out for attention. For a century Deutsche Bank was the leading financial institution in Germany, perhaps in continental Europe. It was a universal bank, selling a full range of financial services to its retail customers and providing investment banking facilities together with both loan and equity funding to its corporate clients. In 1989 its chief executive, Alfred Herrhausen, was murdered by the Red Army Faction, which regarded him and the institution he led as the epitome of finance capitalism.

Following a series of shootings and bombings, Andreas Baader, Ulrike Meinhof and other leaders of the 'Red Army Faction' (now known to have been supported by the Stasi, East Germany's ubiquitous secret police) were arrested and imprisoned. In 1977 the faction kidnapped Hanns Martin Schleyer, president of the German employers' federation. The German government refused to negotiate for the release of the Red Army Faction's leaders.

Four Palestinian hijackers – there was significant cooperation between the German and Palestinian terrorists of the time – took over a Lufthansa jet, which was flown to Somalia; German security forces (which had bungled a rescue operation for the athletes kidnapped during the 1972 Olympics) successfully stormed the plane as it sat on the ground in Mogadishu and freed the passengers. Schleyer was then murdered by his kidnappers; the imprisoned militants were found dead in jail, probably by suicide. The 'Red Army Faction' continued activities, notably the assassination of Herrhausen, but gradually declined and in the 1990s faded away altogether. The armed struggle against capitalism in the Global North, which began with the Bolshevik revolution of 1917, was at an end.

Three decades after Herrhausen's killing, Deutsche Bank might still epitomise finance capitalism but a very different version of finance capitalism. The bank was primarily an ethically and prudentially questionable US hedge fund. For some years Deutsche Bank was the only major institution willing to lend to Donald Trump. Most banks blacklisted Trump during his serial defaults, but different divisions of Deutsche financed him even after he had stiffed others. The bank would probably have failed had financial markets not assumed – reasonably – that neither the German government nor the European Central Bank would allow an institution named Deutsche Bank, which still retained many deposit-taking branches across Germany, to collapse.

From the 1980s European banks were caught up in the wave of financialisation, with regional bankers keen to leave deposit-taking, home mortgages and small business lending behind and become international financiers. In an early series of disasters the French Crédit Lyonnais courted Hollywood and ended up as inadvertent owner of the Metro-Goldwyn-Mayer film studio. Deutsche Bank bought the staid London investment bank Morgan Grenfell and then the scandal-ridden US Bankers Trust. These acquisitions became the basis of a rapid expansion of a wide range of speculative lending and trading activities. In 2002 CEO Josef Ackermann announced a target of a 25 per cent return on equity, a target that would be achieved in 2005. But, in a familiar pattern, never again.

When the global financial crisis broke in 2007–8, Deutsche Bank had substantial exposure to the subprime mortgage market through its acquisition of MortgageIT; but at the same time Greg Lippmann, head of Deutsche's securities trading, was promoting 'the Big Short'. (Lippmann would be played by Ryan Gosling in *The Big Short*, the film version of Michael Lewis's account of the trades.) The bank would subsequently pay fines and compensation of over $7 billion for its actions at that time. The dominance of the investment banking arm was recognised by the promotion of its head, Anshu Jain (who spoke no German), to be chief executive of the whole concern.

But the scandals kept coming: LIBOR fixing; money launder-ing for Russian oligarchs; funding notorious sex offender Jeffrey Epstein; facilitating Iranian sanctions-busting; heavy exposure to weak eurozone economies. Britain's softly spoken Finan-cial Conduct Authority noted 'a culture of generating profits without proper regard to the integrity of the market'.[15] Amer-ica's Department of Justice more bluntly described 'pervasive fraud and collusion'.[16] In 2016 the International Monetary Fund labelled the bank 'the most important net contributor to systemic risks in the global banking system'.[17] A long-running dispute in which Congress sought to subpoena details of Trump's financial dealings from the bank petered out in 2023, when the Republi-cans gained control of the House of Representatives.

In 2018 the supervisory board finally appointed Christian Sewing, who had begun his lifetime in the bank as an officer in a retail branch, as CEO. Sewing began the process of winding down investment banking activities. But the shares, which had been worth €70 when Ackermann announced the 25 per cent return on equity target, had lost most of their value. In 2023 they traded below €10.

23

THE FINANCE CURSE

I would rather see finance less proud and industry more content.

Winston Churchill (1925)[1]

ICI and the General Electric companies (American GE and British GEC); Sears Roebuck and Marks & Spencer. The details are very different, but there is a common theme to the narratives. Each company experienced a twentieth-century history characterised by exceptional success. But between 1981, when Welch took control at GE, and 2005, when Lampert took control of Sears, a new approach to business developed. Managers like Sir Denys Henderson and Simon Marks, Alfred Sloan and Owen Young, had seen themselves as public figures with associated responsibilities to a wide range of constituencies. The generation that succeeded them had a narrower conception of their role. A successor generation of corporate executives paid close attention to quarterly reporting and the stock price.

The results of this greater emphasis on financial metrics were initially pleasing to the stock market. ICI shares reached an all-time peak in 1997. GEC shares achieved their highest-ever value in 2000. GE stock rose from a little over $2 at the beginning of Welch's tenure to almost $50 at its end. Sears stock doubled in value in the two years after diversification into financial services was announced in 1981 and continued to rise steadily for almost two decades thereafter. After a setback in 2002–3 Wall Street greeted Lampert's arrival at Sears with enthusiasm, and the stock price peaked in 2007. And London celebrated Greenbury's billion-pound profit with that £6 share valuation in 1999.

If you had invested in these household names in the 1990s era of shareholder value, you would have lost all your money in GEC and Sears and most of it in the others. Your least bad bet would have been on ICI, whose shares were acquired in 2007 for about one-third of their price a decade earlier. Both GE and Marks and Spencer subsequently lost more than 80 per cent of their peak value. Almost all financial advisers would have agreed in 1995 that a portfolio that consisted of these stocks was a safe and conservative, if unexciting, choice. And that advice would have been spectacularly wrong.

In every case, the activities that analysts and investment bankers applauded diverted attention from the central issues facing the operating businesses, and this diversion was the source of the long-term decline of the corporation. All of these companies cut costs and raised prices in ways that reduced the long-term attractiveness of the business, as exemplified by Marks & Spencer. They engaged in earnings management, effectively borrowing money from the future to enhance reported profits now. As in GE's financial services businesses. They adopted accounting practices that accelerated the recognition of profits that might be earned in the future but often were not. As at Enron. They were enthusiastic dealmakers, engaging in activities that excited the investment community but which rarely created value and frequently destroyed it. As exemplified by GE. In each case, the short-term boost to the share price was followed by a lengthy – or, in the case of GEC, abrupt – decline. The leaks from the pipes became a flood.

Some companies were able to resist the demands of shareholder value. Notable among these stand-outs were some of the leading producers of fast-moving consumer goods (FMCG): corporations such as Proctor and Gamble, Colgate–Palmolive, Coca-Cola, Unilever and Nestlé. The culture of these businesses was and still is dominated by marketing people, for whom responsiveness to the needs of customers is a preoccupation.

And that responsiveness is the key to the durability of these companies.

The private equity house 3G burst on the US scene in 2010 with the acquisition of Burger King. These financiers asserted that more value could be derived from these FMCG businesses through 'zero-based budgeting': a cost-cutting drive. And of course, more value *could* be derived from these activities – for a time. Until their pipes began to leak. The two principal businesses of 3G were brewing and food. A series of acquisitions made AB Inbev the world's largest brewer, owning brands from Stella to Anheuser-Busch to Corona. In an uncharacteristic misstep, Warren Buffett backed 3G's creation of the Kraft Heinz conglomerate, uniting macaroni cheese with baked beans.

It would prove an unappealing combination. In 2017 Kraft Heinz announced a bid for Anglo-Dutch Unilever, a deal quickly stymied by opposition from the European company's board, institutional investors and the British government. By then it was already becoming clear that Kraft Heinz sales were suffering under the new management. Market share fell first, and then so did profits. Today Buffett's investment has lost half its value. The rise of AB Inbev was slower than that of Kraft Heinz, and so was the decline, but the shape of the trajectory was similar.

Halifax – my part in its downfall

I cannot leave the subject of financial services or end this chapter without reference to my own part in the fall of an icon. The Halifax Building Society was formed in 1853 in the Yorkshire town of that name. It was one of several similar British institutions established by prudent local small traders to help each other and fellow members of their community to buy houses. Halifax proved to be the most successful of these organisations and expanded throughout Britain. Under two long-serving general managers (CEOs), Enoch Hill and Raymond Potter, the Society both stimulated and benefited from the growth of owner-occupation in UK housing.

When I joined the board in 1991, 'the Halifax' was the largest mortgage lender in the world. Its head office was still in the modest Yorkshire town of Halifax (which it now dominated), and most of the people who worked there had been born and brought up locally. The organisation – like the Marks & Spencer of that time – was a powerful illustration of how strong systems and culture can enable otherwise unremarkable people to do remarkable things. The contrast with Oxford University, which relied on the services of remarkable people but as an organisation was remarkable only for its ineptitude, was striking. I could not help noticing that even the most junior teller in the Halifax would use the pronoun 'we' in talking about the organisation, while in Oxford even the vice-chancellor would talk about 'the University' as though it were an organisation over which he had little real influence – which was perhaps true.

In common with other building societies, the Halifax retained the mutual structure which followed from its cooperative origins. The board was, in principle, elected by its customer members. In practice, as is also true in businesses with shareholders and a conventional corporate structure, the board was self-perpetuating. Legislation in 1986 brought change. Reflecting the deregulatory spirit of the age, it loosened restrictions on the activities building societies could undertake and allowed them to incorporate.

A side effect of the shareholder value doctrine was a widely held view in business and political circles that the shareholder corporation was the only appropriate vehicle for large businesses. The effects of this belief were seen across the economy. State utilities were privatised with shares offered on the stock exchange – the privatisation of British Telecom and the water and electricity industries are still seen as signature measures of the Thatcher era. Activities traditionally carried out by partnerships – such as investment banking, law firms and estate agencies – became public or private corporations. The Goldman Sachs partnership became Goldman Sachs Inc. in 1999, opening the way for Arkansas Teacher to take a stake. Mutual and cooperative businesses – common in some areas of financial services and in retailing – were either transformed in capital markets or overtaken in product markets. One consequence, which certainly did not go unnoticed, was the windfall profits received by favoured recipients of shares in state enterprises and those who happened to be partners in or members of the organisations at the time of corporate transition.

But few of these changes worked out well for the businesses. And this would certainly be true of the 1986 Building Societies Act. In 1989 Abbey National Building Society handed out shares to its members and became a company listed on the London Stock Exchange. That obliged Halifax to consider its status. My engagement with the Society began when I wrote a paper refuting the predictable conclusion of investment bankers that similar conversion was essential to the development of the business. I knew that those who, like me, were sceptical of the dealmakers' viewpoint had won the argument at a meeting of board members, executives and advisers when a speaker began 'what convinced me of the urgent necessity for conversion ...' and the director sitting next to me finished the sentence with the sotto voce comment '... was the prospect of a fat fee'.

But the issue was only deferred. In April 1994 I awoke and turned on the radio to hear that Lloyds Bank had offered to distribute £1.8 billion to the members of the Cheltenham & Gloucester Building Society if they voted to approve its takeover by the bank. I knew that morning that the days of mutual building societies were over. Few members could resist such an offer, and no board could reasonably recommend that they should. In 1997 I was re-elected to the Halifax Building Society board with more than 2 million votes. (I believe that this is more than any other candidate has received in a British election. This may have had less to do with my personal popularity than the promise of free shares with a total value of £20 billion – probably the largest giveaway in world history. Or the largest bribe, depending on your point of view.)

The only large building society not to convert in the 1990s was the Nationwide, at the time probably the weakest of the majors. In 1998 the board of the society successfully fought off a proposal to float the business, persuading the members to reject the plan by the narrowest of margins (50.7 per cent against 49.3 per cent in favour).[2] Nationwide also implemented measures to prevent new customers from benefiting from a windfall. Abbey struggled with losses following diversification into new business areas and was acquired in 2004 by the Spanish bank Santander. Two other former building societies – Bradford & Bingley and Northern Rock – failed in the 2008 financial crisis and were nationalised. In 2013 Lloyds closed the entire Cheltenham and Gloucester business.

Many people now see conversion as the nemesis of the Halifax, and there is truth in that. But I trace the beginning of decline to an earlier board decision to establish Treasury, which managed day-to-day cash balances, as a profit centre in its own right. Earnings would be enhanced by successful speculation in money markets.

For an economist who taught that profit could be sustained only as a result of competitive advantage, this diversification raised a simple question. And some businessmen on the board, accustomed to a world in which profit is earned only by meeting customer needs, encountered the same difficulty. Trading in short-term money market instruments is essentially a zero-sum game – one party's gain is another's loss. So what was the source of the trading profits that not just our company, but every company in this business, claimed to make? The experienced bankers would shake their heads at this naïvety. If they deigned to answer the question at all, it was to say that our traders were uniquely perceptive and prescient, although it was difficult to remain convinced of that once you had met them. This fantasy that sustainable earnings could be achieved through sleight of hand was dispelled by the 2008 crisis – and was a principal cause of it.

But for many executives the most exciting and potentially

profitable diversification was into corporate lending. In 2001 – after I had left the board – this ambition led to a merger with Bank of Scotland. The new entity, HBOS, retained the Bank's impressive Edinburgh head office but the reality was a takeover by Halifax. (I might have supported the plan – senior executives and some board members were hell-bent on sidelining the organisation's unparalleled retail franchise in favour of developing commercial banking, and if there was to be such a development it was better to merge with a business with some of the necessary skills.)

But the acquired bank did not have enough of these skills for the expansion it undertook. Peter Cummings, the Bank of Scotland employee who became head of corporate banking for the merged group, was eventually fined £500,000 by the Financial Services Authority (FSA) for his reckless conduct – the only such penalty imposed on a British banker after the global financial crisis. In the years that followed, HBOS and its Scottish rival the Royal Bank of Scotland (then led by (Sir) Fred Goodwin) competed vigorously to attract poor-quality commercial business spurned by other lenders. Particular low points were the dismissal in 2004 of the head of regulatory risk, allegedly for drawing attention to the dangers of an aggressive sales culture, and the egregious corruption of the Reading branch. Commercial customers there were induced to take on loans they could not afford and then to obtain the services of bogus 'turn-around experts' associated with the bank staff. Businesses were destroyed: both the bank and its customers incurred substantial losses. The saga culminated in an eleven-year jail sentence for one manager and long terms of imprisonment for five others. But it did not end there.[3] More than a decade later, claims for compensation remain unresolved.

In 2008 both Scottish banks collapsed under the impact of bad loans and inept money market trading. They were bailed out by the Bank of England, which provided liquidity, and the government, which took equity stakes. Prime Minister Gordon Brown personally brokered the takeover of HBOS by Lloyds Bank, which had weathered the crisis relatively successfully because it had maintained a focus on retail business. Lloyds thus snatched defeat from the jaws of victory.

> A report on the HBOS failure by the regulators the Prudential Regulation Authority (PRA) and Financial Conduct Authority (FCA) took the view that the board 'lacked non-executives with sufficient experience and knowledge of banking, particularly corporate banking'.[4] While this may have been true, I believe it is also important to have non-executives with little experience and knowledge of an industry who can offer challenge to the conventional wisdom of those who have spent their working lives in it. Diversity of thought and perspective is necessary, and not the same as the appointment of 'diverse persons'.

Halifax is now only a trading name of the Lloyds Banking Group, which has slowly recovered from its disastrous acquisition – the UK government stake in the combined entity was finally sold at a small profit in 2017. One hundred and fifty years creating an astonishingly successful mortgage and savings business in Halifax ended in a single decade as a failing bank. And those windfall shares, which were worth £7.32 at flotation in 1997 and reached £8.34 upon the merger with Bank of Scotland, now represent 0.6 of a share in Lloyds.[5] This equates to a value of 25p in 2023, a loss of more than 95 per cent of the value of the shares at conversion twenty-five years ago.

The finance curse is the elevation of the achievement of financial metrics over satisfaction of the needs of stakeholders – a priority that has often worked to the long-run detriment of all stakeholders, including shareholders themselves. Neither quarterly earnings management nor merger and acquisition activity is a source of sustainable competitive advantage. And it is sustainable competitive advantage – which all the companies described in this chapter and the preceding one once enjoyed – that is the basis of business success. And the only long-term source of shareholder value.

PART 6

THE CORPORATION IN THE TWENTY-FIRST CENTURY

At the beginning of the twenty-first century, the 'nexus of contracts' and 'shareholder value' approaches held sway in many business schools and consultancies and influenced both discussion and decisions in corporate boardrooms. But there were other schools of thought. Some observers and participants recognised that the successful twenty-first-century corporation is necessarily a cooperative community. That technical progress and business development is based on deploying collective intelligence in innovative combinations of capabilities. That few twenty-first-century corporations can be run as traditional hierarchies. That stakeholders mostly deal with each other in the context of ongoing relationships rather than formal contracts. And that, at least in the Global North, the age of the integrated manufacturing corporation is over.

24

COMBINATIONS AND CAPABILITIES

Maybe we are burning some of the social capital we built up
in this phase where we are all working remote.

Satya Nadella, CEO, Microsoft,
interview with *The New York Times*, 14 May 2020[1]

I do think for a business like ours, which is an innovative,
collaborative apprenticeship culture, this [working from
home] is not ideal for us. And it's not a new normal. It's an
aberration that we're going to correct as soon as possible.

David Solomon, CEO of Goldman Sachs,
Conference talk, 24 February 2021[2]

I know I'm not alone in missing the hum of activity, the
energy, creativity and collaboration of our in-person
meetings and the sense of community we've all built …
For all that we've been able to achieve while many of
us have been separated, the truth is that there has been
something essential missing from this past year: each other

Tim Cook, CEO of Apple, email to employees, 27 May 2021[3]

As I began writing this book in 2020, the Covid-19 pandemic
had paralysed societies through lockdowns. Almost half of the
working population, and a larger proportion of high earners,
were 'working from home'.[4] Before the eighteenth century,
most of the population had been 'working from home'. Then
the Industrial Revolution had taken them into factories, where
they operated the machines and worked the materials provided

by their capitalist employer.

Through the nineteenth and twentieth centuries, the work-place defined the business. If you asked someone where they worked, they might respond either with a location or the name of an organisation. They worked at 'the Rouge' or at Ford, in 'the City' or for Barclays Bank. They went to Dearborn because that was where the assembly line was. They went to the office or branch of the bank because that was where they kept the books and met the customers. The lockdowns of the pandemic illustrated how modern business had changed. The employees of Microsoft, Goldman Sachs and Apple didn't need the physical attributes of the office. They could take their equipment home.

Perhaps they didn't need to be in the office every day. But, as Tim Cook explained, they did need each other. They needed to learn from each other; they needed to trust each other; they needed to access the collective knowledge and intelligence of the organisation. The rather costly offices in which they met were costly mainly because they were in locations such as Seattle, lower Manhattan and Cupertino; places which were popular with people who were rather like them, both professionally and socially, even if many of them worked for other organisations. Geography still matters.

Clusters

I am writing this while sitting on a chair made in Meda. Meda is a town north of Milan, on the way to Lake Como. As you enter the town, a multiplicity of signs advertise and point the way to the showrooms and workshops of the numerous manufacturers of furniture – especially sofas. If you buy a high-end sofa in a fancy New York or London store, it is quite likely that it is made in Meda.

Meda's sofa cluster is characteristic of the industry of north-ern Italy. Drive on a little further north and you reach the town of Como, which specialises in the design and production of silk ties. Drive south into Tuscany and you will come to Prato, for long the principal source of Italian tailored suits. That town has recently become a favoured destination for Chinese (often illegal) immigrants, and today you may buy clothing truthfully labelled 'Made in Italy' but never touched by an Italian hand.[5] The Chinese have travelled thousands of miles to access the collective intelligence accumulated in Prato, which has been a centre of the garment industry for almost a thousand years.

A century ago Alfred Marshall described the effective combination of cooperation and competition in the cluster. 'Great are the advantages', he wrote,

> which people following the same skilled trade get from near neighbourhood to one another. The mysteries of the trade become no mysteries; but are as it were in the air, and children learn many of them unconsciously. Good work is rightly appreciated, inventions and improvements in machinery, in processes and the general organization of the business have their merits promptly discussed; if one man starts a new idea it is taken up by others and combined with suggestions of their own; and thus becomes the source of yet more new ideas.[6]

In Marshall's world, the initial location of the cluster was the result of resource availability. He observed:

> Staffordshire makes many kinds of pottery, all the materials of which are imported from a long distance; but she has cheap coal and excellent clay for making the heavy 'seggars' or boxes in which the pottery is placed while being fired. Straw plaiting has its chief home in Bedfordshire, where straw has just the right proportion of silex to give strength without brittleness; and Buckinghamshire beeches have afforded the material for the Wycombe chairmaking. The Sheffield cutlery trade is due chiefly to the excellent grit of which its grindstones are made.[7]

In Silicon Valley also, 'the mysteries of the trade are in the air'. The resources of Silicon Valley are intellectual rather than material, but the outcomes were similar. To elaborate the clichéd joke, Silicon Valley is not the product of its reserves of silicon, but its concentration of collective intelligence. Around San Francisco, you find Stanford University and the now autonomous Stanford Research Institute. The reputation of the university attracts faculty and students. The density of people with original technical ideas attracts others who enjoy discussing them and business-oriented individuals and organisations interested in supporting them. The success of some of the businesses that emerge from these processes ensures that there are wealthy angels with both the expertise and financial capability to back new ventures. And it helps that the Bay Area is a nice place to live – the weather and access to sea and mountains helped persuade people to locate there in the first place, and the location now benefits from the proximity of other smart people and the social and cultural facilities that cater to them. And that is why you will find Apple, Facebook, Google, Tesla and many others within a 20-mile radius. If there is any negative to this virtuous circle, it is the unaffordable house prices which result. Stanford, not straw, was the initiating resource for the cluster, but the outcome was similar.

The persistence of history

The collective intelligence created by local competition and cooperation means that, as in Staffordshire and Sheffield, the cluster may remain, possibly in attenuated form, after the original rationale for concentration has disappeared. You can still tour the Wedgwood factory in Stoke-on-Trent, named after Josiah Wedgwood, the eighteenth-century founder (and early campaigner for the abolition of slavery), although production of the many cheaper ceramics that carry the Wedgwood label is outsourced from Staffordshire to Asia. Sheffield is still known for cutlery, but long-established Sheffield brand names such as Arthur Price and Richardson are attached to knives made elsewhere – in a similar manner to the ceramic cluster. In the twentieth century, furniture by Parker Knoll of Wycombe would become an icon of Art Deco interiors. (The Parker family, skilled in straw chairmaking, recognised the potential of German Willi Knoll's springing techniques.) Sadly (perhaps) there is now no demand for straw-plaited hats from Bedfordshire.

This persistence of history is as true of services as of man-ufacturing. Britain's historic dominance of the sea is long gone, but London remains a centre for maritime insurance and ship-broking. In the 1920s film-makers flocked to southern California to take advantage of the light; that factor is no longer relevant, but the name Hollywood is still synonymous with the global film industry. And today the most powerful clusters of all are the financial centres of lower Manhattan and the City of London, the places where more than two centuries ago brokers gathered under the Buttonwood tree and exchanged gossip in Jonathan's coffee house.

Land is an important factor of production today – but in a manner very different from that which James Anderson and David Ricardo had described. Land is valuable because it offers proximity to commercially valuable collective intelligence, as in Silicon Valley and Wall Street. Or to the contacts and ideas of smart people, in Cambridge, England, or Cambridge, Massa-chusetts. Or to all these things, as in Mayfair and on the Upper East Side.

Marshall had recognised the tension between the com-petitive and the cooperative character of the cluster. 'Social forces here co-operate with economic,' he wrote. 'There are often strong friendships between employers and employed; but neither side likes to feel that in case of any disagreeable incident happening between them, they must go on rubbing against one another: both sides like to be able easily to break off old associ-ations should they become irksome.'[8]

This recombination routinely occurs in Silicon Valley. Fric-tion within Nobel laureate William Shockley's company led to a seminal event in the Valley's history when the 'traitorous eight', led by Robert Noyce, quit to establish Fairchild Semiconductor. Only three years later a similar 'disagreeable incident' within Fairchild resulted in Noyce leaving, with Gordon Moore and Andy Grove, to form Intel. Hesitate to hire a traitor lest he betray you!

Entrepreneurship

The modern firm is a community, rather than an office or a factory. It is defined not by its plant and machinery but by its capabilities. The successful business is characterised by the distinctive nature of its collection of capabilities and the match between these capabilities and the needs of its customers – and other stakeholders.

The claim that George W. Bush told Tony Blair that 'the problem with the French is that they don't have a word for entrepreneur' is, sadly, apocryphal.[9] But the French origin of the word is revealing – from *entre*, 'between', and *preneur*, 'taker'. The original meaning of the term 'entrepreneur' describes a coordinator, someone who brings things together. Modern American usage represents the entrepreneur as a heroic individual who sees what others do not and takes bold risks. While there is some truth in such a description, it understates the essential cooperative and evolutionary character of economic progress. The business founders we identify as legendary modern entrepreneurs – Jeff Bezos, Bill Gates, Steve Jobs – rode the wave of evolving collective intelligence. Online retailing and the personal computer revolution would have happened even if Bezos, Gates and Jobs had never been born. These developments occurred around the end of the twentieth century because all the necessary pieces of collective knowledge and collective intelligence were then developed. These individuals and their associates pieced together relevant capabilities. When innovative firms succeed, as Amazon, Microsoft and Apple did but most new firms do not, it is because of the distinctive character of the capabilities of their organisation and the combinations they put together.

Lionel Messi, uniquely talented, scores goals only because of the many complementary capabilities that support him. The Great Western Railway, among Victorian England's greatest engineering achievements, came about because the Bristol merchants who conceived it hired the brilliant young Isambard Kingdom Brunel. But also because – less famously but no less importantly – they recruited Charles Saunders, who conceived and promoted the idea of raising capital in small amounts from families like the Brontës.

Thomas Carlyle did not offer to teach a parrot to repeat 'supply and demand', although it is often attributed to him (it was actually Irving Fisher, quoting a wit he does not identify, as we saw in Chapter 11). But he did call economics 'the dismal science'. Joseph Schumpeter may have been the most colourful practitioner of the subject. Briefly finance minister of Austria, Schumpeter supposedly claimed an aspiration to be the world's greatest economist, greatest horseman and greatest lover, adding laconically that the horsemanship was not going well.[10] Having emigrated to the US in anticipation of Nazi hegemony in Europe, he took up a professorship at Harvard. The title of his most famous work, *Capitalism, Socialism and Democracy*, is similarly immodest.[11]

Carlyle's denigration of economics as 'the dismal science' appeared in a pamphlet advocating the restoration of slavery or similar subjugation of the black population of the West Indies, a project that he correctly believed most practitioners of the dismal science would oppose.[12] Carlyle famously wrote that 'The History of the World is but the Biography of great men.'[13] A central theme of this book is that The History of Business is not the Biography of Great Men, although many business biographers and especially autobiographers might seek to tell us otherwise. Economists might reasonably reciprocate Carlyle's contempt. His contemporary, the novelist Samuel Butler, wrote that 'It was very good of God to let Carlyle and Mrs Carlyle marry one another and so make only two people miserable instead of four.'[14]

Schumpeter is especially remembered for his discussion of entrepreneurship, and for his coinage of the vivid term 'creative destruction'. According to Schumpeter, 'it is the carrying out of new combinations that constitutes the entrepreneur'.[15]

The successful entrepreneur turns individual or collective knowledge into a product innovation or novel business process. Combination is therefore the crucial element in entrepreneurship. Silicon Valley's most famous and successful business incubator is called Y Combinator – facilitating fresh and productive combinations of capabilities is the essence of what it does.

And 'the gale of creative destruction' is the process by which the repeated application of such entrepreneurship leads to economic progress.

Capabilities

Edith Penrose, distinctly less flamboyant than the Austrian horseman, was an American economist at Johns Hopkins University. With her husband, who was also an economist, she was active in the defence of their colleague Owen Lattimore, falsely accused in the McCarthy era of being a Soviet spy. The incident led the Penroses to leave the US, and after some international travel she obtained a teaching post at the School of Oriental and African Studies (SOAS) in London. Penrose's magnum opus, published in 1959, took as its subject the appropriate boundaries of the firm and the limits to its growth.[16]

For Penrose, the firm was defined not by the assets it owned or the contracts it made but by its capabilities and its ability to deploy those capabilities in productive services: 'All the evidence we have indicates that the growth of firms is connected with the attempts of a particular group of people to do something.'[17] Perhaps that seems obvious. But her emphasis on 'the group' recognises the centrally cooperative nature of business activity, and her identification of purpose – 'to do something' – establishes its problem-related focus. This recognition of the essentially social nature of the firm differentiated Penrose's thinking from the mainstream economic thinking of Coase, Jensen and Meckling, and Williamson and Hart, which was firmly rooted in individualism.

The collaboration between Sam Mussabini and Harold Abrahams was 'the attempt of a particular group of people with distinct but complementary skills to do something' – to run faster. The merchants of Bristol perceived an opportunity to travel to London in only two hours and assembled a collection of technical and organisational capabilities to achieve that goal. Apple was similarly 'the attempt of a particular group of people to do something'. The group initially comprised Jobs and Wozniak (and Ronald Wayne, who sold back his 10 per cent stake in the company for $800 and now reportedly lives in a mobile home). But Apple would not have been the business we recognise without the complementary business capabilities of financier Mike Markkula. And Apple would not have been the corporation we recognise without the film director Ridley Scott (whose 1984 ad for the Macintosh is rated the best advertisement of all time by Advertising Age) and the marketing capabilities of the now reviled John Sculley.[18] And Apple would not have been the business we recognise without the flair of designer Jony Ive and the steady hand of Tim Cook and and … Apple was a Real Business: not, to use the words of Easterbrook and Fischel, a 'legal fiction' but the ongoing 'attempt of a particular group of people to do something'. People who had often fractious relationships with each other – but who mostly managed to achieve the necessary balance of competition and cooperation that is key to economic progress.

Attention to capabilities focuses on a question elided by the description of the firm as a production function and in the 'markets and hierarchies' and 'structure-conduct-performance' frameworks traditionally favoured by economists. Why do firms in broadly the same industry differ from each other? Why did Apple succeed and Blackberry fail? Why did Microsoft and Apple both succeed, and both then fail, and both then succeed again?

And perhaps the question of why firms facing the same 'five forces' (in Michael Porter's framing) differ *could* be elided when each ironworks or automobile plant was recognisably similar to every other ironworks or automobile plant. When market structure, common to all firms in the industry, determined conduct and thus performance. That was why Ansoff, pioneering the field of business strategy in the 1960s, claimed to find little help from the economic theory of the time.

But by the late twentieth century the multiple ironworks and the several automobile plants had ceased to be the focal points of economic activity. Students of business were interested in the rivalry between Apple and Microsoft, Google and Facebook; between Nucor (which came to market via an IPO in 1972 and is now America's largest steel producer) and US Steel; between Southwest Airlines and Delta; between Tesla and General Motors. And it seems obvious that the explanations were to be found in the different capabilities and combinations of capabilities of these organisations. Each firm in these pairs was engaged in what was broadly the same industry as the other, but each had approached that industry in a different way. (Curiously, although all modern technology firms operate from office blocks, their campuses have distinct characters.)

Yet Penrose's work made little impact on subsequent theorising in economics – her name is not to be found in the index of standard economics texts such as those of Meyer, Milgrom and Roberts or of Tirole. But ideas similar to those of Penrose did have influence in business schools. The resource-based theory of strategy, as it has become known, was developed by Jay Barney and Birger Wernerfelt. The task of corporate strategy is to match the capabilities of the firm to its external environment. The boundaries of the firm are defined less by transaction costs than by the appropriate scope of the firm's capabilities. That is why Apple sells music but not groceries but Amazon sells both. David Teece, an economist known for his work on innovation, added an emphasis on *dynamic* capabilities – the capacity of the firm to adapt its capabilities over time and in response to change.[19] Only through the progressive evolution of the firm's collective intelligence could it respond to the changing needs of its marketplaces.

The resource-based view of strategy was widely popularised in the 'core competencies' approach of C. K. Prahalad and Gary Hamel. But application of this thinking has been made problematic by the absence of sharp criteria for distinguishing core and other competencies, an imprecision that allows wishful thinking. Core competencies became pretty much whatever the senior management of the corporation wanted them to be, and 'focusing on core competencies' a prelude to dealmaking.

The critical resource for a firm lies in its distinctive capabilities or distinctive combinations of capabilities. Apple's smartphone offered a pocket computer with an astonishing range of functions. But without the facility that enabled app developers to provide constant additions to that range of functions and the capability to repeatedly innovate new, well-designed products, Apple Inc. could have commanded only a fraction of the product sales or of the market capitalisation it has achieved. Distinctive capabilities, such as those of Apple's design team, are those characteristics of a firm that cannot be replicated by competitors or can only be replicated with great difficulty, even after these competitors realise the benefits which they yield for the originating company. That distinctiveness could never be true of the hierarchical organisation run in the spirit of Frederick Taylor or as a cascade of principal–agent problems formulated by reference to the solutions in leading economic journals.

25

A LETTER FROM ARNOLD WEINSTOCK

If you want to hire great people and have them stay, you have to be run by ideas, not hierarchy. The best ideas have to win.

Steve Jobs, 2010[1]

Early commercial organisations, such as the East India Company and the Great Western Railway, were organised in rigid hierarchies, even expecting their staff to wear uniforms of their rank.[2] The large manufacturing plants of the twentieth century with their assembly lines similarly exemplified hierarchy. In Frederick Taylor's steelworks, and also in Sloan's General Motors, production workers were not encouraged to think for themselves and were responsible only for doing what they were told.

The term 'bureaucracy' is now pejorative. But when the sociologist Max Weber popularised the term a century ago, his purpose was to contrast the rational structure of authority within the modern organisation with systems based on traditional styles of leadership such as that of Louis XIV, or the charismatic authority of Napoleon Bonaparte.

Frederick the Great made Prussia the greatest military power on the continent of Europe through a highly disciplined hierarchy based on rigid class distinctions, building an army that he led personally. Orders were handed down through a chain of command, and dissent was not contemplated, far less tolerated. In an essay Frederick put forward the notion of 'enlightened absolutism' in the functioning of the state. His theory was that the ruler did not govern by divine right but led, mirroring the 'social contract' theories of Hobbes and Rousseau, with the consent of and for the benefit of the ruled. This was the foundation of the Prussian state bureaucracy, in its time an effective governing machine.

Weber was the son of a Prussian civil servant. Observing the efficiency with which Prussia's military had unified Germany and with which Prussia's civil service was beginning to govern it, he viewed bureaucracy as the modern approach to the management of large organisations, including businesses. Weber observed the further extension of hierarchy: 'It is the peculiarity of the modern entrepreneur that he sees himself as the first official of the enterprise in the very same way in which the ruler of the specifically modern bureaucratic state [Frederick II of Prussia] spoke of himself as "the first servant" of the state. The idea that the bureau activities of the state are intrinsically different in character from the management of private offices is a continental European notion,' Weber wrote, 'and, by way of contrast, is totally foreign to the American way.'[3] Weber denied the validity of this public/private distinction. His list of historical examples of developed large bureaucracies comprised New Kingdom Egypt, Diocletian's Rome, the Catholic Church, China's Ming and Qing dynasties, twentieth-century European states, and *the large modern capitalist enterprise.*[4]

Weber's list of the defining characteristics of bureaucracy – the command structure, the identification of roles and responsibilities, the impersonality, the value of technical expertise – remains influential. And the military origins of this conception of hierarchy are evident.

The bureaucratic hierarchy

Hierarchy requires chains of authority, responsibility and accountability. These three words are often used more or less interchangeably, but it is useful to distinguish them. Authority is the power to make decisions, including the power to delegate that authority. Responsibility is the duty to consider the consequences of these decisions: a teacher is responsible to his or her students, but accountable to the head teacher or school governors. Account-ability is the process by which the consequences of decisions – including the decision to delegate authority – are evaluated.

In 1944 the US Office for Strategic Services (the precursor of the CIA) produced a 'sabotage manual' to advise people in occupied European states on how to obstruct the conduct of the war with little personal risk.[5] Suggestions included:

- Insist on doing everything through 'channels'. Never permit short-cuts to be taken in order to expedite decisions.
- Make 'speeches'. Talk as frequently as possible, and at great length. Illustrate your 'points' by long anecdotes and accounts of personal experiences.
- When possible, refer all matters to committees, for 'further study and consideration'. Attempt to make the committee as large as possible – never less than five.
- Bring up irrelevant issues as frequently as possible.
- Haggle over precise wordings of communications, minutes, resolutions.
- Refer back to matters decided upon at the last meeting and attempt to re-open the question of the advisability of that decision.
- Advocate 'caution'. Be 'reasonable' and urge your fellow-conferees to be 'reasonable' and avoid haste which might result in embarrassments or difficulties later on.

Many readers, especially academic ones, will be able to testify to the continuing effectiveness of these techniques even in peacetime.

Many people find the exercise of authority attractive but the obligations of responsibility and accountability burdensome. So they seek to accrete authority but shed responsibility and avoid accountability. People lower or higher in the hierarchy attempt to resist these natural human tendencies. The tensions arising from these processes, and their consequences, account for much of why bureaucracy has a bad reputation.

The most common device for diluting or deflecting responsibility is the meeting – better still, the committee. If many people are associated with a decision, then no one is really responsible for it. The form and the check box are common means of creating the appearance of accountability without the reality. Meetings, form-filling and box-ticking take time – often a lot of time. That is how bureaucracies come to waste resources while making bad decisions.

Arnold Weinstock was one of the most effective British managers of his generation. In 1968 his company, GEC, acquired its sclerotic rival, English Electric. On completing the takeover, Weinstock observed that 'administrative, commercial and similar overheads are uniformly too high throughout the group'. A letter he wrote to the executives of English Electric set out a new approach:

> Our philosophy of personal responsibility makes it completely unnecessary for you to spend time at meetings of subsidiary boards or of standing committees. Therefore all standing committees are by this direction disbanded and subsidiary boards will not need to meet again except perhaps for statutory purposes once a year. If you wish to confer with colleagues by all means do so; even set up again any committee you and the other members feel you must have for the good of the business. But remember that you will be held personally accountable for any decision taken affecting your operating unit and also remember that you are not obliged to join any such gathering. Incidentally, on this matter of personal responsibility, prior permission

from HQ is required for any proposal to employ management consultants.[6]

This letter should be on the desks of business executives but especially those of university administrators, hospital managers and civil servants. Meetings, both formal and informal, are essential to cooperative activity. But there is an important difference between the meeting that occurs to exchange information and agree on actions and the meeting that takes place because it is 2:30pm on the second Wednesday of the month and it is your turn to serve on the Procrastination Committee.

Military discipline no more

By the end of the twentieth century it was no longer possible even to run an army in the hierarchical style of Frederick's Prussia. Perhaps it never had been. The exemplar of the destructive power of pure hierarchy was the notorious Charge of the Light Brigade by Lord Cardigan's men at Balaclava in 1854. 'Theirs not to make reply, theirs not to reason why,' the poet Tennyson observed, a sentiment later reiterated less eloquently by Frederick Taylor. The French commander in Crimea, Bousquet, took a different view. 'C'est magnifique, mais ce n'est pas la guerre.'[7]

The most powerful military machine the world had ever seen was defeated in Vietnam and Afghanistan and failed in Iraq. It is hard to imagine a more compelling demonstration that the scale of an organisation is less important than the match between the capabilities of the organisation and the problems it is asked to solve.

And the most powerful manufacturing organisation the world had ever seen was defeated in global automobile markets when Asian businesses successfully challenged the hegemony of General Motors. Toyota famously introduced the Andon cord, which enabled individual workers to stop the production line if they identified a defect or a problem. The system restored personal initiative and encouraged workers to take pride in their work.

Consumers noticed the difference in the quality of the product. Today most tasks that consist only of following the instructions of superiors are better done by robots and computers.

In 1974 Frederick Thayer, professor of public administration at the University of Pittsburgh, published *An End to Hierarchy*. Thayer's provocative style limited the application of his argument even within the field of public administration. But more recently the phrase has won wide traction among managers. In 2010 Bill George, professor of management practice at Harvard Business School, wrote: 'The hierarchical model simply doesn't work anymore. The craftsman–apprentice model has been replaced by learning organizations, filled with knowledge workers who don't respond to "top down" leadership.'[8] Somewhat paradoxically, George concluded that the solution was a new style of leadership. (Popular business writing makes frequent reference to leadership because it is addressed to those who are or aspire to be leaders.)

But the death of hierarchy is easily exaggerated. Formal structures are required to coordinate a complex organisation or to create a complex artefact such as an Airbus. Every production process and every organisation requires *some* hierarchy because people need to know when decisions have been made and what they are. When the management consultants Coopers and Lybrand prepared a report on the governance structures of the University of Oxford, they observed that 'in many cases, University decisions are not specifically made at all, they just emerge and it is often difficult to tell at what point a discussion becomes a decision.'[9] This was my own experience also, and it is a recipe for muddle and frustration. The requirement for a degree of clarity about the outcome of the decision-making process is relevant whatever the nature of that process.

Ratifying hierarchy

Nominally, the king of England has powers similar to those of Frederick the Great. He is the commander in chief of Britain's armed forces and may declare war or peace. He can appoint the prime minister, the archbishop of Canterbury, and the regius professor of history at Oxford University. He can veto laws, pardon criminals, prorogue Parliament, award or remove honours. He can appoint or remove the governor-general of Australia, who has similar powers in that country. He is also king of Scotland, Canada, the Caribbean island of St Lucia and several other states.

But everyone knows that the king does not really have these powers. (Well, not quite everyone – I recall a heated conversation in an Arizona diner many years ago with locals who were appalled by my craven submission to Queen Elizabeth's hereditary authority.) The king ratifies decisions that have already been made by appropriate groups of other people – members of parliament, senior clergy and academics and the elected governments of England, Scotland, Wales, Australia, Canada and St Lucia. I read with pleasure a notice on a patch of rough ground in St Lucia: 'No grazing of animals by order of the Queen.'

In 2019 the Conservative British government led by Boris Johnson advised the queen to prorogue (adjourn) Parliament to prevent elected members obstructing the government's plans to exit the European Union. The prorogation was quickly overturned by the Supreme Court, and Parliament resumed its sitting. The Court did not doubt that the queen had the power to prorogue but determined that the advice to prorogue was unlawful because the processes and procedures needed to justify that advice had not been properly followed. The queen was the titular head of a *ratifying hierarchy*. Her assent – which was required not just for prorogation but for all new laws – signified not that the decision was a good one, or that it was a course of action which she favoured, but that it had been the subject of appropriate consideration and consultation.

The monarch, and the position of the monarch, is unique. But an orchestra has a conductor, and a sports team has both a captain and a coach. The players do not, to any large degree, do things because they are the things the conductor, captain or coach has told them to do. The violinist follows the score; the footballer uses his talent and experience to move into position, to pass or to shoot. The music and the game would continue even if the conductor dropped his baton and the coach fell asleep. The great conductor, captain or coach will be a source of inspiration and imagination to his colleagues. But if these leaders understand their responsibilities they never assume the role of Big Boss or The Man Who Knows.

Lyndall Urwick, founding partner of British management consultants Urwick Orr, expected to be addressed as Colonel Urwick and drew heavily on his military experience. But he wrote of that experience:

> The 'proper channels, the official channels', were there and were used to confirm and to record agreement already reached by far quicker and friendlier means of communication. If an officer had to use them before that point was attained, it was rightly regarded as a confession of failure, an admission that his organisational arrangements were not supported by good personal relations.[10]

Even the military hierarchy was, in Urwick's perception, essentially a *ratifying hierarchy*.

Mediating hierarchy

Bill George was right to identify many modern corporations as 'learning organizations, filled with knowledge workers who don't respond to "top down" leadership'. But he was wrong to imply that such organisations could operate without hierarchy. The quotation from Steve Jobs with which this chapter began repays re-reading. Jobs was notorious for his tantrums and for his abuse of people. But a perfectionist, which Jobs seems to have been, is not the same as The Man Who Knows. His critique was not that his instructions had not been followed sufficiently carefully, but that the product was not good enough. His bouts of temper contributed to his inspirational style of leadership (a style of leadership that works better if you really are a genius, respected for your ideas rather than feared for your temper).

However, there are few people with the talents of Steve Jobs or Elon Musk. Andy Grove was another manager of exceptional ability, co-founding and eventually becoming CEO of Intel. Grove's 1983 book *High Output Management* deserves the cult status it achieved in Silicon Valley. In information technology businesses 'a rapid divergence develops between power based on position and power based on knowledge, which occurs because the base of knowledge that constitutes the foundation of the business changes rapidly'.[11] Grove understood clearly that the competitive advantage of Intel, and businesses like it, depended on evolving collective knowledge.

All organisations – whether they are Google or a university department of philosophy – require both managerial authority and technical expertise. The potential conflict between authority and expertise is easier to handle when organisations are small and products simple – as in the partnership between Matthew Boulton and James Watt – or where a few people with specialist skills can act as internal consultants on the rare technical issues that arise in a repetitive manufacturing process such as that of the car factory. But the tension between the manager and the professional is a particularly acute problem for organisations such as universities and hospitals, in which a large proportion of the staff are hired for their high-level specialist skills – which is why these activities are typically so badly run. The Silicon Valley start-ups that could grow into successful businesses were necessarily those few which could handle well the interaction between authority and knowledge. And the same is true of the modern military.

Margaret Blair and Lynn Stout describe the modern business as a *mediating hierarchy*:

A public corporation is a team of people who enter into a complex agreement to work together for their mutual gain.

Participants … yield control over outputs and key inputs (time, intellectual skills, or financial capital) to the hierarchy. They enter into this mutual agreement in an effort to reduce wasteful shirking and rent-seeking by relegating to the internal hierarchy the right to determine the division of duties and resources in the joint enterprise. They thus agree not to specific terms or outcomes (as in a traditional 'contract'), but to participate in a process of internal goal setting and dispute resolution.[12]

I suspect many readers nodded approvingly at the passage above without recognising its radicalism, or how much it differs from the account favoured by the mainstream law and economics movement, with its nexus of contracts created to manage a cascade of principal–agent problems. That radicalism relates more to the way we *describe* business than to how it actually operates; mediating and ratifying hierarchies are the reality of most successful businesses, but it is easier for the lazy journalist to attribute such success to the all-seeing, all-knowing, CEO. Yet the caricature is influential; we should not underestimate the importance of the ways business is described for the practice of business, and the importance of both description and practice for the legitimacy of commercial activity in the broader community.

In this description, Blair and Stout do not prioritise any particular group of stakeholders. The mediating hierarchy – and ultimately its executives and board of directors – can and must 'determine the division of duties and resources in the joint enterprise'. In a corporation, the shareholders collectively have the power to change the directors or sack the executives if they do not like the division of duties and resources that has been implemented. But, especially in Delaware, that right is not easily or often exercised. In practice, unhappy shareholders sell, just as the employees have the right to leave and the customers and suppliers have the right to take their business elsewhere if they do not like the division of duties and resources. As Albert Hirschman famously observed, exit and voice are alternative

responses to organisational failure. And the modern corporation experiences both. But more often, and more powerfully,
dissatisfied stakeholders exit.

A successful management team in a business strikes a
balance with which most stakeholders are content. Investors are
satisfied with their dividend (or now more usually share price
appreciation); employees are happy with their jobs; customers
and suppliers believe they are getting a good deal. So staff turnover is low, customers and suppliers remain loyal and the share
price remains buoyant. And so does the business.

In a market economy exit may be a more important and
effective mechanism of imposing accountability – and expressing one's opinion of the quality of the decisions of the executives
of the business – than voice. But voice and exit operate in parallel. Exit is the remedy of those who feel their ideas or needs are
ignored. The voice that matters to most people in organisations
is not loud. It is the internal voice that says that people in this
organisation care about me, and care about what I do, and about
what I think. That sense of engagement does not require, and is
often inconsistent with, formal processes of consultation, such
as town hall meetings or, particularly, worker representation
on the board. A common feature of these processes is that the
people who take an active part in them are unrepresentative by
virtue of the very fact of being there. Most people have other
things to do, and hesitate to express themselves publicly; participants in consultations are often present simply because they are
particularly opinionated.

While as corporate lawyers Blair and Stout were writing
about business corporations, nothing in their description is in
any way specific to a commercial enterprise. The mediating hierarchy is descriptive of how the *faculty* of most schools, almost
all universities and the medical staff of a hospital, comprised of
articulate professionals, are organised. And a functioning sports
club or charity will need to seek a similar structure. The concept
of mediating hierarchy is relevant to almost any collective or
community activity, private or public. There are some activities

– schools and a few churches, and parts of the military – in which acknowledgement of a hierarchy is intrinsic to the nature of the enterprise. But these are the exceptions rather than the norm. Mediating hierarchy is necessary for any organisation based on collective intelligence to be cohesive and effective. An organisation based on trust and respect rather than obligation and contract.

I once attended a 'public consultation' held to seek popular views on proposed changes to telecoms regulations. As far as I could tell, almost all of the hundred or so attendees worked for telecoms companies or advised telecoms companies, or hoped to do so. I could identify only two bona fide members of the public. One had an incomprehensible grievance against his telecom supplier, which he aired frequently. The other was a pensioner, benefiting from the warm room and a cup of tea, who expressed his gratitude for the opportunity the industry provided for him to phone his grandchildren and was heartily thanked for his contribution to the proceedings.

26

THE MACNEIL RETURNS TO BARRA

Lawyers who will prepare sixty-page contracts for their
clients (because they know that businessmen can't be
trusted) will organize their own office on a scribbled piece
of notepaper that may not even be signed by anybody
because they know they can trust their partners.

Ian Macneil, 1973–4[1]

The MacNeil of Barra, forty-sixth chief of the Scottish Clan
MacNeil, was also an American legal scholar – for almost twenty
years Henry Wigmore professor of law at Northwestern University. In the 1960s he introduced the concept of the relational
contract.[2] Stewart Macaulay, sometimes described as a founder
of the 'law and society' movement – to be contrasted with the
'law and economics' movement – wrote in a similar vein.[3] Both
scholars emphasised that almost all contracts are made within a
context of continuing social and commercial relationships and
that these relationships constitute the substantive agreement.

To those lawyers for whom the firm is a nexus of contracts,
the firm's management is a matter of contract design and spec-
ification. For the economist who sees the firm as a collection of
rational individuals, management is a collection of principal–
agent problems.

For the pedant steeped in the world of law and economics, life is one contract after another, as he encounters a series
of principals and their agents. Daily he fulfils his employment
obligations before entering an agreement with Transport for
London to take him home. He is attentive to the terms and

conditions which the small print on his ticket tells him TfL will make available on demand, though the staff member he approached seemed somewhat reluctant to read them out. Having returned home to enjoy the ninety-eight years remaining on the apartment lease, with whose extensive terms he has familiarised himself, he bribes the dog to bring his slippers as he powers up his computer. He had hoped to resolve some unfinished business with a colleague using Microsoft Teams, but after the two and a half hours it takes him to read the terms and conditions under which the company permits the use of the application (according to an estimate by *PC* magazine) he decides to leave the matter till the following morning.[4] After reviewing Deliveroo's terms and conditions in anticipation of ordering a takeout meal, he is no longer hungry. It is time for bed, an opportunity to refresh himself before navigating the next day's nexus of contracts.

But real people do not – could not – operate in this way, in either their personal or their business lives. They rely on their previous experience, the seller's reputation, the personal relationships they have with the representatives of the supplier and the shared desire of company and customer to continue doing business together. Exchange is embedded in a social context, and that context determines the commercial reality.

You may be reading this text in a printed book, or an ebook, or listening to it as audio; in each case, you almost certainly have a different and lengthy agreement with a different provider. But you don't really care. The terms of the legal contract are unlikely to be of practical significance. The legal contract becomes relevant only, and even then not necessarily, when the relationship breaks down. If you don't like this book, you will put it down and exit; you may send an abusive email to me, but your lawyer will tell you that you and I have no contractual relationship. Sorry. But if you do like it and buy my other books, we have entered a relational exchange. And I hope we can develop it on a basis of trust and respect – and mutual benefit, not exclusively of a financial kind.

Northwestern University occupies an attractive campus with its own beaches on the shore of the decidedly fresh-water Lake Michigan. Barra is a small island in the Outer Hebrides of Scotland with a population of 1,000, golden sandy beaches and an airstrip usable only when the saltwater Atlantic tide is out. Barra has been described as 'the island the Reformation did not reach'; islanders are predominantly Catholic, in contrast to the stern Protestantism of the islands to the north of Barra.

Most of the population of Barra emigrated to North America in the nineteenth century. The profligate forty-first chief was forced to sell most of the property to pay his debts and ownership of the island passed to John Gordon, a main-land landowner who had done well out of investment in Caribbean slave plantations. When the forty-first MacNeil died in 1838, the chiefship passed to a cousin resident in Canada. A century later Professor Macneil's American father, the forty-fifth chief, repurchased most of the island and its derelict castle. Professor Macneil settled in Scotland after retirement and subsequently donated the land on the island to the Scottish government for the benefit of the com-munity and leased the castle for the annual rent of one bottle of whisky.[5] Macneil's subtle understanding of the nature of ownership and obligation was reflected in his actions as well as his academic writing.

Trust and respect

Cooperation – whether it is between a team of workers driving an engine, a board of directors planning a new line or many indi-vidual savers providing capital to the business – requires trust. Successful collective action requires that you believe what others tell you and that you can expect others to do what they say they will do. Trust begins in personal relations; humans are strongly predisposed to trust family members and to form friendship groups. But generalised trust – a rebuttable presumption that one can trust individuals one does not know – is necessary for complex economic products and institutions. Joseph Henrich has argued that the growth of such trust follows the development of social practices that encourage people to seek marriage partners outside their kinship groups.[6]

Polls seek to measure the extent of generalised trust in different countries, posing questions such as 'Do you find that most people can be trusted?' or 'Do you agree that you can't be too careful in dealing with strangers?'[7] Positive generalised trust is strongly correlated with per capita national income. The top performers are all the small, socially homogeneous, rich states of the Global North: Denmark, Luxembourg, Norway and Switzerland. (And New Zealand, geographically located in the South Pacific but culturally part of the Global North.) These states also report the lowest levels of corruption.[8] Larger countries with strong institutions, such as Canada, Germany and the UK, also score well on measures of generalised trust and perceived freedom from corruption. The US ranks behind these, although still far ahead of most of the Global South.

There is a striking exception to this general relationship between trust and prosperity. China is still classified as a middle-income country with income per head below the global average. But the mainland Chinese population is more likely to report that 'most people can be trusted' than respondents in Britain or the United States. This counter-intuitive finding has been the subject of considerable investigation and speculation.[9] It may be simplest to conclude that these questions simply do not have the same meaning in Confucian, authoritarian China as in Lutheran, social-democratic Sweden.

Honesty is a character trait, not a policy

Selfishness of motive, narrowness of objective and instrumentality of behaviour are corrosive of collaborative and cooperative activities such as parenthood or education or scientific research.

Some parents are selfish; some teachers are narrow in their conception of the purposes of education; some scientists select results to make claims insufficiently supported by evidence. But we are glad not to be members of those families; we avoid those classes and are reluctant to join those research groups. We are inclined to think that these behaviours make these individuals poor parents, inferior teachers and bad scientists.

We do not believe that people whose selfish, narrow and instrumental aim is to ensure that children supplement their parents' pensions when they grow old could be good parents. We observe, however, that good parents generally maintain mutually loving and supportive relationships with their children into old age. Great teachers measure themselves and are measured by others, not by their own achievements but by the achievements of their pupils. When we talk of great scientists, we admire not just what they achieved but the way they did it. We applaud Galileo's insistence on observation in the face of the authority of the Church and Barry Marshall infecting himself with bacteria in order to investigate the origins of stomach ulcers.[10]

The relationships with others essential to activities such as parenthood, education and research are valued for themselves, not just for their consequences. Most humans are good at detecting instrumentality – the false bonhomie of the used car salesman, the cynical hypocrisy of the vote-seeking politician – and are repelled by it. There is a difference between the firm that promotes the welfare of its employees because its executives care, and the firm that promotes the welfare of its employees because its finance department has calculated the net present value of reduced staff turnover. And employees can usually tell which is which.

The later Michael Jensen expressed the issue clearly if wordily:

> The application of cost-benefit analysis to one's integrity guarantees you will not be a trustworthy person (thereby reducing the workability of relationships); and, with the

exception of some minor qualifications, also ensures that you will not be a person of integrity (thereby reducing the workability of your life). Your performance, therefore, will suffer.[11]

Two centuries earlier Archbishop Whately had expressed the point more succinctly: 'Honesty may be the best policy, but he who adopts that policy is not an honest man.'[12]

Religion and the rise of capitalism

The link to religious tradition is significant. Trust is markedly higher in societies with predominantly Judaeo-Christian traditions than in countries that are predominantly Buddhist, Hindu or Muslim. The Protestant religion seems to have been particularly favourable to the development of commerce and business. Over a century ago, the sociologist Max Weber linked the Protestant ethic and the rise of capitalism in Western European societies, and his observation remains valid even as religious practice declines. If you want to live in a prosperous society in the twenty-first century, it is wise to be born into a Judaeo-Christian environment and better to be part of a historically Protestant culture than a predominantly Catholic one.

Many religions reinforce their moral teaching with the promise that the virtuous will be rewarded after death. The medieval Catholic church had undermined this doctrine by suggesting that the rich man could also pass through the eye of the needle with the aid of sufficiently generous contributions to the construction of St Peter's Basilica; the salesman–priest Johann Tetzel was so successful in propagating this theory that he provoked Martin Luther's wrath and laid the groundwork for the Protestant Reformation. The purchase of indulgences – the belief that generosity in giving wealth relieves iniquity in its acquisition – today takes only slightly different forms, as in the benevolence of the Sackler family.

The doctrine of predestination posited that honesty and hard work demonstrated one's existing membership of the

Elect rather than providing a means of earning the cash to pay the subscription. Although I was brought up in the Church of Scotland, with its strong Calvinist tradition, I learned that pre-destination was a foundational doctrine not from ministers at the kirk or from teachers at Sunday school but from reading Weber when studying economic history at university. The link between religion and success in business is not a simple, causal one but a matter of the co-evolution of religious doctrine and prevailing culture.

> 'The blessing of the LORD, it maketh rich, and he addeth no sorrow with it.'[13] This is a biblical teaching favoured by some modern televangelists, a phenomenon of the Southern US and Nigeria. Many such evangelists, such as Oral Roberts and Joel Osteen, could give personal testimony to its truth from their own experience. But the prosperity gospel is not what Weber had in mind. 'A good name is rather to be chosen than great riches.'[14] The two biblical texts were not inconsistent, but the latter was the one my Scottish Sunday school recommended.

Thus by the twentieth century 'the Protestant ethic' had become a cultural norm rather than a religious dogma. But its historic influence was central to Western Europe's Industrial Revolution – and the transformation of Scotland from a wild and impoverished frontier on the fringes of Europe to one of the most prosperous places in the world. In continental Europe, industrialisation was concentrated in the Protestant regions of countries such as Germany and the Netherlands although both states had Protestant and Catholic concentrations.

Economically successful minorities

The Pilgrim Fathers were members of an extreme and perse-cuted Protestant sect who had raised funds to establish a colony in North America, and the early European settlers who followed them there were overwhelmingly Protestant. Huguenots, Protestant refugees from Catholic France, exerted economic influence wherever they went. John Houblon, the first governor of the Bank of England (founded by the Scotsman William Patterson), was a Huguenot; his older brother was also a director of the Bank, and his younger brother succeeded him as Governor. Persecution of Protestants left France with only a tiny historically Protestant minority but that minority, which includes Bernard Arnault, France's (and Europe's) richest man, is even today disproportionately represented in French business.

The Huguenots in London (and in the Netherlands and South Africa) are an example of the economically successful minority – often an émigré group – that plays a major role in, or even dominates, commerce and finance in the countries where its members settle. This economic success often exacerbates existing envy, resentment and worse – the persecution of Jews through pogroms and ultimately the Nazi genocide is the extreme example. Other economically successful minorities include Chinese populations in many parts of South-East Asia (the huaren), Christian Lebanese in many countries, Armenians in Turkey, Koreans in the modern United States and Indians in Fiji and East Africa. After the trading community of Indian émigrés in East Africa was expelled in the 1970s, the group reproduced its economic success in Britain.

Outsiders to the established English class system – Quakers, Jews and other immigrant groups, such as Huguenots – played a disproportionate role in the Industrial Revolution and especially in its finance. Darby of Coalbrookdale was a Quaker, as were other steelmakers, such as Samuel and William Lloyd, relatives of the Lloyds of the eponymous bank. Barclays Bank was also founded by Quakers. The Quaker contribution to the chocolate industry is particularly striking – the Cadburys, Frys and Rowntrees were all Quakers. The motive may have been to promote cocoa as an alternative to alcoholic beverages. (The Cadbury and Fry businesses are now part of the US food conglomerate Mondelez and Rowntree has been absorbed into Nestlé.) Quaker

Oats was not, however, established by Quakers; the founders adopted the mark as a symbol of quality and integrity in an early example of cultural appropriation.

The doctrines of Protestant sects were individualistic, but they instilled respect for virtue in others (though mainly others with similar skin colour and traditions to themselves). Cooperation and competition can coexist only if competitors show mutual regard. Here again, the sporting analogy illustrates the point. When we talk of a good sportsperson, the word good is used in two senses. It describes both talent and morality. The good track athlete runs to win but does not trip his competitors up, even if he thinks he will get away with it. Alasdair McIntyre's influential modern exposition of Aristotelian virtue ethics consciously conflates these two senses of the word *good* – talent and morality – as we do in British English when we describe someone as 'a good sport' or enjoin participants to 'play the game'.[15] Relationships with others are important to us, and our own fulfilment is largely derived from these relationships, which are frequently both competitive and cooperative.

Where there are opportunities for mutually advantageous cooperation, businesspeople usually find ways of achieving that. The Domenico fisherman case (Chapter 14) ended in court, in large part, because of the cultural differences among the numerous parties – the WASP managers of the Alaskan canneries supervised native Alaskans and Chinese labourers from very different backgrounds, and the fishermen were recent immigrants to the US who spoke little English.

Large, idiosyncratic projects are a common source of contractual dispute because there is little prospect of establishing relational exchange. Indeed it is common practice in such cases for contractors to offer low prices in the expectation that they will profit from 'variations': once on the job, the hold-up problem will work to their advantage. Public sector contracting raises difficulties because rules are put in place to require that contracts of any size are placed only after open and public competitive tendering. For good reason: the relationship between the minister and his brother-in-law is not a good basis for public procurement. But the demand for transparency and specificity has its own substantial costs. Birmingham City Council negotiated an agreement with construction company Amey for the maintenance of the city's highways. The contract was over five thousand pages long, including two hundred pages of definitions.

Relational contracts and the law

In my *Foundations of Corporate Success*, published in 1993, I singled out Marks & Spencer as an example of the power of architecture – an irreproducible structure of commercial relationships. Suppliers such as William Baird and Nottingham Manufacturing enjoyed exclusive relationships with Marks & Spencer, and manufacturer and retailer discussed every detail of design and production.

Richard Greenbury, who became chairman in 1991, described the company's approach:

> The special partner relationship which M&S developed with all its suppliers of goods and services was, from its inception some 70 years ago, a cornerstone principle of the company. Furthermore, it was at the very heart of the way we did business with our suppliers and a fundamental part of that philosophy was that M&S was going to carry on doing business with the manufacturer season after season, year after year. Continuity of production into the foreseeable future was the basis of all discussions and negotiations. Indeed it was clearly understood that once a major supplier to M&S, always a supplier – unless the manufacturer's performance was considered to be poor in which case high level meetings would be arranged to discuss the situation.

And then Marks & Spencer was struck by the finance curse. In Chapter 22 I described how Greenbury's drive for the billion pound profit had at first succeeded – and then failed. With

profits falling, his tenure ended in 1999 amid acrimonious board-
room conflict. Under Greenbury, an M&S lifer, the supplier
relationships had remained sacrosanct. But within weeks of his
departure, suppliers were notified that they would not receive
new orders. Marks & Spencer would now scour the world for
sources of supply. The company once boasted that more than 90
per cent of its merchandise was made in Britain. If British readers
check their underwear today, the labels will take them on a tour
of Asia.

The law comes into play only when the relationship breaks
down. And at Marks & Spencer, the relationship *did* break down
and the law came into play. William Baird, a privately owned
company which had been one of the four suppliers who provided most of the clothing for Marks & Spencer stores for thirty
years, went to court.[16]

Greenbury's account of Marks & Spencer's historic relationships with its suppliers above is drawn from his evidence
to the court. But in rejecting Baird's claims, Lord Justice Mance
emphasised that the courts could not be used to turn the relationship into a formal contract:

> It is evident that Baird felt, quite rightly, that it had achieved a
> long and very close relationship, an informal business 'part-
> nership', with M&S, and that it could, as a practical matter,
> rely on this and on M&S's management's general goodwill
> and good intentions. But managements, economic condi-
> tions and intentions may all change, and businessmen must
> be taken to be aware that, without specific contractual pro-
> tection, their business may suffer in consequence. I do not
> think that the law should be ready to seek to fetter business
> relationships, even – and perhaps especially – those as long
> and as close as the present.[17]

Lord Mance, and his fellow Court of Appeal judges, were alive
to the near-impossibility of a court writing the explicit terms of
a commercial contract in circumstances where the parties had

explicitly declined to make one.

But what if the parties *had* made one? Despite the five thousand pages of legalese, the contract between Birmingham City Council and Amey could not cover all contingencies. Amey insisted on a literal interpretation of the agreement and the matter went to court. Giving judgment, Lord Justice Jackson opined that 'Any relational contract of this character is likely to be of massive length, containing many infelicities and oddities. Both parties should adopt a reasonable approach in accordance with what is obviously the long-term purpose of the contract. They should not be latching onto the infelicities and oddities, in order to disrupt the project and maximise their own gain.'[18]

The very different approaches and judgments of Jackson and Mance have a common theme. The English courts, at least, have little sympathy for the notion of business as a nexus of contracts. Both the Birmingham and Marks & Spencer cases involved vertical relationships with suppliers, and the judges took the view that businesspeople should work things out in productive mutual relationships and avoid recourse to the law. Baird could not use the courts to insist that Marks & Spencer should continue its long-established business partnership. Amey and Birmingham City Council should make sensible arrangements to resolve the contingencies that, given radical uncertainty, would inevitably emerge in the life of a complex contract. This is different from the tradition begun by Coase and continued by Williamson, Hart and many others, which emphasises the central role of contract design and property rights.

Black and brown coal

In 2016 Oliver Hart was awarded the Nobel Prize for his work on contract design. In his Nobel Lecture he illustrated his thinking with reference to the co-location of an electricity generating plant and a coal mine – a quixotic choice of activity for an era preoccupied with climate change. Commendably, he explained that 'It is useful to illustrate the model with a real-world example. Consider a power plant that locates next to a coal mine with the purpose of burning coal to make electricity.'[19] Need the power company own the provider of the fuel? Hart describes the complications this question entails, given the inevitable asymmetry of information between power company and mine owner. He notes possible contractual solutions, particularly favouring a formal requirement on the parties to resolve any disagreement through a game, refereed by an honest and impartial third party: a solution proposed in a 1999 article by two other Nobel laureates, Eric Maskin and Jean Tirole.[20]

Hart's 'real world' does not refer to any particular plant. The largest coal-fired power station in the Global North is the Scherer plant, operated by Georgia Power. The coal it uses is mined over 2,000 miles away in Wyoming, where there are many competing producers and an active market. Fuel for the Scherer plant is shipped by a dedicated shuttle operated by Berkshire Hathaway's subsidiary Burlington Northern Railroad. Black coal is not heavy or bulky relative to its value and is therefore cheap to transport. Australian black coal is shipped to China and even Europe.

Brown coal, also found in Australia, is another matter. Lignite has a much lower density and hence much higher transport costs relative to its calorific content. There are large deposits in Eastern Europe on both sides of the border between Poland and the former DDR. Much of south-east Australia's electricity has historically come from the Latrobe Valley, in the state of Victoria. When I flew there, I could recognise my destination many miles away because of the clouds of steam above.

In the Latrobe Valley, giant bulldozers shovel brown coal into the furnaces that power the turbines. AGL (Australia Gas and Light), a company founded in 1837, and one of the founding stocks on the Sydney Stock Exchange, owns the Loy Yang mine. AGL also owns Loy Yang A, one of the two adjacent power stations. The other power station is Loy Yang B, and ownership of Loy Yang B has been separate from the mine since the privatisation of Victorian electricity generation more than thirty years ago. It has passed through the hands of Edison Mission (a US corporation), Mitsui (a Japanese corporation) and Engie (a French corporation) and is now owned by the Chinese Chow Tai Fook Enterprises Limited (CTFE). The legal relationships and ownership structures didn't matter much. The parties had good reasons to find commercial arrangements that worked – and did.

It is perhaps unnecessary to say that no one I met in the Latrobe Valley had heard of the Maskin/Tirole solution, far less considered implementing it. Hart acknowledges that to the best of his knowledge no one has done so anywhere.[21] He ascribes this failure to a lack of economic rationality on the part of businesspeople. My preferred explanation is that these businesspeople sensibly have a different concept of rationality, derived from the broader social context within which business is conducted.

Many legal forms appear to be consistent with economic efficiency. The skill of businesspeople is to find arrangements that work, and the best of these people are those who succeed in this pragmatic activity. The mechanisms to implement these arrangements are the product of history and the social and political context in which they operate. There are similarities between the mixtures of competition and cooperation we find in Silicon Valley, the sofa town of Meda, the keiretsu of associated firms that surround titans of Japanese industry such as Toyota and the power plants of the Latrobe Valley, but the particularities are different in the different cultures of California, northern Italy, Japan and Australia.

27

THE HOLLOW CORPORATION

Did [He] who made the lamb make thee,
Or an external franchisee?

Robin Johnson, 2022[1]

Henry Ford, like many founding entrepreneurs, had a very clear view of the structure of vertical relationships. He wanted control over every detail of production. His vision was that raw materials would arrive at the River Rouge and leave as finished automobiles. An area of Brazil is still known as Ford-landia, following Henry's unsuccessful attempt to grow rubber for use in the company's tyres.[2] William Morris, whose Morris Motor works loomed over Oxford, was similarly insistent on control; when I joked that the only part of the car Morris Motors did not produce was the owner's manual, a business historian friend warned me to check. Morris Motors did indeed establish a wholly owned subsidiary, the Nuffield Press, to do just that.

Make or buy

At General Motors (GM), however, Sloan believed in a more decentralised management style. Perhaps that is why that decision by GM in 1926 to buy Fisher Body, which made body parts for the corporation's vehicles, has gone down in history – at least if historical significance is measured by the number of academic articles that discuss the transaction. Peter Klein recalls that

at the inaugural meeting of the International Society for
New Institutional Economics [which he co-founded with
Coase] in 1997, a discussion [began] about the best empirical strategy for that emerging discipline. Harold Demsetz
stood up and said, 'Please, no more papers about Fisher
Body and GM!' ... Ronald Coase, who was at the podium,
replied (I'm paraphrasing from memory) 'Sorry, Harold,
that is exactly the subject of my next paper!'[3]

And in the 2000 issue of the *Journal of Law and Economics* no
fewer than five papers, including that of Coase, discussed the
Fisher Body story.

In his 2000 paper Coase explained that he had been hesitant
to make explicit reference to the Fisher transaction in his 1937
article because he had learned that A. O. Smith, which manufactured the chassis into which the Fisher Body parts were fitted,
had remained an independent company. Smith was based several
hundred miles away from GM, in Milwaukee; Fisher had built a
plant at Detroit to be close to GM. The two cases were similar
in nature, but one relationship was contractual, the other hierarchical. GM executives had offered conflicting accounts of their
motivations.

Despite his obsession with vertical integration, Ford had
bought the bodywork for the Model T from Briggs, a Detroit
firm which supplied other manufacturers, including Chrysler;
and when Ford opened a plant in Dagenham, England, Briggs
followed. Henry bought the Buffalo company Keim Mills to
make axle casings; when the workers went on strike, he simply
shipped the equipment and senior executive team to Detroit
and closed the plant. (That team included Bill Knudsen, who, as
described in Chapters 5 and 6, would be a key right-hand man
first for Henry and subsequently for Alfred Sloan.)

William Morris in Oxford faced similar issues. Impressed
by the bodywork fabricated by the Budd company in the US,
he persuaded Budd to bring its technology to the UK and take
a share in the company he established on a site opposite his

Cowley plant. The arrangement did not work well, and after acrimonious legal proceedings Morris was required to sell his stake. Budd also divested, and from 1935 Pressed Steel was an independent company – until in 1965 it was acquired by the British Motor Corporation, formed by the merger of Morris Motors and its principal British rival, Austin. (William Morris, ennobled as Lord Nuffield, had died in 1963. Nuffield had proposed to establish an engineering college in Oxford University, but a wily vice-chancellor persuaded him that social sciences were almost the same thing and Nuffield College was the venue for my graduate studies.)

Why did GM buy Fisher Body and not A. O. Smith? Perhaps the Fisher brothers had aspirations to achieve executive roles in the largest and most successful corporation in the world while the Smith family cherished their independence. Dealmakers planning mergers and acquisitions talk, quietly, about 'social issues'. By this they do not mean the effects of their activities on employees and communities. They are discussing who will get the top jobs.

This 'make or buy' decision has been an important practical question for businesspeople over the last few decades, as opinion has shifted from the obsessive search for control of every aspect of production displayed by Henry Ford and William Morris to the 'hollow corporation' of the modern era. The term 'hollow corporation' seems to have been used first by Norman Jonas in an extended article in *Business Week* in 1986.[4] Jonas described how modern firms were outsourcing more and more of their activity to independent, specialist suppliers – a development that would steadily gather pace in the years that followed. And 'make or buy' has also become a central political question. Have western economies been damaged, or their social fabric weakened, by outsourcing of activities to countries further south or east? Which traditionally public sector activities should the government undertake itself, and which should be contracted to private businesses?

Production lines analogous to those of the Carron Works or

River Rouge still exist. But in Mexico and Asia rather than the US and Europe. Paradoxically, the traditional rhetoric of capitalism today provides a better description of business in ostensibly communist China than in ostensibly capitalist America.

A century after the Triangle disaster, the Tazreen Fashions factory owned by Delwar Hossain caught fire: there were no fire exits and gates were locked; 112 people died. But the Tazreen factory is in Dhaka, Bangladesh. The trial of Hossain on homicide charges began in 2015 and has not yet been completed.[5] Bangladesh is a major exporter of ready-to-wear garments, made in plants such as Tazreen, and largely staffed by young women fleeing the overpopulated land in search of better wages. The Bangladeshi Industrial Revolution is at an early stage, and this is reflected in both the nature of production and the treatment of workers. History does not repeat itself, but it rhymes.[6]

And so do patterns of economic development. Bangladesh is defined by its constitution as a socialist republic; in practice, it is ruled by a powerful military and a political elite that imposes both legal taxes and corrupt demands on the country's nascent industry. Business is better understood by reference to the stage of industrialisation, which differs across the United States, China and Bangladesh, than it is through the language of capitalism and socialism.

Globalisation

A series of books and articles published from the 1990s made *The New York Times* journalist Thomas Friedman the leading prophet of globalisation. Friedman observed the importance of the emergence of global branding and international supply chains: 'the world is flat.'

For many, Nike, the largest retailer of sports footwear, exemplified the 'hollow corporation'. Gerald Davis has even written of the 'Nikefication' of the American economy.[7] Nike itself manufactures nothing; all the garments and shoes that carry its famous 'swoosh' logo are made in factories in Asia, including

Bangladesh. (Tazreen was not a supplier to Nike but did manufacture products for other US corporations, including Walmart.) Even the design of the swoosh logo was outsourced (for a fee of $35).

Friedman famously asserted 'the Golden Arches theory' of international relations: no two countries with McDonald's restaurants had ever gone to war with each other.[8] The first McDonald's in a former Communist country opened in Belgrade in 1988, and it is claimed that before the Serbia-Croatia war which followed (not as a direct result) Serb football fans would chant 'We have a McDonald's, where is yours?'[9] The first Croatian branch opened in 1996, soon after the 1995 Dayton Accords ended the Yugoslav conflict (again, probably not as a direct result).[10] Friedman went on to refine his argument: the Dell theory claimed that the existence of integrated supply chains precluded armed conflicts. The Golden Arches theory was finally refuted by Russia's invasion of Ukraine in 2022.

Davis did not intend 'Nikefication' to be a term of approbation. There are two principal grounds of criticism. Most opprobrium is directed at outsourcing, which has transferred much manufacturing activity from Britain and the United States, mostly to Asia. Some of this concern is the product of irrational manufacturing fetishism. But there are grounds for real concern over the destruction of communities associated with the demise of large manufacturing plants.

This effect is experienced in the *outsourcing* country. But another source of criticism focuses on effects in the *insourcing* country.[11] Earnings and working conditions in factories in countries such as Bangladesh are far below those that would be acceptable in the Global North. Pressure from 'activists' has led many companies that buy from Bangladesh and similar countries to try to improve the standards of their suppliers, but the effects are modest – and inevitably so. Most of the population of Bangladesh lives in poverty, as defined by the hardly generous World Bank standard, which sets the poverty level at an income of $2.15 per day.[12]

So the retail price of the T-shirt you buy might represent more than a week's wages for the worker who makes it. Yet your purchase is not the cause of Bangladesh's miserable economic state – in fact, it offers that country's most promising hope of escape from it. If your proper embarrassment at the contrast between the circumstances of consumer and producer leads you to eschew the purchase, then you are harming, not helping, the economy of Bangladesh.

The garment industry accounts for more than 80 per cent of Bangladeshi exports, and much of this production comes from small enterprises whose members learned their modest capabilities in the sweatshops.[13] You, and the retailers you patronise, may be enriching undeserving intermediaries such as Delwar Hossain, but although he strays beyond any possible acceptable boundaries, it is unrealistic to seek to impose universal values. Western corporations can best help poor countries by exporting their capabilities to them, and by operating to standards that are good relative to local expectations even if well below the norms of their home countries. Sometimes, of course, the tension between the two may be so great – as when corruption is endemic or abuse of child labour pervasive – as to render it impossible to do business there.

Apple has outsourced the manufacturing of its products to businesses such as Foxconn, a Chinese subsidiary of the Taiwanese Hon Hai group. The Apple-designed processors now used to power Mac computers are manufactured by TSMC, another Taiwanese company.[14] The pace of post-war economic development in East Asia is among the most remarkable in economic history. Since 1980, when data begins, Taiwan's GDP has grown, on average, 7.2 per cent per year; since 1972 Korea's has grown 10.8 per cent per year.[15] There is justified scepticism about Chinese statistics, but that country's growth rate has been similarly remarkable.

The experience of these economies illustrates the potential of *convergence*. States such as these, formerly held back by institutional dysfunction and internal and external strife, are able to adopt the technology and business methods already employed by countries at the *production frontier*, which describes the most efficient utilisation of resources attainable with known technologies and business processes. These successful Asian economies have accessed the available collective intelligence of the world and exploited it more fully and consequently are now themselves both insourcers and outsourcers. Taiwanese Hon Hai manufactures Apple products in mainland China, and Korean Samsung has diverted lower value-added activities to poorer countries such as Vietnam. Globalisation has many critics and is far from a universal benefit. But it has allowed a division of labour far beyond the imagination of Adam Smith. The spectacular reductions in Asian poverty demonstrate that there is more benefit to globalisation than cheap clothes at Primark and Walmart. Following Korea and Taiwan, China and India are growing economies with a burgeoning middle class and many fewer in abject straits.

The Covid pandemic raised questions about the resilience of global supply chains. Perhaps there were instances of leaky pipe syndrome: companies had pursued short-term cost savings at the expense of making themselves more vulnerable to disruption. The emergence of new geopolitical threats – Russia's invasion of Ukraine, conflict in Gaza and Chinese sabre rattling over Taiwan – increases these concerns.

Franchising and platforms

Franchising has a long history. The European imperialist project was in effect franchised to private businesses, such as the Dutch VOC, the English Company of Virginia and the East India Company – and, most scandalously, in King Leopold's personal annexation of the Congo. But in the twentieth century franchising took on a greater scale, a new significance and a much more benign character.

Ray Kroc was a salesman for a struggling producer of mixing machines used in diners to prepare milkshakes. His customers included Maurice and Richard McDonald, who owned a hamburger restaurant in San Bernardino, California. The McDonald brothers had developed what they called the Speedee Service System, with a limited menu and a repetitive process that Frederick Taylor and Bill Knudsen would have admired. The brothers were interested in selling their methods to other restaurants and hired Kroc as their agent.

Everyone knows how the story evolved. The franchising model Kroc implemented involved a process of rigorous standardisation which gave the customer a predictable product. Today you can enjoy, or at least buy, an almost identical Big Mac in familiar surroundings in thousands of outlets in more than a hundred countries. The formula also enabled inexperienced individuals to establish their own businesses with modest capital and a high probability of success.

That formula was imitated by other fast food chains and in many service businesses, from print shops to pharmacies to hotels. Common branding helps with marketing and gives the collective franchise far more bargaining power with suppliers than any individual franchisee could enjoy. Today franchising even extends to global accounting firms, with country-specific operations trading under one name worldwide. And both McDonald's and KPMG need to inspect the work of their franchisees to ensure that their brand and reputation are sustained.

The customers of Facebook, Twitter and YouTube are also these companies' suppliers. And much the same is true of eBay and Google. The digital age has created a new type of corporation. The disastrous merger of AOL and Time Warner was rationalised by the misconception that the platform needed to own the content: the same error that William Morris made when he thought he needed to print his own user manuals, though one with far more destructive consequences for the individuals and businesses concerned.

The key to understanding all these cases is once more to see that to collect much of the economic rent you need only control the source of your competitive advantage. Sloan had understood that; Ford did not. Time Warner did not need to own AOL to be able to distribute *Casablanca* or 'Happy Birthday' – competing firms would fight to obtain the rights to offer access to the product on their platforms. And AOL was quickly outclassed by numerous other social media platforms. Time Warner's competitive advantage was clear and enduring; AOL's was weak and transient.

Warner Music purported to own the copyright of the song 'Happy Birthday'. The world's most popular song is thought to have been written in the late nineteenth century by Mildred and Patty Hill, kindergarten teachers. In 2015 the company finally abandoned this claim and agreed to pay $15 million to settle a class action suit brought by people who had been charged royalties. You can now sing 'Happy Birthday' with your family without fear of your celebration being interrupted by attorneys representing whoever owns Warner Music at the time. (The struggling AOL-TimeWarner disposed of Warner Music to a consortium led by Canadian businessman Edgar Bronfman, who in turn sold it on to a group led by the Ukrainian-born London resident Len Blavatnik.)

The 'gig economy' has taken this disintegration of supply chains a stage further. IKEA's TaskRabbit and Amazon's Mechanical Turk connect individuals looking for tasks with consumers requiring services. A Gallup survey which included such diverse services as contract nursing and freelance graphic designers found that more than one third of working Americans derived at least some of their incomes from these freelance activities.[16]

Airbnb and Uber have characteristics of both platforms and franchises. As platforms they link hosts with guests, passengers with drivers; as franchises they must try to monitor the quality of their lodgings and the reliability of their chauffeurs. In 2019 Uber reported 5 million drivers, although this number has fallen since the pandemic; Airbnb claims 4 million hosts and over 7 million listings.[17] (The world's largest employers are Walmart and the Chinese army, each with a labour force of slightly over 2 million.)

These hollow corporations share the characteristic that the activities of the business have been pared down to the single link in the chain of production at which the corporation holds a distinctive capability and enjoys a competitive advantage. Richard Langlois, a business historian, identifies this as a key reason for the change in the corporate landscape, enabled by the growth of 'market-supporting institutions' which enabled entrepreneurs to easily access support for business functions where they didn't have a comparative advantage.[18] If the assembly line was the defining innovation in business method of twentieth-century manufacturing activity, the hollow corporation may be the defining innovation in business method of twenty-first-century digital activity.

PART 7

CAPITAL IN THE TWENTY-FIRST CENTURY

The word 'capital' is used in many different senses. Capital is a factor of production for the twenty-first-century corporation; much of it takes the form of plant and machinery, offices and warehouses bought from specialist suppliers. The term 'capital' is also used to describe the value of the net assets, tangible and financial, actually owned by the firm itself. In the early Industrial Revolution these measures were often similar but no longer are.

And the term 'capital' is also often used with reference to personal or national wealth, tangible and financial. This conflation also dates from an era of much simpler economic and social organisation. Finally, in the twentieth century several new usages of 'capital' – such as human, social and natural capital – have been created. The word capital is indispensable but should be used certainly more carefully and perhaps more sparingly. And if the meaning of 'capital' is ambiguous, who should we identify as the 'capitalists' of the twenty-first century? Perhaps 'capitalist' is a historic term we should manage without.

28

CAPITAL AS A SERVICE

When we buy an automobile we no longer buy an object in the old sense of the word, but instead we purchase a three- to five-year lease for participation in the state-recognized private transportation system, a highway system, a traffic safety system, an industrial parts-replacement system, a costly insurance system ...

J. Burnham, *Beyond Modern Sculpture*, 1968[1]

The hollow corporation is a combination of capabilities. Some of these capabilities are distinctive to the firm; sometimes it is the combination itself that is distinctive. Apple is distinguished by the capabilities of its product design and development teams: its products are technically advanced but not uniquely so, but they are incorporated in devices of unrivalled elegance that are very easy to use. And every distinctive capability or combination of capabilities requires the support of other complementary capabilities which are necessary but may not be distinctive, such as accounting and marketing competencies. These can be purchased in a (fairly) competitive market in which there are multiple suppliers.

In a modern business capital and labour are purchased services: like accounting and marketing; like electricity and water. It is correct to describe Apple products as the output of the combination of capital and labour, just as it is correct to describe Apple products as the output of the combination of silicon and glass. But these descriptions are of little help in understanding the organisation that is Apple, nor do they explain why people queue to buy its products. And it would be foolish to think that, if one went out to buy the quantities of capital and labour that Apple purchases, one would be able to produce iPhones and MacBooks – any more than one could do so by purchasing appropriate quantities of silicon and glass. The ingredients list is not the recipe. Thomas Thwaites laboriously demonstrated the fallacy of this mechanistic analysis of production through his efforts to make a far simpler item. Capital and labour, silicon and glass: all these factors of production are necessary but no physical description is ever sufficient, or even close to sufficient.

The ironmasters and textile magnates of the Industrial Revolution built plants and mills very like the plants and mills that other ironmasters and textile magnates built. They recruited similar workforces from the fields and villages in similar ways and gave them similar and minimal training. The collective intelligence that built the ironworks and textile mills of the later eighteenth century was more or less common property. Francis Cabot Lowell learned how to build a plant in Massachusetts by touring existing plants around Manchester. A modern Mancunian would gain little insight into how to create an English version of Apple by visiting Cupertino. He might move to Silicon Valley and benefit from the 'mysteries of the trade in the air' – the collective intelligence that is common property and the area's strength. But the visitor would only be at the beginning of the journey to a successful business. Today the hallmark of successful business is access to collective intelligence that is *not* common property.

Capitalism without capital

As I write, Amazon is valued on the stock market at over $2,000 billion. The assets on its balance sheet totalled $464 billion.[2] But that figure repays closer inspection. The business of Amazon requires large warehouses, vehicles and stocks of goods. But Amazon owns few of these things. Its property assets are largely rented from real estate investors, and most of its mechanical assets are leased from financial institutions. And then there is the stock in the sheds. Amazon reports inventories of $34 billion and accounts receivable of $38 billion – payments due for goods sold but not yet paid for (typically the amount charged to your credit card which neither you nor your bank has yet settled). But there are also amounts payable to suppliers of $67 billion.[3] Put simply, on average Amazon has sold its goods before it has paid for them.

The $464 billion of assets Amazon reports are small relative to the company's market value, but a large number nonetheless. However, most of this figure is an artificial accounting construct. Accounting standards require that the 'right of use' of leased property assets be valued and entered on the balance sheet. Of course, there is a corresponding obligation to pay for the use of the asset, and this can be found as a liability elsewhere on the balance sheet. And there is 'goodwill'. This term does not here have its everyday meaning; the item has nothing to do with any affection employees or customers have for the company. Amazon's 'goodwill' is principally the amount the company paid out to buy the Whole Foods chain.

This analysis may be difficult and disturbing to people unfamiliar with accounts. The key point is that Amazon owns virtually no assets akin to the Carron ironworks, the rail line from London to Bristol or Henry Ford's River Rouge complex. When Henry posted a sign saying 'Ford Motor Company' above the door, he meant that the plant was the property of the Ford Motor Company, manager and principal shareholder Henry Ford. That's what capitalism once meant.

But modern business is different – the economists Jonathan Haskel and Stian Westlake have described it as 'capitalism without capital'.[4] The idea of 'software as a service' was pioneered by Salesforce in 1999, following a realisation that what people wanted was not software itself, but the outputs software could produce. Today, abbreviated to SaaS, 'software as a service' is a major industry.

The concept of buying capital goods 'as a service' is hardly new. Housing 'as a service' has existed for centuries. But even as the rental sector of the housing market declined, rental contracts became more common in other fields. The Xerox Corporation, whose name was long synonymous with photocopying, introduced the managed printing service. Users paid not for the machine and consumables but for the number of copies printed. Companies leased cars for their employees, who might fill the tank and arrange servicing without ever knowing – or caring – who was the legal owner of the vehicle. The shift from the provision of goods to the provision of services was increasingly widespread and often gave both buyer and seller greater predictability of costs and revenues.

This development of 'as a service' can be seen in consumer as well as producer markets. You can buy a mobile phone – or a contract which bundles use of the phone with calls, texts and data; your Amazon Prime subscription covers doorstep delivery for a year; and you pay a monthly fee for your gym and your television programming. By 2020 the 'subscription model' had become a business fashion – even a business cliché.

The owners of capital

The Amazon warehouse you pass is probably owned by Prologis, the largest real estate investment trust (REIT) in the world. Headquartered in San Francisco, its shares are traded on the New York Stock Exchange. However, its market capitalisation is far smaller than that of Amazon, to which it is a principal supplier. Another REIT, Equinix, provides data centres for Amazon's businesses. These transactions, outsourcing the provision of capital, parallel Apple's outsourcing of manufacturing. Modern business has pursued specialisation and the division of labour to degrees that Adam Smith could never have imagined.

Equinix is one of several large data centre companies that provide server space for large corporations. The ubiquitous masts that allow your smartphone to receive calls anywhere are largely owned by specialist companies such as American Tower or (in Europe) Connex. It is unlikely that the plane you fly in is owned by the airline whose logo is on the fuselage. There are several large aircraft leasing companies – the biggest is AerCap – but planes may also be owned by partnerships of small investors. And the engine is usually owned by yet another business. The airline will typically make a long-term contract for the supply and service of engines from a manufacturer such as Rolls-Royce. The manufacturer has in turn transferred ownership of the engines to a specialist business such as GATX, which also owns many railway carriages (including the one that derailed at East Palestine, Ohio, in February 2023, filling the sky with toxic chemicals and necessitating a $1 billion clean-up operation).

If you want to ship a load of widgets from China, you will want to employ an agent to lease a container from a container-leasing company (Triton is the largest) and also to lease space on a ship from a company such as the Taiwanese Evergreen group. Evergreen came briefly into the public eye when the *Ever Given* container ship, more than ten times the length of Eddie Lampert's yacht, ran aground and blocked the Suez Canal. (Sadly it was not the same company's *Ever Lucky* or *Ever Lovely*.) The *Ever Forward* became stuck in Chesapeake Bay the following year. The Egyptian government sought and eventually received compensation – from the actual owners of the *Ever Given*, the Japanese company Shoei Kisen Kaisha. The provision of capital as a service has many components and many participants.

Apple is also a trillion-dollar corporation. The centrepiece of its operations is the Norman Foster-designed campus at Cupertino, built at an estimated cost of $5 billion.[5] But that deliberately spectacular headquarters is the corporation's principal tangible asset. The company's New York flagship store is in Grand Central Station, a memorial to Cornelius Vanderbilt, as the Cupertino complex is to Steve Jobs. But that store, and the whole Grand Central building, is owned by New York's Metropolitan Transit Authority. Apple's European flagship, in London's Regent Street, is jointly owned by the king of England and the sovereign wealth fund of Norway.[6] Like Amazon, Apple expects you to pay on the nail (although your credit card company may take a more relaxed view). But, like Amazon, Apple does not display the same urgency in paying its suppliers, so it has no net working capital. The company has assets of more than $300 billion, but two-thirds of these are cash and marketable securities.[7]

This extremely profitable company has more money than it knows what to do with. Far from raising new money on stock markets to invest in its business, it is buying back its own existing shares. In 2023 Apple spent $90 billion in this way. This number might be compared with the $26 billion total raised in the Americas by *all* IPOs in the same year.[8]

> Increasingly, large public companies are eschewing dividends in favour of share buybacks, which can have a tax advantage for shareholders and mechanically increases earnings per share, a key metric for management. In 2022 the firms in the S&P 500 spent $923 billion on share buybacks, compared with just $565 billion in dividend payments.[9] In the UK the situation is less extreme, but buybacks are still prominent: the firms in the FTSE 100 spent £56 billion on buybacks and £77 billion on dividends in 2022.[10]

Modern businesses also buy routine labour as a service, especially for tasks such as cleaning, security and catering. The largest companies in this sector are European, perhaps because European businesses use subcontracting to circumvent the protections that European laws give to direct employees. But also because, as Adam Smith had observed, there are efficiency gains from specialisation. Compass (British), G4S (British) and ISS (Danish) each have around 500,000 staff.[11]

While these businesses focus on relatively low-paid activities such as catering, security and facilities management, other firms offer more sophisticated specialisations. IBM, once known for its dominance of the mainframe computer business, is today the largest global consultancy company.[12] Not only does it sell software as a service; it also sells labour as a service. Amazon Web Services (AWS) provides cloud computing facilities and Application Programming Interfaces (APIs) – the power behind the apps you use every day – to thousands of corporations, and it is AWS, not the retail juggernaut with which we are all familiar, that provides most of Amazon's profits.

Jeff Bezos founded Amazon with some money of his own and the support of his family – less than half a million dollars in total. Subsequently, the business received an $8 million injection from the Silicon Valley venture capital firm Kleiner Perkins, and when it became a public company in 1997 it raised around $50 million from investors.[13] Steve Jobs and Steve Wozniak obtained a small amount of finance but also 'adult supervision' from Mike Markkula and his Silicon Valley friends. Apple finally obtained $100 million from new shareholders at its 1980 IPO.

Neither Amazon nor Apple has raised any money from shareholders since their IPO, and neither is ever likely to in the future. Past stockholder investment represents less than .01 per cent of the current value of these businesses. Modern companies are typically cash-generative before they reach a scale at which they become eligible for a listing on a public market. The purpose of the IPO is not to raise capital but to demonstrate to earlier investors and employees that there is value in their shareholdings and to enable some to realise that value. The objective of listing on a stock exchange is not to put money *into* the business but to make it possible to take money *out of* the business.

The place of the shareholder

Once, people bought shares in the hope and expectation of receiving dividends. The 'Gordon growth model' suggested that the value of stocks was underpinned, even determined, by the net present value of the expected stream of dividends. Successful companies would pay out a share of their profits and would demonstrate their success by providing a steadily increasing dividend stream.

But the yield on Alphabet (Google), Apple or Meta (Facebook) shares is derisory and Amazon, Berkshire Hathaway and Tesla pay no dividend at all. The only reason for buying these shares is a hope that the stock price will rise – a hope that has been amply justified for long-term holders of these particular stocks, but these are the winners in a crowded field. The practice of share buybacks may help to validate the elevated market values of 'tech stocks'. But the connection between financial assets and physical assets has never been more tenuous.

> If you want a dividend yield, you might prefer to buy shares in a provider of capital as a service. Prologis pays out essentially all its net income as dividends. The REIT regime which is used by most suppliers of capital as a service is designed to treat stockholders for tax purposes as if they were 'part owners' of the physical assets of the company. AerCap, however, does not pay dividends: each year it aims to buy more planes.

In a speculative bubble, the dominant motive for trade is not the continuing benefit of ownership of the purchased asset. It is the hope and expectation that the asset can be sold on at a higher price to someone else. Well-known historical examples include the Dutch tulip craze, the South Sea Bubble and the railway mania. The last thirty years have witnessed the emerging market debt crisis of the 1990s, the 'new economy' boom in 1997–2000 and the credit market expansion of 2003–8. Often the madness has some basis in real economic developments: the arrival of the railways; the rapid growth of Asian economies; the spread of the internet. But the reaction to all these events vindicates the widely repeated maxim that people tend to overestimate the short-run impact of change while underestimating its long-run effect.

The near-collapse of the world financial system in 2008 might have triggered greater transparency of, and more emphasis on, the relationship between wealth and tangible assets, and between the ownership of capital and control of the means of production. It did not. Central banks and governments of the world propped up the failing institutions and sought little substantive change.

Indeed an outcome of the crisis was the development of financial instruments that were not just unrelated to the real economy of productive activity and tangible assets but divorced from any reality at all. In 2009 someone using the pseudonym Satoshi Nakamoto launched the first cryptocurrency, Bitcoin, secured by a blockchain, or distributed ledger – no central agency monitored or assured transactions. The utility of this innovation, aside from supporting criminality and circumventing regulation, was and remains unclear; many cynical observers, including this one, have described blockchain as a solution in search of a problem.

But adopters of Bitcoin traded enthusiastically with each other. As in all speculative bubbles, the sceptics were confounded by the profits made by the early proponents of the new craze. Many other cryptocurrencies followed, as did other related products such as Initial Coin Offerings (ICOs) and Non-Fungible Tokens (NFTs). In another corner of the financial universe Special Purpose Acquisition Companies (SPACs) became popular. These were closer to real business – they were launched, often with celebrity backing (Leonardo DiCaprio and Serena Williams among them) in the hope that someone would suggest an activity they might engage in, or an existing business they could buy (most bizarrely Donald Trump's loss-making TruthSocial). The divergence of finance from industry, of traded securities from physical assets, has never been so extreme.

29

CAPITAL AND WEALTH

> If only Karl had made Capital, instead of just writing about it.
>
> Attributed to his mother, Henriette Pressburg,
> by Marx in a letter to Engels in 1868[1]

The term 'capital' is today widely used in both popular and technical language. In both contexts the word has a variety of meanings. Capital is a factor of production. Businesses need factories and offices, plant and machinery, and stocks of goods. But the term 'capital' is also used as a measure of personal, or more frequently institutional, wealth – as when we talk about the capital of a business or the endowment of a university. This multiplicity of interpretations is a legacy of the historical equivalence of personal wealth and productive assets – an equivalence that no longer exists now that the tripartite linkage of wealth, productive capital and management control that was characteristic of most businesses of the Industrial Revolution has largely dissolved.

Capital as a factor of production must now be distinguished from *capital as a measure of personal wealth*. And neither of these is closely linked to *control of modern business*, which is mostly in the hands of professional managers. These executives derive their authority and their economic power not from their ownership of the physical means of production, nor from their wealth, but from their role in an organisation. If senior managers are wealthy – and many of them now are – their role in directing business is not derived from their wealth; rather, their wealth is derived from their role in directing business. The causal relationship is thus reversed: it runs not from the prior accumulation of wealth to the control of economic activity but from control of economic activity, both financial and industrial, to the posterior accumulation of wealth. This is true of business founders such as Jeff Bezos and Elon Musk, whose wealth is mostly based on the value of their shareholdings, and also of 'salarymen' – such as Jack Welch and Jamie Dimon (CEO of GE and J. P. Morgan respectively for two decades) – who accumulate considerable fortunes through generous remuneration packages. (Welch died in 2021 with an estate estimated at $750 million; in October 2023 Dimon announced a plan to realise $141 million by selling a little under 10 per cent of his shareholding in the bank, a holding almost entirely acquired as a result of awards of options and bonuses.)

Capital and wealth

In his widely cited *Capital in the Twenty-First Century* Thomas Piketty acknowledges the different uses of the term 'capital'.[2] However, he continues, 'To simplify the text, I use the words "capital" and "wealth" interchangeably, as though they were perfectly synonymous.'[3] Mystifyingly, Piketty seems to suggest that the key problem in conflating capital and wealth is the need to distinguish between wealth created by humans (buildings, machinery, infrastructure etc.) and land and natural resources (with which humans have been endowed – or, in a plausible alternative explanation, which humans have appropriated).

But while the distinction between produced and natural inputs to production is sometimes helpful, it is not central to an understanding of the modern business organisation. And it offers a potentially misleading account of the role of land in modern production. The cost and value of a central London office reflect both the cost and value of the (produced) building and the cost and value of the land on which it sits. But land in Mayfair and on Threadneedle Street is more valuable than the

fields of East Lothian as a result of human action, not differences in nature's bounty. Both land and location are factors of
production, and most of the value of land today is derived from
its location rather than its fertility.

Despite the historic association between capital and wealth,
the terms are *not* now synonymous and cannot be used interchangeably without confusion. Today we benefit from the
investment that built the motorways and bridges (as well as the
automobile assembly plants) that would have enabled Adam
Smith to drive to his Kirkcaldy birthplace or the Carron Works.
We appreciate the investment that built railways and railroads
and laid out the grid pattern of Manhattan. And the investment
that installed the cables, pipes and subway lines beneath our
feet. Little of this transport, energy and communications infrastructure – without which our modern lives would be severely
restricted and modern business could not function – is part of
the personal wealth of individuals. (Although governments can,
and sometimes do, create and sell financial claims related to
these assets through franchising and similar devices.)

Conversely, government debt and bank deposits are key components of personal and institutional wealth but are not factors
of production. And the value of shares in companies such as
Amazon and Apple does not correspond to the cost or value of
any tangible factor of production, such as the Carron Works or
the River Rouge complex; these valuations reflect claims over
future revenues of these companies. Almost all the wealth of
the people who are at the top of the 'rich lists' compiled by
newspapers and magazines is composed of financial assets of
these kinds; very little corresponds to factors of production such
as plant and machinery or personal trophies such as houses and
yachts. At the same time, the tangible assets – the warehouses,
data centres and Chinese assembly lines that are necessary for
the businesses of Amazon and Apple – are of much less value
than the value of Amazon and Apple as listed companies, and
are owned by people who have no engagement with the management of Amazon and Apple.

Importantly for Piketty's purposes r – one of the terms in his famous inequality $r>g$ – relates to capital as wealth; the other, g, relates to capital as factor of production. The two cannot therefore sensibly be compared with each other, far less be expected to exhibit stability over time or in their relation. In the absence of a clearer and more relevant definition of the underlying concepts, it is impossible to attach the claimed significance to the relationship between the two.

Piketty concludes: 'To summarise, I define "national wealth" or "national capital" as the market value of everything owned by the residents and government of a country at a given point in time, provided that it can be traded on some market.'[4] The *Mona Lisa* and Central Park (owned by the French state and the City of New York respectively) *could* be traded on some market – there are many potential purchasers of old master paintings, and Central Park probably represents the world's most valuable development land. But since there is no possibility that these assets *will* be so traded, it is hard to see any issue in economic or societal relations to which a calculation of their market value would have relevance. Schools and universities would seem to represent an important element of national capital and national wealth, on any reasonable definition – they are both factors of production and collective assets – but they have no ascertainable market value.

Measuring the value of capital as a factor of production

The value of capital as a factor of production – as distinct from capital as wealth – is usually measured by aggregating what has been spent to create it. Estimates of this national capital are compiled by government statistics offices using a method called 'perpetual inventory'. The statisticians record the amount of new investment in each year in each category. They add that to their estimate of national capital reported in the previous year. (The relevant statistics do not extend back to the eighteenth century, so the draining of the Nor' Loch, which improved the quality of Adam Smith's life and aided the delivery of supplies to his baker and brewer, is not included. Nor is the cost of building the seventeenth-century Palace of Versailles.)

Allowance is then made for depreciation, reflecting both physical deterioration – equipment wears out with use – and obsolescence – typewriters were thrown away, not because they had worn out but because they were no longer wanted. In practice, given the inevitable absence of a detailed annual survey of all assets, allowance for depreciation is a very rough and ready measure.

Perpetual inventory is broadly similar to the methods of historic cost accounting, traditionally the basis of company financial reporting. But for many purposes we are more interested in the current benefits of capital items than we are in their historic cost. The Great Western Railway line to Bristol cost £6.5 million to build almost 200 years ago, but even, or perhaps especially, if we estimated depreciation over that period and used an index of construction costs to update the figure to the present day, it is hard to think of any current question or decision to which the answer might be relevant.[5]

Modern business accounting practice, reflected in International Financial Reporting Standards (IFRS) and Generally Accepted Accounting Principles (GAAP), has tended to move away from historic cost in favour of 'fair value'. But the term 'fair value' raises questions rather than offering answers. What does 'fair' mean in this context? European standards favour market values of assets where such markets exist – or almost exist. American accountants, more conservative, support downward adjustments but not upward revaluations.

Estimating the value of capital as a factor of production

Fig. 1 below shows the composition of the capital stock of four major Western economies calculated on this basis.[6]

Everywhere, housing is the largest component. On average, half of the value of the physical assets of a modern economy

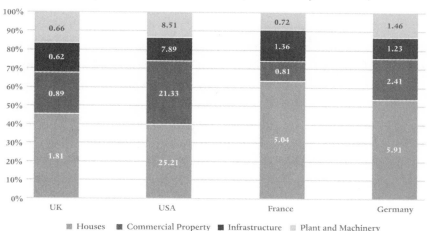

Physical Assets of Nations, 2020 (local currency in trillions)

	UK	USA	France	Germany
(top)	0.66	8.51	0.72	1.46
	0.62	7.89	1.36	1.23
			0.81	2.41
	0.89	21.33	5.04	5.91
(bottom)	1.81	25.21		

■ Houses ■ Commercial Property ■ Infrastructure ▦ Plant and Machinery

takes the form of residential property. At the Carron Works, the owners built houses for the labourers they had recruited from the fields. This was common practice until well into the twentieth century; Ford and General Motors each promoted housing development for their workers.

> The UK Office for National Statistics defines the capital stock as follows: 'Capital stock is the quantity of produced non-financial assets with a lifespan of more than a year (for example, buildings and machinery), which contribute to the production of goods and services, without being completely used up or transformed in the process. Capital stock produces a flow of capital services into the production process.'[7]

Before the twentieth century, wealthy people – mainly landed aristocrats – owned or bought land and made it available to builders for speculative housing development. The properties were usually rented or leased, so that the promoters retained an element of ultimate control over their urban estates: a phenomenon you can still see in central London, where the Crown and Grosvenor estates continue to own many of the freeholds of the city's most prized properties. But the humble dwellings that housed labourers in the burgeoning cities were also developed for lease or rent.

All this changed in the twentieth century. The financial innovation that had begun in places like Halifax made it possible for people of modest – but some – means to buy their own homes. In Britain, France and the US almost two-thirds of residential properties are owner-occupied; in Germany, where apartment rental continues to be popular, the proportion is half.[8] The share of the housing stock that is in owner occupation is higher by value than the share calculated by number of dwellings, since it is generally the more expensive properties that are owner-occupied. Put simply, nineteenth-century housing was owned by capitalists; in the twenty-first century housing is owned by workers.

Other elements of the capital stock

Much infrastructure, such as roads and sewers, is state-owned; once constructed by a mixture of profit-seeking businesspeople, municipalities and public-spirited merchants, most of these assets were taken over by governments in the twentieth century. But in the later part of that period franchising of the operation, and even 'sale' of the infrastructure, including of basic utility services such as water and electricity, became common.

Commercial property includes shops, offices, warehouses – though also bowling alleys, pubs and doctors' surgeries, often now described as 'alternatives'. The final element of national capital is the plant and machinery operated by business. Both business real estate and business equipment are now largely owned by specialist capital service providers, typically REITs, large institutional investors or subsidiaries of financial institutions.

When Al-Qaeda aeroplane hijackers hit the Twin Towers in 2001, the terrorists were able to destroy what they perceived as an iconic symbol of modern capitalism and kill 3,000 people. The buildings were owned by the Port Authority of New York;

only nine weeks earlier Silverstein Properties, a family-owned real estate company, had paid $3.2 billion for a ninety-nine-year lease on the buildings. Years of negotiation and political infighting secured a settlement with the insurers of the buildings and the hijacked aircraft that helped fund the modern rebuilding.

But what could it mean, for example, to 'own' the sewers of London? They are maintained by Thames Water Utilities, which operates under a licence granted by the Water Services Regulation Authority. Thames Water Utilities enjoys certain rights explicitly conferred on it by statute and contract and is a company whose shares are ultimately owned by a consortium of institutional investors. The largest of these equity investors are the Ontario Municipal Employees Retirement Scheme and the (British) Universities Superannuation Scheme. The company is in fact mostly funded by debt provided by other institutional investors and, as I write, teeters on the edge of bankruptcy.

This precarious financial position does not arise because the provision of drinking water and sewage disposal to London is not a commercially viable business; nor would the taps in Buckingham Palace (or my apartment) run dry if the corporate entity that is Thames Water Utilities failed. In the event of such failure government and its agencies would resume responsibility for these essential services. The financial situation is the result of financial engineering encouraged by poor regulation and anomalous fiscal rules.

If one applies Honoré's tests of ownership (see Chapter 15), it would seem that only two of the eleven (right to manage and right to income) apply to the pipes and sewers of Thames Water Utilities. Ultimate control lies with the British government and its agencies, which have the ability to pass relevant laws and formulate regulations and frequently do so. Here, as so often, the concept of 'ownership' is simply not helpful in describing economic relations in the modern economy.

The (mainly financial) companies that had been attacked quickly resumed operations from other sites. I read with interest a Harvard Business School case in which a senior Morgan Stanley executive recounted the company's response to the incident.[9] I anticipated at least a mention of Rick Rescorla, the head of security for that company, who ordered evacuation in defiance of the Port Authority's advice to occupants to stay put, with the result that only thirteen of Morgan Stanley's 3,700 employees in the towers died.[10] They included Rescorla himself, who returned to the South Tower to ensure that no one remained inside the wrecked structure, and who is now buried in the Cornish village where he was born. There was no such mention, but considerable self-congratulation for the contingency planning which enabled trading to resume less than an hour after the first plane hit the North Tower. Such are the priorities of modern financiers.

Westward Ho!

The capital initially subscribed by the English middle class to the Great Western Railway was used to build the line to Bristol, the stations and rail sheds and the Swindon engineering works. The most capital-intensive industrial project in history at the time, it was completed in 1841 at a cost of £6.5 million – then 1.3 per cent of British GDP. An equivalent proportion today would be around £30 billion. Fresh public offerings raised further capital to extend the line to Wales and Cornwall.

In 1921 the British government forced the amalgamation of all railways into four companies of which the Great Western Railway was one; nationalisation followed in 1948, and a complex restructuring, described as privatisation, was effected in 1995. At the time of writing, GWR is operated under an 800-page franchise agreement between the British government and FirstGroup, which is principally a bus company. The trains are owned by specialist rolling stock leasing companies Angel Trains and Porterbrook. The track is owned and maintained by

Network Rail, a state-owned company formed after the failure of Railtrack, a company that had been listed on the London Stock Exchange. If the GWR franchise is not renewed – and it won't be, since the government has announced yet another reorganisation of the structure of Britain's railways – then the agreement provides for most of the few rail assets that First-Group does own to be transferred to a new operator.

Who are Angel Trains and Porterbrook? The two largest shareholders of Angel Trains are Allianz, the German insurance company, and AIMCo, each with 30 per cent of the stock of the company. AIMCo was established in 2008 by the government of the Canadian province of Alberta. It manages funds on behalf of various provincial pension funds and invests the reserves of that oil-rich province. Fifty-five per cent of the stock of Porter-brook is held by AMP, an Australian financial services business (formerly Australian Mutual Provident) now mainly engaged in the management of 'super funds' (Australian for individual and collective pension funds).

What is missing from this account of the operation of the 'privatised' British railways is the figure of caricature in commu-nist posters – the capitalist with porcine girth and features and a fat cigar, the successor to George Hudson and Leland Stanford. The nearest approximation I have found is Li Ka-shing, a refugee from China who is now Hong Kong's richest man. Li left school at the age of fifteen and set up a small business manufacturing plastic flowers. From these modest beginnings he developed the massive Hutchison Whampoa group, of which Eversholt, another rail rolling stock leasing company, is a subsidiary. None of the, admittedly small, sample of railway employees I inter-viewed had ever heard of Li, far less experienced resentment at his oppression or exploitation. If they did express resentment, it was – appropriately – directed at the management of First-Group and most of all at the Department for Transport. Li is svelte, noted for his relatively modest habits and second only to Bill Gates for the scale of his global philanthropy.

THE CONDITION OF THE LABORING MAN AT PULLMAN.—

The divorce of ownership

AerCap and Prologis are both quoted on US stock exchanges and their identified shareholders are large asset managers such as Fidelity. These companies are not the beneficial owners. The stakes are mostly held on behalf of funds similar to those that invest in rolling stock, such as AIMCo and Allianz, and in the expectation of stable long-term returns.

Prologis and Aercap, AMP and the investment arm of the province of Alberta, have neither the desire nor the competence to involve themselves in the management of Amazon, British Airways or the Great Western Railway.

The phrase 'the divorce of ownership and control' was coined by Berle and Means in 1932 to describe the rise of the professional manager who owned little, if any, of the stock of the corporation. Two decades later Berle noted that 'major corporations in most instances do not seek capital. They form it themselves.'[11] Corporations by then largely financed investment through their retained earnings rather than through capital markets. But the development of extensive markets for capital services described in this chapter is a much more fundamental change in the nature of business and our understanding of it.

All these capital services are essential to the operation of the businesses. But the necessity of buying these means of production does not imply that their provider controls, far less owns, the business that depends on them. As the economic historian Deirdre McCloskey has pointed out, we do not talk about water-ism, essential though running water is to our personal and commercial lives.[12] Or power-ism, although the new availability of first steam and then electric power may have been a more important contributor to the modernity of economic life than any change in the availability of capital.

If the managers of a modern business do not want to succumb to the demands of their capital supplier, they can buy their capital services elsewhere. In fact, it is often rather easier for them to exercise that choice than it is to change their water or electricity provider. That these points seem novel, even disturbing, is a measure of the extent to which outdated rhetoric developed to describe the Carron Works and the plant at the River Rouge continues to frame our thought.

Most commercial property is now owned either by real estate investment trusts like Prologis or directly by institutions such as insurance companies and pension funds. A recent trend, particularly in Britain, is for business property assets to be acquired by opaque offshore entities. These are mostly believed to represent individuals from Eastern Europe, the Gulf and Asia who see London as a safe haven for their wealth. National and local government occupies extensive property, but much of this has been divested – Britain's iconic Treasury building is 'owned' by a consortium of investors. Yet again, the transaction raises the question of what such ownership means. But it plainly does *not* mean that the owner of the property controls, or even has influence over, the actions of the officials in the building that once housed the offices of David Lloyd George and Winston Churchill.

Many readers will never have heard of AerCap or Equinix or

GATX or Prologis. The Amazon employee does not know who owns the warehouse where he works and probably his boss does not know either. They don't know because it doesn't matter. They work for the organisation that is Amazon, with its collective intelligence and management structure.

About two-thirds of AerCap's $70 billion aircraft fleet is financed by debt, mostly provided by major banks, with the balance in equity, mostly held by asset managers on behalf of institutions such as pension funds. If political and economic power in modern economies still rested with the owners of business assets, that is where it would be found. But political and economic power obviously does not rest with the owners of business assets. If the forces of revolution were to storm the bastions of capitalism, the Dublin headquarters of AerCap would not be on their itinerary.

A century ago the awakened proletariat might have made their way to Ford's River Rouge plant. Or, more recently, ridden the subway to the General Motors building at Fifth Avenue in New York, which the company erected in the 1960s just as its hegemony was starting to fade. The new sans-culottes could have smashed the plate glass windows that fronted the display of Cadillacs and ascended to invade the executive suites. But GM is not there any more and, after a dalliance with Donald Trump, the former GM building is now owned by a consortium that includes a REIT, Zhang Xin (a female Chinese real estate billionaire) and the secretive Safra banking family. If today's revolutionaries made their way to Cupertino or Seattle or Wilmington, Delaware to sack Apple or Amazon, they would discover that the means of production of modern businesses are elusive.

30

WHO ARE THE CAPITALISTS NOW?

The class of big capitalists, who, in all civilized countries,
are already in almost exclusive possession of all the means
of subsistence and of the instruments (machines, factories)
and materials necessary for the production of the means of
subsistence.

Friedrich Engels, *Principles of Communism*, 1847

The Cardells and Garbetts founded the business of the Carron
Works, funded and built the plant and financed its operations.
They were directly involved in determining strategy, took all
executive decisions and supervised day-to-day operations. The
'robber barons' of the 'gilded age' – men like Carnegie, Rockefeller and Vanderbilt – were recognisable as their successors.
However, the scale and capital intensity of the businesses they
controlled meant that much of the funding of their companies
came from external sources. And securities markets and the
banking industry were developing to make that possible.

But the functions these heroes or villains of capitalism
once exercised are now dispersed among many individuals and
groups. Many might today lay claim to the title 'capitalist'.

Business founders

If we were searching for a modern Carnegie, Rockefeller or Vanderbilt, we might look to Bezos, Gates or Musk. These modern
businesspeople own financial assets – stock in the businesses
they helped create. Unlike their predecessors, they do not own

tangible productive assets, such as steelworks, oil wells and pipe-lines, and no longer do the companies own them; these titans of twenty-first-century business control only their companies.

But while people like Bezos, Gates and Musk top the modern 'rich list' and capture the public imagination, most large corporations are controlled by men in suits, if no longer in ties, whose careers have been spent ascending corporate bureaucracies. Of the ten largest companies in the *Fortune* list discussed in Chapter 7, none was founder-controlled.

Leading executives in large corporations

At Amazon, Bezos has given way to Andy Jassy, who joined the company in 1997, not long after it was established. Jassy established the web services business which has become the profit engine of the company. At Microsoft Gates handed over to Steve Ballmer, also an early recruit, in a transition that did not work well. Satya Nadella, who replaced Ballmer, had come to Microsoft as a graduate recruit to what was by 1992 a well-established business. Musk remains an active manager not only of Tesla but also of SpaceX and, following his eccentric purchase, of X (formerly Twitter), although an increasing number of his followers wish that he were less hyperactive.

The skills of the successful professional manager are different from the inspiration of the founder, and Nadella may be to Microsoft what Sloan was to General Motors – the man who imposed the bureaucratic discipline required by large-scale organisation. Sloan maintained a low public profile, and Jack Welch may have been the first career professional manager to attract wide public attention. Still, the people for whom management is a career and being CEO is a job do not command the legion of followers who await the tweets of Elon Musk. Doug McMillon is boss to more people than any other business executive but not well known even to Walmart shoppers – or to many Walmart employees. While Françoise Bettencourt plays piano, the business in which she is the principal stockholder is in the charge of Nicolas Hieronimus (CEO of L'Oréal). (Yes, I had to look it up too.)

Rentiers

Françoise Bettencourt and Alice Walton are modern rentiers. This group was once epitomised by Mr Darcy and Emily Brontë – people whose income is derived from interest and dividends on inherited capital who do not seek or engage in paid employment. A shrunken class today – unless one stretches the definition to include 'retirees' such as Bill Gates and Jeff Bezos.

Banks

At the beginning of the twentieth century, J. P. Morgan promoted the formation of the most valuable company in the world, US Steel. Morgan was not only the leading global financier; he also conformed to everyone's picture of the leading global financier. Today the bank he founded is led by Jamie Dimon, lieutenant to Sandy Weill until that dealmaking titan feared that Dimon sought his crown and fired him. Dimon moved to a smaller regional bank, which was acquired by J. P. Morgan, and quickly became CEO of the whole operation.

Venture capital and private equity

Other financiers focus on more specialist roles. Examples include leaders of venture capital partnerships such as John Doerr of Kleiner Perkins and Michael Moritz of Sequoia Capital. Venture capital firms are providers of finance to early-stage businesses, generally to cover the operating losses most will incur in their activities. These investors hope to profit from an IPO or a trade sale of the business to an established corporate purchaser.

More developed businesses may be subject to the attention of private equity titans such as Steve Schwarzman of Blackstone and Henry Kravis of KKR. Private equity firms buy established businesses and hope to enhance earnings before selling the business on, typically after three to five years.

Specialist providers of capital as a service

Examples: Prologis and AerCap, Evergreen and Triton – firms that supply the capital services that constitute the means of production in modern business. Their funds are, directly or indirectly, mostly derived from the retirement and other savings of small investors and loans from conventional banks.

Leading executives of international economic organisations

Examples: Christine Lagarde (president, European Central Bank), Kristalina Georgieva (Managing Director of the International Monetary Fund, previously at the World Bank), Ngozi Okonjo-Iweala (World Trade Organization), Ajay Banga (World Bank). Note the predominance of women in this group; the exception is the presidency of the World Bank, by convention appointed by the US. Women have advanced further and more rapidly in politics than in business and – especially – finance.

Influencers

Examples: Charles Koch, Robert Mercer, George Soros. These rich men have attempted to parlay their wealth into political influence. Koch funded right-wing think tanks and academic research. Mercer and Soros made fortunes through the success of their hedge funds. Mercer attracted public attention with his involvement in Cambridge Analytica, which played an unsavoury role in the Brexit campaign. Soros promoted liberal democracy in post-communist Eastern Europe through his Open Society Foundations and has contributed to left-of-centre causes in the United States.

Media barons

Alfred Harmsworth (publisher of the *Daily Mail*) and William Randolph Hearst (the model for Orson Welles's *Citizen Kane*) pioneered tabloid journalism and attempted to use their positions to exert political influence. Today Rupert Murdoch-controlled companies publish *Fox News* and the *Wall Street Journal*, as well as *The Times* of London, and Jeff Bezos owns the *Washington Post*.

Traders

Examples: Goldman Sachs, Renaissance Technologies. Most of the activity of the modern financial sector is concerned with creating, buying and selling claims to existing assets rather than the provision of capital to fund new businesses or new productive capital. Despite the nomenclature of 'investment bank', secondary market trading is the main source of revenues of a business such as Goldman Sachs. The Abacus and Timberwolf transactions, which were straightforwardly designed to fleece naïve investors, are extreme examples. But it is generally unlikely that such activity yields much public value. Renaissance is the algorithmic trading fund established by mathematician Jim Simons and computer scientist Robert Mercer. Ken Griffin of Citadel, another large hedge fund, featured in Chapter 11 as the owner of some of the world's most desirable residences.

Asset managers

Examples: Blackrock, Fidelity, Vanguard. Blackrock is the largest such business and manages assets of under just $10 trillion.[1] This total includes investments in almost every listed company in the world through its *passive* funds, which attempt to replicate the performance of the widely publicised equity indices, such as the S&P 500. These asset managers also offer *active* management, involving the purchase and sale of individual stocks and also, but secondarily, engage in the provision of funds to early-stage companies that are not traded on any stock exchange.

Institutional investors

Examples: the Norwegian Oil Fund, the Californian Public Employees Retirement System (CalPERS). With assets of over $1 trillion Norway's sovereign wealth fund, managed by Norges Bank Investment Management (NBIM), is the world's largest single investor. CalPERS, with 1.6 million members, is the biggest US pension scheme. Large asset holders such as these may undertake some or all of their own asset management, but smaller ones will delegate this to asset managers such as Blackrock.

All capitalists now?

AerCap and Prologis, major owners of the modern means of production, are nevertheless rather unimportant intermediaries in the modern economy. Both corporations are listed on the New York Stock Exchange (NYSE). The largest holders of Prologis stock are Blackrock, State Street and Vanguard. These asset managers are the largest providers of passive funds, which replicate a stock market index and therefore simply hold the same proportion of all listed shares in them. But most of the funding of these capital service providers comes not from equity but through loans from other financial institutions: banks, insurance companies and pension funds.

Whether the long chain of intermediation runs through shares or deposits, pension funds or mutual funds, at its end we find individuals. The beneficiaries of NBIM are the people of Norway. CalPERS invests on behalf of the teachers, firefighters and police of the Golden State. Depositors in J. P. Morgan Chase and BNP Paribas provide the cash which is lent to providers of capital as a service. Few of these individuals know how, or even that, they have themselves funded the planes they fly in. Or that they finance the Amazon warehouses which are key to another chain of intermediation that brings gadgets from south China to their homes.

So are we all capitalists now? People of my generation,

going through the papers of their deceased parents, often find in the attic a certificate for the handful of shares mum and dad were allotted in the 1984 privatisation of British Telecom. Those ageing share certificates testify to a 1980s British illusion of a shareholder democracy. Few people – and very few outside the United States – own shares directly. But very many people are *beneficiaries* of share ownership. Wealth is today more *widely* distributed than ever before. This is not the same as saying wealth is more *equally* distributed. But more people have *some* wealth than in the past.

Several factors have contributed to this wider distribution of wealth. One is the housing market: in the immediate post-war decades, owner-occupation became the norm in most developed countries. And then low interest rates and restrictions on house building resulted in house prices rising relative to most other economic variables.

Another is the invention of retirement. At the beginning of the twentieth century, life expectancy at birth in England was forty-four for men and forty-seven for women (although those who survived to age five might expect to live till they were fifty-eight and sixty respectively).[2] Still, most people died before reaching what would either now or then have been considered retirement age. And if people survived to the end of their working life they rarely lived long thereafter. Today someone aged sixty-five can expect to live for another twenty years and will have accumulated rights to state and private pensions that will support their retirement.

Meanwhile rising incomes allow people who would once have lived from hand to mouth to accumulate some savings. And at the same time a variety of financial innovations – from mutual funds to mobile banking – have transformed retail finance. Once, most workers were paid on a weekly cycle and budgeted on the same cycle; today a smartphone gives instant and almost universal access to the financial system and a wide variety of financial instruments.

In Britain today, even the poorest households are likely to

have some wealth. The second-lowest decile, for example, has wealth of £70,000, of which about 20 per cent is financial or in a pension; the third-lowest decile has £180,000, with 35 per cent in financial assets.[3] And this is not accounting for age: household assets, if all goes well, grow up to the point of retirement. The median retiree lives in a household with assets above £500,000; more than a quarter are in households with assets above £1,000,000.[4] Wealth is not equally, or even equitably, distributed, but it is more broadly distributed than in the past. To see a modern capitalist, perhaps you should go to the mirror in the home you own.

31

IN SEARCH OF CAPITAL

People are the most important asset in the company.
                    Mary Barra, CEO General Motors, 2018[1]

How can you buy or sell the sky, the warmth of the land?
The idea is strange to us.
    If we do not own the freshness of the air and the sparkle
of the water, how can you buy them from us?
                    Attributed to Chief Seattle, 1854

> The myth of Chief Seattle's eloquence (in English, which he did not speak) is more than a century old. The words cited were written much more recently by Ted Perry for a film script for the documentary *Home* (produced by the Southern Baptist Radio and Television Commission, 1972). Perry's 'speech' was subsequently popularised by Al Gore (1992).[2]

The terminology of capitalism is so pervasive that new types of 'capital' are invented to describe recent developments in society. This usage enables people of all political persuasions to continue to apply familiar categories of dialogue and enables economists to apply familiar analytic models. So we encounter intangible capital, human capital, social capital, natural capital and even Surveillance Capitalism.[3] For something to count and be counted, it seems necessary to label it as some form of capital. Would Marx applaud – or wonder what on earth these writers were talking about?

Intangible assets

Companies such as Apple and Amazon have market capital-
isations far in excess of their tangible assets. One common
explanation of this difference is the scale of their 'intangible
assets'. But unless one can be specific about what these intangible assets are, this statement provides no additional explanation
or insight. The two sources of intangible assets most frequently
cited are research & development and brand value.

The phrase 'research & development' brings to mind an
image of white-coated scientists in laboratories occasionally
coming up with astonishing discoveries. And a few industries,
such as pharmaceuticals and some areas of electronics, may
seem like that. This kind of work is undoubtedly important:
the economic historian Brad DeLong identifies the research
laboratory as one of the three key factors behind the take-off
in economic growth seen in the last two centuries.[4] But even
in these industries, the business reality is one of incremental
improvement, continued tinkering with products and processes.
Apple and Amazon are technologically sophisticated companies,
constantly innovating. But their distinctive capability lies in the
combination and recombination of well-known and generally
available ideas rather than pioneering scientific breakthroughs.
In a twenty-first-century company it is almost impossible to
draw a line around a facility or an element of the management
accounts and say 'This is our research & development department' and 'This is what it cost us to develop that product.'

When governments offer tax advantages to 'research &
development' expenditures, specialist consultants are needed
to enable businesses to frame their claims. And while the link
between the capital expenditure on a production line at General
Motors and the cars that rolled off it in the years that followed
was direct and quantifiable, today the connection between
development expenditure and future returns is tentative and
uncertain. What part of the market value of Amazon and Apple
is attributable to their past development expenditure? There
seems no sensible answer short of 'all of it'.

Human capital

When executives deliver that routine cliché of modern management – 'Our people are our greatest asset' – the commercial value of the collective intelligence developed within the corporation is probably what they have in mind. The asset is the capability of individuals and teams within the business to solve problems, to devise and deliver new products and to win the commitment of suppliers and the trust of customers. Collective intelligence is the basis of the competitive advantage of most successful corporations, and it is enshrined in its people.

'Our people are our greatest asset' was literally true for the slave owners of the West Indies and the Confederate States, and that history is probably why it was not until well into the twentieth century that the term 'human capital' came again into use. And a little longer before managers could say 'Our people are our greatest asset' without embarrassment. That 'our people' are not 'our property' but are free to leave makes a big difference.

> Adam Smith described human capital without using the term: its popularisation begins with Gary Becker in the 1960s. Smith believed that slavery was both immoral and inefficient, the product of a pervasive desire to dominate others, a trait sometimes observable in the heroic CEO of the modern era. The question of whether the institution was inefficient as well as immoral has remained controversial since it was famously challenged by Robert Fogel and Stanley Engerman in *Time on the Cross* (1974).

There are some valid analogies between 'human capital' and physical capital. Human capital entails investment in schooling, apprenticeship and on-the-job training. Wisely managed, the resulting knowledge and skills yield returns for many years while requiring maintenance and incurring depreciation. Some of Honoré's 'badges of ownership' can be applied to brands, research & development and human capital.

But there are also many reasons why human capital is

different. Most fundamentally, you can rent human capital as a service but you cannot buy or sell it. (Even when slavery was legal, what you could buy or sell was labour as a service rather than the problem-solving capabilities of slaves. The coercive nature of the relationship minimised its economic value.) Education yields social and cultural benefits as well as economic ones, and not just to the recipient. The most important function of education is to prepare its beneficiaries to be part of a civilised society and democratic polity. The Protestant Reformation did not have economic benefits in mind when it laid emphasis on teaching children to read, but the economic consequences were transformational.

The name most associated with human capital is that of the Chicago economist Gary Becker, who won the Nobel Prize in 1992 for 'having extended the domain of microeconomic analysis to a wide range of human behaviour and interaction, including nonmarket behaviour'.[5] While many of the extensions of this rational choice framework to non-economic spheres such as family life or crime and punishment are simply silly,[6] some of these developments yield insight. There is purpose and value to quantitative research on the economic dimensions and value of education and training.

Prospective students needing loans to finance their studies would do well to review evidence on the returns to higher education. Research on the role of such education as a device for signalling the abilities needed to gain admission to the course rather than as a means of acquiring knowledge is illuminating – I have certainly encountered more than one student for whom time spent listening to me is the price to be paid for three otherwise pleasurable and certainly career-enhancing years at Oxford. But whatever the mechanism by which the human capital created by formal education is developed or expressed, the product belongs to the student.

The human capital provided by formal education is merely preliminary to the human capital developed by individuals within firms. Some of the latter will be general, the kind of knowledge and intelligence gained through apprenticeship, whether that apprenticeship is of the formal kind leading to qualification – the plumber's training or the barrister's pupillage – or the informal development of personal capability that everyone experiences when they begin work. And some of that acquired intelligence – the ability to solve work-related problems – is specific to particular businesses, either because these are the kinds of problems that such businesses solve or because you learn the proprietary solutions that that business proffers – whether appropriately or not – to all its customers. Old Macdonald's farm would rear beef, McDonald's restaurants will serve a Big Mac and McKinsey will deliver a PowerPoint presentation. And their employees will learn the skills of animal husbandry, the contents of the McDonald's manuals and the templates of PowerPoint. Workers share in and contribute to the development of the collective intelligence which defines the capabilities of the business. And in the meantime robots have been taking over the assembly line jobs at General Motors, where in the past commoditised labour had been told what to do and incentivised to do it as quickly as possible.

Social capital

The term 'social capital' is today indelibly associated with the Harvard political scientist Robert Putnam, who equates it with 'the features of social life – networks, norms and trust – that enable participants to act together more effectively to pursue shared objectives'.[7] This definition is obviously consonant with the description of the firm developed in the preceding chapters. The capabilities of the firm are a reflection of the features of *working* life – networks, norms and trust – that enable participants to act together to pursue shared objectives more effectively. In this manner, collective intelligence is built within the firm and also within society more broadly. Society is, as Margaret Thatcher observed, made up of individuals; but in both its economic and its social dimensions it is comprised of Burke's 'little platoons' and the communities of work and place that are part of our everyday lives.

> To be attached to the subdivision, to love the little platoon we belong to in society, is the first principle (the germ, as it were) of public affections. It is the first link in the series by which we proceed towards a love to our country and to mankind.
>
> Edmund Burke, 1790[8]

Putnam's research on the considerable variations in the quality of regional government across Italy emphasised the importance of networks, norms and trust. And Italy demonstrates powerfully the productivity of industrial clusters. Moreover, the differences in social capital were related to the considerable variations in the economic performance of different regions – the industrial success of Meda (the Italian centre of sofa manufacturing we came across earlier) versus the Mafia-blighted backwardness of Sicily. Of course, these factors had received attention from economists since Adam Smith; and in the 1830s Tocqueville had identified 'the spirit of association' as the source of American exceptionalism. 'The spirit of association' which Tocqueville observed created a civic society in which agency was no longer polarised between the individual and the state.

But more than a century after Tocqueville the United States would generally be seen as more individualistic than the European societies from which so many of its citizens' ancestors had emigrated. And it was from the United States that an approach to political philosophy and economic theory based on exactly that polarisation betweeen individual and state became a dominant strand of thought globally in the late twentieth century.

Putnam's critique was one of the most eloquent responses to this evolution in political theory and social practice. His claim that this wide American participation in voluntary organisation was in decline put his concept of social capital at the centre of a developing debate. And the striking phrase 'bowling alone' drew attention to his analysis. In a more recent book Putnam would claim to see signs of some revival of 'social capital'.[9]

Putnam's work is important, and his thinking is consistent with the themes of this book. But 'social capital' has few of the characteristics normally associated with the term 'capital'. No one owns it (there are no 'social capitalists'); it is not convertible to or from other kinds of capital; it cannot be bought or sold. It does not depreciate through use – if anything, the opposite is true. And it has defied attempts to measure it. As I described in Chapter 26, the most illuminating approach to measurement is the extent of generalised trust: how do people respond to the question 'Do you think that most people can be trusted?'

Natural capital

The Organisation for Economic Cooperation and Development (OECD) offers a definition of natural capital: 'Natural capital are [*sic*] natural assets in their role of providing natural resource inputs and environmental services for economic production.' The report goes on to explain that 'Natural capital is generally considered to comprise three principal categories: natural resource stocks, land and ecosystems. All are considered essential to the long-term sustainability of development for their provision of "functions" to the economy, as well as to mankind outside the economy and other living beings.'[10]

The language is not felicitous, but the attempt to account for the contribution the natural environment makes to economic production and welfare is admirable. However, the attempt to measure it borders on the ludicrous. Britain's Office for National Statistics (ONS) identifies natural capital in the UK totalling £1.8 trillion, a figure that might be compared with physical capital of £2.7 trillion.[11] The largest component of this 'natural capital' is Britain's attractive countryside, with the opportunities that it offers for recreation and tourism.

But recreation is valued at what it costs to benefit from it – a measure that sounds useful until you stop to think about it. I often take a break by walking in Regent's Park, a magnificent open space in central London. But since I walk to it, no value is attributed to my recreation, as it is free. If I took a taxi to the entrance, the cab fare would contribute to the nation's natural capital. If I drive to the lovely Perthshire countryside my family comes from, the ONS would count the cost of my petrol and the cost of my hiking boots. If the oil price rises, so does the value of the hills and lochs – in fact, the maximum value is reached just before the point at which I decide it is too expensive to go at all. In 2023, vandals cut down an iconic tree in Northumberland. The loss of the tree was valued at £622,191 (sic) and the damage to the two thousand year old Hadrian's Wall put at £1,144.[12]

This is not the only point in this book at which it is useful to recall the observation of the long-deceased Chicago economist Frank Knight:

> the saying often quoted from Lord Kelvin … that 'where you cannot measure your knowledge is meagre and unsatisfactory,' as applied in mental and social science, is misleading and pernicious. This is another way of saying that these sciences are not sciences in the sense of physical science, and cannot attempt to be such, without forfeiting that proper nature and function. Insistence on a concretely quantitative economics means the use of statistics of physical magnitudes, whose economic meaning and significance is uncertain and dubious. (Even 'wheat' is approximately homogeneous only if measured in economic terms.) And a similar statement would even apply more to other social sciences. In this field, the Kelvin dictum very largely means in practice, 'if you cannot measure, measure anyhow!'[13]

The anxiety of many people to call attention to something they think is important – education, trust, the environment – by describing it as 'capital' is a tribute to the impact Marxist rhetoric continues to make on those who would run from any suggestion of Marxist association. 'Capital' is not a word we can do without, but we should use it much more sparingly.

PART 8

THE BEST OF TIMES,
THE WORST OF TIMES

'Now this is not the end. It is not even the beginning of the end. But it is, perhaps, the end of the beginning.'[1]

I long for a better description of business than one which treats 'our clients always come first' as a 'mere puff', a generic statement of the kind that 'all companies make'. It will be a difficult task to retrace the 'long march through the institutions' which began with the Powell memorandum fifty years ago. But the very success of these 'long marches', that of the right in the footsteps of Milton Friedman and that of the left in the spirit of Rudi Dutschke, illustrates that change is possible. In the famous words of Keynes, 'the ideas of economists and political philosophers, both when they are right and when they are wrong, are more powerful than is commonly understood. Indeed the world is ruled by little else.'[2] This book is written in that hope.

32

AMBIGUITY IS A FEATURE, NOT A BUG

> On the road from the City of Skepticism, I had to pass
> through the Valley of Ambiguity.
> > Adam Smith (actually George Goodman, financial journalist
> > and broadcaster writing under the pseudonym
> > Adam Smith), 1975[1]

It was the best of times, it was the worst of times, it was
the age of wisdom, it was the age of foolishness, it was the
epoch of belief, it was the epoch of incredulity, it was the
season of Light, it was the season of Darkness, it was the
spring of hope, it was the winter of despair, we had everything before us, we had nothing before us, we were all going
direct to Heaven, we were all going direct the other way.[2]

Dickens begins *A Tale of Two Cities* with one of the most powerful opening paragraphs of English literature.

Dickens's story begins in 1775 and ends in 1792. Events during
that period set in train many of the forces that define, and
brought about, the democracy and prosperity of the modern
world. It was the epoch of the French Revolution – and the
American Revolution. It was also the age of the Industrial Revolution. In these years Thomas Paine wrote of *Rights of Man*
and Adam Smith of *Wealth of Nations*. For twenty-three-year-old
William Wordsworth, 'Bliss was it in that dawn to be alive, / But
to be young was very heaven.'[3]

Nineteenth-century writers, of whom the most influential was Karl Marx, documented and analysed the business

*"I wish you would make up your mind, Mr. Dickens.
Was it the best of times or was it the worst of times?
It could scarcely have been both."*

environment that developed subsequently. And yet perhaps the most profound insight into that environment would come from a quite different source: Charles Darwin's exposition of evolution. Earlier thinkers, including Adam Smith's contemporaries in the Scottish Enlightenment, had foreshadowed the notion of design without designer, of coordination without coordinator. Indeed Adam Ferguson (the earlier beneficiary of Diderot's depiction of a pin factory) had written that 'nations stumble upon establishments, which are indeed the result of human action, but not the execution of any human design', and Smith's famous, perhaps notorious, reference to the 'invisible hand' is often interpreted in this sense.[4] Adaptation with selection, the basic mechanism of evolution, is the process through which collective intelligence develops and the means by which successful firms find products and business processes appropriate to the needs of their customers. Disciplined pluralism, which allows freedom to experiment but is quick to end unsuccessful experiment, is inseparable from economic progress.

Disciplined pluralism

The Protestant Reformation substituted decentralised authority for the rigid hierarchy of Catholicism, whose papal authority exemplified The Man Who Knows. In Presbyterian churches the elders – the wise and virtuous of the parish – elected their own pastor. Congregants were encouraged to read the Bible for themselves, and universal (male) literacy was therefore treated as a prerequisite. The resulting levels of educational achievement equipped young men to contribute to intellectual and scientific advances, to assume roles in business and to administer empires. Some other Protestant sects, such as the Quakers, were similarly sceptical of priestly dogma. Pluralism – freedom of thought and the opportunity to make mistakes – was encouraged rather than repressed. Future Galileos would no longer fear the Inquisition; the scientific revolution and the Enlightenment followed.

And it was the collective knowledge and collective intelligence which arose then that made the Industrial Revolution possible. The economies and societies that emerged from the scientific revolution advanced through disciplined pluralism. Pluralism is the freedom to try new ideas or new ways of doing old things or promoting new products. A society with freedom of speech and a vibrant research community enjoys a surfeit of claims to new knowledge. Likewise, a competitive business environment stimulates the adoption of new business processes and the offer of new goods and services. An economy characterised by disciplined pluralism will applaud these novelties but weed out those not worth pursuing from those that are. In these ways humans navigate radical uncertainty – and prosper from it.

Economic advance through disciplined pluralism is an evolutionary process, resembling natural selection. The Darwinian recognition that evolution might establish complex systems beyond anyone's capacity to design offers a profound insight into the nature of the contemporary firm. But the history of economic development shows more deliberation in both mutation and selection. Genetic modification is random, but businesspeople launch new products and introduce new business processes only because they believe (not necessarily correctly) that they will succeed. The parentheses are important. In a well-run business or economic system failed mutations are killed rather than left to die a natural death. Multiple mechanisms of evolution – genetic, cultural and commercial – have been crucial to the development of modern society.

This disciplined pluralism is the genius of the market economy. Both pluralism and discipline are essential. State-directed economies find each difficult to achieve. Established organisational structures resist experimentation. Britain opens its National Archives after thirty years and I still treasure recently finding there an internal assessment by the Inland Revenue (as it then was) of a report on taxation I had helped write in the 1970s. 'Everything which is practical is not new, and everything which is new is not practical.' Nothing more eloquently captures a certain bureaucratic mindset – so eloquently that I suspected the formulation was not being used for the first time. How fortunate we are that there was no one with authority to deliver that message to James Watt, Thomas Edison, Bill Gates or Steve Jobs.

And when centralised organisations finally adopt new approaches, they tend to deploy them on too large a scale. State agencies are slow to acknowledge failure and prone to cover it up or even to proclaim that failure is success. The same is true of large corporate organisations, which is why disruptive innovation most often comes from outside.

Flourishing

This book is written in the spirit of Aristotelian virtue ethics, in which *eudaimonia*, most often today translated as flourishing, is the goal of human existence. *Eudaimonia* is the outcome of a life well lived, the product not just of worldly possessions but of relations with others: their esteem, their friendship and their love. *Eudaimonia* required, in line with the expectations of the *polis* of classical Athens, a contribution to the life of the community. There are many elements of *eudaimonia*, and its achievement requires the maintenance of a balance among all these elements.[5] In commentary on Aristotle and his modern followers, this requirement of balance is often called the doctrine of the mean.

I believe it is appropriate – indeed necessary – to view the business organisation in the same way. The proper goal of corporate activity is the flourishing of the multiple stakeholders of the corporation: employees, investors, suppliers and customers, the communities in which it operates and the corporation itself. For the corporation to flourish, it must contribute to the flourishing of the society in which it operates. And 'the doctrine of the mean' is as relevant to the business organisation as it is to the individual. The directors and executives of a flourishing company operate within a mediating hierarchy, which meets the needs of all its stakeholders, gives them an opportunity for voice and protects the business from the adverse consequences of stakeholder exit.

To be clear, this is not a view of business that Aristotle shared. 'In the state which is best governed', he wrote, 'the citizens must not lead the life of mechanics or tradesmen, for such a life is ignoble, and inimical to virtue.'[6] But Aristotle's world was one in which even complex – for the time – products could be fabricated by a single skilled artisan. Aristotle could not have conceived of the modern division of labour and the associated complexity of supply chains; in short, he could not have conceived of industrialisation. Or of corporate organisation. But human nature may have changed less than technology, or legal forms, and Aristotle could perhaps have all too easily imagined the contemptible ethics and behaviour of some of those who live a modern mercantile life.

Vagueness and ambiguity

Dickens's language captured the complex ambiguities of the French Revolution – and of British and American responses to it. Dickens and Wordsworth both expressed the excitement and trepidation that the uncertainty surrounding momentous events creates; as Wordsworth continued:

> *the meek and lofty*
> *Did both find, helpers to their heart's desire,*
> *And stuff at hand, plastic as they could wish;*
> *Were called upon to exercise their skill.*[7]

But everyone – well, almost everyone – will laugh at the picture of the punctilious editor who cannot accept ambiguity or understand the insights and opportunities uncertainty offers.

I had practised economics for too long before learning about the Sorites paradox. How many grains of sand can be removed from a heap, Greek philosophers asked, before it ceases to be a heap?[8] Two millennia later, there is still no answer. Nor will there be; no further research or discussion will establish that the minimum size of a heap of sand is 987,216 grains. And if we were to *define* a heap in that precise manner, we would need a different word such as 'pile' to describe the (former) heap of sand that contained only 987,215 grains, and the Sorites paradox would now involve the definition of the word 'pile'. The National Bureau of Economic Research claims authority to define 'recession' and maintains a committee to determine whether the US economy is, or is not, in that state.[9] Some economists declare that a 'recession' is two consecutive quarters of negative GDP growth. And as I write this book there is endless speculation in the economic press as to whether there is, or will be, a recession.

But the answer to that question is not what businesspeople or policymakers want to know – or ought to want to know. They want the answer to a question less specific but more pertinent to their decisions. 'What is going on here?' That formulation sounds trite. But we live in a world of radical uncertainty, and every situation, every point of decision, is unique. And in that world, the question 'What is going on here?' needs to be posed again and again.

There is today substantive philosophical literature on the topic of *vagueness* – the necessary deployment of terms that are useful in narrative description but are not susceptible to precise definition. Ambiguity and vagueness are, in the language of today's digitised world, a feature, not a bug; they reflect the inescapable complexity of reality rather than our incompetence at describing that reality. Only a cartoon character could have accused Dickens of that incompetence – he remains the finest chronicler of nineteenth-century English society.

The architects of the modern digital world quickly encountered *fuzzy logic*. There is something inherently binary about digitisation – switches are either on or off. But 'fuzzy logic' is needed when truth values lie between 0 and 1. As when the computer must decide 'Is this a heap?' Or the sensor on the tumble dryer asks 'Is the washing dry?' Everyone wants a 'dry' towel but everyone, including the manufacturers of modern electronic dryers powered by fuzzy logic, knows that too dry a towel may be uncomfortable to use.

In writing this book, I have been repeatedly struck by the frequency with which discussion is clouded, not illuminated, by the imposition of false binaries where no clear-cut distinction actually exists. Just as there is no usefully sharp distinction between heap and not heap, between dry and wet, so there is no sharp distinction between market and hierarchy, between public and private sectors, between profit and not-for-profit organisations, even – and critically – no sharp distinction between capital and labour. The concept of ownership is often complicated, and the 'badges of ownership' may be divided among several agents so that the 'owner' is hard to identify.

Binaries are the natural currency of both lawyers and economists because, for different but related reasons, both law and mathematics demand precision. Stewart Macaulay attributed to his co-creator of the relational contract concept, Ian Macneil, the metaphor:

Classic contract law assumes a light switch. A light is either

on or off; the parties have agreed to a contract or they
haven't. Often, however, in a long-term continuing relationship, the situation resembles a rheostat. As more and
more power is sent to the bulb, we get more and more
light. It is hard to say when the light has been turned on.
On and off are not useful terms.[10]

The world often does not offer the precision of on and off. Nobel
laureate Paul Romer, he of neoclassical endogenous growth
theory, and for a time chief economist at the World Bank, coined
the term 'mathiness' to describe the wide use of symbolic nota-
tion by economists to give a misleading impression of rigour.
The practice, he said, 'leaves ample room for slippage between
statements in natural versus formal language and between statements with theoretical as opposed to empirical content'.[11]

Binary categorisation raises another problem. Economists
have employed concepts such as 'market efficiency' in securities
markets and 'contestability' of markets for goods and services,
without sufficient recognition that 'approximately efficient' or
'very contestable' may be very different in their implications
from 'perfectly efficient' or 'perfectly contestable'.

Concepts of market, hierarchy, public, private, capital, labour
and ownership are nevertheless useful – in fact, indispensable
– even if they defy precise definition. To insist, with Dickens's
hypothetical editor, on identifying things we observe as falling
into one category or the other detracts from, rather than adds
to, our understanding. Better, as Dickens did, to describe the
rich and ambiguous reality. Writing in 1859, seventy years after
the French Revolution, Dickens concluded that famous paragraph with an acknowledgement that the period in which his
novel was set was far from unique in its polarisation, turbulence
and radical uncertainty. 'In short,' he wrote, 'the period was so
far like the present period, that some of its noisiest authorities
insisted on its being received, for good or for evil, in the superlative degree of comparison only.'[12] We might say the same today.

33

AFTER CAPITALISM

> If capitalism had built up science as a productive force, the
> very character of the new mode of production was serving
> to make capitalism itself unnecessary.
>
> J. D. Bernal, *Marx and Science*, 1952[1]

Marx died in 1883. A century later the Berlin Wall crumbled, an event that symbolised the death of Marxism as an economic doctrine of practical relevance. Yet the rhetoric promoted by Marx, developed in the nineteenth century by both his acolytes and his critics, continues to play a major role in current debate. The tripartite linkage from personal wealth to ownership of capital to control of business was fundamental both to an understanding of business and to ideas about the distribution of income and wealth. But no longer. There is a linkage, but it runs from control of business to personal wealth, and the development of capital as a service renders ownership of capital largely irrelevant to managerial authority.

The ironworks and the textile mill were representative workplaces of the Industrial Revolution. Then they would be supplemented and superseded by steel mills, automobile assembly lines and meat-packing plants. But these facilities no longer represent the commanding heights of the twenty-first-century economy: Apple and Google, J. P. Morgan and Verizon, Pfizer and PwC now occupy that terrain. The employees of these companies are not the labouring poor (of the 1834 Poor Law report of Nassau Senior and Edwin Chadwick) or the lumpenproletariat (of the Communist Manifesto). They go to offices, not factories. In the eighteenth century, before the Industrial Revolution, they had mostly worked from home. In the twenty-first century, many of them want to do so again.

The products they produce are smartphones and internet search, bank accounts and connectivity, pills and accounting services. Items that fit in your pocket – or your head. Materials constitute a negligible proportion of the cost of these products. What you are paying for is the collective intelligence within these companies which is incorporated in the product design, rather than the transformation of raw materials into finished goods. This dematerialisation of the value of product is associated with dematerialisation of the means of production. Twenty-first-century business needs little capital, mostly does not own the capital it uses and is not controlled by the people who provide that capital. A modern firm buys capital services just as it buys water, electricity and transport – and as it purchases the services of workers, accountants, executives and suppliers.

In the business environment that followed the Industrial Revolution, production resulted from the combination of physical capital and physical labour. The distribution of income was the outcome of a class struggle between the providers of these two factors of production, between the owners of capital and the suppliers of labour. That description remained true of parts of business through much of the twentieth century. But in the twenty-first-century business, labour – often many different kinds of labour in combination – is the key factor of production. Output results from the associated skills of the software engineer and the designer, the accountant and the marketer, the rainmaker and the dealmaker.

The factory was once the front line of the class struggle, with trade unions leading the demand for better wages and conditions. When Marx wrote, 40 per cent of the British workforce was employed in manufacturing; today that figure is less than 10 per cent. In Britain and the United States trade unionism is now mainly a public sector phenomenon. (Germany and Scandinavia, where union officials have been co-opted into political and managerial roles, are different.) The totemic strikes of the late nineteenth century were those of the London match girls in 1888 and the Pullman dispute of 1894, with workers demanding better pay and conditions from their well-heeled employers. The totemic strikes of the late twentieth century were those of US air traffic controllers in 1982 and British mineworkers in 1984–5. To see either of these more recent events as a battle between capital and labour is, at best, a considerable oversimplification. In both cases, the employers were agencies of the state. The dismissed controllers and defeated miners were victims of the political ambitions of egotistical union leaders, who had mounted challenges that almost any democratically elected government, far less the administrations of Reagan and Thatcher, was bound to resist.

Until the end of the twentieth century political parties were defined by the economic interest – capital or labour – that they represented. And since the capitalists were less numerous, they could succeed in democracies only in alliance with conservative interests – religious groups, the military, traditionalists and libertarians – which also feared collectivism or social upheaval. As the capital/labour dichotomy became less descriptive of business, and the collapse of the Soviet Union ended the international promotion of communism, the historic rationale of these parties fractured. Across the Global North, this paved the way for the populism, identity politics and culture wars that have come to characterise the politics of the twenty-first century.

The modern business is defined by its combination of capabilities, not its production function. The success of twenty-first-century firms is derived almost entirely from the diverse capabilities of the people who work in them. The workers *are* the means of production. Is this still capitalism, or has socialism finally arrived? That is a good question for a student essay, but is of little relevance to practical business. These terms have ceased to have much explanatory value in the analysis of business organisations or economic systems.

It is impossible to construct a theory of the firm without

insights from organisational theory, psychology, anthropology and other social sciences. An emphasis on principal–agent models within a nexus of contracts diverts attention from the many issues raised by organisational theory, business history and corporate strategy. The focus on the firm as a collection of capabilities gives a different and more illuminating perspective for understanding the extraordinary diversity of business organisations and of businesspeople over geographies and over time.

The core ideas in this book – collective intelligence, radical uncertainty, disciplined pluralism, relational contracts and the mediating hierarchy – have been extensively developed and discussed by earlier writers, though much of that work has been outside the context of business organisation. The relevance of each to the argument of this book arises from a belief that in the modern world successful commercial relationships are not simply instrumental and transactional; they are social and are embedded in a wider framework of communities and teams. That transactional view was both incorrect and unattractive. This book is written in the hope that a better account of how business and its stakeholders flourish will point the way not just to a better understanding of business but to the better conduct of business itself. In a successor volume I will try to explain some of the implications of that understanding for both business policy and public policy.

'The pain of parting is nothing to the joy of meeting again.'
Charles Dickens [2]

ACKNOWLEDGEMENTS

The origins of this book go back almost forty years, when I joined the faculty of the London Business School. I hoped to diversify my interests, which had focussed on issues of fiscal policy into a wider understanding of the economic issues raised in business and finance. This book and another that will follow are the product of the journey that began then – a journey that has taken me not only into the halls of academia but into corporate board-rooms, through financial institutions and along the corridors of Whitehall. It would be impossible to list the very many people whose wisdom – and sometimes foolishness – have contributed to my education. But special thanks for ideas and inspiration to Paul Collier, Mervyn King, Colin Mayer and David Sainsbury. To Jo Charrington, who kept the many strands of my life in order for twenty years. And to the readers who commented on earlier versions of this book – James Anderson, Paul Davies, Leslie Hannah, Jonathan Haskell, Bill Janeway, John McLaren, Saurabh Mukherjee, Adam Ridley, Paul Seabright and Andrew Dilnot. They have helped remove errors of fact and opinion but those that remain are my responsibility alone.

But most of all, the intellectual journey has taught me how much there is still to learn. The study of business is still at a very early stage of development, and may be advancing no more rapidly than business itself is changing. If this book encourages a few young readers to embark on that study, my journey will have been worthwhile.

Matthew Ford has been my research assistant since 2017, before this book was more than a gleam in my eye – or his. His contribution has been stellar. We have been ably supported by Conor Callaghan, Doris Nikolic and Ying Yao. The Salvia Foundation has provided moral and financial support. I am grateful to Andrew Franklin of Profile Books, an enthusiastic promoter of the book since the day I mentioned the project to him. Seth Ditchik at Yale University Press was very ready to accept that a British author's business book might be appropriate for an American audience. And of course bound-less thanks to my wife Mika Oldham, who has had much to put up with in the course of authorship, and has been a meticulous editor of the text.

NOTES

Introduction

1   Mark 2:22. The original King James Version recites the more familiar 'And no man putteth new wine into old bottles: else the new wine doth burst the bottles, and the wine is spilled, and the bottles will be marred: but new wine must be put into new bottles.' The New King James Version is more faithful to the original – and makes more sense. The practice in those times was to use animal skins to store liquids, which came under pressure during fermentation.

2   Chandler, A. D., *Strategy and Structure: Chapters in the History of the American Industrial Enterprise* (Boston, MA: MIT Press, 1962).

3   Berle, A., and Means, G., *The Modern Corporation and Private Property* (New Brunswick, NJ: Transaction, 1932).

4   Drucker, P., *Concept of the Corporation* (New York: John Day, 1946).

PART 1: THE BACKGROUND

1. Love the Product, Hate the Producer

1   'Wall Street and the Financial Crisis: The Role of Investment Banks', Hearing before the Permanent Subcommittee on Investigations of the Committee on Homeland Security and Governmental Affairs, vol. 4, 111th Congress (27 April 2010), p. 121.

2   CNBC, 'CNBC Exclusive: CNBC Transcript: Goldman Sachs Chairman & CEO David Solomon Speaks with CNBC's Jim Cramer on *Mad Money* Today' (18 July 2022), https://www.cnbc.com/2022/07/18/cnbc-exclusive-cnbc-transcript-goldman-sachs-chairman-ceo-david-solomon-speaks-with-cnbcs-jim-cramer-on-mad-money-today.html (accessed 24 January 2023).

3   Goldman Sachs, 'Code of Business Conduct and Ethics' (23 February 2023), <https://www.goldmansachs.com/about-us/purpose-and-values/code-of-business-conduct-and-ethics.html> (accessed 8 November 2023); see *Arkansas Teacher Retirement System et al. v. Goldman Sachs Group, Inc.*, no. 16–250 (2d. Cir. 2018), pp. 6–8.

4   'Event studies', a concept I shall describe in Chapter 21.

5   And characterised explicitly so in Brief for the Chamber of
    Commerce of the United States of America as Amici Curiae
    Supporting Defendants-Appellants, *Arkansas Teacher Retirement System
    et al. v. Goldman Sachs Group, Inc.* (2018), p. 6.

6   *ECA v. J. P. Morgan Chase*, No. 07-1786 (2d. Cir. 2009), pp. 7, 30–31.

7   *Johannes T. Martin v. Living Essentials, LLC*, No. 15 C 01647 (Northern
    District, Eastern Illinois 2016), Memorandum Opinion and Order,
    <https://cases.justia.com/federal/district-courts/illinois/
    ilndce/1:2015cv01647/307113/17/0.pdf?ts=1454410266> (accessed 17
    September 2020), p. 1.

8   Kannon Shanmugam, quoted in Dewey, K., and Hemingway, M.,
    'Building a Top-Flight Supreme Court Practice with Kannon
    Shanmugam', *Lawdragon* (25 January 2024), <https://www.lawdragon.
    com/lawyer-limelights/2024-01-25-building-a-top-flight-supreme-
    court-practice-with-kannon-shanmugam> (accessed 31 January 2024).

9   Taibbi, M., 'The Great American Bubble Machine', *Rolling Stone* (5
    April 2010), <https://www.rollingstone.com/politics/politics-news/
    the-great-american-bubble-machine-195229/> (accessed 17 September
    2020).

10 Goldman Sachs, 'Goldman Sachs' Commitment to Board Diversity' (4
    February 2020), <https://www.goldmansachs.com/our-
    commitments/diversity-and-inclusion/launch-with-gs/pages/
    commitment-to-diversity.html> (accessed 24 January 2023).

11 Brief for the Chamber of Commerce of the United States of America
    as Amici Curiae Supporting Defendants-Appellants, *Arkansas Teacher
    Retirement System et al. v. Goldman Sachs Group, Inc.* (2018), p. 8.

12 The Chamber also led opposition to the proposed introduction of an
    obligation on advisers on retirement savings to put the client's
    interests first. The Trump administration dropped the plan.

13 Muilenburg, D., 'Statement from Boeing CEO Dennis Muilenburg:
    We Own Safety – 737 MAX Software, Production and Process Update'
    (5 April 2019), <https://boeing.mediaroom.com/2019-04-05-
    Statement-from-Boeing-CEO-Dennis-Muilenburg-We-Own-Safety-737-
    MAX-Software-Production-and-Process-Update> (accessed 17
    September 2020).

14 Majority Staff of the Committee on Transportation and
    Infrastructure, 'Final Committee Report: The Design, Development
    & Certification of the Boeing 737 MAX' (September 2020), <https://
    transportation.house.gov/imo/media/doc/2020.09.15%20FINAL%20

737%20MAX%20Report%20for%20Public%20Release.pdf> (accessed
12 November 2020), p. 13.

15 U.S. Department of Justice, Office of Public Affairs, 'Boeing Charged
with 737 Conspiracy and Agrees to Pay over $2.5 Billion' (7 January
2021), <https://www.justice.gov/opa/pr/boeing-charged-737-max-
fraud-conspiracy-and-agrees-pay-over-25-billion> (accessed 10 October
2023).

16 U.S. Securities and Exchange Commission, 'Boeing to Pay $200 Million
to Settle SEC Charges that it Misled Investors about the 737 Max' (22
September 2022), <https://www.sec.gov/news/press-
release/2022-170> (accessed 10 October 2023).

17 The Volkswagen case is still before the German courts. Prosecutors
had sought a jail term for Carrie Tolstedt, the Wells Fargo executive
who acknowledged responsibility for the falsification, but the court
released her on probation.

18 *Jeffrey Ross Blue v. Michael James Wallace Ashley* [2017] EWHC 1928
(Comm), para 142.

19 LaFrance, A., 'The Largest Autocracy on Earth', *The Atlantic* (27
September 2021), <https://www.theatlantic.com/magazine/
archive/2021/11/facebook-authoritarian-hostile-foreign-
power/620168/> (accessed 16 June 2023).

20 Pew Research Center, 'Modest Declines in Positive Views of
"Socialism" and "Capitalism" in U.S.' (19 September 2022), <https://
www.pewresearch.org/politics/2022/09/19/modest-declines-in-
positive-views-of-socialism-and-capitalism-in-u-s/> (accessed 16 June
2023).

21 Orwell, G., 'Politics and the English Language', *Horizon*, vol. 13, no. 76
(1946), pp. 257–8.

22 Lowrey, A., 'Why the Phrase "Late Capitalism" Is Suddenly
Everywhere', *The Atlantic* (1 May 2017), <https://www.theatlantic.
com/business/archive/2017/05/late-capitalism/524943/> (accessed 30
January 2024).

23 The first place I have found the expression 'Love the product, hate the
producer' recorded is in Alasdair Spark's 'Wrestling with America'
(1996), which comments on the ambivalence much of the world felt
towards the 'American model of consumer capitalism'. However, the
text suggests that this formulation is not original to Sparks but was in
common usage.

24 Edelman, 'Edelman Trust Barometer 2020' (2020), <https://www.
edelman.com/sites/g/files/aatuss191/files/2020-01/2020 %20Edelman

%20Trust%20Barometer%20Global%20Report.pdf> (accessed 19 September 2020), p. 28; Gallup, 'Confidence in Institutions' (2020), <https://news.gallup.com/poll/1597/confidence-institutions.aspx> (accessed 19 September 2020): 2020 figures for 'Great deal/Quite a lot'. (News in general is more trusted than big business, but television news is slightly less trusted. Large technology companies are significantly more trusted.)

25 Department for Business, Energy & Industrial Strategy, 'Business Population Estimates for the UK and Regions 2022: Statistical Release' (6 October 2022), <https://www.gov.uk/government/statistics/business-population-estimates-2022/business-population-estimates-for-the-uk-and-regions-2022-statistical-release-html> (accessed 16 June 2023), Tab 4. (The ONS dataset covers businesses registered for VAT: those not included will typically be sole proprietors with few or no employees.); U.S. Small Business Administration Office of Advocacy, '2022 Small Business Profile' (2022), <https://advocacy.sba.gov/wp-content/uploads/2022/08/Small-Business-Economic-Profile-US.pdf> (accessed 16 June 2023), p. 2.

2. A History of Pharmaceuticals: A Case for Treatment

1 Thomas, Z., and Swift, T., 'Who is Martin Shkreli – "the Most Hated Man in America"?', *BBC News* (4 August 2017), <https://www.bbc.co.uk/news/world-us-canada-34331761> (accessed 27 September 2021).

2 Redman, M., 'Cocaine: What Is the Crack? A Brief History of the Use of Cocaine as an Anesthetic', *Anesthesiology and Pain Medicine*, vol. 1, no. 2 (2011), pp. 95–7; Reinarz, J., and Wynter, R., 'The Spirit of Medicine: The Use of Alcohol in Nineteenth-Century Medical Practice', in Schmid, S., and Schmidt-Haberkamp, B. (eds.), *Drink in the Eighteenth and Nineteenth Centuries* (Abingdon: Pickering & Chatto, 2014), pp. 127–40.

3 Haynes, A., 'The History of Snake Oil', *Pharmaceutical Journal*, vol. 294, no. 7850 (21 February 2015).

4 U.S. Food and Drug Administration, 'Milestones in US Food and Drug Law', <https://www.fda.gov/about-fda/fda-history/milestones-us-food-and-drug-law> (accessed 28 September 2021); Cassidy, J., 'Muckraking and Medicine: Samuel Hopkins Adams', *American Quarterly*, vol. 16, no. 1 (1964), pp. 85–99.

5 Connelly, D., 'A History of Aspirin', *Clinical Pharmacist*, vol. 6, no. 7

(2014), <https://pharmaceutical-journal.com/article/infographics/a-history-of-aspirin> (accessed 14 October 2021) .

6   Otten, H., 'Domagk and the Development of the Sulphonamides',
     Journal of Antimicrobial Chemotherapy, vol. 17, no. 6 (June 1986),
     pp. 689–90.

7   Ballentine, C., 'Sulfanilamide Disaster', *FDA Consumer Magazine* (June
     1981).

8   Anthony, R. S., and Kim, J. H., 'Thalidomide: The Tragedy of Birth
     Defects and the Effective Treatment of Disease', *Toxicological Sciences:
     An Official Journal of the Society of Toxicology*, vol. 122, no. 1 (2007),
     <https://doi.org/10.1093/toxsci/kfr088>, pp. 1–6.

9   Laurence, J., 'Government's £80m for Victims of Thalidomide – But
     Still No Apology', *The Independent* (21 December 2012), <https://
     www.independent.co.uk/life-style/health-and-families/health-news/
     government-s-ps80m-victims-thalidomide-still-no-apology-8427855.
     html> (accessed 1 September 2021).

10   Phillips, S., 'How a Courageous Physician-Scientist Saved the U.S.
     from a Birth-Defects Catastrophe', *UChicagoMedicine* (March 2020),
     <https://www.uchicagomedicine.org/forefront/biological-sciences-
     articles/courageous-physician-scientist-saved-the-us-from-a-birth-
     defects-catastrophe> (accessed 28 September 2021).

11   American Chemical Society International Historic Chemical
     Landmarks, 'Discovery and Development of Penicillin', <https://
     www.acs.org/content/acs/en/education/whatischemistry/
     landmarks/flemingpenicillin.html> (accessed 28 September 2021).

12   Merck & Co., 'Merck's 1899 Manual', Project Gutenberg, https://
     www.gutenberg.org/files/41697/41697-h/41697-h.htm (accessed 28
     September 2021).

13   Merck KGaA, 'Company History', <https://www.merck.com/
     company-overview/history/> (accessed 28 September 2021).

14   Kannabus, A., 'History of TB Drugs', <https://tbfacts.org/history-of-
     tb-drugs/> (accessed 30 September 2021).

15   Bernard, D., 'How a Miracle Drug Changed the Fight Against
     Infection During World War II', *Washington Post* (11 July 2020),
     <https://www.washingtonpost.com/history/2020/07/11/penicillin-
     coronavirus-florey-wwii-infection/> (accessed 28 September 2021);
     Lydon, C., 'A Tough Infighter', *The New York Times* (20 August 1976),
     <https://www.nytimes.com/1976/08/20/archives/a-tough-infighter.
     html> (accessed 28 September 2021).

16   Bastian, H., 'Down and Almost Out in Scotland: George Orwell,

Tuberculosis and Getting Streptomycin in 1948', *Journal of the Royal Society of Medicine*, vol. 99, no. 2 (2006), pp. 95–8, <doi: 10.1258/jrsm.99.2.95>.

17 Collins, J. C., and Porras, J. I., *Built to Last: Successful Habits of Visionary Companies* (New York: HarperBusiness, 1997), p. 48.

18 Johnson & Johnson, 'Our Credo', <https://www.jnj.com/credo/> (accessed 28 September 2021).

19 Solomon, M., 'Poison Pill', *Medium* (14 July 2022), <medium.com/truly-adventurous/poison-pill-d98f366522a7> (accessed 20 July 2023).

20 U.S. Department of Defense, 'Crisis and Communication Strategies Case Study: The Johnson and Johnson Tylenol Crisis', <https://www.ou.edu/deptcomm/dodjcc/groups/02C2/Johnson%20&%20Johnson.htm> (accessed 28 September 2021).

21 Stokes, A., 'Merck Continues Campaign against River Blindness in the DRC' (September 2014), <https://www.pri.org/stories/2014-09-29/merck-continues-campaign-against-river-blindness-drc-video> (accessed 28 September 2021).

22 Reese, J. and Sookdeo, R., 'America's Most Admired Corporations', *Fortune* (8 February 1993), pp. 44–53.

23 Collins and Porras (1997), p. 49.

24 Prakash, S., and Valentine, V., 'Timeline: The Rise and Fall of Vioxx', *npr* (10 November 2007), <https://www.npr.org/2007/11/10/5470430/timeline-the-rise-and-fall-of-vioxx?t=1632949540924> (accessed 28 September 2021).

25 Collins, J. C., *How the Mighty Fall* (London: Random House, 2009), p. 50.

26 Kavilanz, P., 'Johnson and Johnson CEO: We Made a Mistake' (30 September 2010), <https://money.cnn.com/2010/09/30/news/companies/hearing_johnson_fda_drug_recalls/index.html> (accessed 28 September 2021).

27 Fortune, 'Merck, World's Most Admired Companies' (2020), <https://fortune.com/ranking/worlds-most-admired-companies/2020/merck/> (accessed 30 September 2023).

28 Court, E., 'Valeant Gets a New Name to Shed Its Scandals, but Will It Work?', *MarketWatch* (17 July 2018), <https://www.marketwatch.com/story/valeant-will-get-a-new-name-again-hoping-to-shed-its-scandals-2018-05-08> (accessed 28 September 2021); Bloomberg News, 'Valeant's Former Boss Michael Pearson Is Suing the Pharma for Not Paying Him 3 Million Shares Promised When He Left', *Financial Post* (28 March 2018); Scott, B., 'Valeant CEO Michael Pearson Lost $180

Million Yesterday, and \$750 Million in Past Year', *Forbes* (16 March 2016), <https://www.forbes.com/sites/bartiescott1/2016/03/16/valeant-ceo-michael-pearson-lost-two-thirds-of-his-billion-dollar-fortune-in-a-year/?sh=3d917b446c41> (accessed 28 September 2021).

29   Pollack, A., 'Drug Goes from \$13.50 a Tablet to \$750, Overnight', *The New York Times* (20 September 2015), <https://www.nytimes.com/2015/09/21/business/a-huge-overnight-increase-in-a-drugs-price-raises-protests.html> (accessed 20 July 2023). Shkreli was subsequently sentenced to seven years' imprisonment for an unrelated securities fraud.

30   Mylan, 'Mylan Launches the First Generic for EpiPen ® (epinephrine injection, USP) Auto-Injector as an Authorized Generic' (16 December 2016), <https://investor.mylan.com/news-releases/news-release-details/mylan-launches-first-generic-epipenr-epinephrine-injection-usp> (accessed 20 July 2023). A generic drug is a product pharmacologically similar to an existing drug whose patent has expired.

31   Jeffrey, A., 'Mylan Finalizes \$465 Million EpiPen Settlement with Justice Department', *CNBC* (17 August 2017), <https://www.cnbc.com/2017/08/17/mylan-finalizes-465-million-epipen-settlement-with-justice-department.html> (accessed 28 September 2021).

32   Mylan, 'Mylan and Pfizer Announce Viatris and the New Company Name in the Planned Mylan – Upjohn Combination' (12 November 2019), <https://investor.mylan.com/news-releases/news-release-details/mylan-and-pfizer-announce-viatris-new-company-name-planned-mylan> (accessed 28 September 2023).

33   *Guardian* Staff and Agencies, 'Johnson & Johnson to Pay \$5bn in Landmark \$26bn US Opioid Settlement', *The Guardian* (21 July 2021), <https://www.theguardian.com/us-news/2021/jul/21/us-opioid-settlement-state-attorneys-general-johnson-and-johnson> (accessed 28 September 2021); Case, A., and Deaton, A., *Deaths of Despair and the Future of Capitalism* (Princeton, NJ: Princeton University Press, 2020); Hoffman, J., 'Purdue Pharma Is Dissolved and Sacklers Pay \$4.5 Billion to Settle Opioid Claims', *New York Times* (1 September 2021), <https://www.nytimes.com/2021/09/01/health/purdue-sacklers-opioids-settlement.html> (accessed 28 September 2021).

34   Bodleian Libraries, 'The University of Oxford's Relationship with the Sackler Family – Statement' (15 May 2023), <https://www.bodleian.

ox.ac.uk/about/media/university-oxford-relationship-sackler-family-statement> (accessed 20 July 2023).

35 Durkin Richer, A., 'Witness: Drug Company Hired Ex-Stripper to Increase Sales', *abcNews* (1 March 2019), <https://abcnews.go.com/US/wireStory/witness-drug-company-hired-stripper-increase-sales-61419793> (accessed 28 September 2021).

36 Kuchler, H., et al., 'Opioid Executive Admits to "No Morals" Ahead of Prison Term', *Financial Times* (23 January 2020).

37 McCarthy, J., 'Big Pharma Sinks to the Bottom of U.S. Industry Rankings', Gallup (3 September 2019), <https://news.gallup.com/poll/266060/big-pharma-sinks-bottom-industry-rankings.aspx> (accessed 29 September 2021).

38 World Health Organization (WHO), 'WHO Timeline Covid-19', <https://www.who.int/news/item/27-04-2020-who-timeline---covid-19> (27 April 2020).

39 Khazan, O., 'The One Area Where the U.S. COVID-19 Strategy Seems To Be Working', *The Atlantic* (22 February 2021), <https://www.theatlantic.com/politics/archive/2021/02/america-vaccination-speed-europe-better/618094/> (accessed 29 September 2021).

40 Gallup, 'Business and Industry Sector Ratings' (17 August 2021), <https://news.gallup.com/poll/12748/business-industry-sector-ratings.aspx> (accessed 29 September 2021).

41 Wellcome Trust, 'Who We Are', <https://wellcome.org/who-we-are> (accessed 29 September 2021).

42 Novo Nordisk Fonden, 'History', <https://novonordiskfonden.dk/en/about-the-foundation/history/> (accessed 29 September 2021).

3. Economic Motivation

1 Smith, A., *An Inquiry into the Nature and Causes of the Wealth of Nations*, vol. II (London: W. Strahan and T. Cadell, 1776), p. 232.

2 Ibid.

3 Broadberry, S., Campbell, B. M. S., Klein, A., Overton, M., and Van Leeuwen, B., *British Economic Growth, 1270–1870* (Cambridge: Cambridge University Press, 2015) via Bank of England (2020)

4 Razzell, P., and Spence, C., 'The History of Infant, Child and Adult Mortality in London, 1550–1850', *London Journal*, vol. 32, no. 3 (2007), pp. 271–92; Roser, M., Ortiz-Ospina, E., and Ritchie, H., 'Life Expectancy', *Our World In Data* (2013), <https://ourworldindata.org/life-expectancy> (accessed 6 November 2023). Raw life expectancy data can be misleading, as childbirth and the first five years were

especially dangerous. However, even accounting for this, Smith did well. See 'Life Expectancy by Age in England and Wales' (we assume the Scottish experience is similar, and that, since the data series begin in 1841, extrapolation backwards is possible) in Roser, M., Ortiz-Ospina, E., and Ritchie, H., 'Life Expectancy', Our World in Data (2013), <https://ourworldindata.org/life-expectancy> (accessed 6 November 2023) (data drawn from the Human Mortality Database) to get a sense of life expectancy around that time for people who had survived the first five years. Supporting this analysis is Houston, R., "Mortality in Early Modern Scotland: The Life Expectancy of Advocates", *Continuity and Change*, vol. 7, no. 1 (1992), Table 1, which constructs conditional life expectancies for advocates, who would have inhabited a similar social class to Smith. (In fact, Smith's father was one.)

5   Smith (1776), p. 6.

6   Thwaites, T., *The Toaster Project: or, A Heroic Attempt to Build a Simple Electric Appliance from Scratch* (Princeton, NJ.: Princeton Architectural Press, 2011).

7   Rousseau, J.-J., *A Discourse upon the Origin and Foundation of the Inequality among Mankind* (London: R. and J. Dodsley, 1761).

8   Peterson, C., and Seligman, M. E. P., *Character Strengths and Virtues: A Handbook and Classification* (Oxford: Oxford University Press, 2004).

9   Csikszentmihalyi, M., *Flow: The Psychology of Optimal Experience: Steps toward Enhancing the Quality of Life* (New York: Harper Collins, 1991).

10   YouTube video of Messi *v.* Getafe: https://www.youtube.com/watch?v=mMiL4_1Yewg. Steve Jobs's iPhone launch in San Francisco: https://www.youtube.com/watch?v=MnrJzXM7a60. YouTube video of Claudio Abbado: https://www.youtube.com/watch?v=4YcmIohczpQ.

11   Jobs, S., 'Commencement Address', Stanford Report (12 June 2005) <https://news.stanford.edu/stories/2005/06/youve-got-find-love-jobs-says> (accessed 12 June 2024).

12   Service, T., 'The Abbado Effect', *The Guardian* (19 August 2008), <https://www.theguardian.com/music/tomserviceblog/2008/aug/19/theabbadomoment> (accessed 15 August 2023).

13   Schofield, R. S., 'Dimensions of Illiteracy, 1750–1850', *Explorations in Economic History*, vol. 10, no. 4 (1973), p. 443.

14   Matthew, H. C. G., McKibbin, R. I., and Kay, J. A., 'The Franchise Factor in the Rise of the Labour Party', *English Historical Review*, vol. 91, no. 361 (1976), pp. 723–52. Voting rights were extended in 1868, but

only a few working-class men and no women qualified. The First World War was the trigger for a major extension in 1918, which was completed only in 1928.

15 MacDermot, E. T., and Clinker, C. R., *History of the Great Western Railway* (London: Ian Allan, 1982), p. 15, provides a list of directors.

16 Quoted in *New York Daily Tribune* (25 March 1888), p. 11.

17 Jensen, M. C., and Meckling, H. W., 'Theory of the Firm: Managerial Behaviour, Agency Costs and Ownership Structure', *Journal of Financial Economics*, vol. 3, no. 4 (1976), pp. 305–60.

18 Haldeman, P., 'The Return of Werner Erhard, Father of Self Help', *New York Times* (28 November 2015), <https://www.nytimes.com/2015/11/29/fashion/the-return-of-werner-erhard-father-of-self-help.html> (accessed 7 November 2023).

19 Welkos, R. W., 'Founder of est Targeted in Campaign by Scientologists: Religion: Competition for Customers Is Said To Be the Motive behind Effort to Discredit Werner Erhard', *Los Angeles Times* (29 December 1991).

20 Pavlov, I. P., *Conditioned Reflexes: An Investigation of the Physiological Activity of the Cerebral Cortex* (Oxford: Oxford University Press, 1927); Skinner, B. F., *The Behavior of Organisms: An Experimental Analysis* (New York: Appleton-Century-Crofts, Inc., 1938).

PART 2: A BRIEF HISTORY OF BUSINESS
4. The Mechanical Firm

1 Solow, R. M., 'The Production Function and the Theory of Capital', *Review of Economic Studies*, vol. 23, no. 2 (1955–6), p. 101.

2 There is a literature on 'agglomeration economics', but it is small relative to the salience of the phenomenon. For an introduction see Glaeser, E. L., *Agglomeration Economics* (Chicago, IL: University of Chicago Press, 2010).

3 Cobb, C. W., and Douglas, P. H., 'A Theory of Production', *American Economic Review*, vol. 18, no. 1 (supplement) (1928), pp. 139–65.

4 See Romer, P. M., 'The Origins of Endogenous Growth', *Journal of Economic Perspectives*, vol. 8, no. 1 (1994), pp. 3–22, for a summary of the literature.

5 Quoted in Adams, R., 'Does Brown Need Balls?', *The Guardian* (27 February 2007).

6 Kanigel, R., *The One Best Way: Frederick Winslow Taylor and the Enigma of Efficiency* (London: MIT Press, 2005), p. 165.

7   Taylor, F. W., *Shop Management* (New York: Harper & Brothers, 1912), p. 132.

8   Ibid., pp. 139–40.

9   Ibid., p. 196.

10 Marx, K., F. Engels (ed.), S. Moore and E. Aveling (trans.), *Capital*, vol. I (London: Swan Sonnenschein, Lowrey, & Co., 1887), p. 556.

5. The Rise of Manufacturing

1   Carnegie, A., in J. B. Freeman, *Behemoth: A History of the Factory and the Making of the Modern World* (New York: W. W. Norton & Co., 2018).

2   Clapham, J. H., *Bibliography of English Economic History* (London: Historical Association, 1913), p. 401. 'Cannonades' is presumably a reference to the carronade [*sic*], the gun produced at the Carron Works, to which Napoleon attributed his defeat at Trafalgar.

3   Peaucelle, J.-L., and Guthrie, C., 'How Adam Smith Found Inspiration in French Texts on Pin Making in the Eighteenth Century', *History of Economic Ideas*, vol. 19, no. 3 (2011), pp. 41–67. The dispute was noticed in Hamowy, R., 'Progress and Commerce in Anglo-American Thought: The Social Philosophy of Adam Ferguson', *Interpretation*, vol. 14, no. 1 (1986), pp. 61–88.

4   Robert Burns, 'At Carron Ironworks' (1787): 'We did not come to visit your works; In the hope of acquiring greater wisdom. But only, so that if we are predestined for hell It will not come as a surprise.'

5   Pennant, T., *A Tour in Scotland, 1769* (London: 1771), p. 261.

6   Hume, D., Letter to Adam Smith (27 June 1772), in J. H. Burton (ed.), *Life and Correspondence of David Hume*, vol. II (1846), pp. 459–61.

7   'At Carrons Ironworks': 'When we rattled at your door, the porter declined to hear us. So when we come to the gates of hell, May your friend Satan treat us similarly.'

8   Bossidy, J. C., 'A Boston Toast' (1910), quoted in Juster, A. M., 'Cabots, Lowells, and a Quatrain You Don't Really Know', *Light Poetry Magazine* (2015), <https://lightpoetrymagazine.com/historical-and-hysterical-winterspring-2015/> (accessed 21 March 2024). 'A Boston Toast' appears to have been given at a dinner of Holy Cross alumni in 1910, although it seems that the general form of the poem may have already existed. Holy Cross is a highly exclusive Jesuit-founded college in Worcester, Massachusetts.

9   Smith, A., *An Inquiry into the Nature and Causes of the Wealth of Nations*, vol. I (London: W. Strahan and T. Cadell, 1776), p. 17.

10 Marçal, K., *Who Cooked Adam Smith's Dinner?* (London: Portobello Books, 2015), p. 17.

11 Gross, D., and editors of *Forbes* magazine, *Forbes Greatest Business Stories of All Time* (New York: John Wiley & Sons, 1996); Lewis, D. L., *The Public Image of Henry Ford: An American Folk Hero and His Company* (Detroit, MI: Wayne State University Press, 1976), pp. 42, 44.

12 Hamilton, H., 'The Founding of Carron Ironworks', *Scottish Historical Review*, vol. 25, no. 99 (1928), p. 189.

13 National Museums Scotland, *Boulton & Watt Engine* (2021), <https://www.nms.ac.uk/explore-our-collections/stories/science-and-technology/boulton-and-watt-engine/> (accessed 9 November 2023).

14 Marx (1887), p. 713; Smith (1776), p. 328.

15 Pennant (1771), pp. 261–2.

16 Saltaire Village Website, 'The Saltaire Village Website, World Heritage Site', <https://saltairevillage.info/> (accessed 30 October 2023).

17 Port Sunlight Village Trust, 'A Brief History of Port Sunlight', <https://www.portsunlightvillage.com/about-port-sunlight/history-and-heritage/> (accessed 6 October 2023).

18 Cornell School of Industrial and Labour Relations Web Exhibit 'The 1911 Triangle Factory Fire' (2018), https://trianglefire.ilr.cornell.edu/index.html (accessed 30 January 2024) collates a collection of sources describing this incident.

19 Knoema, 'Top Vehicle Manufacturers in the US Market, 1961–2016' (21 May 2020), <https://knoema.com/infographics/floslle/top-vehicle-manufacturers-in-the-us-market-1961-2016> (accessed 17 September 2020). The latest data is for 2016.

20 The incongruous name is that of the long-serving former leader of the Italian Communist party.

6. The Rise of Corporation

1 Bierce, A., *The Collected Works of Ambrose Bierce*, vol. VII, *The Devil's Dictionary* (New York: Neale Publishing, 1911).

2 The corporation changed its name in 2006.

3 Legally, the City of London is incorporated by prescription, which means that the law considers it to be incorporated because it has been considered to be incorporated for a very long time – hence its origins being lost. Its liberties are reaffirmed in clause 13 of Magna Carta, one of the four clauses still valid today.

4 Kwai, I., 'Murderer Who Wielded Narwhal Tusk to Stop Terrorist Gets Royal Pardon', *The New York Times* (19 October 2020), <https://

www.nytimes.com/2020/10/19/world/europe/london-bridge-narwhal-tusk-pardon.html> (accessed 7 November 2023).

5   Though King Leopold of Belgium 'owned' the Congo until 1908, when international outcry over his abuses and those of his subordinates forced the Belgian government to take control.

6   Dreazen, Y. J., 'How a 24-Year-Old Got a Job Rebuilding Iraq's Stock Market', *Wall Street Journal* (28 January 2004).

7   As Turner observes, the legislation that became known as the Bubble Act was actually promoted by the South Sea Company, which wished to prevent other companies from competing for the funds of speculative investors.

8   Givner, J., 'Industrial History, Preindustrial Literature: George Eliot's *Middlemarch*', *ELH*, vol. 69, no. 1 (2002), pp. 223–43.

9   Odlyzko, A., 'The Collapse of the Railway Mania, the Development of Capital Markets, and the Forgotten Role of Robert Lucas Nash', *Accounting History Review*, vol. 21, no. 3 (2011), p. 332.

10   Brontë, C., Letter to Margaret Wooler (30 January 1846), <https://www.annebronte.org/2020/09/27/2164/> (accessed 7 November 2023).

11   Checkland, S. G., *Scottish Banking: A History, 1695–1973* (Glasgow: Collins, 1975), pp. 469–71. The Western Bank, at one point the second most prominent in Scotland, had failed twenty-one years earlier, with similar, though lesser, consequences.

12   Drummond, H., *The Dynamics of Organizational Collapse: The Case of Barings Bank* (Abingdon: Routledge, 2008), p. 17.

13   Ziegler. P., *The Sixth Great Power: A History of One of the Greatest of All Banking Families, the House of Barings, 1762–1929* (New York: Alfred A. Knopf Inc., 1988).

14   Catherwood, J., 'Drunk Valuations, and Frothy Markets: The Guinness IPO', *Investor Amnesia* (30 August 2018), <https://investoramnesia.com/2018/08/30/drunk-valuations-and-frothy-markets-the-guinness-ipo/> (accessed 18 September 2020).

15   Take a look via https://www.ardingtonhouse.com/history/.

16   Baer, J., and Zuckerman, G., 'Branded a Villain, Lehman's Dick Fuld Chases Redemption', *Wall Street Journal* (6 September 2018).

17   Hannah, L., 'J. P. Morgan in London and New York before 1914', *Business History Review*, vol. 85, no. 1 (2011), p. 126.

18   Hannah, L., *The Rise of the Corporate Economy* (London: Routledge, 1976).

7. Changing Fortunes

1 Boethius, H. R. James (trans.), *The Consolation of Philosophy* [AD 524], (London: Elliot Stock, 1897).

2 Clark, A., 'Chrysler – How a Great Car Firm Crashed', *The Guardian* (1 May 2009), <https://www.theguardian.com/business/2009/may/01/chrysler-bankruptcy-car-industry-us> (accessed 27 September 2023).

3 Motavalli, J., 'Stellantis: Fiat Chrysler Merges with PSA, Becoming World's Fourth-Largest Automaker', *Forbes* (4 October 2021), <https://www.forbes.com/wheels/news/stellantis-fiat-chrysler-merges-with-psa-becoming-worlds-fourth-largest-automaker/> (accessed 27 September 2023).

4 Tichy, N., and Charan, R., 'Speed, Simplicity, Self-Confidence: An Interview with Jack Welch', *Harvard Business Review* (1989 updated to 2020), <https://hbr.org/1989/09/speed-simplicity-self-confidence-an-interview-with-jack-welch> (accessed 26 September 2023)

5 Saudi Aramco, which is not a business in the ordinary sense of the word, is also valued at more than a trillion dollars.

8. The Decline of Manufacturing

1 Greenspan, A., 'Question: Is There a New Economy?', Haas Annual Business Faculty Research Dialogue, University of California, Berkeley (4 September 1998).

2 Biden, J., 'Remarks by President Biden on Economic Progress since Taking Office: Speech at Springfield, Virginia' (26 January 2023), <https://www.whitehouse.gov/briefing-room/speeches-remarks/2023/01/26/remarks-by-president-biden-on-economic-progress-since-taking-office/> (accessed 26 July 2023).

3 Herrendorf, B., Rogerson, R., and Valentinyi, A., 'Growth and Structural Transformation', National Bureau of Economic Research, Working Paper 18996 (2013), <https://www.nber.org/system/files/working_papers/w18996/w18996.pdf> (accessed 7 November 2023), and Our World in Data, 'Share of Agriculture in Total Employment, 1801 to 2011', <https://ourworldindata.org/grapher/share-of-agriculture-in-total-employment?country=~GBR> (accessed 18 March 2024). Note: The calculations are by Our World in Data; Herrendorf et al. (2013) is the underlying data source that they have used.

4 Bank of England, 'Inflation Report' (2018), <https://www.bankofengland.co.uk/-/media/boe/files/inflation-report/2018/

february/inflation-report-february-2018.pdf> (accessed 26 July 2023); Office for National Statistics (ONS), 'UK Labour Market: September 2020' (15 September 2020), <https://www.ons.gov.uk/releases/uklabourmarketseptember2020> (accessed 26 May 2023); U.S. Bureau of Labor Statistics, 'Injuries, Illnesses and Fatalities' (2020), <https://www.bls.gov/iif/snapshots/isn-manufacturing-2016-20.htm> (accessed 9 November 2023). For UK figures we use Bank of England (2018) and, for data since 2016, ONS (15 September 2020). For US figures, we use U.S. Bureau of Labour Statistics (2020).

5   Aristotle, B. Jowett (trans.), *Politics* (350 BC), <https://classics.mit.edu/Aristotle/politics.html> (accessed 27 March 2024), Book I, Chapter 10.

6   Ibid.

7   European Commission, 'Labour Market Information: Switzerland (6 June 2023)', <https://eures.ec.europa.eu/living-and-working/labour-market-information/labour-market-information-switzerland_en> (accessed 26 September 2023).

8   'The Truth behind the Tories' Northern Strongholds', *The Economist* (31 March 2021), <https://www.economist.com/britain/2021/03/31/the-truth-behind-the-tories-northern-strongholds> (accessed 3 October 2021). The 'red wall' is a term in English politics for the constituencies in the midlands and north of England, many the victims of industrial decline, which elected Conservative members of Parliament for the first time in 2019.

9   Similar to the British term 'red wall', 'rustbelt' refers to the US regions that experienced the aftermath of deindustrialisation after the 1950s.

10 Wolf, M., *The Crisis of Democratic Capitalism* (London: Penguin, 2024).

11 Derks, S., *The Value of a Dollar: Prices and Incomes in the United States, 1860–1999* (Lakeville, CT: Grey House Publishing, 1999).

12 Ford Motor Company, 'The Model T' (2023), <https://corporate.ford.com/articles/history/the-model-t.html> (accessed 1 August 2023).

13 Author's own calculations, with rounding. Dollars are converted to sterling at the 1 January 2020 rate of £1:$1.325. US inflation data is from McCusker, J. J., 'How Much Is That in Real Money? A Historical Price Index for Use as a Deflator of Money Values in the Economy of the United States', *Proceedings of the American Antiquarian Society*, vol. 101, no. 2 (1991), Table A2, CPI Index and U.S. Bureau of Labor Statistics, 'CPI for all Urban Consumers (CPI-U), All Items in U.S. City Average, All Urban Consumers, Not Seasonally Adjusted, CUUR0000SA0' (4 May 2023).

14 Roberts, W., 'That Imperfect Arm: Quantifying the Carronade', *Warship International*, vol. 33, no. 3 (1996), pp. 231–40.

15 British Army, 'Equipment: Small Arms and Support Weapons' (2020), <https://www.army.mod.uk/equipment/small-arms-and-support-weapons/> (accessed 28 January 2021).

16 Ford Motor Company (2023).

17 Airbus Media Relations, 'Airbus Aircraft 2018 Average List Prices (USD Millions)' (2018), <http://www.airbus.com/content/dam/corporate-topics/publications/backgrounders/Airbus-Commercial-Aircraft-list-prices-2018.pdf> (accessed 28 January 2021).

18 Penafiel, K., "The Empire State Building: An Innovative Skyscraper", *Buildings* (28 June 2006), <https://www.buildings.com/industry-news/article/10193728/the-empire-state-building-an-innovative-skyscraper> (accessed 3 April 2024); Empire State Realty Trust, 'Empire State Building Fact Sheet', <https://www.esbnyc.com/sites/default/files/esb_fact_sheet_final_0.pdf> (accessed 3 April 2024).

19 Burj Khalifa, 'Fact Sheet', <https://www.burjkhalifa.ae/img/FACT-SHEET.pdf> (accessed 3 May 2023).

20 Mobile Phone Museum, 'MOTOROLA DYNATAC 8000X', <https://www.mobilephonemuseum.com/phone-detail/dynatac-8000x> (accessed 3 May 2023).

21 Ashton, T. S., 'The Records of a Pin Manufactory, 1814–21', *Economica*, no. 15 (1925), pp. 281–92.

22 Medicines and Healthcare Products Regulatory Agency (26 January 2021), <https://www.gov.uk/government/collections/new-guidance-and-information-for-industry-from-the-mhra> (accessed 10 November 2023), p. 2.

23 Nordhaus, W. D., 'Do Real-Output and Real-Wage Measures Capture Reality? The History of Lighting Suggests Not', in Bresnahan, T. F., and Gordon, R. J. (eds.), *The Economics of Real Goods* (Chicago, IL: University of Chicago Press, 1996), pp. 29–70.

24 At the time of writing, a Philips LED Ultra Efficient 2.3W Bulb retails for £8.99 and promises 50,000 hours of use. Typical electricity costs of 27p per kWh account for about three-quarters of the cost.

25 We assume a 60W incandescent bulb costing £1 with a typical life of 1,000 hours and typical luminosity of 840 lumens.

PART 3: THE SECRET OF OUR SUCCESS
9. Better at Everything

1 The Beatles, 'Getting Better' (1967).

2   Olympics, 'The Story of Abrahams and Liddell at Paris 1924' (27 June 2023), <https://olympics.com/en/news/the-story-of-abrahams-and-liddell-at-paris-1924> (accessed 21 July 2023).

3   Nag, U., 'Usain Bolt's Records: Best Strikes from the Lighting Bolt' (27 June 2023), <https://olympics.com/en/news/usain-bolt-record-world-champion-athlete-fastest-man-olympics-sprinter-100m-200m> (accessed 21 July 2023).

4   In the film, Mussabini, as a professional coach, is denied admittance to the stadium and learns of Abrahams's success by hearing the playing of the British national anthem.

5   Scottish FA, 'Kenny Dalglish', <https://www.scottishfa.co.uk/players/?pid=113766&lid=1> (accessed 7 September 2023).

6   Littlewood, M., 'Sir James Mirrlees Obituary', *The Guardian* (24 September 2018), <https://www.theguardian.com/politics/2018/sep/24/sir-james-mirrlees-obituary> (accessed 7 September 2023).

7   An attempt was made to revive Dalmarnock, which had once been a centre of locomotive engineering, by building the competitors' village for the 2014 Commonwealth Games on some of the derelict sites. But the athletes came – and went.

8   Internet Movie Database (IMDB), 'Alec Guinness', <https://www.imdb.com/name/nm0000027/> (accessed 7 September 2023).

9   For different perspectives see: Hamilton, B., 'East African Running Dominance: What Is behind It?', *British Journal of Sports Medicine*, vol. 34, no. 5 (2000), pp. 391–4; Wilber, R. L., and Pitsiladis, Y. P., 'Kenyan and Ethiopian Distance Runners: What Makes Them So Good?', *International Journal of Sports Physiology and Performance*, vol. 7, no. 2 (2012), pp. 92–102; and Mooses, M., and Hackney, A. C., 'Anthropometrics and Body Composition in East African Runners: Potential Impact on Performance', *International Journal of Sports Physiology and Performance*, vol. 12, no. 4 (2017), pp. 422–30.

10   Genesis 3:6.

11   Henrich, J., *The Secret of Our Success: How Culture Is Driving Human Evolution, Domesticating Our Species, and Making Us Smarter* (Princeton, NJ: Princeton University Press, 2015).

12   Tomasello, M., Page-Barbour Lecture at the University of Virginia (2010).

10. Better at Business

1   Tesla, N., 'A Story of Youth Told by Age (Dedicated to Miss Pola

Fotitch)' (1939), <https://www.pbs.org/tesla/ll/story_youth.html> (accessed 4 September 2023).

2 Regis, E., 'No One Can Explain Why Planes Stay in the Air', *Scientific American* (1 February 2020), <https://www.scientificamerican.com/article/no-one-can-explain-why-planes-stay-in-the-air> (accessed 21 July 2023).

3 Boeing, 'Boeing 737 Facts' (2014), <https://www.boeing.com/farnborough2014/pdf/BCA/fct%20-737%20Family%20Facts.pdf> (accessed 21 July 2023).

4 Wright, T., 'The Learning Curve of the Cumulative Average Model: What is Wright's Law?', Ark Invest, <https://ark-invest.com/wrights-law/> (accessed 21 July 2023).

5 Henderson, B., 'The Experience Curve – Reviewed (Part II)', *BCG* (1973), <https://www.bcg.com/publications/1973/corporate-finance-strategy-portfolio-management-experience-curve-reviewed-part-ii-the-history> (accessed 5 September 2023).

6 Wright (accessed 2023).

7 Surowiecki, J., *The Wisdom of Crowds: Why the Many Are Smarter than the Few and How Collective Wisdom Shapes Business, Economies, Societies and Nations* (New York: Doubleday, 2004).

8 Galton, F., 'Vox Populi', *Nature*, vol. 75 (1907), pp. 450–51. Galton used the median, which is much easier to calculate without mechanical or electronic assistance. The mean was in fact closer to the actual weight – as Galton observed, the distribution of guesses was non-normal.

9 Kay, J., *Other People's Money: Masters of the Universe or Servants of the People?* (London: Profile, 2015).

10 Aristotle, *Politics*, Book 3.

11. Value

1 Fisher, I., *The Rate of Interest: Its Nature, Determination and Relation to Economic Phenomena* (New York: Macmillan, 1907), p. 6.

2 Wilde, O., *Lady Windermere's Fan: A Play about a Good Woman* (London, 1892), p. 40.

3 Marshall, A., *Principles of Economics* (London: Macmillan & Co., 1890), p. 348.

4 Either the real Maharajah trek of the Rajahs of Anandapur or the one you can visit at Disney World.

5 Kirkpatrick, D., 'Mystery Buyer of $450 Million *Salvator Mundi* was a Saudi Prince', *The New York Times* (6 December 2017), <https://www.

nytimes.com/2017/12/06/world/middleeast/salvator-mundi-da-vinci-saudi-prince-bader.html> (accessed 21 July 2023).

6   'The Upper East Side's Most Expensive 5th Avenue Apartment Buildings', *MPA* (5 February 2013), <https://www.mpamag.com/us/news/general/the-upper-east-sides-most-expensive-5th-avenue-apartment-buildings/13476> (accessed 21 July 2023).

7   Hirsch, F., *Social Limits to Growth* (London and Henley: Routledge & Kegan Paul, 1977).

8   Mayer, C., *Capitalism and Crises* (Oxford: Oxford University Press, 2023)

12. Stanley Matthews Changes Trains

1   Messi, L., <https://www.brainyquote.com/quotes/lionel_messi_473553> (accessed 25 July 2023).

2   Settimi, C., 'The World's Highest-Paid Soccer Players 2017: Cristiano Ronaldo, Lionel Messi Lead the List', *Forbes* (26 May 2017), <https://www.forbes.com/sites/christinasettimi/2017/05/26/the-worlds-highest-paid-soccer-players-2017-cristiano-ronaldo-lionel-messi-lead-the-list/?sh=3b8e254b210e> (accessed 25 July 2023).

3   Shread, J., 'Lionel Messi Reveals He Chose to Join Paris Saint-Germain in Order to Win Fifth Champions League', *SkySports* (12 August 2021), <https://www.skysports.com/football/news/11095/12378621/lionel-messi-reveals-he-chose-to-join-paris-saint-germain-in-order-to-win-fifth-champions-league> (accessed 30 September 2021).

4   Matthews, S., *The Way It Was: My Autobiography* (London: Headline Publishing, 2001), pp. 301–2.

5   Hollander, J. H., 'Adam Smith 1776–1926', *Journal of Political Economy*, vol. 35, no. 2 (1927), p. 86.

6   Smith, A., *An Inquiry into the Nature and Causes of the Wealth of Nations*, vol. I (London: W. Strahan and T. Cadell, 1776), p. 75.

7   Anderson, J., *Observations on the Means of Exciting a Spirit of National Industry; Chiefly Intended to Promote the Agriculture, Commerce, Manufactures and Fisheries of Scotland* (Edinburgh: T. Cadell & C. Elliot, 1777), p. 376.

8   Alton, R., 'A New Biography of Stanley Matthews', *The Spectator* (1 June 2013), <https://www.spectator.co.uk/article/a-new-biography-of-stanley-matthews/> (accessed 6 September 2023).

9   Porter, J., 'How Jimmy Hill's Strike Threat Turned £20 Footballers into Multi-Millionaires', *The Sportsman* (18 January 2021), <https://

www.thesportsman.com/features/how-jimmy-hill-s-strike-threat-turned-20-footballers-into-multi-millionaires> (accessed 25 July 2023).

10 Carlson, M., 'For F.J. Titmus Read Titmus, F.J.' (23 March 2011), <http://irresistibletargets.blogspot.com/2011/03/for-fj-titmus-read-titmus-fj.html> (accessed 25 July 2023).

11 Taylor, M., *The Association Game: A History of British Football* (Abingdon: Routledge, 2013), p. 196.

12 I wisely didn't take up the offer. The match took place before a crowd of 22,500, one quarter of the stadium's normal capacity, owing to covid restrictions. In a lacklustre match on a wet evening, neither side managed to score. The £200 price in the secondary market indicates that scalpers were appropriating much of the rent.

13 Leicester City, 'Emotional Khun Vichai Tribute Played on Big Screen', YouTube (11 November 2018), <https://www.youtube.com/watch?v=LCLRawxqhWg> (accessed 4 October 2023).

14 True Faith, 'Premier League – Owner Financing Last 10 Years (2012–21)', (2022), <https://true-faith.co.uk/wp-content/uploads/2022/05/acc8.jpg> (accessed 4 October 2023).

15 Maidment, N., 'Could the Glazers Lose Their Public Enemy No. 1 Tag at Manchester United?', *Reuters* (15 June 2015), <https://www.reuters.com/article/manchester-united-glazers/feature-could-the-glazers-lose-their-public-enemy-no-1-tag-at-manchester-united-idUSL1N0XW0O620150615> (accessed 17 July 2023).

16 Anderson, J., *An Enquiry into the Nature of the Corn Laws; with a View to the New Corn Bill Proposed for Scotland* (Edinburgh: Mundell, 1777), pp. 48, 50.

17 Hint – what would happen to the earnings of farmers?

18 Webb in Shaw, G. B. (ed.), *Fabian Essays in Socialism* (London: W. Scott, 1899), p. 44.

19 Hayes, A., 'Economic Rent: Definition, Types, How It Works, and Example', *Investopedia* (1 September 2023), <https://www.investopedia.com/terms/e/economicrent.asp> (accessed 30 January 2024).

PART 4: THE AGE OF INDIVIDUALISM
13. Money Can't Buy You Love

1 Larkin, P., 'Annus Mirabilis', in *High Windows* (London: Faber and Faber, 1974). The poem was written by Larkin in 1967, but the collection was not published until 1974.

2 Eisenhower, D., 'President Dwight D. Eisenhower's Farewell Address'

(1961), <https://www.archives.gov/milestone-documents/president-dwight-d-eisenhowers-farewell-address> (accessed 6 November 2023); Galbraith, J. K., *The New Industrial State* (Boston, MA: Houghton Mifflin, 1967), pp. 211–13.

3   Willy Brandt, Social Democrat Chancellor from 1969 to 1974, is given credit for restoring a respected place in world affairs for Germany after the Second World War through his *Ostpolitik* détente with the Soviet Union.

4   Marcuse, a German Jew, had emigrated to the US as the Nazis came to power.

5   Reich, C. A., *The Greening of America* (New York: Random House, 1970).

6   Ehrlich, P. R., *The Population Bomb* (New York: Ballantine Books, 1968), p. 11.

7   Friedman, F., 'A Friedman Doctrine – "The Social Responsibility of Business Is to Increase Its Profits"', *The New York Times* (13 September 1970), <https://www.nytimes.com/1970/09/13/archives/a-friedman-doctrine-the-social-responsibility-of-business-is-to.html> (accessed 3 October 2021).

8   Powell, L. F., 'Attack on American Free Enterprise System', *U.S. Chamber of Commerce* (23 August 1971), <https://law2.wlu.edu/deptimages/Powell%20Archives/PowellMemorandumTypescript.pdf> (accessed 5 October 2021).

9   Biskupic, J., and Barbash, F., 'Retired Justice Lewis Powell Dies at 90', *Washington Post* (26 August 1998), <https://www.washingtonpost.com/wp-srv/national/longterm/supcourt/stories/powell082698.htm> (accessed 5 October 2021).

14. Or Perhaps It Can: The Modern Theory of the Firm

1   Attributed to Ely Devons by Coase, R. H., 'Opening Address to the Annual Conference: International Society of New Institutional Economics, Washington, DC, USA', The Ronald Coase Institute (17 September 1999), <https://www.coase.org/coasespeech.htm> (accessed 16 October 2023).

2   Clapham, J. H., 'Of Empty Economic Boxes', *Economic Journal*, vol. 32, no. 127 (1922), pp. 305–14.

3   Sainsbury, D., *Windows of Opportunity* (London: Profile, 2019)

4   Ansoff, H. I., *Corporate Strategy: An Analytic Approach to Business Policy for Growth and Expansion* (New York: McGraw-Hill, 1965), pp. 2–3.

5   Ansoff (1965), p. 16.

6   American Economic Association, 'Distinguished Fellows', <https://www.aeaweb.org/about-aea/honors-awards/distinguished-fellows> (accessed 30 October 2023).

7   Bain, J. S., *Industrial Organisation: A Treatise* (London: John Wiley, 1959), pp. vii–viii.

8   Scherer, F. M., *Industrial Market Structure and Economic Performance* (Chicago, IL: Rand McNally, 1970).

9   Porter, M., 'How Competitive Forces Shape Strategy', *Harvard Business Review* (1979), <https://hbr.org/1979/03/how-competitive-forces-shape-strategy> (accessed 30 October 2023).

10 Gardner, D., and Tetlock, E. P., *Superforecasting: The Art and Science of Prediction* (London: Random House, 2016).

11 Hayek, F. von, 'Friedrich von Hayek Prize Lecture', The Nobel Prize (11 December 1974), <https://www.nobelprize.org/prizes/economic-sciences/1974/hayek/lecture/> (accessed 1 November 2023).

12 Ibid.

13 Kay, J., and King, M., *Radical Uncertainty: Decision-Making for an Unknowable Future* (London: Bridge Street Press, 2020).

14 Hall, R. E., 'Notes on the Current State of Empirical Macroeconomics' (June 1976), <https://web.stanford.edu/~rehall/Notes%20Current%20State%20Empirical%201976.pdf> (accessed 30 October 2023). While Pittsburgh, where Ansoff was located, is closer to Lake Erie than to the Atlantic, Carnegie-Mellon's intellectual milieu was more fresh than salty.

15 Coase, R. H., 'Prize Lecture', *The Nobel Prize* (9 December 1991), <https://www.nobelprize.org/prizes/economic-sciences/1991/coase/lecture/> (accessed 3 May 2023).

16 Kay, J., 'Ronald Coase: Nobel Prize Winner Who Explored Why Companies Exist', *Financial Times* (3 September 2013), <https://www.ft.com/content/d1c4aa66-ef9d-11e2-a237-00144feabdc0> (accessed 30 October 2023).

17 Williamson, O. E., *Markets and Hierarchies: Analysis and Antitrust Implications* (New York: Free Press, 1975).

18 *Alaska Packers' Association v. Domenico*, 117F. 99 (1902).

19 Alchian, A. A., and Demsetz, H., 'Production, Information Costs, and Economic Organization', *American Economic Review*, vol. 62, no. 5 (1972), pp. 777–95.

20 Posner, R. A., 'A Reply to Some Recent Criticisms of the Efficiency Theory of the Common Law', *Hofstra Law Review*, vol. 9, no. 3 (1981), pp. 775–94; MacFarquhar, L., 'The Bench Burner', *New Yorker* (2

December 2001), <https://www.newyorker.com/
magazine/2001/12/10/the-bench-burner> (accessed 5 October 2021).

21 Jensen and Meckling (1976), pp. 305–36.

22 Easterbrook, F. H., and Fischel, D. R., 'Limited Liability and the Corporation', *University of Chicago Law Review*, vol. 52, no. 1 (1985), p. 89.

23 Meyer, M., Milgrom, P., and Roberts, J., 'Organisational Prospects, Influence Costs, and Ownership Changes', *Journal of Economics & Management Strategy*, vol. 1, no. 1 (1992), p. 17.

15. The Myth of Ownership

1 Rousseau (1761).

2 Friedman (1970).

3 Ibid.

4 *Treasury Commissioners v. Short Brothers*, UKHL J0729 – 2 (1948), Summary.

5 *Inland Revenue v. Laird Group*, EWCA Civ 576 (2003), Para 35.

6 Ibid., *Inland Revenue Commissioners v. Crossman* [1937] AC 26 p. 66.

7 *Inland Revenue v. Laird Group* (2003) Para 36; *Inland Revenue Commissioners v. Joiner* [1975] 1 WLR 1701, 1705E *per* Lord Wilberforce.

8 Davies, P. L., Worthington, S., and Hare, C., *Gower: Principles of Modern Company Law*, 11th edn (London: Sweet & Maxwell, 2021), p. 787. The latest version of *Gower* is essentially unchanged.

9 *Inland Revenue v. Laird Group* (2003), Para 35.

10 Basic Law for the Federal Republic of Germany', European Union Agency for Fundamental Rights (1949), <https://fra.europa.eu/en/law-reference/basic-law-federal-republic-germany-13> (accessed 13 June 2024).

11 *Marex Financial Ltd v. Sevilleja* (2020), UKSC 31.

12 Chancellor J. L. Wolcott in *Bodell v. Gen. Gas & Elec. Corp.*, 132 A. 442 (Del. Ch. 1926).

13 Delaware became known as the First State in 1787, when it was the first colony to ratify the US Constitution.

14 Stout, L., *The Shareholder Value Myth: How Putting Shareholders First Harms Investors, Corporations, and the Public* (San Francisco, CA: Berrett-Koehler Publishers, 2012).

15 Hart is also the co-author of a 2016 article extolling 'formal relational contracts', a seeming oxymoron. The article does not explain how the difficulties of legal implementation identified by Lord Mance in the Court of Appeal are to be overcome.

16 Hart, O., *Firms, Contracts, and Financial Structure* (Oxford: Clarendon Press, 2009), p. 30.

17 Honoré, A. M., 'Ownership', in Guest, A. G. (ed.), *Oxford Essays in Jurisprudence* (Oxford: Oxford University Press, 1961), p. 108.

18 Bohn, J., and Choi, S., 'Fraud in the New-Issues Market: Empirical Evidence on Securities Class Actions', *University of Pennsylvania Law Review*, vol. 144, no. 3 (1996), pp. 904–5.

19 Garry, P. M., Spurlin, C., Owen, D. A., and Williams, W. A., 'The Irrationality of Shareholder Class Action Lawsuits: A Proposal for Reform', *South Dakota Law Review*, vol. 49, no. 2 (2004), p. 278.

20 Handy, C., 'What Is a Company for?', *RSA Journal*, vol. 139, no. 5416 (1991), pp. 231–41.

16. Must Companies Maximise Profits?

1 *Bank of Tokyo Ltd v. Karoon*, EWCA Civ J0524 -1 (24 May 1987).

2 Regierungskommission, Deutscher Corporate Governance Kodex, 'German Corporate Governance Code 2017, Press Release' (14 February 2017), <https://www.ecgi.global/code/german-corporate-governance-code-2017-press-release> (accessed 7 November 2023).

3 *Dodge v. Ford Motor Co.*, 204 Mich. 459, 170 N.W. 668 (Mich. 1919).

4 Ford, H., and Crowther, S., *My Life and Work* (New York: Garden City Publishing Company, Inc., 1922), p. 73.

5 *Dodge v. Ford* (1919).

6 Macey, J. R., 'A Close Read of an Excellent Commentary on *Dodge v. Ford*', *Virginia Law and Business Review*, vol. 3, no. 1 (2008), p. 184.

7 Wise, D. B., 'Dodge: Hell Raisers from Michigan', in Ward, I. (ed.), *The World of Automobiles: An Illustrated Encyclopedia of the Motor Car*, vol. (New York: Purnell Reference Books, 1977), p. 552.

8 Macrotrends, 'Dow Jones – DJIA – 100 Year Historical Chart', <https://www.macrotrends.net/1319/dow-jones-100-year-historical-char> (accessed 31 October 2023); Federal Reserve Bank of Minneapolis, 'Consumer Prize Index, 1913', <https://www.minneapolisfed.org/about-us/monetary-policy/inflation-calculator/consumer-price-index-1913> (accessed 31 October 2023).

9 *eBay Domestic Holdings, Inc. v. Newmark*, 16 A.3d 1 (Del. Ch. 2010).

10 *Revlon, Inc. v. MacAndrews & Forbes Holdings, Inc.*, 506 A.2d 173 (Del. 1986).

11 *eBay v. Newmark* (2010), para. 34.

12 *Burwell v. Hobby Lobby Stores, Inc.*, 573 U.S. 682 (2014).

13 *Autronic AG v. Switzerland*, No. 12726/87 (1990); *Colas Est SA and Others*

v. France, No. 37971/97 (ECHR, 2002); Emberland, M., *The Human Rights of Companies: Exploring the Structure of ECHR Protection* (Oxford: Oxford University Press, 2006), pp. 129–35.

14   Citizens United is a decision with major implications, but these relate to the US political system rather than to the conduct of business.

17. Leaky Pipes and Overflowing Sewage

1   Philips, M., 'Remembering Hatfield – 20 Years On', *Rail Safety and Standard Board* (17 October 2020), <https://www.rssb.co.uk/what-we-do/insights-and-news/blogs/remembering-hatfield-20-years-on> (accessed 30 October 2023).

2   Kornai, J., 'The Soft Budget Constraint', *Kyklos: International Review for Social Sciences*, vol. 39, no. 1 (1986), pp. 3–30.

3   McLean, B., and Elkind, P., *The Smartest Guys in the Room: The Amazing Rise and Scandalous Fall of Enron* (London: Penguin, 2013), p. 42.

4   Brantley, B., 'Titans of Tangled Finances Kick Up Their Heels Again', *The New York Times* (27 April 2010).

5   Companies listed in the US, regardless of place of legal incorporation, are required by the Securities and Exchange Commission to issue quarterly earnings reports. In 2014, following a report to the government on short-termism, it no longer applies to UK businesses, but most issue quarterly announcements anyway.

6   Quoted in McLean and Elkind (2013), p. 39.

18. The Dumbest Idea in the World

1   Quoted in Guerrera, F., 'A Need to Reconnect', *Financial Times* (12 March 2009).

2   Buffet, quoted in Rattner, S., 'Who's Right on the Stock Market?', *The New York Times* (14 November 2013).

3   Langley, M., *Tearing Down the Walls* (New York: Simon & Schuster, 2003), pp. 324–5.

4   Rappaport, A., *Creating Shareholder Value: A Guide for Managers and Investors* (New York: The Free Press, 1986).

5   Guerrera (2009).

6   Bloomberg, 'Jack Welch Elaborates: Shareholder Value', Bloomberg (16 March 2009), <https://www.bloomberg.com/news/articles/2009-03-16/jack-welch-elaborates-shareholder-value?leadSource=uverify%20wall> (accessed 30 October 2023).

7   Jensen, M. C., 'Some Anomalous Evidence Regarding Market Efficiency', *Journal of Financial Economics*, vol. 6, no. 2–3 (1978), p. 95.

8   Grossman, S. J., and Stiglitz, J. E., 'On the Impossibility of
      Informationally Efficient Markets', American Economic Review, vol.
      70, no. 3 (1980), pp. 393-408.

9   Buffett, W. E., 'Chairman's Letter 1989' (28 February 1989), <https://
      www.berkshirehathaway.com/letters/1988.html> (accessed 26 June
      2023).

10   And there is evidence for this: there are rules restricting executives in
      trading their firm's stock *because* they know more about the firm's
      prospects. Studies indicate that, even with these safeguards, their sales
      tend to be well timed: see, for example, Jeng, L. A., Metrick, A., and
      Zeckhauser, R., 'Estimating the Returns to Insider Trading: A
      Performance-Evaluation Perspective', *Review of Economics and
      Statistics*, vol. 85, no. 2 (2003), pp. 453–47, and Mazza, P., and Ruh, B.,
      'The Performance of Corporate Legal Insider Trading in the Korean
      Market', *International Review of Law & Economics*, vol. 71 (2022).

11   Capen, E. C., Clapp, R. V., and Campbell, W. M., 'Competitive
      Bidding in High-Risk Situations', *Journal of Petroleum Technology*, vol.
      23, no. 6 (1971), pp. 641–53.

PART 5: HOW IT ALL WORKED OUT
19. The Evolution of Finance

1   Wolfe, T., *The Bonfire of the Vanities* (New York, Farrar Straus and
      Giroux, 1987), p. 57.

2   Chernova, Y., 'Sequoia Capital Goes on Fundraising Spree', *Wall Street
      Journal Pro Venture Capital* (5 March 2018), <https://www.wsj.com/
      articles/sequoia-capital-goes-on-fundraising-spree-152025304>
      (accessed 17 October 2023).

3   Darmouni, O., and Papoutsi, M., 'The Rise of Bond Financing in
      Europe' (May 2022), <https://www.ecb.europa.eu/pub/pdf/scpwps/
      ecb.wp2663~06c26039e0.en.pdf> (accessed 5 October 2023).

4   Morgan Grenfell pre-dated both J. P. Morgan and Morgan Stanley.
      It was founded by the American George Peabody, whose Peabody
      Trust still provides social housing in London. Peabody took on
      J. P. Morgan's father as his junior, American, partner.

20. The Art of the Deal

1   Schanche, A. D., 'It Is Theoretically Possible for the Entire United
      States to Become One Vast Conglomerate, Presided over by Mr
      James. J. Ling', *Saturday Evening Post* (January 2024), <https://files.

saturdayeveningpost.com/uploads/reprints/One_Vast_
Conglomerate/index.html> (accessed 18 January 2024), p. 49.

2   Trump, D. J., and Schwartz, T., *Trump: The Art of the Deal* (New York:
Random House, 1987).

3   Southey, R., 'The Battle of Blenheim' (1796), in *Metrical Tales, and
Other Poems* (London: Longman, Hurst, Rees, and Orme, 1805).

4   Manne, H. G., 'Mergers and the Market for Corporate Control',
Journal of Political Economy, vol. 73, no. 2 (1965), pp. 110–20.

5   Clutterbuck, D., and Devine, M., *Clore: The Man and His Millions*
(London: Weidenfeld and Nicolson, 1987).

6   Cao, X., Chan, K., and Kahle, K., 'Risk and Performance of Bonds
Sponsored by Private Equity Funds', *Journal of Banking and Finance*,
vol. 93 (2018), pp. 41–53.

7   Reuters Staff, 'Quote Box-Trump, Business Leaders Comment on Jack
Welch's Death', Reuters (2 March 2020), <https://www.reuters.com/
article/people-jackwelch-quote-idUSL4N2AV4TB> (accessed 1
November 2023).

21. Not a Pretty Picture

1   Roosevelt, T., 'The Duties of a Great Nation', in *The Works of Theodore
Roosevelt*, vol. XIV, *Campaigns and Controversies* (New York: Charles
Scribner's Sons, 1926), pp. 290–2 (p. 291). The speech was delivered in
1898.

2   Bewkes, quoted in Butterworth, T., 'The Biggest Mistake in
Corporate History', *Forbes* (30 September 2010).

3   AT&T, 'AT&T to Acquire Time Warner' (22 October 2016), <https://
about.att.com/story/att_to_acquire_time_warner.html> (accessed 9
October 2023).

4   'A Steal?', *The Economist* (24 October 2002); McIntosh, B., 'Vodafone
Faces Pounds 400m Bill as It Posts Bid for Mannesmann', *The
Independent* (24 December 1999).

5   McKinsey, 'Global M&A Market Defies Gravity in 2021 Second Half'
(16 March 2022), <https://www.mckinsey.com/capabilities/m-and-a/
our-insights/global-m-and-a-market-defies-gravity-in-2021-second-
half> (accessed 9 October 2023).

6   Orcel, quoted in Jenkins, P., and Saigol, L., 'UBS's Orcel Admits Banks
Must Change', *Financial Times* (9 January 2013).

7   Bowers, S., 'RBS Invested Billions in Complex Loans That Bosses Did
Not Understand', *The Guardian* (12 December 2011), <https://www.

theguardian.com/business/2011/dec/12/rbs-invested-billions-complex-loans-fsa> (accessed 1 November 2023).

8　Wilson, H., Aldrick, P., and Ahmed, K., 'The Bank that Went Bust', *Sunday Telegraph* (6 March 2011), p. B6.

9　Sabbagh, D., 'Ackermann Agrees to Pay €3.2 Million Towards Settlement', *The Times* (25 November 2006), <https://www.thetimes.co.uk/article/ackermann-agrees-to-pay-32-million-towards-settlement-zp7kqj57w8z> (accessed 31 October 2023).

10　Board of Governors of the Federal Reserve System, 'Currency in Circulation [CURRCIR]', retrieved from FRED, Federal Reserve Bank of St. Louis, <https://fred.stlouisfed.org/series/CURRCIR> (accessed 29 January 2024).

11　Mondelez International, 'Oreo Fact Sheet' (2017), <https://web.archive.org/web/20190826235732/https://www.mondelezinternational.com/en/~/media/MondelezCorporate/Uploads/downloads/OREO_Fact_Sheet.pdf> (accessed 9 October 2023).

22. The Fall of the Icons

1　Callahan, P., 'So Why Does Harry Stonecipher Think He Can Turn Around Boeing?', *Chicago Tribune* (29 February 2004).

2　Kay, J., *Obliquity: Why Our Goals Are Best Achieved Indirectly* (London: Profile, 2010).

3　Ibid.

4　Hosking, P., 'I Made Money at Marconi: Mayo', *This is Money* (21 January 2002), <https://www.thisismoney.co.uk/money/news/article-1544765/I-made-money-at-Marconi-Mayo.html> (accessed 7 November 2023). Mayo, J., 'Marconi Under the Microscope: In the Final Part of his Account John Mayo Reflects on Mistakes that were Made and the Responsibility he Feels Towards Shareholders', *Financial Times* (21 January 2002).

5　It is now the Willis Tower, named after the London-based financial services business which rents space in it. However, the largest tenant is United Airlines, and the owner is Blackstone.

6　Serling, R. J., *Legend and Legacy: The Story of Boeing and Its People* (New York: St. Martin's Press, 1992), p. 68.

7　Ibid., p. 285

8　Useem, J., 'The Long-Forgotten Flight that Sent Boeing Off Course', *The Atlantic* (20 November 2019).

9   Ford, J., 'Boeing and the Siren Call of Share Buybacks', *Financial Times* (4 August 2019).

10 Majority Staff of the Committee on Transportation and Infrastructure, 'Final Committee Report: The Design, Development & Certification of the Boeing 737 MAX' (September 2020), p. 6.

11 Kay, J., 'Boeing and a Dramatic Change of Direction', johnkay.com (10 December 2003), <https://www.johnkay.com/2003/12/10/boeing-and-a-dramatic-change-of-direction/> (accessed 18 January 2024).

12 Insinna, V., 'Boeing Hits 2023 Jet Delivery Goal but Lags Airbus', Reuters (10 January 2024), <https://www.reuters.com/business/aerospace-defense/boeing-hits-2023-jet-delivery-goal-blockbuster-sales-year-2024-01-09/> (accessed 18 January 2024).

13 IBM, 'A History of Progress' (2008), <https://www.ibm.com/ibm/history/interactive/ibm_history.pdf> (accessed 7 November 2023), p. 34.

14 Francis, T., 'Revisiting IBM's Palmisano Equation' (13 March 2012), <https://footnoted.com/revisiting-ibms-palmisano-equation/> (accessed 27 September 2021).

15 Financial Conduct Authority (FCA), 'Deutsche Bank Fined £227 Million by Financial Conduct Authority for LIBOR and EURIBOR Failings and for Misleading the Regulator' (24 April 2015), <https://www.fca.org.uk/news/press-releases/deutsche-bank-fined-%C2%A3227-million-financial-conduct-authority-libor-and-euribor> (accessed 12 November 2020).

16 Cited in Enrich, D., *Dark Towers: Deutsche Bank, Donald Trump, and an Epic Trail of Destruction* (New York: HarperCollins, 2020), p. 290, which asserts that it was found in 'Justice Department Statement of Facts (draft), 15 April 2015, disclosed in *USA v. Connolly*, Exhibit 399-12', although I have not been able to locate this document.

17 International Monetary Fund (IMF), 'Germany: Financial Sector Assessment Program – Stress Testing the Banking and Insurance Sectors – Technical Notes' (29 June 2016), <https://www.elibrary.imf.org/view/journals/002/2016/191/article-A001-en.xml> (accessed 30 January 2024), p. 29.

23. The Finance Curse

1   Churchill quoted in Moggridge, D., *British Monetary Policy, 1924–31* (Cambridge: Cambridge University Press, 1972), p. 76. This was Churchill's comment on the tension between finance and industry back in 1925, when he was the Chancellor of the Exchequer – a

tension that he foolishly resolved in favour of finance by returning Britain to the gold standard.

2 'Building Society Members Vote by Narrowest of Margins against the Organisation Becoming a Bank: Nationwide Rejects Float', *The Herald* (24 July 1998).

3 Croft, J., 'Rogue HBOS Banker Sentenced to 11 Years in Prison', *Financial Times* (2 February 2017), <https://www.ft.com/content/ff5aa796-e963-11e6-967b-c88452263daf> (accessed 9 October 2023).

4 Bank of England, 'The Failure of HBOS plc (HBOS)' (November 2015), <https://www.bankofengland.co.uk/-/media/boe/files/prudential-regulation/publication/hbos-summary-and-recommendations> (accessed 9 October 2023).

5 Kendall, T., and Chesworth, N., 'Money Watch: Windfalls in Freefall as Shares Crash to Earth; Millions Lose Out as Bank Values Plunge', *Sunday Mirror* (12 March 2000), <https://www.thefreelibrary.com/Money+Watch%3A+Windfalls+in+freefall+as+shares+crash+to+earth%3B+Millions...-a060960200> (accessed 26 October 2023); Unclaimed Assets, 'Halifax Unclaimed Demutualisation Shares', <https://unclaimedassets.co.uk/halifax-unclaimed-shares> (accessed 9 October 2023).

PART 6: THE CORPORATION IN THE TWENTY-FIRST CENTURY
24. Combinations and Capabilities

1 'What Satya Nadella Thinks', *New York Times* (14 May 2020), <https://www.nytimes.com/2020/05/14/business/dealbook/satya-nadella-microsoft.html> (accessed 10 October 2023).

2 BBC News, 'Goldman Sachs: Bank Boss Rejects Work from Home as the "New Normal"', *BBC News* (25 February 2021), <https://www.bbc.co.uk/news/business-56192048> (accessed 10 October 2023).

3 Schiffer, Z., 'Apple Asks Staff to Return to Office Three Days a Week Starting in Early September', *The Verge* (2 June 2021), <https://www.theverge.com/2021/6/2/22465846/apple-employees-return-office-three-days-week-september> (accessed 3 October 2021).

4 Office for National Statistics (ONS), 'Characteristics of Homeworkers, Great Britain: September 2022 to January 2023' (13 February 2023), <https://www.ons.gov.uk/employmentandlabourmarket/peopleinwork/employmentandemployeetypes/articles/characteristicsofhomeworkersgreatbritain/september2022tojanuary2023> (accessed 1 October 2023).

5   Max, D. T., 'The Chinese Workers Who Assemble Designer Bags in Tuscany', *The New Yorker* (9 April 2018), <https://www.newyorker.com/magazine/2018/04/16/the-chinese-workers-who-assemble-designer-bags-in-tuscany> (accessed 12 April 2023).

6   Marshall, A., *Principles of Economics* (London: Macmillan & Co., 1890), p. 332.

7   Ibid., p. 330.

8   Ibid. p. 333.

9   Mikkelson, B., 'Bush and French Word for Entrepreneur', *Snopes* (23 September 2007), <https://www.snopes.com/fact-check/french-lesson/> (accessed 20 October 2023).

10   McCraw, T. K., *Prophet of Innovation: Joseph Schumpeter and Creative Destruction* (Cambridge, MA: Belknap Press, 2007), p. 4.

11   Schumpeter is sometimes accused of having had Nazi sympathies and was indeed investigated by the FBI after the outbreak of war, but without result; he helped many European scholars escape to the US and was a strong supporter of Paul Samuelson, who moved to MIT after failing to obtain recognition at Harvard, a failure attributed by many to anti-Semitism.

12   Carlyle, T., 'Occasional Discourse on the Negro Question', *Fraser's Magazine for Town and Country*, vol. 40 (1849), pp. 670–79.

13   Carlyle, T., *On Heroes, Hero-Worship, and the Heroic in History* (New York: Wiley and Putnam, 1846), p. 26.

14   Butler, S., 'Letter to Carlyle', (21 November 1884), <https://www.oxfordreference.com/display/10.1093/acref/9780191866692.001.0001/q-oro-ed6-00002407> (accessed 24 October 2023).

15   Schumpeter, J. A., R. Opie (trans.), *The Theory of Economic Development*, (Cambridge, MA: Harvard University Press, 1959), p. 75.

16   Penrose, E. T., *The Theory of the Growth of the Firm* (Oxford: Oxford University Press, 1995).

17   Ibid., p. 2.

18   Isaacson, W., *Steve Jobs: A Biography* (New York: Simon & Schuster, 2011), p. 151; Mac History, '1984 Apple's Macintosh Commercial', YouTube (1 February 2012), <https://www.youtube.com/watch?v=VtvjbmoDx-I> (accessed 1 October 2023).

19   Teece, D. J., Pisano, G., and Shuen, A., 'Dynamic Capabilities and Strategic Management', *Strategic Management Journal*, vol. 18, no. 7 (1997), pp. 509–33.

25. A Letter from Arnold Weinstock

1 In his last interview with Walt Mossberg and Kara Swisher at the All Things Digital's D8 Conference in 2010: <https://www.youtube.com/watch?v=i5f8bqYYwps>.

2 The new employee – they used the term 'servant' – of the East India Company would go to Messrs Grindlay to obtain the manifold requirements for his passage to India. Grindlay's Bank survived until it was finally absorbed into Standard and Chartered Bank in 2000.

3 Weber, M., G. Roth, and C. Wittich, (eds.), *Economy and Society* (Berkeley, CA: University of California Press, 1978), pp. 957–8.

4 Ibid., p. 964.

5 Office of Strategic Services, *Simple Sabotage Field Manual* (Washington, DC: Office of Strategic Services, 1944), p. 28.

6 Freund, C. J., *Anatomy of a Merger: Strategies and Techniques for Negotiating Corporate Acquisitions* (New York: Law Journal Press, 1975), p. 394.

7 Fenton, Roger, *General Pierre François Joseph Bosquet (1810–1861)*, 1855, Royal Collection Trust, <https://www.rct.uk/collection/2500328/general-pierre-franccedilois-joseph-bosquet-1810-1861> (accessed 11 October 2023). 'It is magnificent, but it is not war.'

8 George, B., 'The New 21st Century Leaders', *Harvard Business Review* (30 April 2010), <https://hbr.org/2010/04/the-new-21st-century-leaders-1> (accessed 9 November 2023).

9 Quoted in Kay, J. A., 'The Management of the University of Oxford... Facing the Future', johnkay.com (20 November 2000), <https://www.johnkay.com/2000/11/20/the-management-of-the-university-of-oxford-facing-the-future/> (accessed 1 November 2023).

10 Urwick, L., *The Elements of Administration* (London: Pitman, 1947), p. 47.

11 Grove, A., *High Output Management* (New York: Souvenir Press, 1984), p. 82.

12 Blair, M. M., and Stout, L. A., 'A Team Production Theory of Corporate Law', *Virginia Law Review*, vol. 85, no. 2 (1999), p. 278.

26. The MacNeil Returns to Barra

1 Macneil, I. R., 'The Many Futures of Contracts', *Southern California Law Review*, vol. 47, no. 691 (1973–4), p. 767.

2 Macaulay, S., Friedman, L. M., and Stookey, J., *The Law and Society – Readings on the Social Study of Law* (New York & London: W. W. Norton & Co., 1996).

3   Ibid.

4   Cohen, J., 'It Would Take 17 Hours to Read the Terms & Conditions of the 13 Most Popular Apps', *PCMag* (4 December 2020), <https://uk.pcmag.com/security/130336/it-would-take-17-hours-to-read-the-terms-conditions-of-the-13-most-popular-apps> (accessed 10 October 2023).

5   'Obituary: Ian Macneil, Clan Chief and Lawyer', *The Scotsman* (19 February 2010), <https://www.scotsman.com/news/obituaries/obituary-ian-macneil-clan-chief-and-lawyer-2442857> (accessed 26 October 2023).

6   Henrich, J., *The WEIRDest People in the World* (New York: Farrar Straus and Giroux, 2020).

7   Pew Research Center, 'Religion's Relationship to Happiness, Civic Engagement and Health around the World' (31 January 2019).

8   Transparency International, 'Corruption Perceptions Index 2022' (2023), <https://images.transparencycdn.org/images/Report_CPI2022_English.pdf> (accessed 1 November 2023).

9   Steinhardt, M., *Jewish Pride* (New York: Simon and Schuster, 2022).

10 Heilbron, J. L., *Galileo* (Oxford: Oxford University Press, 2012); Charisius, H., 'When Scientists Experiment on Themselves: H. Pylori and Ulcers', *Scientific American* (5 July 2014), <https://blogs.scientificamerican.com/guest-blog/when-scientists-experiment-on-themselves-h-pylori-and-ulcers/> (accessed 20 October 2023).

11 Erhard, W., Jensen, M. C., and Zaffron, S., 'Integrity: Where Leadership Begins – A New Model of Integrity', presented at the Center for Public Leadership, John F. Kennedy School of Government, Harvard University (10 May 2007), Abstract.

12 Whately, R., *Detached Thoughts and Apophthegms: Extracted from Some of the Writings of Archbishop Whately* (London, 1854), p. 127.

13 Proverbs 10:22.

14 Proverbs 22:1.

15 MacIntyre, A., 'The Nature of the Virtues', *The Hastings Center Report*, vol. 11, no. 2 (1981), pp. 27–34.

16 *Baird Textiles Holdings Ltd v. Marks & Spencer plc* (2002).

17 Ibid.

18 *Amey Birmingham Highways Ltd v. Birmingham City Council* [2018] EWCA Civ 264.

19 Hart, O., 'Incomplete Contracts and Control', Nobel Prize Lecture (8 December 2016), <https://www.nobelprize.org/uploads/2018/06/hart-lecture.pdf> (accessed 1 November 2023).

20 Ibid.
21 Ibid

27. The Hollow Corporation

1   Johnson, R., 'Tyger! Tyger! Burning Bright', *Twitter* (23 April 2022), <https://twitter.com/rdouglasjohnson/status/1517804673998237697?s=20> (accessed 7 November 2023).
2   Grandin, G., *Fordlandia: The Rise and Fall of Henry Ford's Forgotten Jungle City* (New York: Metropolitan Books, 2009).
3   Klein, P. G., 'Coase and the Myth of Fisher Body', *Organizations and Markets* (12 September 2006), <https://organizationsandmarkets.com/2006/09/12/coase-and-the-myth-of-fisher-body/> (accessed 25 June 2023).
4   Jonas, N., 'The Hollow Corporation', *Business Week* (3 March 1986), pp. 57–9.
5   Tipu, Md. S. I., 'Tazreen Fire Tragedy: Trial Proceedings of Cases in Limbo', *Dhaka Tribune* (23 November 2020), <https://www.dhakatribune.com/bangladesh/dhaka/2020/11/23/tazreen-fire-tragedy-trial-proceedings-of-cases-in-limbo> (accessed 5 October 2021).
6   Attributed, as so much else is, to Mark Twain.
7   Davis, G. F., 'What Might Replace the Modern Corporation? Uberization and the Web Page Enterprise', *Seattle University Law Review*, vol. 39, no. 2 (2016), pp. 501–15.
8   Friedman, T. L., 'Foreign Affairs Big Mac I', *The New York Times* (8 December 1996), <https://www.nytimes.com/1996/12/08/opinion/foreign-affairs-big-mac-i.html> (accessed 8 November 2023).
9   Lynch, L., 'I'm Lovin' It (Most of the Time): A Brief History of McDonald's in Serbia', *Balkanist* (27 August 2014), <https://balkanist.net/im-lovin-it-mcdonalds-serbia/> (accessed 19 October 2023).
10 Thomas, M., 'McDonalds Coming to Dubrovnik – Location Known!', *Dubrovnik Times* (27 January 2023), <https://www.thedubrovniktimes.com/news/dubrovnik/item/14431-mcdonalds-coming-to-dubrovnik-location-known> (accessed 30 October 2023).
11 I am not sure if 'insourcing' exists, but my spellcheck accepts it.
12 World Bank, 'Creating Jobs and Diversifying Exports in Bangladesh' (14 November 2017), <https://www.worldbank.org/en/news/feature/2017/11/14/creating-jobs-and-diversifying-exports-in-bangladesh> (accessed 30 January 2024).
13 International Finance Corporation, 'Safety First: Bangladesh Garment

Industry Rebounds' (11 November 2019), <https://www.ifc.org/en/stories/2010/bangladesh-garment-industry> (accessed 19 October 2023).

14 Barboza, D., 'An iPhone's Journey, from the Factory to Floor to the Retail Store (And Why the Product Costs More in China)', *The New York Times* (29 December 2016), <https://www.nytimes.com/2016/12/29/technology/iphone-china-apple-stores.html> (accessed 19 October 2023).

15 World Bank, 'World Development Indicators: NY.GDP.MKTP.CD' (30 March 2023), and IMF, 'GDP, Current Prices (Billions of U.S. Dollars)' (2022), for Taiwan.

16 Gallup, 'The Gig Economy and Alternative Work Arrangements' (2018), p. 2.

17 Uber, '2020 Annual Report' (26 February 2021), <https://s23.q4cdn.com/407969754/files/doc_financials/2021/ar/FINAL-Typeset-Annual-Report.pdf> (accessed 30 October 2023), p. 7; Airbnb, 'About Us', <https://news.airbnb.com/about-us/> (accessed 7 November 2023).

18 Langlois, R. N., *The Corporation and the Twentieth Century* (Princeton, PA: Princeton University Press, 2023).

PART 7: CAPITAL IN THE TWENTY-FIRST CENTURY
28. Capital as a Service

1 Burnham, J., *Beyond Modern Sculpture* (New York: G. Braziller, 1968), p. 11.

2 Amazon, 'Form 10-Q' (2023), <https://www.sec.gov/Archives/edgar/data/1018724/000101872423000008/amzn-20230331.htm> (accessed 19 March 2024), p. 6.

3 Ibid.

4 Haskel, J., and Westlake, S., *Capitalism without Capital* (Princeton, PA: Princeton University Press, 2018).

5 Burrows, P., 'Inside Apple's Plans for Its Futuristic, $5Billion Headquarters', Bloomberg (5 April 2013), <https://www.bloomberg.com/news/articles/2013-04-04/inside-apples-plans-for-its-futuristic-5-billion-headquarters> (accessed 18 October 2023).

6 Norges Bank Investment Management, 'Fund Signs Regent Street Agreement' (13 January 2011), <https://www.nbim.no/en/the-fund/news-list/2011/fund-signs-regent-street-agreement/> (accessed 17 May 2023).

7 Apple, 'Apple Inc. FORM 10-K' (2019), <https://www.annualreports.

com/HostedData/AnnualReportArchive/a/NASDAQ_AAPL_2019. pdf> (accessed 7 November 2023), p. 31.

8   Dealogic via PwC, 'Global IPO Watch 2023 and Outlook for 2024', <https://www.pwc.co.uk/services/audit/insights/global-ipo-watch. html> (accessed 19 January 2024).

9   Anelli, M., 'FTSE 100 Firms Announce £26.9bn Buybacks, but will this Reward them?', *TrustNet* (3 May 2023), <https://www.trustnet. com/news/13376434/ftse-100-firms-announce-269bn-buybacks-but-will-this-reward-them> (accessed 26 March 2024); AJ Bell, 'Dividend Dashboard Q2 2023', (2023), <https://www.ajbell.co.uk/group/sites/ ajbell.co.uk/files/AJB_Dividend_dashboard%20July%202023_0.pdf> (accessed 26 March 2024).

10   Miao, H., 'Buybacks from S&P 500 Companies Set Record in 2022', *Wall Street Journal* (21 March 2023); Greenwald, I., 'Companies Pay Record Dividends in 2022 Despite Dismal Year', *Investopedia* (30 December 2022), <https://www.investopedia.com/companies-pay-records-dividends-2022-7090440> (accessed 26 March 2024).

11   Compass Group, 'Our People Are the Heart of Our Business', <https://www.compass-group.com/content/dam/compass-group/ corporate/Investors/factsheet/People%20Factsheet.pdf> (accessed 7 November 2023); G4S, 'G4S UK: Socio-Economic Impact Assessment', <https://www.g4s.com/social-responsibility/securing-our-communities//-/media/g4s/corporate/indexed-files/files/csr/ cc_g4s_socio-economic_impact_assessment_-_2018-19.ashx> (accessed 7 November 2023), p. 2; International Service System, 'Annual Report 2019' (2020), https://inv. issworld.com/static-files/77620900-c25e-4bd6-9260-ac725a5a1a65 (accessed 19 October 2023), p. 8.

12   IBM, 'Annual Report 2019' (2019), <https://www.ibm.com/ annualreport/assets/downloads/IBM_Annual_Report_2019.pdf> (accessed 30 January 2024), p. 64.

13   Rosoff, M., 'Jeff Bezos Told What Might Be the Best Startup Investment Story Ever', *Business Insider* (20 October 2016), <https:// www.businessinsider.com/jeff-bezos-on-early-amazon-investors-2016-10?r=US&IR=T> (accessed 6 October 2021).

29. Capital and Wealth

1   McLellan, D., *Karl Marx: A Biography*, 4th edn (London: Palgrave Macmillan, 2006), p. 356.

2   Widely cited though perhaps less widely read: an entertaining *jeu*

d'esprit by Jordan Ellenburg finds Piketty's *Capital in the Twenty-First Century* behind only the memoirs of Hillary Clinton among works whose owners – *correction, licensees of the electronic text from Amazon* – struggled to complete: Ellenburg, J., 'The Summer's Most Unread Book Is …', *Wall Street Journal* (3 July 2014). Ellenburg comes to his conclusions based on the distribution of highlighted passages in the work – this assumes that, were people to have read the entire work, they would have found passages worthy of being highlighted distributed uniformly throughout the text.

3   Piketty, T., *Capital in the Twenty-First Century* (Cambridge, MA: Belknap Press, 2014), p. 47.

4   Ibid., p. 48.

5   Rolt, L. T. C., *Victorian Engineering* (London: Penguin, 1970), p. 37.

6   Organisation for Economic Cooperation and Development (OECD), 'National Accounts: 9B. Balance Sheets for Non-Financial Assets', <https://stats.oecd.org/Index.aspx?QueryId=104323> (accessed 6 October 2023). Data from N1111, 'Dwellings'; N11121, 'Buildings other than dwellings'; N11122, 'Other structures'; N1113, 'Machinery and equipment and weapons systems'. Note that there are other relevant categories, but owing to measurement differences between countries we do not include these.

7   Office for National Statistics (ONS), 'Capital Stocks and Fixed Capital Consumption, UK: 2023', *Office for National Statistics* (8 December 2023), <https://www.ons.gov.uk/economy/nationalaccounts/uksectoraccounts/bulletins/capitalstocksconsumptionoffixedcapital/2023> (accessed 30 January 2024).

8   Eurostat, 'House or Flat – Owning and Renting', <https://ec.europa.eu/eurostat/cache/digpub/housing/bloc-1a.html> (accessed 19 October 2023).

9   Walsh, C., 'Leadership on 9/11: Morgan Stanley's Challenge', *Harvard Business School* (17 December 2001), <https://hbswk.hbs.edu/archive/leadership-on-9-11-morgan-stanley-s-challenge> (accessed 30 October 2023).

10 Stewart, J., 'The Real Heroes Are Dead', *The New Yorker* (3 February 2002), <https://www.newyorker.com/magazine/2002/02/11/september-11th-attacks-world-trade-center-rick-rescorla-the-real-heroes-are-dead> (accessed 30 October 2023).

11 Berle, A., *The 20th Century Capitalist Revolution* (New York: Harcourt, Brace & Co., 1954), p. 40.

12 McCloskey, D., *Beyond Positivism, Behaviorism, and Neoinstitutionalism in Economics* (Chicago, IL: University of Chicago Press, 2022), p. 46: 'Having liquid water at the usual temperatures, or a reasonably stable government, is necessary for a Great Enrichment, too. But nobody wants to speak of "water-ism" or "stable-ism".'

30. Who Are the Capitalists Now?

1 Rees, K., 'BlackRock's Assets Seen Topping $15 Trillion in Five Years' Time', Bloomberg (17 April 2023), <https://www.bloomberg.com/news/articles/2023-04-17/blackrock-assets-to-top-15-trillion-in-five-years-analyst-says?leadSource=uverify%20wall> (accessed 7 November 2023).

2 Office for National Statistics (ONS), 'How Has Life Expectancy Changed over Time?' (9 September 2015), <https://www.ons.gov.uk/peoplepopulationandcommunity/birthsdeathsandmarriages/lifeexpectancies/articles/howhaslifeexpectancychangedovertime/2015-09-09> (accessed 19 October 2023). Data is for 1891–1900.

3 ONS, 'Total Wealth in Great Britain: April 2016 to March 2018' (5 December 2019), <https://www.ons.gov.uk/peoplepopulationandcommunity/personalandhouseholdfinances/incomeandwealth/bulletins/totalwealthingreatbritain/april2016tomarch2018> (accessed 19 October 2023), Table 2.2. Data is from April 2016–March 2018. 'Financial' refers to Aggregate Financial Worth (net) and Aggregate Private Pension Wealth.

4 ONS (5 December 2019), Table 2.11. Data is from April 2016–March 2018. 'Retiree' here means 65+: of course some people retire earlier, but, in general, doing so is a sign one has amassed considerable wealth, so these data provide a conservative estimate.

31. In Search of Capital

1 Wharton School, University of Pennsylvania, 'How GM's Mary Barra Drives Value', *Knowledge at Wharton*, <https://knowledge.wharton.upenn.edu/article/how-gms-mary-barra-drives-value/> (accessed 3 May 2018).

2 Abruzzi, W., 'The Myth of Chief Seattle', *Human Ecology Review*, vol. 7, no. 1 (2000), pp. 72–5.

3 Zuboff, S., *The Age of Surveillance Capitalism: The Fight for a Human Future at the New Frontier of Power* (London: Profile, 2018).

4 DeLong, J. B., *Slouching towards Utopia* (London: Basic Books, 2022).

5   Becker, G., 'Gary Becker Facts', The Nobel Prize (1992), <https://
     www.nobelprize.org/prizes/economic-sciences/1992/becker/facts/>
     (accessed 2 November 2023).

6   See, for example, Becker's theory of marriage, satirised by the young
     Alan Blinder, future vice chair of the Fed, in the economics of
     teeth-brushing.

7   Putnam, R. D., 'Tuning In, Tuning Out: The Strange Disappearance
     of Social Capital in America', *Political Science and Politics*, vol. 28, no. 4
     (1995), p. 667.

8   Burke, E., *Reflections on the Revolution in France* (London: J. Dodsley,
     1790), p. 68.

9   Putnam, R., and Garrett, S. R., *The Upswing: How America Came
     Together a Century Ago and How We Can Do It Again* (New York: Simon
     & Schuster, 2020).

10   OECD, 'Biodiversity, Natural Capital and the Economy: A Policy
     Guide for Finance, Economic and Environment Ministers', *OECD
     Environment Policy Papers*, no. 26 (2021).

11   ONS, 'UK Natural Capital Accounts: 2022' (10 November 2022),
     <https://www.ons.gov.uk/economy/environmentalaccounts/
     bulletins/uknaturalcapitalaccounts/2022> (accessed 7 November
     2023); ONS, 'National Balance Sheet' (31 October 2022), <https://
     www.ons.gov.uk/economy/grossdomesticproductgdp/
     compendium/unitedkingdomnationalaccountsthebluebook/2022/
     nationalbalancesheet> (accessed 7 November 2023), Table A. We reach
     the physical capital figure by summing Buildings and Structures
     (AN.112), Machinery, Equipment and Weapons Systems (AN.113 &
     AN.114), and Inventories (AN.12).

12   BBC News, 'Sycamore Gap: Man Pleads not Guilty to Cutting Down
     Tree', (16 May 2024) https://www.bbc.co.uk/news/uk-england-
     tyne-69011665 (accessed 20 May 2024).

13   Knight, F. H., '"What is Truth" in Economics?', *Journal of Political
     Economy*, vol. 48, no. 1 (1940), fn. 10.

PART 8: THE BEST OF TIMES, THE WORST OF TIMES

1   Winston Churchill, Mansion House speech (1942).

2   Keynes, J. M., *The General Theory of Employment Interest and Money*
     (London: MacMillan and Co., 1936), p. 383.

32. Ambiguity is a Feature, Not a Bug

1   Goodman, G. J. W., *Powers of Mind* (New York: Random House, 1975), p. 209.

2   Dickens, C., *A Tale of Two Cities* (London: Chapman & Hall, 1859), p. 1.

3   Wordsworth, W., 'The French Revolution: as It Appeared to Enthusiasts at Its Commencement', in de Selincourt, E. (ed.) *The Poetical Works of William Wordsworth*, vol. 2 (Oxford: Oxford University Press, 1952), pp. 264–5.

4   Ferguson, A., *An Essay on the History of Civil Society* (Dublin: Boulter Grieson, 1767), p. 183.

5   Aristotle, *Nicomachean Ethics* (350 BC), Book I.

6   Aristotle, *Politics* (350 BC), Book VII, Part 9.

7   Wordsworth, (1952), pp. 264–5.

8   The first formulation of the paradox has been attributed to Eubulides.

9   National Bureau of Economic Research (NBER), 'Business Cycle Dating', <https://www.nber.org/research/business-cycle-dating> (accessed 3 September 2023).

10 Macaulay, S., 'Relational Contracts Floating on a Sea of Custom? Thoughts about the Ideas of Ian Macneil and Lisa Bernstein', *Northwestern University Law Review*, vol. 94, no. 3 (2000), p. 778.

11 Romer, P., 'Mathiness in the Theory of Economic Growth', *American Economic Review: Papers & Proceedings*, vol. 105, no. 5 (2015), pp. 89–93.

12 Dickens (1859), p. 1.

33. After Capitalism

1   Bernal, J. D., *Marx and Science* (New York: International Publishers, 1952).

2   Dickens, C., *Nicholas Nickleby* (London: Chapman and Hall, 1839), p. 22.

BIBLIOGRAPHY

'A Steal?', *The Economist* (24 October 2002) <https://www.economist.com/business/2002/10/24/a-steal> (accessed 19 June 2024>

Abruzzi, W., 'The Myth of Chief Seattle', *Human Ecology Review*, vol. 7, no. 1 (2000), pp. 72–5

Adams, R., 'Does Brown Need Balls?', *The Guardian* (27 February 2007)

Airbnb, 'About Us', <https://news.airbnb.com/about-us/> (accessed 7 November 2023)

Airbus Media Relations, 'Airbus Aircraft 2018 Average List Prices (USD Millions)' (2018), <http://www.airbus.com/content/dam/corporate-topics/publications/backgrounders/Airbus-Commercial-Aircraft-list-prices-2018.pdf> (accessed 28 January 2021)

AJ Bell, 'Dividend Dashboard Q2 2023', (2023), <https://www.ajbell.co.uk/group/sites/ajbell.co.uk/files/AJB_Dividend_dashboard%20July%202023_0.pdf> (accessed 26 March 2024)

Alaska Packers' Association v. Domenico, 117F. 99 (1902)

Alchian, A. A., and Demsetz, H., 'Production, Information Costs, and Economic Organization', *American Economic Review*, vol. 62, no. 5 (1972), pp. 777–95

Alton, R., 'A New Biography of Stanley Matthews', *The Spectator* (1 June 2013), <https://www.spectator.co.uk/article/a-new-biography-of-stanley-matthews/> (accessed 6 September 2023)

Amazon, '2019 Annual Report' (2020), <https://s2.q4cdn.com/299287126/files/doc_financials/2020/ar/2019-Annual-Report.pdf> (accessed 27 July 2020)

—, 'Form 10-Q' (2023), <https://www.sec.gov/Archives/edgar/data/1018724/000101872423000008/amzn-20230331.htm> (accessed 19 March 2024)

American Chemical Society International Historic Chemical Landmarks, 'Discovery and Development of Penicillin', <https://www.acs.org/content/acs/en/education/whatischemistry/landmarks/flemingpenicillin.html> (accessed 28 September 2021)

American Economic Association, 'Distinguished Fellows', <https://www.aeaweb.org/about-aea/honors-awards/distinguished-fellows> (accessed 30 October 2023)

Amey Birmingham Highways Ltd v. Birmingham City Council [2018] EWCA Civ 264

Anderson, J., *An Enquiry into the Nature of the Corn Laws; with a View to the New Corn Bill Proposed for Scotland* (Edinburgh: Mundell, 1777)

—, *Observations on the Means of Exciting a Spirit of National Industry; Chiefly Intended to Promote the Agriculture, Commerce, Manufactures and Fisheries of Scotland* (Edinburgh: T. Cadell & C. Elliot, 1777)

Anelli, M., 'FTSE 100 Firms Announce £26.9bn Buybacks, but will this Reward them?', *TrustNet* (3 May 2023), <https://www.trustnet.com/news/13376434/ftse-100-firms-announce-269bn-buybacks-but-will-this-reward-them> (accessed 26 March 2024)

Ansoff, H. I., *Corporate Strategy: An Analytic Approach to Business Policy for Growth and Expansion* (New York: McGraw-Hill, 1965)

Anthony, R. S., and Kim, J. H., 'Thalidomide: The Tragedy of Birth Defects and the Effective Treatment of Disease', *Toxicological Sciences: An Official Journal of the Society of Toxicology*, vol. 122, no. 1 (2007), <https://doi.org/10.1093/toxsci/kfr088>, pp. 1–6

Ardington House, 'History', <https://www.ardingtonhouse.com/history/> (accessed 30 October 2023)

Aristotle, B. Jowett (trans.), *Politics* (350 BC), <https://classics.mit.edu/Aristotle/politics.html> (accessed 27 March 2024)

—, W. D. Ross (trans.), *The Nicomachean Ethics* (350 BC), <https://classics.mit.edu/Aristotle/nicomachaen.html> (accessed 27 March 2024)

Arkansas Teacher Retirement System et al. v. Goldman Sachs Group, Inc., No. 16–250 (2d. Cir. 2018)

Apple, 'Apple Inc. FORM 10-K' (2019), <https://www.annualreports.com/HostedData/AnnualReportArchive/a/NASDAQ_AAPL_2019.pdf> (accessed 7 November 2023)

Ashton, T. S., 'The Records of a Pin Manufactory, 1814–21', *Economica*, no. 15 (1925), pp. 281–92

AT&T, 'AT&T to Acquire Time Warner' (22 October 2016), <https://about.att.com/story/att_to_acquire_time_warner.html> (accessed 9 October 2023)

Autronic AG v. Switzerland, NO 12726/87 (1990)

Baer, J., and Zuckerman, G., 'Branded a Villain, Lehman's Dick Fuld Chases Redemption', *Wall Street Journal* (6 September 2018)

Bain, J. S., *Industrial Organisation: A Treatise* (London: John Wiley, 1959)

The Corporation in the 21ˢᵗ Century

Baird Textiles Holdings Ltd v. Marks & Spencer plc (2002)

Ballentine, C., 'Sulfanilamide Disaster', *FDA Consumer Magazine* (June 1981)

Bank of England, 'The Failure of HBOS plc (HBOS)' (November 2015), <https://www.bankofengland.co.uk/-/media/boe/files/prudential-regulation/publication/hbos-summary-and-recommendations> (accessed 9 October 2023)

—, 'Inflation Report' (2018), <https://www.bankofengland.co.uk/-/media/boe/files/inflation-report/2018/february/inflation-report-february-2018.pdf> (accessed 26 July 2023)

Bank of Tokyo Ltd v. Karoon, EWCA Civ J0524 -1 (24 May 1987)

Barboza, D., 'An iPhone's Journey, from the Factory to Floor to the Retail Store (And Why the Product Costs More in China)', *New York Times* (29 December 2016), <https://www.nytimes.com/2016/12/29/technology/iphone-china-apple-stores.html> (accessed 19 October 2023)

Barney, J., 'Firm Resources and Sustained Competitive Advantage', *Journal of Management*, vol. 17, no. 1 (1991), pp. 99–120

Basic Law for the Federal Republic of Germany', European Union Agency for Fundamental Rights (1949), <https://fra.europa.eu/en/law-reference/basic-law-federal-republic-germany-13> (accessed 13 June 2024).

Bastian, H., 'Down and Almost Out in Scotland: George Orwell, Tuberculosis and Getting Streptomycin in 1948', *Journal of the Royal Society of Medicine*, vol. 99, no. 2 (2006), pp. 95–8, <doi: 10.1258/jrsm.99.2.95>

BBC News, 'Goldman Sachs: Bank Boss Rejects Work from Home as the "New Normal"', *BBC News* (25 February 2021), <https://www.bbc.co.uk/news/business-56192048> (accessed 10 October 2023)

Becker, G., 'Gary Becker Facts', The Nobel Prize (1992), <https://www.nobelprize.org/prizes/economic-sciences/1992/becker/facts/> (accessed 2 November 2023)

Berle, A., *The 20th Century Capitalist Revolution* (New York: Harcourt, Brace & Co., 1954)

Berle, A., and Means, G., *The Modern Corporation and Private Property* (New Brunswick, NJ: Transaction, 1932)

Berliner Philarmoniker, 'Claudio Abbado in Rehearsal with the Berliner Philarmoniker', *YouTube* (3 August 2011), <https://www.youtube.com/watch?v=4YcmIohczpQ> (accessed 9 October 2023)

Berman, M., *All That Is Solid Melts into Air: The Experience of Modernity* (New York: Penguin Books, 1982)

Bernal, J. D., *Marx and Science* (New York: International Publishers, 1952)

Bernard, D., 'How a Miracle Drug Changed the Fight against Infection during World War II', *Washington Post* (11 July 2020), <https://www.washingtonpost.com/history/2020/07/11/penicillin-coronavirus-florey-wwii-infection/> (accessed 28 September 2021)

Biden, J., 'Remarks by President Biden on Economic Progress since Taking Office: Speech at Springfield, Virginia' (26 January 2023), <https://www.whitehouse.gov/briefing-room/speeches-remarks/2023/01/26/remarks-by-president-biden-on-economic-progress-since-taking-office/> (accessed 26 July 2023)

Bierce, A., *The Collected Works of Ambrose Bierce*, vol. VII, *The Devil's Dictionary* (New York: Neale Publishing, 1911)

Biskupic, J., and Barbash, F., 'Retired Justice Lewis Powell Dies at 90', *Washington Post* (26 August 1998), <https://www.washingtonpost.com/wp-srv/national/longterm/supcourt/stories/powell082698.htm> (accessed 5 October 2021)

Blair, M. M., and Stout, L. A., 'A Team Production Theory of Corporate Law', *Virginia Law Review*, vol. 85, no. 2 (1999), pp. 247–328

Bloomberg, 'Jack Welch Elaborates: Shareholder Value', Bloomberg (16 March 2009), <https://www.bloomberg.com/news/articles/2009-03-16/jack-welch-elaborates-shareholder-value> (accessed 30 October 2023)

Bloomberg News, 'Valeant's Former Boss Michael Pearson Is Suing the Pharma for Not Paying Him 3 Million Shares Promised When He Left', *Financial Post* (28 March 2018)

Board of Governors of the Federal Reserve System, 'Currency in Circulation [CURRCIR]', retrieved from FRED, Federal Reserve Bank of St. Louis, <https://fred.stlouisfed.org/series/CURRCIR> (accessed 29 January 2024)

Bodell v. Gen. Gas & Elec. Corp., 132 A. 442 (Del. Ch. 1926)

Bodleian Libraries., 'The University of Oxford's Relationship with the Sackler Family – Statement' (15 May 2023), <https://www.bodleian.ox.ac.uk/about/media/university-oxford-relationship-sackler-family-statement> (accessed 20 July 2023)

Boeing., 'Boeing 737 Facts' (2014), <https://web.archive.org/web/20240119184424/https://www.boeing.com/farnborough2014/pdf/BCA/fct%20-737%20Family%20Facts.pdf>

Boethius, H. R. James (trans.), *The Consolation of Philosophy* [AD 524], (London: Elliot Stock, 1897)

Bohn, J., and Choi, S., 'Fraud in the New-Issues Market: Empirical

Evidence on Securities Class Actions', *University of Pennsylvania Law Review*, vol. 144, no. 3 (1996), pp. 903–82

Bowers, S., 'RBS Invested Billions in Complex Loans That Bosses Did Not Understand', *The Guardian* (12 December 2011), <https://www.theguardian.com/business/2011/dec/12/rbs-invested-billions-complex-loans-fsa> (accessed 1 November 2023)

Brantley, B., 'Titans of Tangled Finances Kick Up Their Heels Again', *New York Times* (27 April 2010)

Brief for the Chamber of Commerce of the United States of America as Amici Curiae Supporting Defendants-Appellants, *Arkansas Teacher Retirement System et al. v. Goldman Sachs Group, Inc.*, No. 16–250 (2d. Cir. 2018)

British Army., 'Equipment: Small Arms and Support Weapons' (2020), <https://www.army.mod.uk/equipment/small-arms-and-support-weapons/> (accessed 28 January 2021)

Broadberry, S., Campbell, B. M. S., Klein, A., Overton, M., and Van Leeuwen, B., *British Economic Growth, 1270–1870* (Cambridge: Cambridge University Press, 2015)

Brontë, C., Letter to Margaret Wooler (30 January 1846), <https://www.annebronte.org/2020/09/27/2164/> (accessed 7 November 2023)

Buffett, W. E., 'Chairman's Letter 1989' (28 February 1989), <https://www.berkshirehathaway.com/letters/1988.html> (accessed 26 June 2023)

'Building Society Members Vote by Narrowest of Margins against the Organisation Becoming a Bank: Nationwide Rejects Float', *The Herald* (24 July 1998) https://www.heraldscotland.com/news/12257020.building-society-members-vote-by-narrowest-of-margins-against-the-organisation-becoming-a-bank-nationwide-rejects-float/

Burj Khalifa, 'Fact Sheet', <https://www.burjkhalifa.ae/img/FACT-SHEET.pdf> (accessed 3 May 2023)

Burke, E., *Reflections on the Revolution in France* (London: J. Dodsley, 1790)

Burnham, J., *Beyond Modern Sculpture* (New York: G. Braziller, 1968)

Burns, R., 'Elegy on the Year Eighty-Eight/Verses, Written on a Window of the Inn at Carron' (1787), <https://en.wikisource.org/wiki/Elegy_on_the_year_eighty-eight/Verses,_written_on_a_Window_of_the_Inn_at_Carron> (accessed 8 November 2023)

Burrows, P., 'Inside Apple's Plans for Its Futuristic, $5Billion Headquarters', Bloomberg (5 April 2013), <https://www.bloomberg.com/news/articles/2013-04-04/inside-apples-plans-for-its-futuristic-5-billion-headquarters> (accessed 18 October 2023)

Burwell v. Hobby Lobby Stores, Inc., 573 U.S. 682 (2014)

Butler, S., 'Letter to Carlyle', (21 November 1884), <https://www.oxfordreference.com/display/10.1093/acref/9780191866692.001.0001/q-oro-ed6-00002407> (accessed 24 October 2023)

Butterworth, T., 'The Biggest Mistake in Corporate History', *Forbes* (30 September 2010)

Callahan, P., 'So Why Does Harry Stonecipher Think He Can Turn Around Boeing?', *Chicago Tribune* (29 February 2004)

Cao, X., Chan, K., and Kahle, K., 'Risk and Performance of Bonds Sponsored by Private Equity Funds', *Journal of Banking and Finance*, vol. 93 (2018), pp. 41–53

Capen, E. C., Clapp, R. V., and Campbell, W. M., 'Competitive Bidding in High-Risk Situations', *Journal of Petroleum Technology*, vol. 23, no. 6 (1971), pp. 641–53

Carbolic Smoke Ball Co., 'Carbolic Smoke Ball', *Illustrated London News* (1893), <https://commons.wikimedia.org/wiki/File:Carbolic_smoke_ball_co.jpg> (accessed 31 January 2024)

Carlson, M., 'For F.J. Titmus Read Titmus, F.J.' (23 March 2011), <http://irresistibletargets.blogspot.com/2011/03/for-fj-titmus-read-titmus-fj.html> (accessed 25 July 2023)

Carlyle, T., 'Occasional Discourse on the Negro Question', *Fraser's Magazine for Town and Country*, vol. 40 (1849), pp. 670–79

—, *On Heroes, Hero-Worship, and the Heroic in History* (New York: Wiley and Putnam, 1846)

Case, A., and Deaton, A., *Deaths of Despair and the Future of Capitalism* (Princeton, NJ: Princeton University Press, 2020)

Cassidy, J., 'Muckraking and Medicine: Samuel Hopkins Adams', *American Quarterly*, vol. 16, no. 1 (1964), pp. 85–99

Catherwood, J., 'Drunk Valuations, and Frothy Markets: The Guinness IPO', *Investor Amnesia* (30 August 2018), <https://investoramnesia.com/2018/08/30/drunk-valuations-and-frothy-markets-the-guinness-ipo/> (accessed 18 September 2020)

Chandler, A. D., *Strategy and Structure: Chapters in the History of the American Industrial Enterprise* (Boston, MA: MIT Press, 1962)

Charisius, H., 'When Scientists Experiment on Themselves: H. Pylori and Ulcers', *Scientific American* (5 July 2014), <https://blogs.scientificamerican.com/guest-blog/when-scientists-experiment-on-themselves-h-pylori-and-ulcers/> (accessed 20 October 2023)

Checkland, S. G., *Scottish Banking: A History, 1695–1973* (Glasgow: Collins, 1975)

Chernova, Y., 'Sequoia Capital Goes on Fundraising Spree', *Wall Street Journal Pro Venture Capital* (5 March 2018), <https://www.wsj.com/articles/sequoia-capital-goes-on-fundraising-spree-152025304> (accessed 17 October 2023)

Citizens United v. Federal Election Commission, 558 U.S. 310 (2012)

Clapham, J. H., *Bibliography of English Economic History* (London: Historical Association, 1913)

—, 'Of Empty Economic Boxes', *Economic Journal*, vol. 32, no. 127 (1922), pp. 305–14

Clark, A., 'Chrysler – How a Great Car Firm Crashed', *The Guardian* (1 May 2009), <https://www.theguardian.com/business/2009/may/01/chrysler-bankruptcy-car-industry-us> (accessed 27 September 2023)

Clutterbuck, D., and Devine, M., *Clore: The Man and His Millions* (London: Weidenfeld and Nicolson, 1987)

CNBC, 'CNBC Exclusive: CNBC Transcript: Goldman Sachs Chairman & CEO David Solomon Speaks with CNBC's Jim Cramer on *Mad Money* Today' (18 July 2022), <https://www.cnbc.com/2022/07/18/cnbc-exclusive-cnbc-transcript-goldman-sachs-chairman-ceo-david-solomon-speaks-with-cnbcs-jim-cramer-on-mad-money-today.html> (accessed 24 January 2023)

Coase, R. H., 'The Nature of the Firm', *Economica*, vol. 4, no. 6 (1937), pp. 386–405

—, 'Opening Address to the Annual Conference: International Society of New Institutional Economics, Washington, DC, USA', The Ronald Coase Institute (17 September 1999), <https://www.coase.org/coasespeech.htm> (accessed 16 October 2023)

—, 'Press Release', The Nobel Prize (15 October 1991), <https://www.nobelprize.org/prizes/economic-sciences/1991/press-release/> (accessed 7 November 2023)

—, 'Prize Lecture', *The Nobel Prize* (9 December 1991), <https://www.nobelprize.org/prizes/economic-sciences/1991/coase/lecture/> (accessed 3 May 2023)

Cobb, C. W., and Douglas, P. H., 'A Theory of Production', *American Economic Review*, vol. 18, no. 1 (supplement) (1928), pp. 139–65

Cohen, J., 'It Would Take 17 Hours to Read the Terms & Conditions of the 13 Most Popular Apps', *PCMag* (4 December 2020), <https://uk.pcmag.com/security/130336/it-would-take-17-hours-to-read-the-terms-conditions-of-the-13-most-popular-apps> (accessed 10 October 2023)

Colas Est SA and Others v. France, no 37971/97 (ECHR, 2002)

Collins, C., *How the Mighty Fall* (London: Random House, 2009)

Collins, J. C., and Porras, J. I., *Built to Last: Successful Habits of Visionary Companies* (New York: HarperBusiness, 1997)

Commissioners v. Joiner [1975] 1 WLR 1701

Compass Group, 'Our People Are the Heart of Our Business', <https://www.compass-group.com/content/dam/compass-group/corporate/Investors/factsheet/People%20Factsheet.pdf> (accessed 7 November 2023)

Connelly, D., 'A History of Aspirin', *Clinical Pharmacist*, vol. 6, no. 7 (2014), <https://pharmaceutical-journal.com/article/infographics/a-history-of-aspirin> (accessed 14 October 2021)

Cornell School of Industrial and Labour Relations Web Exhibit, 'The 1911 Triangle Factory Fire' (2018), <https://trianglefire.ilr.cornell.edu/index.html> (accessed 30 January 2024)

Court, E., 'Valeant Gets a New Name to Shed Its Scandals, But Will It Work?', *MarketWatch* (17 July 2018), <https://www.marketwatch.com/story/valeant-will-get-a-new-name-again-hoping-to-shed-its-scandals-2018-05-08> (accessed 28 September 2021)

Croft, J., 'Rogue HBOS Banker Sentenced to 11 Years in Prison', *Financial Times* (2 February 2017), https://www.ft.com/content/ff5aa796-e963-11e6-967b-c88452263daf> (accessed 9 October 2023)

Csikszentmihalyi, M., *Flow: The Psychology of Optimal Experience: Steps toward Enhancing the Quality of Life* (New York: HarperCollins, 1991)

Darmouni, O., and Papoutsi, M., 'The Rise of Bond Financing in Europe', *European Central Bank Working Paper Series,* no. 2663 (May 2022), <https://www.ecb.europa.eu/pub/pdf/scpwps/ecb.wp2663~06c26039e0.en.pdf> (accessed 5 October 2023)

Davies, P. L., Worthington, S., and Hare, C., *Gower: Principles of Modern Company Law*, 11th edn (London: Sweet & Maxwell, 2021)

Davis, G. F., 'What Might Replace the Modern Corporation? Uberization and the Web Page Enterprise', *Seattle University Law Review*, vol. 39, no. 2 (2016), pp. 501–15

Dealogic via PwC, 'Global IPO Watch 2023 and Outlook for 2024', <https://www.pwc.co.uk/services/audit/insights/global-ipo-watch.html> (accessed 19 January 2024)

DeLong, J. B., *Slouching towards Utopia* (London: Basic Books, 2022)

Department for Business, Energy & Industrial Strategy, 'Business Population Estimates for the UK and Regions 2022: Statistical Release' (6 October 2022), <https://www.gov.uk/government/statistics/business-population-estimates-2022/

business-population-estimates-for-the-uk-and-regions-2022-statistical-release-html> (accessed 16 June 2023)

Derks, S., *The Value of a Dollar: Prices and Incomes in the United States, 1860–1999* (Lakeville, CT: Grey House Publishing, 1999)

Dewey, K., and Hemingway, M., 'Building a Top-Flight Supreme Court Practice with Kannon Shanmugam', *Lawdragon* (25 January 2024), <https://www.lawdragon.com/lawyer-limelights/2024-01-25-building-a-top-flight-supreme-court-practice-with-kannon-shanmugam> (accessed 31 January 2024)

Dickens, C., *A Tale of Two Cities* (London: Chapman & Hall, 1859)

—, *Nicholas Nickleby* (London: Chapman and Hall, 1839)

Dodge v. Ford Motor Co., 204 Mich. 459, 170 N.W. 668 (1919)

Dreazen, Y. J., 'How a 24-Year-Old Got a Job Rebuilding Iraq's Stock Market', *Wall Street Journal* (28 January 2004)

Drucker, P., *Concept of the Corporation* (New York: John Day, 1946)

Drummond, H., *The Dynamics of Organizational Collapse: The Case of Barings Bank* (Abingdon: Routledge, 2008)

Durkin Richer, A., 'Witness: Drug Company Hired Ex-Stripper to Increase Sales', *abcNews* (1 March 2019), <https://abcnews.go.com/US/wireStory/witness-drug-company-hired-stripper-increase-sales-61419793> (accessed 28 September 2021)

Easterbrook, F. H., and Fischel, D. R., 'Limited Liability and the Corporation', *University of Chicago Law Review*, vol. 52, no. 1 (1985), pp. 89–117

eBay Domestic Holdings, Inc. v. Newmark – 16 A.3d 1 (2010)

ECA v. J. P. Morgan Chase, No. 07-1786 (2d. Cir. 2009)

Edelman, 'Edelman Trust Barometer 2020' (2020), <https://www.edelman.com/sites/g/files/aatuss191/files/2020-01/2020 %20Edelman %20Trust %20Barometer %20Global %20Report.pdf> (accessed 19 September 2020)

Ehrlich, P. R., *The Population Bomb* (New York: Ballantine Books, 1968)

Eisenhower, D., 'President Dwight D. Eisenhower's Farewell Address' (1961), <https://www.archives.gov/milestone-documents/president-dwight-d-eisenhowers-farewell-address> (accessed 6 November 2023)

Ellenburg, J., 'The Summer's Most Unread Book Is …', *Wall Street Journal* (3 July 2014)

Emberland, M., *The Human Rights of Companies: Exploring the Structure of ECHR Protection* (Oxford: Oxford University Press, 2006)

Empire State Realty Trust, 'Empire State Building Fact Sheet', <https://

www.esbnyc.com/sites/default/files/esb_fact_sheet_final_o.pdf>
(accessed 3 April 2024)

Engels, F., P. Sweezy (trans.), 'The Principles of Communism', in *Karl Marx and Frederick Engels: Selected Works,* vol. 1 (Moscow: Progress Publishers, 1973), pp. 81–97

Enrich, D., *Dark Towers: Deutsche Bank, Donald Trump, and an Epic Trail of Destruction* (New York: HarperCollins, 2020)

Erhard, W., Jensen, M. C., and Zaffron, S., 'Integrity: Where Leadership Begins – A New Model of Integrity', presented at the Center for Public Leadership, John F. Kennedy School of Government, Harvard University (10 May 2007)

European Commission, 'Labour Market Information: Switzerland (6 June 2023)', <https://eures.ec.europa.eu/living-and-working/labour-market-information/labour-market-information-switzerland_en>
(accessed 26 September 2023)

Eurostat, 'House or Flat – Owning and Renting', <https://ec.europa.eu/eurostat/cache/digpub/housing/bloc-1a.html> (accessed 19 October 2023)

Federal Reserve Bank of Minneapolis, 'Consumer Prize Index, 1913', <https://www.minneapolisfed.org/about-us/monetary-policy/inflation-calculator/consumer-price-index-1913> (accessed 31 October 2023)

Fenton, R., *General Pierre François Joseph Bosquet (1810–1861)*, 1855, Royal Collection Trust, <https://www.rct.uk/collection/2500328/general-pierre-franccedilois-joseph-bosquet-1810-1861> (accessed 11 October 2023)

Ferguson, A., *An Essay on the History of Civil Society* (Dublin: Boulter Grieson, 1767)

Financial Conduct Authority (FCA), 'Deutsche Bank Fined £227 Million by Financial Conduct Authority for LIBOR and EURIBOR Failings and for Misleading the Regulator' (24 April 2015), <https://www.fca.org.uk/news/press-releases/deutsche-bank-fined-%C2%A3227-million-financial-conduct-authority-libor-and-euribor> (accessed 12 November 2020)

Fisher, I., *The Rate of Interest: Its Nature, Determination and Relation to Economic Phenomena* (New York: Macmillan, 1907)

Ford, J., 'Boeing and the Siren Call of Share Buybacks', *Financial Times* (4 August 2019)

Ford, H., and Crowther, S., *My Life and Work* (New York: Garden City Publishing Company, Inc., 1922)

Ford Motor Company, 'The Model T' (2023), <https://corporate.ford.com/articles/history/the-model-t.html> (accessed 1 August 2023)

Fortune, 'Merck, World's Most Admired Companies' (2020), <https://fortune.com/ranking/worlds-most-admired-companies/2020/merck/> (accessed 30 September 2023)

Francis, T., 'Revisiting IBM's Palmisano Equation' (13 March 2012), <https://footnoted.com/revisiting-ibms-palmisano-equation/> (accessed 27 September 2021)

Freeman, J. B., *Behemoth: A History of the Factory and the Making of the Modern World* (New York: W. W. Norton & Co., 2018)

Freund, C. J., *Anatomy of a Merger: Strategies and Techniques for Negotiating Corporate Acquisitions* (New York: Law Journal Press, 1975)

Friedman, F., 'A Friedman Doctrine – "The Social Responsibility of Business Is to Increase Its Profits"', *New York Times* (13 September 1970), <https://www.nytimes.com/1970/09/13/archives/a-friedman-doctrine-the-social-responsibility-of-business-is-to.html> (accessed 3 October 2021)

Friedman, T. L., 'Foreign Affairs Big Mac I', *New York Times* (8 December 1996), <https://www.nytimes.com/1996/12/08/opinion/foreign-affairs-big-mac-i.html> (accessed 8 November 2023)

G4S, 'G4S UK: Socio-Economic Impact Assessment', <https://www.g4s.com/social-responsibility/securing-our-communities//-/media/g4s/corporate/indexed-files/files/csr/cc_g4s_socio-economic_impact_assessment_-_2018-19.ashx> (accessed 7 November 2023)

Galbraith, J. K., *The New Industrial State* (Boston, MA: Houghton Mifflin, 1967)

Gallup, 'Business and Industry Sector Ratings' (17 August 2021), <https://news.gallup.com/poll/12748/business-industry-sector-ratings.aspx> (accessed 29 September 2021)

—, 'Confidence in Institutions' (2020), <https://news.gallup.com/poll/1597/confidence-institutions.aspx> (accessed 19 September 2020)

—, 'The Gig Economy and Alternative Work Arrangements' (2018)

Galton, F., 'Vox Populi', *Nature*, vol. 75 (1907), pp. 450–51

Gardner, D., and Tetlock, E. P., *Superforecasting: The Art and Science of Prediction* (London: Random House, 2016)

Garry, P. M., Spurlin, C., Owen, D. A., and Williams, W. A., 'The Irrationality of Shareholder Class Action Lawsuits: A Proposal for Reform', *South Dakota Law Review*, vol. 49, no. 2 (2004), pp. 275–312

Gavi, The Vaccine Alliance, 'There are Four Different Kinds of COVID-19 Vaccines: Here's How They Work', <https://www.gavi.org/

vaccineswork/there-are-four-types-covid-19-vaccines-heres-how-they-work> (accessed 28 September 2021)

George, B., 'The New 21st Century Leaders', *Harvard Business Review* (30 April 2010), <https://hbr.org/2010/04/the-new-21st-century-leaders-1> (accessed 9 November 2023)

Givner, J., 'Industrial History, Preindustrial Literature: George Eliot's *Middlemarch*', *ELH*, vol. 69, no. 1 (2002), pp. 223–43

Glaeser, E. L., *Agglomeration Economics* (Chicago, IL: University of Chicago Press, 2010)

Goldman Sachs, 'Code of Business Conduct and Ethics' (23 February 2023), <https://www.goldmansachs.com/about-us/purpose-and-values/code-of-business-conduct-and-ethics.html> (accessed 8 November 2023)

—, 'Goldman Sachs' Commitment to Board Diversity' (4 February 2020), <https://www.goldmansachs.com/our-commitments/diversity-and-inclusion/launch-with-gs/pages/commitment-to-diversity.html> (accessed 24 January 2023)

Goodman, G. J. W., *Powers of Mind* (New York: Random House, 1975)

Grandin, G., *Fordlandia: The Rise and Fall of Henry Ford's Forgotten Jungle City* (New York: Metropolitan Books, 2009)

Greenspan, A., 'Question: Is There a New Economy?', Haas Annual Business Faculty Research Dialogue, University of California, Berkeley (4 September 1998)

Greenwald, I., 'Companies Pay Record Dividends in 2022 Despite Dismal Year', *Investopedia* (30 December 2022), <https://www.investopedia.com/companies-pay-records-dividends-2022-7090440> (accessed 26 March 2024)

Gross, D., and editors of *Forbes* magazine, *Forbes Greatest Business Stories of All Time* (New York: John Wiley & Sons, 1996)

Grossman, S. J., and Stiglitz, J. E., 'On the Impossibility of Informationally Efficient Markets', *American Economic Review*, vol. 70, no. 3 (1980), pp. 393-408.

Grove, A., *High Output Management* (New York: Souvenir Press, 1984)

Guardian Staff and Agencies, 'Johnson & Johnson to Pay $5bn in Landmark $26bn US Opioid Settlement', *The Guardian* (21 July 2021), <https://www.theguardian.com/us-news/2021/jul/21/us-opioid-settlement-state-attorneys-general-johnson-and-johnson> (accessed 28 September 2021)

Guerrera, F., 'A Need to Reconnect', *Financial Times* (12 March 2009)

Haldeman, P., 'The Return of Werner Erhard, Father of Self Help', *New*

York Times (28 November 2015), <https://www.nytimes.
com/2015/11/29/fashion/the-return-of-werner-erhard-father-of-self-
help.html> (accessed 7 November 2023)

Hall, R. E., 'Notes on the Current State of Empirical Macroeconomics'
(June 1976), <https://web.stanford.edu/~rehall/Notes%20
Current%20State%20Empirical%201976.pdf> (accessed 30 October
2023)

Hamel, G., and Prahalad, C. K., 'The Core Competence of the
Corporation', *Harvard Business Review* (1990), <https://hbr.
org/1990/05/the-core-competence-of-the-corporation> (accessed 19
October 2023)

Hamilton, B., 'East African Running Dominance: What is Behind It?',
British Journal of Sports Medicine, vol. 34, no. 5 (2000), pp. 391–4

Hamilton, H., 'The Founding of Carron Ironworks', *Scottish Historical
Review*, vol. 25, no. 99 (1928), pp. 185–93

Hamowy, R., 'Progress and Commerce in Anglo-American Thought: The
Social Philosophy of Adam Ferguson', *Interpretation*, vol. 14, no. 1
(1986), pp. 61–88

Handy, C., 'What is a Company for?', *RSA Journal*, vol. 139, no. 5416 (1991),
pp. 231–41

Hannah, L., 'J. P. Morgan in London and New York before 1914', *Business
History Review*, vol. 85, no. 1 (2011), pp. 113–50

—, *The Rise of the Corporate Economy* (London: Routledge, 1976)

Hart, O., *Firms, Contracts, and Financial Structure* (Oxford: Clarendon Press,
2009)

—, 'Incomplete Contracts and Control', Nobel Prize Lecture (8 December
2016), <https://www.nobelprize.org/uploads/2018/06/hart-lecture.
pdf> (accessed 1 November 2023)

Haskel, J., and Westlake, S., *Capitalism without Capital* (Princeton, PA:
Princeton University Press, 2018)

Hayek, F. von, 'Friedrich von Hayek Prize Lecture', The Nobel Prize (11
December 1974), <https://www.nobelprize.org/prizes/economic-
sciences/1974/hayek/lecture/> (accessed 1 November 2023)

Hayes, A., 'Economic Rent: Definition, Types, How It Works, and
Example', *Investopedia* (1 September 2023), <https://www.
investopedia.com/terms/e/economicrent.asp> (accessed 30 January
2024)

Haynes, A., 'The History of Snake Oil', *Pharmaceutical Journal*, vol. 294,
no. 7850 (21 February 2015)

Heilbron, J. L., *Galileo* (Oxford: Oxford University Press, 2012)

Henderson, B., 'The Experience Curve – Reviewed (Part II)', *BCG* (1973), <https://www.bcg.com/publications/1973/corporate-finance-strategy-portfolio-management-experience-curve-reviewed-part-ii-the-history> (accessed 5 September 2023)

Henrich, J., *The Secret of Our Success: How Culture is Driving Human Evolution, Domesticating Our Species, and Making Us Smarter* (Princeton, NJ: Princeton University Press, 2015)

—, *The WEIRDest People in the World* (New York: Farrar Straus and Giroux, 2020)

Herrendorf, B., Rogerson, R., and Valentinyi, A., 'Growth and Structural Transformation', National Bureau of Economic Research, Working Paper 18996 (2013), <https://www.nber.org/system/files/working_papers/w18996/w18996.pdf> (accessed 7 November 2023)

Heyes, C., *Cognitive Gadgets: The Cultural Evolution of Thinking* (Cambridge, MA: Belknap Press, 2018)

Hirsch, F., *Social Limits to Growth* (London and Henley: Routledge & Kegan Paul, 1977)

Hoffman, J., 'Purdue Pharma Is Dissolved and Sacklers Pay $4.5 Billion to Settle Opioid Claims', *New York Times* (1 September 2021), <https://www.nytimes.com/2021/09/01/health/purdue-sacklers-opioids-settlement.html> (accessed 28 September 2021)

Hollander, J. H., 'Adam Smith 1776–1926', *Journal of Political Economy*, vol. 35, no. 2 (1927), pp. 153–97

Honoré, A. M., 'Ownership', in Guest, A. G. (ed.), *Oxford Essays in Jurisprudence* (Oxford: Oxford University Press, 1961), pp. 107–47

Hosking, P., 'I Made Money at Marconi: Mayo', *This is Money* (21 January 2002), <https://www.thisismoney.co.uk/money/news/article-1544765/I-made-money-at-Marconi-Mayo.html> (accessed 7 November 2023)

Houston, R., "Mortality in Early Modern Scotland: The Life Expectancy of Advocates", *Continuity and Change*, vol. 7, no. 1 (1992), 47–69

Hume, D., Letter to Adam Smith (27 June 1772), in Burton, J. H. (ed.), *Life and Correspondence of David Hume*, vol. II (Edinburgh: W. Tait, 1846), pp. 459–61

IBM, 'Annual Report 2019' (2019), <https://www.ibm.com/annualreport/assets/downloads/IBM_Annual_Report_2019.pdf> (accessed 30 January 2024)

—, 'A History of Progress' (2008), <https://www.ibm.com/ibm/history/interactive/ibm_history.pdf> (accessed 7 November 2023)

—, 'What is SaaS (Software-as-a-Service)?', <https://www.ibm.com/
    topics/saas> (accessed 18 October 2023)
Inland Revenue v. Laird Group UKHL 54 Para 35 (2003)
Inland Revenue v. Laird Group, EWCA Civ 576 (2003)
Inland Revenue Commissioners v. Crossman [1937] AC 26
Inland Revenue Commissioners v. Joiner [1975] 1 WLR 1701, 1705E *per* Lord
    Wilberforce
Insinna, V., 'Boeing Hits 2023 Jet Delivery Goal but Lags Airbus', Reuters
    (10 January 2024), <https://www.reuters.com/business/aerospace-
    defense/boeing-hits-2023-jet-delivery-goal-blockbuster-
    sales-year-2024-01-09/> (accessed 18 January 2024)
International Finance Corporation, 'Safety First: Bangladesh Garment
    Industry Rebounds' (11 November 2019), <https://www.ifc.org/en/
    stories/2010/bangladesh-garment-industry> (accessed 19 October
    2023)
International Monetary Fund (IMF), 'GDP, Current Prices (Billions of U.S.
    Dollars)' (2022)
—, 'Germany: Financial Sector Assessment Program – Stress Testing the
    Banking and Insurance Sectors – Technical Notes' (29 June 2016),
    <https://www.elibrary.imf.org/view/journals/002/2016/191/
    article-A001-en.xml> (accessed 30 January 2024)
International Service System, 'Annual Report 2019' (2020), <https://inv.
    issworld.com/static-files/77620900-c25e-4bd6-9260-ac725a5a1a65>
    (accessed 7 November 2023)
Internet Movie Database, 'Alec Guinness', <https://www.imdb.com/
    name/nm0000027/> (accessed 7 September 2023)
Isaacson, W., *Steve Jobs: A Biography* (New York: Simon & Schuster, 2011)
Jeffrey, A., 'Mylan Finalizes $465 Million EpiPen Settlement with Justice
    Department', *CNBC* (17 August 2017), <https://www.cnbc.
    com/2017/08/17/mylan-finalizes-465-million-epipen-settlement-with-
    justice-department.html> (accessed 28 September 2021)
Jeffrey Ross Blue v. Michael James Wallace Ashley, [2017] EWHC 1928 (Comm)
Jeng, L. A., Metrick, A., and Zeckhauser, R., 'Estimating the Returns to
    Insider Trading: A Performance-Evaluation Perspective', *Review of
    Economics and Statistics*, vol. 85, no. 2 (2003), pp. 453–71
Jenkins, P., and Saigol, L., 'UBS's Orcel Admits Banks Must Change',
    Financial Times (9 January 2013)
Jensen, M. C., 'Some Anomalous Evidence Regarding Market Efficiency',
    Journal of Financial Economics, vol. 6, no. 2–3 (1978), pp. 95–101
Jensen, M. C., and Meckling, H. W., 'Theory of the Firm: Managerial

Behaviour, Agency Costs and Ownership Structure', *Journal of Financial Economics*, vol. 3, no. 4 (1976), pp. 305–60

Jobs, S., 'Commencement Address', Stanford Report (12 June 2005) <https://news.stanford.edu/stories/2005/06/youve-got-find-love-jobs-says> (accessed 12 June 2024).

Johannes T. Martin v. Living Essentials, LLC, No. 15 C 01647 (Northern District, Eastern Illinois 2016), Memorandum Opinion and Order, <https://cases.justia.com/federal/district-courts/illinois/ilndce/1:2015cv01647/307113/17/0.pdf?ts=1454410266> (accessed 17 September 2020)

Johnson & Johnson, 'Our Credo', <https://www.jnj.com/credo/> (accessed 28 September 2021)

Johnson, R., 'Tyger! Tyger! Burning Bright', *Twitter* (23 April 2022), <https://twitter.com/rdouglasjohnson/status/1517804673998237697?s=20> (accessed 7 November 2023)

Jonas, N., 'The Hollow Corporation', *Business Week* (3 March 1986), pp. 57–9

Juster, A. M., 'Cabots, Lowells, and a Quatrain You Don't Really Know', *Light Poetry Magazine* (2015), <https://lightpoetrymagazine.com/historical-and-hysterical-winterspring-2015/> (accessed 21 March 2024)

Kanigel, R., *The One Best Way: Frederick Winslow Taylor and the Enigma of Efficiency* (London: MIT Press, 2005)

Kannabus, A., 'History of TB Drugs', <https://tbfacts.org/history-of-tb-drugs/> (accessed 30 September 2021)

Kavilanz, P., 'Johnson and Johnson CEO: We Made a Mistake' (30 September 2010), <https://money.cnn.com/2010/09/30/news/companies/hearing_johnson_fda_drug_recalls/index.html> (accessed 28 September 2021)

Kay, J., 'Boeing and a Dramatic Change of Direction', johnkay.com (10 December 2003), <https://www.johnkay.com/2003/12/10/boeing-and-a-dramatic-change-of-direction/> (accessed 18 January 2024)

—, 'The Management of the University of Oxford … Facing the Future', johnkay.com (20 November 2000), <https://www.johnkay.com/2000/11/20/the-management-of-the-university-of-oxford-facing-the-future/> (accessed 1 November 2023)

—, *Obliquity: Why Our Goals Are Best Achieved Indirectly* (London: Profile, 2010)

—, *Other People's Money: Masters of the Universe or Servants of the People?* (London: Profile, 2015)

—, 'Produced to Price' (13 June 1997), <https://www.johnkay.com/1997/06/13/produced-to-price/> (accessed 26 July 2023)

— , 'Ronald Coase: Nobel Prize Winner Who Explored Why Companies Exist', *Financial Times* (3 September 2013), <https://www.ft.com/content/d1c4aa66-ef9d-11e2-a237-00144feabdc0> (accessed 30 October 2023)

Kay, J., and King, M., *Radical Uncertainty: Decision-Making for an Unknowable Future* (London: The Bridge Street Press, 2020)

Kendall, T., and Chesworth, N., 'Money Watch: Windfalls in Freefall as Shares Crash to Earth; Millions Lose Out as Bank Values Plunge', *Sunday Mirror* (12 March 2000), <https://www.thefreelibrary.com/Money+Watch%3A+Windfalls+in+freefall+as+shares+crash+to+earth%3B+Millions...-a060960200> (accessed 26 October 2023)

Khazan, O., 'The One Area Where the U.S. COVID-19 Strategy Seems To Be Working', *The Atlantic* (22 February 2021), <https://www.theatlantic.com/politics/archive/2021/02/america-vaccination-speed-europe-better/618094/> (accessed 29 September 2021)

Kirkpatrick, D., 'Mystery Buyer of $450 Million *Salvator Mundi* was a Saudi Prince', *New York Times* (6 December 2017), <https://www.nytimes.com/2017/12/06/world/middleeast/salvator-mundi-da-vinci-saudi-prince-bader.html> (accessed 21 July 2023)

Klein, P. G., 'Coase and the Myth of Fisher Body', *Organizations and Markets* (12 September 2006), <https://organizationsandmarkets.com/2006/09/12/coase-and-the-myth-of-fisher-body/> (accessed 25 June 2023)

Knight, F. H., '"What is Truth" in Economics?', *Journal of Political Economy*, vol. 48, no. 1 (1940), pp. 1–32

Knoema, 'Top Vehicle Manufacturers in the US Market, 1961–2016' (21 May 2020), <https://knoema.com/infographics/floslle/top-vehicle-manufacturers-in-the-us-market-1961-2016> (accessed 17 September 2020)

Kornai, J., 'The Soft Budget Constraint', *Kyklos: International Review for Social Sciences*, vol. 39, no. 1 (1986), pp. 3–30

Kuchler, H., et al., 'Opioid Executive Admits to "No Morals" Ahead of Prison Term', *Financial Times* (23 January 2020)

Kwai, I., 'Murderer Who Wielded Narwhal Tusk to Stop Terrorist Gets Royal Pardon', *New York Times* (19 October 2020), <https://www.nytimes.com/2020/10/19/world/europe/london-bridge-narwhal-tusk-pardon.html> (accessed 7 November 2023)

Lackman, C. L., 'The Classical Base of Modern Rent Theory', *American Journal of Economics and Sociology*, vol. 35, no. 3 (1976), pp. 287–300 (p. 291)

LaFrance, A., 'The Largest Autocracy on Earth', *The Atlantic* (27 September 2021), <https://www.theatlantic.com/magazine/archive/2021/11/facebook-authoritarian-hostile-foreign-power/620168/> (accessed 16 June 2023)

Langley, M., *Tearing Down the Walls* (New York: Simon & Schuster, 2003)

Langlois, R. N., *The Corporation and the Twentieth Century* (Princeton, PA: Princeton University Press, 2023), p. 6

Larkin, P., 'Annus Mirabilis', in *High Windows* (London: Faber and Faber, 1974)

Laurence, J., 'Government's £80M for Victims of Thalidomide – But Still No Apology', *The Independent* (21 December 2012), <https://www.independent.co.uk/life-style/health-and-families/health-news/government-s-ps80m-victims-thalidomide-still-no-apology-8427855.html> (accessed 1 September 2021)

Leicester City, 'Emotional Khun Vichai Tribute Played on Big Screen', YouTube (11 November 2018), <https://www.youtube.com/watch?v=LCLRawxqhWg> (accessed 4 October 2023)

Lewis, D. L., *The Public Image of Henry Ford: An American Folk Hero and His Company* (Detroit, MI: Wayne State University Press, 1976)

Littlewood, M., 'Sir James Mirrlees Obituary', *The Guardian* (24 September 2018), <https://www.theguardian.com/politics/2018/sep/24/sir-james-mirrlees-obituary> (accessed 7 September 2023)

Lowrey, A., 'Why the Phrase "Late Capitalism" Is Suddenly Everywhere', *The Atlantic* (1 May 2017), <https://www.theatlantic.com/business/archive/2017/05/late-capitalism/524943/> (accessed 30 January 2024)

Lydon, C., 'A Tough Infighter', *New York Times* (20 August 1976), <https://www.nytimes.com/1976/08/20/archives/a-tough-infighter.html> (accessed 28 September 2021)

Lynch, L., 'I'm Lovin' It (Most of the Time): A Brief History of McDonald's in Serbia', *Balkanist* (27 August 2014), <https://balkanist.net/im-lovin-it-mcdonalds-serbia/> (accessed 19 October 2023)

Mac History, '1984 Apple's Macintosh Commercial', YouTube (1 February 2012), <https://www.youtube.com/watch?v=VtvjbmoDx-I> (accessed 1 October 2023)

Macaulay, S., 'Relational Contracts Floating on a Sea of Custom? Thoughts about the Ideas of Ian Macneil and Lisa Bernstein', *Northwestern University Law Review*, vol. 94, no. 3 (2000), pp. 775–804

Macaulay, S., Friedman, L, M., and Stookey, J., *The Law and Society – Readings on the Social Study of Law* (New York & London: W. W. Norton & Co., 1996)

MacDermot, E. T., and Clinker, C. R., *History of the Great Western Railway* (London: Ian Allan, 1982)

Macey, J. R., 'A Close Read of an Excellent Commentary on *Dodge v. Ford*', *Virginia Law and Business Review*, vol. 3, no. 1 (2008), pp. 177–90

MacFarquhar, L., 'The Bench Burner', *New Yorker* (2 December 2001), <https://www.newyorker.com/magazine/2001/12/10/the-bench-burner> (accessed 5 October 2021)

MacIntyre, A., 'The Nature of the Virtues', *The Hastings Center Report*, vol. 11, no. 2 (1981), pp. 27–34

Macneil, I. R., 'The Many Futures of Contracts', *Southern California Law Review*, vol. 47, no. 691 (1973–4), pp. 691–816

—, 'Whither Contracts?', *Journal of Legal Education*, vol. 21, no. 4 (1969), pp. 403–18

Macrotrends, 'Dow Jones – DJIA – 100 Year Historical Chart', <https://www.macrotrends.net/1319/dow-jones-100-year-historical-char> (accessed 31 October 2023)

Maidment, N., 'Could the Glazers Lose Their Public Enemy No.1 Tag at Manchester United?', *Reuters* (15 June 2015), <https://www.reuters.com/article/manchester-united-glazers/feature-could-the-glazers-lose-their-public-enemy-no-1-tag-at-manchester-united-idUSL1N0XW0O620150615> (accessed 17 July 2023)

Majority Staff of the Committee on Transportation and Infrastructure, 'Final Committee Report: The Design, Development & Certification of the Boeing 737 MAX' (September 2020), <https://transportation.house.gov/imo/media/doc/2020.09.15 %20FINAL %20737 %20MAX %20Report %20for %20Public %20Release.pdf> (accessed 12 November 2020)

Manne, H. G., 'Mergers and the Market for Corporate Control', *Journal of Political Economy*, vol. 73, no. 2 (1965), pp. 110–20

Marçal, K., *Who Cooked Adam Smith's Dinner?* (London: Portobello Books, 2015)

Marex Financial Ltd v. Sevilleja, UKSC31 (2020)

Marshall, A., *Principles of Economics* (London: Macmillan & Co., 1890)

Marx, K., F. Engels (ed.), S. Moore and E. Aveling (trans.), *Capital*, vol. I (London: Swan Sonnenschein, Lowrey, & Co., 1887)

Matthew, H. C. G., McKibbin, R. I., and Kay, J. A., 'The Franchise Factor in the Rise of the Labour Party', *English Historical Review*, vol. 91, no. 361 (1976), pp. 723–52

Matthews, S., *The Way It Was: My Autobiography* (London: Headline Publishing, 2001)

Max, D. T., 'The Chinese Workers Who Assemble Designer Bags in Tuscany', *The New Yorker* (9 April 2018), <https://www.newyorker.com/magazine/2018/04/16/the-chinese-workers-who-assemble-designer-bags-in-tuscany> (accessed 12 April 2023)

Mayer, C., *Capitalism and Crises* (Oxford: Oxford University Press, 2023)

Mayo, J., 'Marconi Under the Microscope: In the Final Part of his Account John Mayo Reflects on Mistakes that were Made and the Responsibility he Feels Towards Shareholders', *Financial Times* (21 January 2002)

Mazza, P., and Ruh, B., 'The Performance of Corporate Legal Insider Trading in the Korean Market', *International Review of Law & Economics*, vol. 71 (2022)

McCarthy, J., 'Big Pharma Sinks to the Bottom of U.S. Industry Rankings', Gallup (3 September 2019), <https://news.gallup.com/poll/266060/big-pharma-sinks-bottom-industry-rankings.aspx> (accessed 29 September 2021)

—, 'Mylan and Pfizer Announce Viatris and the New Company Name in the Planned Mylan – Upjohn Combination' (12 November 2019), <https://investor.mylan.com/news-releases/news-release-details/mylan-and-pfizer-announce-viatris-new-company-name-planned-mylan> (accessed 28 September 2023)

McCloskey, D., *Beyond Positivism, Behaviorism, and Neoinstitutionalism in Economics* (Chicago, IL: University of Chicago Press, 2022)

McCraw, T. K., *Prophet of Innovation: Joseph Schumpeter and Creative Destruction* (Cambridge, MA: Belknap Press, 2007)

McCusker, J. J., 'How Much Is That in Real Money? A Historical Price Index for Use as a Deflator of Money Values in the Economy of the United States', *Proceedings of the American Antiquarian Society*, vol. 101, no. 2 (1991), pp. 297–373

McIntosh, B., 'Vodafone Faces Pounds 400m Bill as It Posts Bid for Mannesmann', *The Independent* (24 December 1999)

McKinsey, 'Global M&A Market Defies Gravity in 2021 Second Half' (16 March 2022), <https://www.mckinsey.com/capabilities/m-and-a/our-insights/global-m-and-a-market-defies-gravity-in-2021-second-half> (accessed 9 October 2023)

McLaughlin, K., 'Burj Khalifa: Everything You Need to Know about the Tallest Building in the World', *Architectural Digest* (26 December 2022), <https://www.architecturaldigest.com/story/burj-khalifa> (accessed 3 May 2023)

McLean, B., and Elkind, P., *The Smartest Guys in the Room: The Amazing Rise and Scandalous Fall of Enron* (London: Penguin, 2013)

McLellan, D., *Karl Marx: A Biography*, 4th edn (London: Palgrave Macmillan, 2006)

Medicines and Healthcare Products Regulatory Agency, (26 January 2021), <https://www.gov.uk/government/collections/new-guidance-and-information-for-industry-from-the-mhra> (accessed 10 November 2023)

Merck & Co., 'Merck's 1899 Manual', Project Gutenberg, https://www.gutenberg.org/files/41697/41697-h/41697-h.htm (accessed 28 September 2021)

Merck KGaA, 'Company History', <https://www.merck.com/company-overview/history/> (accessed 28 September 2021)

Messi, L., <https://www.brainyquote.com/quotes/lionel_messi_473553> (accessed 25 July 2023)

'Messi Magic: Messi vs Getafe', YouTube (7 June 2016), <https://www.youtube.com/watch?v=mMiL4_1Yewg> (accessed 9 October 2023)

Meyer, M., Milgrom, P., and Roberts, J., 'Organisational Prospects, Influence Costs, and Ownership Changes', *Journal of Economics & Management Strategy*, vol. 1, no. 1 (1992), pp. 9–35

Miao, H., 'Buybacks from S&P 500 Companies Set Record in 2022', *Wall Street Journal* (21 March 2023)

Mikkelson, B., 'Bush and French Word for Entrepreneur', *Snopes* (23 September 2007), <https://www.snopes.com/fact-check/french-lesson/> (accessed 20 October 2023)

Mobile Phone Museum, 'MOTOROLA DYNATAC 8000X', <https://www.mobilephonemuseum.com/phone-detail/dynatac-8000x> (accessed 3 May 2023)

Modern Airliners, 'Airbus A380 Super Jumbo', <https://www.modernairliners.com/airbus-a380> (accessed 4 May 2023)

Moggridge, D., *British Monetary Policy, 1924–31* (Cambridge: Cambridge University Press, 1972)

Mondelez International, 'Oreo Fact Sheet' (2017), <https://web.archive.org/web/20190826235732/https://www.mondelezinternational.com/en/~/media/MondelezCorporate/Uploads/downloads/OREO_Fact_Sheet.pdf> (accessed 9 October 2023)

Mooses, M., and Hackney, A. C., 'Anthropometrics and Body Composition in East African Runners: Potential Impact on Performance', *International Journal of Sports Physiology and Performance*, vol. 12, no. 4 (2017), pp. 422–30

Motavalli, J., 'Stellantis: Fiat Chrysler Merges with PSA, Becoming World's

Fourth-Largest Automaker', *Forbes* (4 October 2021), <https://www.
forbes.com/wheels/news/stellantis-fiat-chrysler-merges-with-psa-
becoming-worlds-fourth-largest-automaker/> (accessed 27 September
2023)

Muilenburg, D., 'Statement from Boeing CEO Dennis Muilenburg: We
Own Safety – 737 MAX Software, Production and Process Update' (5
April 2019), <https://boeing.mediaroom.com/2019-04-05-Statement-
from-Boeing-CEO-Dennis-Muilenburg-We-Own-Safety-737-MAX-
Software-Production-and-Process-Update> (accessed 17 September
2020)

Mylan, 'Mylan Launches the First Generic for EpiPen ® (epinephrine
injection, USP) Auto-Injector as an Authorized Generic' (16 December
2016), <https://investor.mylan.com/news-releases/news-release-
details/mylan-launches-first-generic-epipenr-epinephrine-
injection-usp> (accessed 20 July 2023)

Nag, U., 'Usain Bolt's Records: Best Strikes from the Lighting Bolt' (27
June 2023), <https://olympics.com/en/news/usain-bolt-record-
world-champion-athlete-fastest-man-olympics-sprinter-100m-200m>
(accessed 21 July 2023)

National Bureau of Economic Research (NBER), 'Business Cycle Dating',
<https://www.nber.org/research/business-cycle-dating> (accessed 3
September 2023)

National Museums Scotland, *Boulton & Watt Engine* (2021), <https://
www.nms.ac.uk/explore-our-collections/stories/science-and-
technology/boulton-and-watt-engine/> (accessed 9 November 2023)

Nordhaus, W. D., 'Do Real-Output and Real-Wage Measures Capture
Reality? The History of Lighting Suggests Not', in Bresnahan, T. F.,
and Gordon, R. J. (eds.), *The Economics of Real Goods* (Chicago, IL:
University of Chicago Press, 1996), pp. 29–70

Norges Bank Investment Management, 'Fund Signs Regent Street
Agreement' (13 January 2011), <https://www.nbim.no/en/the-fund/
news-list/2011/fund-signs-regent-street-agreement/> (accessed 17
May 2023)

Novo Nordisk Fonden, 'History', <https://novonordiskfonden.dk/en/
about-the-foundation/history/> (accessed 29 September 2021)

'Obituary: Ian Macneil, Clan Chief and Lawyer', *The Scotsman* (19
February 2010), <https://www.scotsman.com/news/obituaries/
obituary-ian-macneil-clan-chief-and-lawyer-2442857> (accessed 26
October 2023)

Odlyzko, A., 'The Collapse of the Railway Mania, the Development of

Capital Markets, and the Forgotten Role of Robert Lucas Nash', *Accounting History Review*, vol. 21, no. 3 (2011), pp. 309–45

O'Donnell, T., 'Pfizer CEO: Company Refused Taxpayer Money for COVID-19 Vaccine Development to "Liberate our Scientists"', *Yahoo!News* (13 September 2020), <https://news.yahoo.com/pfizer-ceo-refused-taxpayer-money-175100171.html> (accessed 28 September 2021)

Office for National Statistics (ONS), 'Capital Stocks and Fixed Capital Consumption, UK: 2023', *Office for National Statistics* (8 December 2023), <https://www.ons.gov.uk/economy/nationalaccounts/uksectoraccounts/bulletins/capitalstocksconsumptionoffixedcapital/2023> (accessed 30 January 2024)

—, 'Characteristics of Homeworkers, Great Britain: September 2022 to January 2023' (13 February 2023), <https://www.ons.gov.uk/employmentandlabourmarket/peopleinwork/employmentandemployeetypes/articles/characteristicsofhomeworkersgreatbritain/september2022tojanuary2023> (accessed 1 October 2023)

—, 'How has Life Expectancy Changed over Time?' (9 September 2015), <https://www.ons.gov.uk/peoplepopulationandcommunity/birthsdeathsandmarriages/lifeexpectancies/articles/howhaslifeexpectancychangedovertime/2015-09-09> (accessed 19 October)

—, 'National Balance Sheet' (31 October 2022), <https://www.ons.gov.uk/economy/grossdomesticproductgdp/compendium/unitedkingdomnationalaccountsthebluebook/2022/nationalbalancesheet> (accessed 7 November 2023)

—, 'Total Wealth in Great Britain: April 2016 to March 2018' (5 December 2019), <https://www.ons.gov.uk/peoplepopulationandcommunity/personalandhouseholdfinances/incomeandwealth/bulletins/totalwealthingreatbritain/april2016tomarch2018> (accessed 19 October 2023)

—, 'UK Business: Activity, Size and Location, 2022' (28 September 2022), <https://www.ons.gov.uk/businessindustryandtrade/business/activitysizeandlocation/datasets/ukbusinessactivitysizeandlocation> (accessed 16 June 2023)

—, 'UK Labour Market: September 2020' (15 September 2020), <https://www.ons.gov.uk/releases/uklabourmarketseptember2020> (accessed 26 May 2023)

—, 'UK Natural Capital Accounts: 2022' (10 November 2022), <https://

www.ons.gov.uk/economy/environmentalaccounts/bulletins/
uknaturalcapitalaccounts/2022> (accessed 7 November 2023)

Office of Strategic Services, *Simple Sabotage Field Manual* (Washington,
DC: Office of Strategic Services, 1944)

Olympics, 'The Story of Abrahams and Liddell at Paris 1924' (27 June
2023), <https://olympics.com/en/news/the-story-of-abrahams-and-
liddell-at-paris-1924> (accessed 21 July 2023)

Organisation for Economic Cooperation and Development (OECD),
'Biodiversity, Natural Capital and the Economy: A Policy Guide for
Finance, Economic and Environment Ministers', *OECD Environment
Policy Papers*, no. 26 (2021)

—, 'National Accounts: 9B. Balance Sheets for Non-Financial Assets',
<https://stats.oecd.org/Index.aspx?QueryId=104323> (accessed 6
October 2023)

Orwell, G., 'Politics and the English Language', *Horizon*, vol. 13, no. 76
(1946), pp. 252–65

Otten, H., 'Domagk and the Development of the "Sulphonamides"',
Journal of Antimicrobial Chemotherapy, vol. 17, no. 6 (June 1986), pp.
689–96

Our World in Data, 'Share of Agriculture in Total Employment, 1801 to
2011', <https://ourworldindata.org/grapher/share-of-agriculture-in-
total-employment?country=~GBR> (accessed 18 March 2024)

Pavlov, I. P., *Conditioned Reflexes: An Investigation of the Physiological Activity
of the Cerebral Cortex* (Oxford: Oxford University Press, 1927)

Peaucelle, J.-L., and Guthrie, C., 'How Adam Smith Found Inspiration in
French Texts on Pin Making in the Eighteenth Century', *History of
Economic Ideas*, vol. 19, no. 3 (2011), pp. 41–67

Penafiel, K., '"The Empire State Building: An Innovative Skyscraper"',
Buildings (28 June 2006), <https://www.buildings.com/industry-
news/article/10193728/the-empire-state-building-an-innovative-
skyscraper> (accessed 3 April 2024)

Pennant, T., *A Tour in Scotland, 1769* (London: 1771)

Penrose, E. T., *The Theory of the Growth of the Firm* (Oxford: Oxford
University Press, 1995)

Peterson, C., and Seligman, M. E. P., *Character Strengths and Virtues: A
Handbook and Classification* (Oxford: Oxford University Press, 2004)

Pew Research Center, 'Modest Declines in Positive Views of "Socialism"
and "Capitalism" in U.S.' (19 September 2022), <https://www.
pewresearch.org/politics/2022/09/19/modest-declines-in-positive-
views-of-socialism-and-capitalism-in-u-s/> (accessed 16 June 2023)

—, 'Religion's Relationship to Happiness, Civic Engagement and Health around the World' (31 January 2019)

Philips, M., 'Remembering Hatfield – 20 Years On', *Rail Safety and Standard Board* (17 October 2020), <https://www.rssb.co.uk/what-we-do/insights-and-news/blogs/remembering-hatfield-20-years-on> (accessed 30 October 2023)

Phillips, S., 'How a Courageous Physician-Scientist Saved the U.S. from a Birth-Defects Catastrophe', *UChicagoMedicine* (March 2020), <https://www.uchicagomedicine.org/forefront/biological-sciences-articles/courageous-physician-scientist-saved-the-us-from-a-birth-defects-catastrophe> (accessed 28 September 2021)

Piketty, T., *Capital in the Twenty-First Century* (Cambridge, MA: Belknap Press, 2014)

Pollack, A., 'Drug Goes from $13.50 a Tablet to $750, Overnight', *New York Times* (20 September 2015), <https://www.nytimes.com/2015/09/21/business/a-huge-overnight-increase-in-a-drugs-price-raises-protests.html> (accessed 20 July 2023)

Port Sunlight Village Trust, 'A Brief History of Port Sunlight', <https://www.portsunlightvillage.com/about-port-sunlight/history-and-heritage/> (accessed 6 October 2023)

Porter, J., 'How Jimmy Hill's Strike Threat Turned £20 Footballers into Multi-Millionaires', *The Sportsman* (18 January 2021), <https://www.thesportsman.com/features/how-jimmy-hill-s-strike-threat-turned-20-footballers-into-multi-millionaires> (accessed 25 July 2023)

Porter, M., 'How Competitive Forces Shape Strategy', *Harvard Business Review* (1979), <https://hbr.org/1979/03/how-competitive-forces-shape-strategy> (accessed 30 October 2023)

Posner, R. A., 'A Reply to Some Recent Criticisms of the Efficiency Theory of the Common Law', *Hofstra Law Review*, vol. 9, no. 3 (1981), pp. 775–94

Powell, L. F., 'Attack on American Free Enterprise System', *U.S. Chamber of Commerce* (23 August 1971), <https://law2.wlu.edu/deptimages/Powell%20Archives/PowellMemorandumTypescript.pdf> (accessed 5 October 2021)

Prakash, S., and Valentine, V., 'Timeline: The Rise and Fall of Vioxx', *npr* (10 November 2007), <https://www.npr.org/2007/11/10/5470430/timeline-the-rise-and-fall-of-vioxx?t=1632949540924> (accessed 28 September 2021)

Putnam, R., and Garrett, S. R., *The Upswing: How America Came Together a*

Century Ago and How We Can Do It Again (New York: Simon & Schuster, 2020)

Putnam, R. D., 'Tuning In, Tuning Out: The Strange Disappearance of Social Capital in America', *Political Science and Politics*, vol. 28, no. 4 (1995), pp. 664–683

Rappaport, A., *Creating Shareholder Value: A Guide for Managers and Investors* (New York: The Free Press, 1986)

Rattner, S., 'Who's Right on the Stock Market?', *New York Times* (14 November 2013)

Razzell, P., and Spence, C., 'The History of Infant, Child and Adult Mortality in London, 1550–1850', *London Journal*, vol. 32, no. 3 (2007), pp. 271–92

Redman, M., 'Cocaine: What Is the Crack? A Brief History of the Use of Cocaine as an Anesthetic', *Anesthesiology and Pain Medicine*, vol. 1, no. 2 (2011), pp. 95–7

Rees, K., 'BlackRock's Assets Seen Topping $15 Trillion in Five Years' Time', Bloomberg (17 April 2023), <https://www.bloomberg.com/news/articles/2023-04-17/blackrock-assets-to-top-15-trillion-in-five-years-analyst-says?leadSource=uverify%20wall> (accessed 7 November 2023)

Regierungskommission, Deutscher Corporate Governance Kodex, 'German Corporate Governance Code 2017, Press Release' (14 February 2017), <https://www.ecgi.global/code/german-corporate-governance-code-2017-press-release> (accessed 7 November 2023)

Regis, E., 'No One Can Explain Why Planes Stay in the Air', *Scientific American* (1 February 2020), <https://www.scientificamerican.com/article/no-one-can-explain-why-planes-stay-in-the-air> (accessed 21 July 2023)

Reich, C. A., *The Greening of America* (New York: Random House, 1970)

Reinarz, J., and Wynter, R., 'The Spirit of Medicine: The Use of Alcohol in Nineteenth-Century Medical Practice', in Schmid, S., and Schmidt-Haberkamp, B. (eds.), *Drink in the Eighteenth and Nineteenth Centuries* (Abingdon: Pickering & Chatto, 2014), pp. 127–40

Reuters Staff, 'Quote Box-Trump, Business Leaders Comment on Jack Welch's Death', Reuters (2 March 2020), <https://www.reuters.com/article/people-jackwelch-quote-idUSL4N2AV4TB> (accessed 1 November 2023)

Revlon, Inc. v. MacAndrews & Forbes Holdings, Inc., 506 A.2d 173 (1986)

Ricardo, D., *On the Principles of Political Economy and Taxation* (London: John Murray, 1817)

Roberts, W., 'That Imperfect Arm: Quantifying the Carronade', *Warship International*, vol. 33, no. 3 (1996), pp. 231–40

Rolt, L. T. C., *Victorian Engineering* (London: Penguin, 1970)

Romer, P., 'Mathiness in the Theory of Economic Growth', *American Economic Review: Papers & Proceedings*, vol. 105, no. 5 (2015), pp. 89–93

—, 'The Origins of Endogenous Growth', *Journal of Economic Perspectives*, vol. 8, no. 1 (1994), pp. 3–22

Roosevelt, T., 'The Duties of a Great Nation', in *The Works of Theodore Roosevelt*, vol. XIV, *Campaigns and Controversies* (New York: Charles Scribner's Sons, 1926), pp. 290–297

Roser, M., Ortiz-Ospina, E., and Ritchie, H., 'Life Expectancy', *Our World in Data* (2013), <https://ourworldindata.org/life-expectancy> (accessed 6 November 2023)

Rosoff, M., 'Jeff Bezos Told What Might Be the Best Startup Investment Story Ever', *Business Insider* (20 October 2016), <https://www.businessinsider.com/jeff-bezos-on-early-amazon-investors-2016-10?r=US&IR=T> (accessed 6 October 2021)

Rousseau, J.-J., *A Discourse upon the Origin and Foundation of the Inequality Among Mankind* (London: R. and J. Dodsley, 1761)

Sabbagh, D., 'Ackermann Agrees to Pay €3.2 Million Towards Settlement', *The Times* (25 November 2006), <https://www.thetimes.co.uk/article/ackermann-agrees-to-pay-32-million-towards-settlement-zp7kqj57w8z> (accessed 31 October 2023)

Sainsbury, D., *Windows of Opportunity* (London: Profile, 2019)

Saltaire Village Website, 'The Saltaire Village Website, World Heritage Site', <https://saltairevillage.info/> (accessed 30 October 2023)

Schanche, A. D., 'It Is Theoretically Possible for the Entire United States to Become One Vast Conglomerate, Presided over by Mr James. J. Ling', *Saturday Evening Post* (January 2024), <https://files.saturdayeveningpost.com/uploads/reprints/One_Vast_Conglomerate/index.html> (accessed 18 January 2024)

Scherer, F. M., *Industrial Market Structure and Economic Performance* (Chicago, IL: Rand McNally, 1970)

Schiffer, Z., 'Apple Asks Staff to Return to Office Three Days a Week Starting in Early September', *The Verge* (2 June 2021), <https://www.theverge.com/2021/6/2/22465846/apple-employees-return-office-three-days-week-september> (accessed 3 October 2021)

Schofield, R. S., 'Dimensions of Illiteracy, 1750–1850', *Explorations in Economic History*, vol. 10, no. 4 (1973), pp. 437–54

Schroter, J., 'Steve Jobs Introduces iPhone in 2007', YouTube (9 October

2011), <https://www.youtube.com/watch?v=MnrJzXM7a60> (accessed 9 October 2011)

Schumpeter, J., *Capitalism, Socialism, and Democracy* (New York: Harper & Brothers, 1942)

Schumpeter, J. A., R. Opie (trans.), *The Theory of Economic Development*, (Cambridge, MA: Harvard University Press, 1959)

Scott, B., 'Valeant CEO Michael Pearson Lost $180 Million Yesterday, and $750 Million in Past Year', *Forbes* (16 March 2016), <https://www.forbes.com/sites/bartiescott1/2016/03/16/valeant-ceo-michael-pearson-lost-two-thirds-of-his-billion-dollar-fortune-in-a-year/?sh=3d917b446c41> (accessed 28 September 2021)

Scottish FA, 'Kenny Dalglish', <https://www.scottishfa.co.uk/players/?pid=113766&lid=1> (accessed 7 September 2023)

'Secrets of Ball-Giving: A Chat with Ward McAllister', *New York Daily Tribune* (25 March 1888)

Serling, R. J., *Legend and Legacy: The Story of Boeing and Its People* (New York: St. Martin's Press, 1992)

Service, T., 'The Abbado Effect', *The Guardian* (19 August 2008), <https://www.theguardian.com/music/tomserviceblog/2008/aug/19/theabbadomoment> (accessed 15 August 2023)

Settimi, C., 'The World's Highest-Paid Soccer Players 2017: Cristiano Ronaldo, Lionel Messi Lead the List', *Forbes* (26 May 2017), <https://www.forbes.com/sites/christinasettimi/2017/05/26/the-worlds-highest-paid-soccer-players-2017-cristiano-ronaldo-lionel-messi-lead-the-list/?sh=3b8e254b210e> (accessed 25 July 2023)

Shaw, G. B., *Fabian Essays in Socialism* (London: W. Scott, 1899)

Short v. Treasury Commissioners, AC 534 (1948)

Shread, J., 'Lionel Messi Reveals He Chose to Join Paris Saint-Germain in Order to Win Fifth Champions League', *SkySports* (12 August 2021), <https://www.skysports.com/football/news/11095/12378621/lionel-messi-reveals-he-chose-to-join-paris-saint-germain-in-order-to-win-fifth-champions-league> (accessed 30 September 2021)

Skinner, B. F., *The Behavior of Organisms: An Experimental Analysis* (New York: Appleton-Century-Crofts, Inc., 1938)

Smith, A., *An Inquiry into the Nature and Causes of the Wealth of Nations*, vol. I (London: W. Strahan and T. Cadell, 1776)

—, *An Inquiry into the Nature and Causes of the Wealth of Nations*, vol. II (London: W. Strahan and T. Cadell, 1776)

Solomon, M., 'Poison Pill', *Medium* (14 July 2022), <medium.com/truly-adventurous/poison-pill-d98f366522a7> (accessed 20 July 2023)

Solow, R. M., 'The Production Function and the Theory of Capital', *Review of Economic Studies*, vol. 23, no. 2 (1955–6), pp. 101–8

Southey, R., 'The Battle of Blenheim' (1796), in *Metrical Tales, and Other Poems* (London: Longman, Hurst, Rees, and Orme, 1805), pp. 44–7

Spark, A., 'Wrestling with America: Media, National Images, and the Global Village', *Journal of Popular Culture*, vol. 29 (1996), pp. 83–98

Steinhardt, M., *Jewish Pride* (New York: Simon and Schuster, 2022)

Stewart, J., 'The Real Heroes Are Dead', *The New Yorker* (3 February 2002), <https://www.newyorker.com/magazine/2002/02/11/september-11th-attacks-world-trade-center-rick-rescorla-the-real-heroes-are-dead> (accessed 30 October 2023)

Stokes, A., 'Merck Continues Campaign Against River Blindness in the DRC' (September 2014), <https://www.pri.org/stories/2014-09-29/merck-continues-campaign-against-river-blindness-drc-video> (accessed 28 September 2021)

Stout, L., *The Shareholder Value Myth: How Putting Shareholders First Harms Investors, Corporations, and the Public* (San Francisco, CA: Berrett-Koehler Publishers, 2012)

Strine Jr., L. E., 'The Dangers of Denial: The Need for a Clear-Eyed Understanding of the Power and Accountability of Structure Established by the Delaware General Corporation Law', *University of Pennsylvania Institute for Law and Economics Research Paper*, no. 15–08 (2015)

Surowiecki, J., *The Wisdom of Crowds: Why the Many Are Smarter than the Few and How Collective Wisdom Shapes Business, Economies, Societies and Nations* (New York: Doubleday, 2004)

Taibbi, M., 'The Great American Bubble Machine', *Rolling Stone* (5 April 2010), <https://www.rollingstone.com/politics/politics-news/the-great-american-bubble-machine-195229/> (accessed 17 September 2020)

Taylor, F. W., *Shop Management* (New York: Harper & Brothers, 1912)

Taylor, M., *The Association Game: A History of British Football* (Abingdon: Routledge, 2013)

Teece, D. J., 'Firm Organisation, Industrial Structure, and Technological Innovation', *Journal of Economic Behavior & Organisation*, vol. 31, no. 2 (1996), pp. 193–224

Teece, D. J., Pisano, G., and Shuen, A., 'Dynamic Capabilities and Strategic Management', *Strategic Management Journal*, vol. 18, no. 7 (1997), pp. 509–33

Tesla, N., 'A Story of Youth Told by Age (Dedicated to Miss Pola Fotitch)'

(1939), <https://www.pbs.org/tesla/ll/story_youth.html> (accessed 4 September 2023)

Thayer, C. F., *An End to Hierarchy, and End to Competition* (New York: New Viewpoints, 1981)

The Beatles, 'Getting Better' (1967)

'The Truth behind the Tories' Northern Strongholds', *The Economist* (31 March 2021), <https://www.economist.com/britain/2021/03/31/the-truth-behind-the-tories-northern-strongholds> (accessed 3 October 2021)

'The Upper East Side's Most Expensive 5th Avenue Apartment Buildings', *MPA* (5 February 2013), <https://www.mpamag.com/us/news/general/the-upper-east-sides-most-expensive-5th-avenue-apartment-buildings/13476> (accessed 21 July 2023)

Thomas, M., 'McDonalds Coming to Dubrovnik – Location Known!', *Dubrovnik Times* (27 January 2023), <https://www.thedubrovniktimes.com/news/dubrovnik/item/14431-mcdonalds-coming-to-dubrovnik-location-known> (accessed 30 October 2023)

Thomas, Z., and Swift, T., 'Who is Martin Shkreli – "the Most Hated Man in America"?', *BBC News* (4 August 2017), <https://www.bbc.co.uk/news/world-us-canada-34331761> (accessed 27 September 2021)

Thwaites, T., *The Toaster Project: or, A Heroic Attempt to Build a Simple Electric Appliance from Scratch* (Princeton, NJ.: Princeton Architectural Press, 2011)

Tichy, N., and Charan, R., 'Speed, Simplicity, Self-Confidence: An Interview with Jack Welch', *Harvard Business Review* (1989), <https://hbr.org/1989/09/speed-simplicity-self-confidence-an-interview-with-jack-welch> (accessed 26 September 2023)

Tipu, Md. S. I., 'Tazreen Fire Tragedy: Trial Proceedings of Cases in Limbo', *Dhaka Tribune* (23 November 2020), <https://www.dhakatribune.com/bangladesh/dhaka/2020/11/23/tazreen-fire-tragedy-trial-proceedings-of-cases-in-limbo> (accessed 5 October 2021)

Tomasello, M., Page-Barbour Lecture at the University of Virginia (2010)

Transparency International, 'Corruption Perceptions Index 2022' (2023), <https://images.transparencycdn.org/images/Report_CPI2022_English.pdf> (accessed 1 November 2023)

Treasury Commissioners v. Short Brothers, UKHL J0729 – 2 (1948)

True Faith, 'Premier League – Owner Financing Last 10 Years (2012–21)', (2022), <https://true-faith.co.uk/wp-content/uploads/2022/05/acc8.jpg> (accessed 4 October 2023)

Trump, D. J., and Schwartz, T., *Trump: The Art of the Deal* (New York: Random House, 1987)

Twain, M., 'Letter to Helen Keller, in Wrentham', (17 March 1903), <https://www.gutenberg.org/files/3197/3197-h/3197-h.htm#link2H_4_0003> (accessed 24 October 2023)

Uber, '2020 Annual Report' (26 February 2021), <https://s23.q4cdn.com/407969754/files/doc_financials/2021/ar/FINAL-Typeset-Annual-Report.pdf> (accessed 30 October 2023)

Unclaimed Assets, 'Halifax Unclaimed Demutualisation Shares', <https://unclaimedassets.co.uk/halifax-unclaimed-shares> (accessed 9 October 2023)

United Nations Commission for Trade and Development, 'Classifications', <https://unctadstat.unctad.org/en/classifications.html> (accessed 21 July 2023)

U.S. Bureau of Labor Statistics, 'CPI for all Urban Consumers (CPI-U), All Items in U.S. City Average, All Urban Consumers, Not Seasonally Adjusted, CUUR0000SA0' (4 May 2023), <https://data.bls.gov/timeseries/CUUR0000SA0> (accessed 21 March 2024)

—, 'Injuries, Illnesses, and Fatalities', <https://www.bls.gov/iif/snapshots/isn-manufacturing-2016-20.htm> (accessed 9 November 2023)

U.S. Department of Defense, 'Crisis and Communication Strategies Case Study: The Johnson and Johnson Tylenol Crisis', <https://www.ou.edu/deptcomm/dodjcc/groups/02C2/Johnson%20&%20Johnson.htm> (accessed 28 September 2021)

U.S. Department of Justice, Office of Public Affairs, 'Boeing Charged with 737 Conspiracy and Agrees to Pay over $2.5 Billion' (7 January 2021), <https://www.justice.gov/opa/pr/boeing-charged-737-max-fraud-conspiracy-and-agrees-pay-over-25-billion> (accessed 10 October 2023)

U.S. Food and Drug Administration, 'Milestones in US Food and Drug Law', <https://www.fda.gov/about-fda/fda-history/milestones-us-food-and-drug-law> (accessed 28 September 2021)

U.S. Securities and Exchange Commission, 'Boeing to Pay $200 Million to Settle SEC Charges that It Misled Investors about the 737 Max' (22 September 2022), <https://www.sec.gov/news/press-release/2022-170> (accessed 10 October 2023)

U.S. Small Business Administration Office of Advocacy, '2022 Small Business Profile' (2022), <https://advocacy.sba.gov/wp-content/uploads/2022/08/Small-Business-Economic-Profile-US.pdf> (accessed 16 June 2023)

Useem, J., 'The Long-Forgotten Flight that Sent Boeing Off Course', *The Atlantic* (20 November 2019)

Video Insider, 'Steve Jobs in 2010, at D8 Conference', YouTube (8 February 2015), <https://www.youtube.com/watch?v=i5f8bqYYwps> (accessed 11 October 2023)

'Wall Street and the Financial Crisis: The Role of Investment Banks', Hearing before the Permanent Subcommittee on Investigations of the Committee on Homeland Security and Governmental Affairs, vol. 4, 111th Congress (27 April 2010)

Walsh, C., 'Leadership on 9/11: Morgan Stanley's Challenge', *Harvard Business School* (17 December 2001), <https://hbswk.hbs.edu/archive/leadership-on-9-11-morgan-stanley-s-challenge> (accessed 30 October 2023)

Wang, E., 'After US IPO Stumbles, Companies under Pressure to Offer Bargains', Reuters (19 October 2023), <https://www.reuters.com/markets/deals/after-us-ipo-stumbles-companies-under-pressure-offer-bargains-2023-10-19/> (accessed 7 November 2023)

Weber, M., G. Roth and C. Wittich (eds.), *Economy and Society* (Berkeley, CA: University of California Press, 1978)

Welkos, R. W., 'Founder of est Targeted in Campaign by Scientologists: Religion: Competition for Customers Is Said To Be the Motive behind Effort to Discredit Werner Erhard', *LA Times* (29 December 1991)

Wellcome Trust, 'Who We Are', <https://wellcome.org/who-we-are> (accessed 29 September 2021)

Wernerfelt, B., 'A Resource-Based View of the Firm', *Strategic Management Journal*, vol. 5, no. 2 (1984), pp. 171–80

Wharton School, University of Pennsylvania, 'How GM's Mary Barra Drives Value', *Knowledge at Wharton*, <https://knowledge.wharton.upenn.edu/article/how-gms-mary-barra-drives-value/> (accessed 3 May 2018)

'What Satya Nadella Thinks', *New York Times* (14 May 2020), <https://www.nytimes.com/2020/05/14/business/dealbook/satya-nadella-microsoft.html> (accessed 10 October 2023)

Whately, R., *Detached Thoughts and Apophthegms: Extracted from Some of the Writings of Archbishop Whately* (London, 1854)

Wilber, R. L., and Pitsiladis, Y. P., 'Kenyan and Ethiopian Distance Runners: What Makes Them So Good?', *International Journal of Sports Physiology and Performance*, vol. 7, no. 2 (2012), pp. 92–102

Wilde, O., *Lady Windermere's Fan: A Play about a Good Woman* (London, 1892)

Williamson, O. E., 'Calculativeness, Trust, and Economic Organization', *Journal of Law & Economics*, vol. 36, no. 1 (1993), pp. 453–86

—, 'The Economics of Organization: The Transaction Cost Approach', *American Journal of Sociology*, vol. 87, no. 3 (1981), pp. 548–77

—, *Markets and Hierarchies: Analysis and Antitrust Implications* (New York: Free Press, 1975)

Wilson, H., Aldrick, P., and Ahmed, K., 'The Bank that Went Bust', *Sunday Telegraph* (6 March 2011)

Wise, D. B., 'Dodge: Hell Raisers from Michigan', in Ward, I. (ed.), *The World of Automobiles: An Illustrated Encyclopedia of the Motor Car, vol. V* (New York: Purnell Reference Books, 1977), pp. 550–558

Wolf, M., *The Crisis of Democratic Capitalism* (London: Penguin, 2024)

Wolfe, T., *The Bonfire of the Vanities* (New York, Farrar Straus and Giroux, 1987)

Wordsworth, W., 'The French Revolution: as It Appeared to Enthusiasts at Its Commencement', in de Selincourt, E. (ed.), *The Poetical Works of William Wordsworth*, vol. 2 (Oxford: Oxford University Press, 1952), pp. 264–5

World Bank, 'Creating Jobs and Diversifying Exports in Bangladesh' (14 November 2017), <https://www.worldbank.org/en/news/feature/2017/11/14/creating-jobs-and-diversifying-exports-in-bangladesh> (accessed 30 January 2024)

—, 'World Development Indicators: NY.GDP.MKTP.CD' (30 March 2023)

World Health Organization, 'WHO Timeline Covid-19' (27 April 2020), <https://www.who.int/news/item/27-04-2020-who-timeline---covid-19> (accessed 21 March 2024)

Wright, T., 'The Learning Curve of the Cumulative Average Model: What is Wright's Law?', Ark Invest, <https://ark-invest.com/wrights-law/> (accessed 21 July 2023)

Yahoo!, 'Amazon.com, Inc. (AMZN) Balance Sheet', <https://finance.yahoo.com/quote/AMZN/balance-sheet/> (accessed 6 November 2023)

Ziegler. P., *The Sixth Great Power: A History of One of the Greatest of All Banking Families, the House of Barings, 1762–1929* (New York: Alfred A. Knopf Inc., 1988)

Zuboff, S., *The Age of Surveillance Capitalism: The Fight for a Human Future at the New Frontier of Power* (London: Profile, 2018)

INDEX